# PRODUCTION AND OPERATIONS MANAGEMENT

# PRODUCTION AND OPERATIONS MANAGEMENT

**M.E. Thukaram Rao**
Head, Department of Commerce
Sri Sathya Sai University
Brindavan Campus, Bangalore
Karnataka

PUBLISHING FOR ONE WORLD
**NEW AGE INTERNATIONAL (P) LIMITED, PUBLISHERS**
New Delhi • Bangalore • Chennai • Cochin • Guwahati • Hyderabad
Jalandhar • Kolkata • Lucknow • Mumbai • Ranchi
Visit us at **www.newagepublishers.com**

Published by New Age International (P) Ltd., Publishers
First Edition: 2010
Reprint: 2012



***Branches:***

- No. 37/10, 8th Cross (Near Hanuman Temple), Azad Nagar, Chamrajpet, **Bangalore** - 560 018. Tel.: (080) 26756823, Telefax: 26756820, E-mail: bangalore@newagepublishers.com
- 26, Damodaran Street, T. Nagar, **Chennai** - 600 017. Tel.: (044) 24353401, Telefax: 24351463 E-mail: chennai@newagepublishers.com
- CC-39/1016, Carrier Station Road, Ernakulam South, **Cochin** - 682 016. Tel.: (0484) 2377004, Telefax: 4051303 E-mail: cochin@newagepublishers.com
- Hemsen Complex, Mohd. Shah Road, Paltan Bazar, Near Starline Hotel, **Guwahati** - 781 008.Tel.: (0361) 2513881 Telefax: 2543669, E-mail: guwahati@newagepublishers.com
- No. 105, 1st Floor, Madhiray Kaveri Tower, 3-2-19, Azam Jahi Road, Nimboliadda, **Hyderabad** - 500 027. Tel.: (040) 24652456, Telefax: 24652457, E-mail:hyderabad@newagepublishers.com
- RDB Chambers (Formerly Lotus Cinema)106A, 1st Floor, S.N. Banerjee Road, **Kolkata** - 700 014. Tel.: (033) 22273773, Telefax: 22275247, E-mail:kolkata@newagepublishers.com
- 16-A, Jopling Road, **Lucknow** - 226 001. Tel.: (0522) 2209578, 4045297, Telefax: 2204098 E-mail: lucknow@newagepublishers.com
- 142C, Victor House, Ground Floor, N.M. Joshi Marg, Lower Parel, **Mumbai** - 400 013.Tel.: (022) 24927869 Telefax: 24915415, E-mail: mumbai@newagepublishers.com
- 22, Golden House, Daryaganj, **New Delhi** - 110 002. Tel.: (011) 23262370, 23262368, Telefax: 43551305 E-mail: sales@newagepublishers.com

**ISBN : 978-81-224-2740-0**

**₹ 250.00**

**C-11-09-5889**

Printed in India at Ramprintograph, Delhi.
Typeset at Akriti Graphics, Delhi.

**PUBLISHING FOR ONE WORLD**
**NEW AGE INTERNATIONAL (P) LIMITED, PUBLISHERS**
4835/24, Ansari Road, Daryaganj, New Delhi-110002
Visit us at **www.newagepublishers.com**

# PREFACE

I have immense pleasure in placing into the hands of my esteemed readers this book, *Production and Operations Management*. Although several books are available on the subject, the need for a comprehensive volume covering all the important aspects of production and operations management has been felt for a long time. Keeping this need in mind the book is written in a simple and lucid style so that it can be easily understood by the readers. At the end of each chapter a few standard questions which serve as objective, very short, short and long questions have been given. They should enable the students to test their skills. A selected bibliography at the end of book would give the students an opportunity to refer to the works of renowned authors for enriching their knowledge on the subject.

In the course of writing this book, I have referred to many standard works of various authors. Some useful definitions and contributions have been incorporated in the book by retaining their originality. I am always thankful to all of them.

The book serves the needs of standards preparing for examinations of BBM, BBA, MBA, M.Com., ICWA, B.E. (Mechanical Engineering and Industrial Production Engineering) and other technical courses, diploma courses in Business Management, Production Management and other allied courses.

I am extremely grateful to Mr Saumya Gupta, Managing Director and Dr R.C. Gupta, Academic Director of New Age International Publishers for publication of this book so nicely and elegantly.

I shall appreciate receiving comments and suggestions from my readers for the improvement of this book.

**M.E. Thukaram Rao**

# CONTENTS

Chapter 1

# PRODUCTION MANAGEMENT

## ■ INTRODUCTION

The term production is used to indicate a process through which raw materials are converted into finished product. In other words, it transforms the various inputs, such as raw materials, labour, money, management, etc. into output, i.e., goods and services. The place where such transformation takes place is known as factory. Production process can be undertaken either manually or mechanically. Now a days, it is undertaken by automatic machines. So, technically speaking, all the processes involved in various productions and service departments of a factory which converts raw materials to a finished product can be designated as production.

In economic sense, the term 'production' connotes an activity through which form utility is created. For example, raw cotton cannot be used as such. But when converted into cloth it has utility. However, the finished product of one organisation can become raw material for another organisation. For example, the component parts manufactured by a small scale industry can be used to assemble into a TV by a large sized industry.

## ■ FEATURES OF PRODUCTION FUNCTION

The following are the features of the production function:

1. It involves transformation of raw materials into finished product.
2. The place where production takes place is known as a factory.
3. Production is undertaken in various departments, such as production and service department of a factory.
4. Production may involve more than one process or operation.
5. It can be undertaken either manually or mechanically.
6. It is based on technology which may be either indigenous or imported.
7. Production is undertaken on large scale basis in recent times.
8. Production process involves combination of resources, such as materials, men, money, machinery, management.
9. Production process leads to uniformity of finished goods.
10. In modern times, production process is highly specialised.

## ■ DIFFERENCE BETWEEN PRODUCTION AND OPERATION

The term production is strictly used in the sense of manufacturing tangible products. In this sense, the term production is used in a narrow sense. In recent times, production is taken to involve services as well. In this sense, the production is viewed in a broad sense. The differences between production and operations are as follows:

| Production | Operation |
|---|---|
| 1. It involves manufacturing of a tangible product | 1. It involves rendering of kind of services, such as electricity, cooking gas etc. |
| 2. It is used in a narrow sense | 2. It is used in a broad sense. |
| 3. It is applied to manufacturing organisations, such as industry | 3. It is applied to non-manufacturing organisations, such as Banks, Insurance, agriculture, transportation, warehousing, etc. |
| 4. It will have closing stock at the end of an accounting year | 4. There is nothing like closing stock. |
| 5. Demand for the product is regular | 5. Demand for services fluctuate time to time. |

## ■ IMPORTANCE OF PRODUCTION FUNCTION IN AN ORGANISATION

Production function is a basic function of an industrial organisation around which all other functions of the organisation, such as purchasing, financing, marketing, storing, personnel, research and development, revolve. It is, therefore, very essential that the production function is managed effectively and efficiently so as to achieve the organisation's goals. The main aim of every production system is to produce the goods and services economically to the full satisfaction of the customer for which they are meant. In order to achieve this aim, it is essential to plan, organise, direct and control the production system. In fact, these functions of planning, organising, directing and controlling comprise the production management.

## ■ DEFINITION OF PRODUCTION MANAGEMENT

Production management is a branch of general management which is concerned with planning, organising, directing and controlling the activities of production function.

According to Elwood S. BUFFA, production management deals with decision-making related to production process, so that the resulting goods or services are produced according to specification in amounts and by the schedule demanded and at minimum cost.

The above definition highlights the following features:

1. It is a function of management which is concerned with production.
2. Output is obtained from input in accordance with the specification laid down.
3. Production is undertaken according to the prevailing demand for goods.
4. Production is undertaken at a minimum cost.

## ■ HISTORICAL DEVELOPMENT OF PRODUCTION MANAGEMENT OR CONTRIBUTIONS TO PRODUCTION MANAGEMENT

### 1. Adam Smith

The first person who attempted production improvement, was Adam Smith in 1776. During this stage, factory system was in its infancy. His main contribution to production management was the extension of the principle of division of labour to industrial activities. The application of division of labour results in three benefits, which are as follows:

(i) Improvement of skill owing to repeated operations.
(ii) Savings in time as it does not need change from one activity to another.
(iii) Specialisation leads to invention in machines and methods.

The above advantages of division of labour result in increased output.

### 2. Charles Babbage

In the year 1832, the British Mathematician Charles Babbage published his book entitled. "*The Economics of Machinery and Manufactures*". His main contribution to production management are as follows:

(a) **Division of labour:** In his masterpiece work on "*The Economy of Machinery and Manufacture*," Babbage explained the benefits arising out of specialization,
(b) **Use of science and mathematics:** He advocated the practice of scientific method of production instead of the traditional manufacturing process, and
(c) **Emphasis on cost reduction:** He suggested that every effort must be made to reduce cost by adopting new and improved methods of production.

### 3. James Watt and Mathew Robinson Boulton

James Watt, the junior and Mathew R. Boulton were the sons of the inventors of steam engine. Their contribution to production management are as follows:

(a) Planned machine layout in factories.
(b) Production planning.
(c) Use of records to calculate cost of production and profit.
(d) Training and development programme for workers.
(e) Work study and payment by output.

### 4. F. W. Taylor

F. W. Taylor's major publications are: "A Piece Rate System (1895), Shop Management (1903) and The Principles of Scientific Management." His major contribution to production management are as follows:

(a) **A clearly defined daily task:** Each man in the establishment, high or low, should daily have a clearly defined task laid out before him.
(b) **Standard conditions:** The workers should be given such standardised conditions and appliances as will enable him to accomplish his task with certainty.
(c) **Higher pay for success:** The worker should be sure of higher pay when he accomplishes his task. The emphasis is on the importance of "the coupling of high wages for workmen with low labour cost for the employer" and as a result, the public will benefit from lower prices.
(d) **Loss in the case of failure:** When, a workman fails, he should be sure that sooner or later he will be the loser for it.

### 5. Subsequent developments

After the World War II the theory and technique of production management began to improve. Many researches were conducted the latest development being linear programme. This technique helped in solving allocation of limited resources. Introduction of computers and internet further helped in automation. The process of information dissemination.

### 6. Present Position

Since Adam Smith, we have progressed in every field of production. Production and productive capacity have increased and design, equipment and house building technologies have developed. We have improved industrial relations and quality of our products and services.

## ■ SCOPE OF PRODUCTION MANAGEMENT

The scope of any subject refers to the areas of study. The production management has a wide scope. The following aspects are said fall under the purview of production management.

### 1. Planning physical facilities

Whenever an idea of starting production in a factory is conceived by an industrialist, he has to plan its formative aspects. This involves determining the place of incorporation and selection of a suitable site to construct a factory building. Next follows the plan relating to the layout of the factory and design of the factory building. The factory building must be constructed so as to provide better working conditions to the employees. So, this involves provision of adequate physical facilities with the factory for lighting, ventilation, air-conditioning, sanitation and noise control. Planning must also be done for the proper maintenance of plant, machineries and other equipments. Finally, industrial security is to be provided for men, materials, machineries and finished goods. All these aspects go to ensure a smooth flow of production in the factory.

### 2. Organisation of production

The term production organisation is used both in a broad and narrow sense. In its broad sense, it implies the arrangement of all the factors of production, such as raw materials, labourers, machines, money and management required for production. Having procured these factors, necessary efforts are made to utilise them to the fullest extent possible so as to maximise production. In its narrow sense, the term organisation is concerned with setting up the internal organisation structure of the factory. In modern days, the structure of a factory is becoming more and more complex owing to the increase in the size of factories, the ever increasing application of scientific methods of production and diversity in the production process. It is highly impossible for a single individual to perform all the functions in a factory. So, in order to improve efficiency, the functions to be performed are identified in various categories. Then, these functions are entrusted to various persons by means of fixing responsibilities for them. Finally, the persons to whom duties are assigned are made accountable to their immediate superior. Thus, a sense of awareness is created in the minds of persons for discharging their duties satisfactorily. The internal organisation of a factory helps in coordinating the efforts of all employees which is very essential for the successful conduct of operations in the factory.

### 3. Factory management

'Factory Management' is mainly concerned with the implementation of policies into actions. This requires the performance of certain important functions, such as planning of the various aspects in the factory. Directing various activities, motivating the employees so as to increase their efficiency, communication of various reports to all levels of management, staffing the factory with required personnel, making decisions from alternative proposals, providing leadership ability in order to guide the subordinates, coordinating the efforts of people and, lastly, controlling the efficiency of operations of the factory. In order to perform all these functions, various levels of management, such as top level, middle level and bottom level management can be created. With the network of all the above functions, it is possible to attain the objectives of a factory in this way.

### 4. Materials management

'Materials Management' is concerned with controlling the kind, amount, location, movement, and timing of the various commodities used and produced by the factory. Materials use up substantial portion of the capital invested in the factories and thus demand continuing and considerable attention from the management. Many factories failures of the direct result outgrowth of excessive inventories. Too much materials canbe lock idle funds, and can result storage and obsolescence problems. On the other hand, if the materials are not adequate to meet the needs of the operating and distributing segments of the factory efficiency suffers and costs increase. Effective control of materials embrace four phases namely, (1) procurement of materials, i.e., purchases (2) external transportation, i.e., receiving, traffic and shipping, (3) internal transportation, i.e., material handling and (4) inventory control, i.e., storekeeping.

### 5. Labour administration

The importance of human labour cannot be underestimated in spite of the fact that machines have come to occupy a predominant place in factories. "Labour administration" is concerned with the scientific recruitment and selection of required number of employees with different types of skills. This is followed by training of employees to acquire perfection in their respective field of work. The formulation of promotional and transfer policy is an essential aspect of labour administration. The implementation of a particular system of wage payment has a direct bearing upon the efficiency of employees. Assessment of the performance morale of employees through job evaluation and merit rating techniques considerably improve the productivity of a factory. The provision of safety, health and welfare facilities enhances the morale of employees. The study of labour turnover and behavioural control of employees helps us restricting the change in labour force, thereby retaining experienced workers within the factory. Workers' participation in management enables us to solve labour problems in a more amicable way. Thus, labour administration deals with various aspects of labour with a view to utilise the available labour factor to the fullest possible extent.

### 6. Production and administrative control

The managerial function of control consists of a comparison of the actual performance with planned performance with the object of discovering whether everything is proceeding according to plan and if not why? Control is an essential feature of all factories. Effective control of men, materials, machines and money is essential for the proper running of any factory. In order to measure performance and to adjust to the changing environment, the efforts of individuals must be channelised into the desired directions. Control is necessary to ascertain the deviations and to guide the development of the firm towards chosen goals. The important types of control in a factory are: (1) administrative control, (2) financial or budgetary control, (3) production control, and (4) quality control, etc.

## ■ DUTIES AND RESPONSIBILITIES OF PRODUCTION MANAGER

The production manager is the head of the production department. He is responsible to the general manager for the accomplishment of the target output. The production manager must necessarily possess the technical knowledge of the production process. He takes the assistance of staff officers, such as the industrial engineer and production engineer for efficient production. His duties are as follows:

1. To prepare the production budget and achieve the budgeted output.
2. To receive work orders from customers and to distribute the same for execution to the production control department.
3. To design the factory building and equip it with the most up-to-date and efficient operating plant in consultation with the chief engineer.
4. To undertake efficient designs, productive efficiency and reduction of the cost by simplification and standardisation.
5. To compare actual results of production with the targeted production and ascertain how far the target has been attained.
6. To provide the best possible working conditions to the employees in the production department.
7. To organise a system of periodic meeting of work executives and workers so as to bring about greater coordination and create a spirit of fullest cooperation among all.
8. To engage in constant research and development programme so as to discover new methods of production to minimise wastages and ensure economical production.
9. To investigate into actual running time and idle time of the machines as that would often reveal the weak spots in the production work and thus strict control could be exercised.
10. To inspect the manufacturing processes, machinery and equipment and to control the production cost.

## PROBLEMS OF PRODUCTION MANAGEMENT

The problems faced by production manager are as follows:

### 1. Problem of plant location

Before the production process is determined, the production manager has to decide the place at which he has to set-up his factory. He has to choose the best locality in order to economise the cost of production. In order to select the best locality, he has to weigh the pros and cons of various factors, such as nearness to raw materials, transportation, warehousing, banking and other related facilities. All these factors are discussed in detail in chapter 5.

### 2. Problem of plant layout

It implies arrangement of plant and machineries and furniture and fixture in such a way that it occupies minimum space in the factory. This minimises not only the space but also facilitates easy movement of materials, men and finished goods. In addition to the layout of building, production manager has to solve other problems such as lighting, ventilation, air-conditioning, sanitation, noise control, etc. The various methods of overcoming these problems are discussed under Part-II of this book.

### 3. Problem of product designing

The selection of the design of the product is another problem faced by production manager. Any change in the design of the product will affect the design of the plant and its layout which will prove costly and complex for the enterprise. So, the design problem should be considered in advance.

### 4. Problem of material and production control

One of the problems faced by production manager is to ensure ready availability of materials to ensure continuity in production. With a view to take advantage of reduced cost of material and to avoid excess losses and wastages, various techniques of material control, such as deciding Economic Order Quantity (EOQ), level setting, ABC analysis, perpetual stock taking system must be decided.

Production planning and control techniques are essential to keep up promised delivery date. The production manager must also decide the production capacity. He has to plan the flexible schedules, work load of men and machines and assess the flow of production from machine to machine.

### 5. Problem of quality

Customer satisfaction, to a greater extent, depends upon the quality of the products. The quality of goods must fulfill the norm set by ISI and ISO series. The production manager must consider product inspection and statistical quality control techniques to ensure quality of goods.

### 6. Problem of personnel

By far this is the most serious problem faced by production manager. If demand of the workers is not fulfilled, they can resort to strikes and lockouts. Labour unrest will lead to inefficiency and consequently loss of output, both in terms of quantity and quality.

### 7. Problem of cost of production

The selling price depends upon the cost of production. If the cost of production is high, selling price will also be high. Consumers may find it difficult to buy costlier products. On the other hand, if the competitor's price is less, his sales will increase. Thus, the production manager is in a dilemma as to what price he has to charge for the goods.

### 8. Problem of environment

The functioning of a factory is affected by various economic and non-economic environmental factors, such as social, cultural, political, technological, natural, and historical. The production manager has to take into account all these factors so that the adverse effects may be solved by taking suitable measures.

## ■ STRATEGIC MANAGEMENT

Strategic management embraces a set of decisions, actions and interactions which help in designing an effective strategic network to facilitate the accomplishment of organisation's mission. In other words, it can be stated that the emphasis of strategic management is on innovative strategic programme, looks for changes in programme, identifies the potential for changes and makes critical appraisal of programme of attaining enterprise's mission.

### Meaning of strategy

The term 'strategy' is drawn from Military Science. It refers to actions that can be taken in the light of action taken by the opposite party. In business field, it refers to the actions of a businessman to offset the potential actions of competitors.

### Features of strategy

1. Strategy relates the firm to its environment, particularly the external environment. It is related to all actions whether objective setting or actions and resources required for its achievement.
2. Strategy is the right combination of factors, both external and internal. In relating an organisation to its environment, the management must also consider the internal factors too, particularly its strengths and weakness to take various courses of action.
3. Strategy is relative combination of actions. The combination is to meet a particular condition, to solve certain problems or to attain a desirable objective. It may take any form for every situation varies and therefore requires a somewhat different approach.
4. Strategy may also involve contradictory action. Since strategy depends on environmental variables, a manager may be forced to take action today and he may reverse or revise his steps later, depending on the situation.
5. Strategy is always forward looking and hence it has to do orientated towards the future. Strategic action required in a new situation.

### Need for strategic management

The need for strategic management can be discussed under the following points:

1. Today's bussiness has become more dynamic because of ever-changing environmental factors. Consequently, the organisations have to live and thrive in an atmosphere of continuous flux of threats and opportunities. Hence the pressing problem of modern organisation is to find out the ways for their survival in a highly volatile and transient environment. Under these circumstances, the only way of keeping the business, in momentum is by adopting several techniques of strategic management by exploring opportunities and minimizing threats. Today, the corporations either survive or acquit themselves well only by adopting "strategic management" in the present-day competitive world.
2. It helps the employees to carry out their tasks very effectively as they have clear role perception with well defined objectives, goals, rules which direct them clearly as to the work they have to do. In short, it gears the efficiency of workers.
3. It furnishes as a strong base for unified decision making and every one knows what are the objectives of the organisation. The success of strategic management depends on the competence of the strategist who owes the responsibility of defining the firm's objectives.

### Importance of strategic management in operation management

In the past, production was based on the number of orders received and the finance available with the organisation. But, in recent time, production function is affected by many environmental factors, such as economic, social, legal and such other factors. Besides, there environmental factors — the global market, foreign technology, foreign capital also influence production function. It is in this context, that strategic management has become useful to operations management.

Operation strategies involve the following elements:

(a) **Goal of the organisation**

1. Profit earning
2. Survival
3. Growth

4. Producing a targeted quantity of output
5. Attaining a targeted share of market
6. Compete successfully with others.

(b) **Reducing the cost of production:** In order to attain the above objectives, the cost of production should be minimised.

(c) **Decide method of production:** With a view to take benefit of economies of large-scale production one has to decide between manual or mechanical production and the relative advantages and disadvantages arising therefrom.

(d) **Quality of product:** The quality should be consistent with the expected quality of costumers. It should neither be too superior nor too inferior.

(e) **Delivery date:** In order to win the confidence of customers the goods should be delivered on the promised delivery date.

Operations strategies provide a blue print for attaining the operations objectives. It also involves other important decisions, such as introducing new line of product, expanding or contraction of production volume, continuance or discontinuance of a line of product, shuting down or continuance of a particular department which is responsible for incurring losses. It also involves provision of good working conditions and adoption of latest technology. All these are incorporated in the production plan of the organisation.

## QUESTIONS

### A. Very short answer type

1. What do you mean by production?
2. What do you mean by an operation?
3. State any four differences between production and operation.
4. Define production management.
5. List out the problems which a production manager encounters.

### B. Short answer type

1. State the features of production function or a manufacturing unit.
2. State the duties of production manager.
3. Explain problems faced by production manager.

### C. Long answer type

1. Define production management. Discuss its scope.
2. Give a brief history of development of production management.
3. Explain the major contributions to production management by
   (a) Charles Babbage
   (b) James Watt and M.R. Boulton
   (c) F.W. Taylor.

Chapter 2

# PRODUCTION SYSTEM

## MEANING OF SYSTEM

A system may be described as an entity arrangement of logically inter-related parts. Each inter-related part is known as a sub-system. The production function is considered to be a part of the industry. The sub-systems are inter-related and integrated so as to achieve the purpose of the main-system.

## PRODUCTION SYSTEM

If we consider production as a main-system, we see the following sub-systems in it:

1. **Input:** The various resources that are used in the production process, such as raw materials, human resources, capital resources, physical resources, monetary resources, etc. constitute input as a sub-system.
2. **Conversion process:** This sub-system involves various operations carried out for transforming inputs into output.
3. **Output:** The outcome of conversion process of input as known as output. It is the end result of production process. It generates revenue to the factory.
4. **Storage:** This sub-system exists to store the new materials until they are issued to production departments. Similarly, work in progress or semi-finished goods are also stored until they are further processed. The finished goods are also stored until demand for such goods arise.
5. **Transportation:** This sub-system is also known as internal transportation. It carries the raw materials from storeroom to various production departments.
6. **Information:** This sub-system connects all other sub-systems by providing required information. The information also facilitates in decision-making-process.

   A production system is said to be efficient when it achieves maximum output for a given minimum input.

## Types of production system

The types of production system can be shown under the following chart:

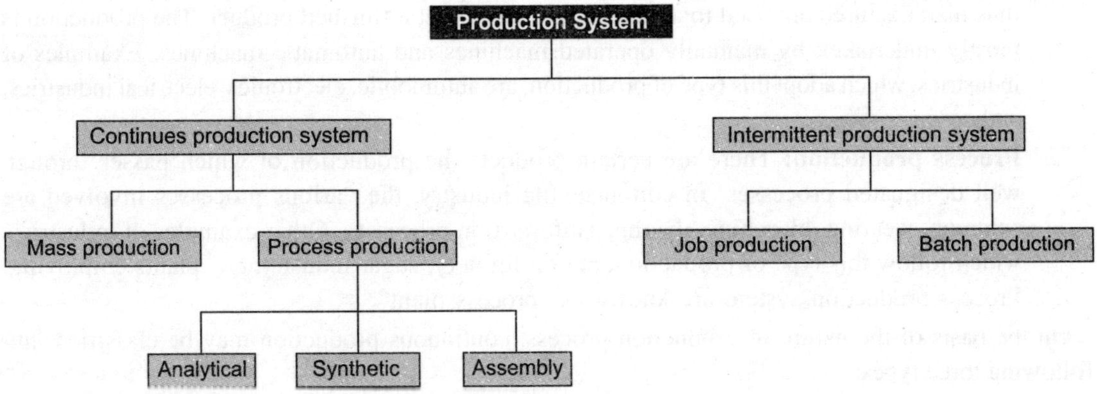


## Continuous production system

As the name itself indicates under this system, production is undertaken on a regular basis. The production process is standardised and involves a forward flow of materials and semi-finished products from machine to machine. The sequence of production is pre-determined and there is no back tracking of either materials or semi-finished goods. The examples of industries, which follow this system of production, are glass industries, steel mills, oil mill, sugar mill, paper mill, textile mill, etc.

## Characteristic features

1. Production is undertaken on continuous basis in anticipation of demand for such goods.
2. Production is undertaken on mass scale basis.
3. The end products are uniform in all respects.
4. Production is standardised, i.e., the design, production process and sequence of production are decided in advance.
5. There is a systematic arrangement of plant and machinery.
6. A good system of material handling exists under this system.

### Merits

1. Because of continuous production the work in progress inventory is minimised.
2. Production time is minimised because of continuous production.
3. Material handling cost is minimised.
4. Storage space is also minimised.
5. Cost per unit is minimised.
6. Quality is kept uniform.

### Demerits

1. It is a rigid system i.e., once it is installed it is difficult to alter it.
2. Break down of one machine leads to stoppage of production by other machines.

The two types of continuous production are given below:

1. **Mass production:** Mass production implies production of a standard component on a large-scale basis. The entire production process is standardised under this type. The components thus manufactured are used to assemble in order to get a finished product. The production is mostly undertaken by manually operated machines and automatic machines. Examples of industries, which adopt this type of production, are automobile, electronics, electrical industries, and so on.
2. **Process production:** There are certain products the production of which passes through well designated processes. In cotton textile industry, the various processes involved are spinning, wearing, bleaching, dyeing, sanforisation processes. Other examples of industries, which follow this type of production, are oil refinery, sugar industry, etc. plants employing. Process production system are known as "process plant".

On the basis of the nature of production process, continuous production may be classified into the following three types:

(a) **Analytical process:** In analytical process of production, a raw material is broken into different products. For example, crude oil is analysed into petrol, diesel, kerosene, gas, naphtha, etc. Similarly, coal is processed to obtain coke, coal gas, coal tar, ammonia, etc.

(b) **Synthetic process:** Under this system of production, two or more materials are mixed to manufacture a single product. For example, sand, bauxite, lime stone etc. are mixed to obtain cement.

(c) **Assembling process:** This type of production is followed in assembly type of industries, where the many component parts are assembled to get a finished product. The examples of such industries are: T.V., refrigerators, automobiles, washing machines, etc.

## ■ INTERMITTENT PRODUCTION

Under this type, production does not take place continuously. Hence, standardisation of production is not possible. The features of this type of production are as follows:

1. The volume of production is low.
2. The production process is intermittent.
3. Many varieties of products are produced.
4. General purpose machines are used instead of special purpose machines.
5. The production process may take place in more than one department.

Intermittent production may be of two types, viz.

### (a) Job production

Under this type, production is undertaken according to costomer's specification. The production process depends upon the number of orders received from customers. As such, production is not standardised and is intermittent in nature. The goods manufactured are not stocked but are for immediate delivery once it is complete in all respects. Its features are as follows:

1. Each job is dissimilar in nature requiring special treatment. Hence, the operations, process and the sequence may differ from job to job.
2. Production is intermittent and not continuous.

3. Production is undertaken against customer's order and not for stock.
4. Each job is distinctively identified by a production order throughout the production stage.
5. The cost of production of every job is ascertained after the completion of the job.

**Merits**

1. This type of production involves comparatively small investment.
2. It is flexible and capable of adapting to change.
3. Any stoppage of production in one department does not affect production in other departments.

**Demerits**

1. It involves accumulation of work in progress at various places because of intermittent production. This requires more storage space and involves high material handling cost.
2. Because of frequent movement of employees and equipments, production is delayed and thereby involving high cost of production.

### (b) Batch production

H. A. Harding defines batch production as "the manufacture of a product in small or large batches or lots at intervals by a series of operations, each operation being carried out in the whole batch before any subsequent operation is performed." Its features are as follows:

1. Economic batch quantity is determined before production is undertaken.
2. It involves setting up of machines and therefore setting up cost in addition to production cost.
3. The production in batches repeats after the completion of batch cycle.

**Merits**

1. It takes the benefit of reduced cost of production arising out of economic batch quantity.
2. Supervision becomes easy and more effective by means of spreading over the supervisor's time over all the units constituting the batch. Thus, the idle time of supervisors as well as workers is eliminated.
3. The loss of time under job production, arising out of inter-job transfer of materials, labours and tools is minimised.

**Demerits**

1. If the production of a batch is wrongly undertaken, say, owing to sub-standard materials or defective operations, the whole batch of articles are to be discarded which will become a great loss to the manufacturers. Drugs and pharmaceutical products are the best example to this point of disadvantage.
2. Due to frequent changes in product design, no standard sequence of operation can be used.
3. It involves frequent changes in machine set-ups and tooling arrangements which also increases the cost of production.

# QUESTIONS

## A. Very short answer type

1. What do you mean by a system?
2. What do you mean by a sub-system?
3. State the sub-systems involved in the production system.
4. What do you mean by continuous production?
5. What is mass production?
6. What is process production?
7. What is analytical production?
8. What is synthetic production?
9. What is assembly production?
10. What is intermittent production?
11. What is job production?
12. What is batch production?

## B. Short answer type

1. State the features, merits and demerits of continuous production.
2. State the features, merits and demerits of job production.
3. State the features, merits and demerits of batch production.

Chapter 3

# PRODUCT SELECTION AND DESIGNING

## ■ INTRODUCTION

The term 'product' is used in a wider sense. It includes not only tangible product but also services which are intangible. Selection of product is based not only on the decision of the manufacturer but also on the requirements of the customer. For example, when a book is published it should not only enhance knowledge but also enable the students to understand the subject matter and score better marks in the examination.

In some cases, a manufacturer may decide to choose a product from product mix. The selection of product depends not only on the decision of the production manager but also on other factors, such as competition, availability of materials, demand for the product, technology and financial availability.

Having selected a product, the production manager must design the product, decide the quality of the product, estimate the cost of product, and assess the difficulties involved in production. The other factors which determine the selection of a product are the availability of plant and machineries, flexibility of production process, availability of substitute raw materials and available infrastructure facilities.

## ■ PROCEDURES INVOLVED IN PRODUCT SELECTION

Product selection is one of the steps involved in production planning. It involves the following steps:

1. Conceiving an idea to produce a product: The idea may generate owing to the knowledge and experience of production manager, through conducting research and development, by suggestions made by customers or even by salesman.
2. If more than one product is conceived it involves shortlisting the product. This depends upon customers' choice or their tastes and preferences, production capacity available, profit margin expected, policy and philosophy of the organisation and goal pursued by the organisation. A check-list can be prepared or ranking method can be followed for shortlisting the product.
3. To undertake a detailed business analysis, including risk analysis, break-even analysis, cash flow analysis, etc. so as to know the feasibility of the product.
4. The next step involved is product development. In this stage, the product idea takes a definite shape. A miniature of the product is developed. This can be improved upon by engineering department. It can be tested so that it meets the requirements of customer and it has no side-effects.

There is always exists a gestation period in this, i.e., the time of conceiving a product to the time of launching the product. This time lag must be minimized so that the competitors do not take over such product. This can be reduced by constantly undertaking various product proposals in such a way as one stage is reached it should enter into the subsequent stage. Such a practice indicates innovation in the organization and product development becomes a continuous process.

## ■ PRODUCT DESIGN

According to Indian Patent and Designs Act., design means the feature or shape, configuration, pattern or ornament applied to any article by any industrial process which, in the finished article, appeal to eye and does not include any trade mark.

Designing a product plays an important role in the development of a product. A detailed specification of the product is listed at the design stage. From these specifications a design is made. The success and profitability of a product depends upon the design of the product. The product is designed with the coordinated efforts of various departmental heads, such as production manager, plant engineer, marketing manager, etc. In some cases, standard specifications are available, as for example standard specification of drugs and pharmaceutical products.

A design once prepared need not be used on a permanent basis. It can be improved over a period of time. It can also be redesigned in case of need.

In modern days, computers are used on a large scale to design a product. The various factors which influence a design are:

(a) The mechanical problems involved in the economical manufacturing methods.
(b) Ease in handling.
(c) The overall weight and dimension of the machinery.
(d) The type and the number of personnel required to run the plant and to undertake repairs.
(e) The capital cost of plant and cost of maintenance.
(f) Smoothness in operation.
(g) Selling consideration.
(h) Appearance of the product.

## ■ PROCEDURE IN DESIGNING

Designing a product involves the following steps:

1. Research should be conducted about the product.
2. Functional drawings and design be prepared on a scientific basis.
3. Construction and test of experimental phototypes should be prepared.
4. To undertake analysis of experimental phototype performance.
5. Analysis of design for standardisation simplification, and production method is to be undertaken.
6. Production drawing is to be detailed.
7. The issue of manufacturing drawing be carefully checked and authorised to avoid any duplication.
8. Supervision of assembly and test of production phototype.
9. Full-scale test of pilot production model be carried out.
10. Release for production on a full scale output.

## ■ OBJECTS OF DESIGNING

The objects of designing are as under:

1. To create attention in product for maximizing sales.
2. To enlarge the importance of product from customers' point of view.
3. To make product more effective and create more utility in the product for the consumers.
4. To produce better quality at the lower possible price.

## ■ PRODUCT DEVELOPMENT

Product development means devising a product to meet the exact requirement of the market. In case of existing product, if it is not up to the satisfaction of customers, it should be improved to meet the requirement of customers. It involves creations of new product to overcome the defects of old product and to suggest ways and means of improving old product with a new to earn more profit and increase efficiency of the production process. There are two elements in product development, viz., (a) Introduction of a new product, and (b) improvement of existing product.

The following check-list can be used to decide the product development in a factory:

1. Whether the product satisfy customers' preference, size, colour, shape, etc.?
2. Whether the product been designed for economy in factory production to ensure a reasonable price?
3. What is the possibility of production protection?
4. What will be probable effect of product development on the products in the line?
5. What are the manufacturing and distributing facilities available for the product?
6. Is the stock and display of the product convenient?
7. To what extent will the by-product or waste be utilised.
8. Can the product be sold or distributed through the existing channel of distribution?
9. Whether the product afford stable supply?
10. Is the product within the buying capacity of the consumer?
11. Is the product convenient to handle, carry out of stores and to use?
12. Whether the product is durable and can prevent the spoilage during the course of its transfer to the customer?
13. Is the quality of product appeals to the people which may help in increasing the demand continuously?
14. What relationship it has between development and research and manufacturing cost and the returns expected?
15. Is the product pleasing to the eyes?

## ■ SPECIALISATION

Kimball and Kimball in their book "Industrial organisation" define specialisation as "the concentration of efforts upon a limited field of endeavour. The concentration, in its widest sense, may involve labour, the use of machinery or other facilities of production". In its narrow sense, where the production of an article is divided up among a number of workers, each worker performing a very limited range of work, constitutes specialisation. The specialisation is based on the following principles :

(a) The size of the production unit should be big enough so that large-scale production is possible.
(b) There must be a scientific division of activities and sub-activities. Each sub-activity must be complete in itself.
(c) 'Interest' and 'ability' should be the main criteria for the allocation of work among persons.
(d) Thc arca of work and responsibility should be clearly defined.
(e) There must be coordination among various sub-activities.

**Advantages**

1. Specialisation in production leads to achieve higher productivity through the use of standardised methods of production.
2. By the application of division of labour it helps to increase output and thereby decrease cost of production.
3. It enables a person to become a specialist and thus he can speed up the process of production.
4. It eliminates wastages and losses because a specialist alone can avoid its recurrence.
5. Because of inter-dependence of all departments it promotes cooperation in the organisation.
6. It improves quality of products.

**Disadvantages**

1. Specialisation takes flexibility. A person who specialises in an activity may not be able to do another task with some efficiency.
2. Specialisation may involve danger in the stoppage of production as closure of production in one department may lead to stoppage of production in another department.
3. It gives rise to groupism. Non-cooperation may lead to production problems, such as delay etc.
4. Seasonal fluctuation in demand may also affect the specialised plant.

## ■ DIVERSIFICATION

According to James Lundy in *Effective Industrial Management*, diversification involves the broadening of the line through addition of new products or new models of old products. Diversification may be in the form of new products, new product line, new markets or a new technology. Diversification may take place owing to the following reasons:

(a) Technological development may lead to development of a new product.
(b) Expansion in the existing market.
(c) To improve goodwill and reputation of the business.
(d) To overcome threat to the existing product owing to change in fashion.
(e) To utilise the untapped capacity of production.
(f) To overcome the problem of seasonality of the product or seasonal fluctuation of demand.
(g) To utilise the existing selling and distribution methods effectively.

The product diversification is undertaken to achievc thc following objectives:

(a) To maintain stability in earnings.

(b) To utilise the resourcces more efficiently.

(c) To undertake marketing more efficiently.

## QUESTIONS

### A. Very short answer type

1. What do you mean by product design?
2. List out any four factors which influence product design.
3. State four objects of product design.
4. What do you mean by product development?
5. What do you mean by specialisation?
6. State the principles on which specialisation is based.
7. What do you mean by product diversification?
8. State the objects of product diversification.

### B. Short answer type

1. What do you mean by product selection? State the procedure involved in it.
2. List out the steps involved in designing a product.
3. State the advantages and disadvantages of specialisation.
4. Enumerate the factors which determine product diversification.

Chapter 4

# SALES FORECASTING

## ■ INTRODUCTION

Production of goods or services has no meaning unless they are sold. So, management of a manufacturing enterprise gives serious thought to sales. For this purpose, sales are forecasted so that the production may be carried on accordingly and there should be no problem of under or over stocking because it would lead to many other problems like storing and warehousing, quality deterioration, etc. So, sales forecasting is necessary.

Forecasting means forseeing the future. As future is unknown, in the past businessmen used to involve certain systematic and scientific methods to know the future by scientific analysis based on facts and possible consequences. This is systematic method of assessing the future is called forecasting. Forecast of sales refers to an act of under taking production according to future sales followed by a detailed analysis of facts related to future situations and forces which may affect the business as a whole.

Sales forecasting is an important event in the production field and the whole production system revolves around this concept of sales forecasting. Production activities are planned according to the sales estimates. The buying, selling, advertising, sales promotion, storage, packaging, etc. are planned accordingly. Thus, sales forecasting may be said to be the very basis of planning whether concerned with marketing, production, finance or personnel and, therefore, for the successful achievement of overall objectives of the organisation accurate sales forecasting is necessary. It is advisable that the figures of sales forecasting once estimated should be reviewed periodically so that plans may be adjusted accordingly. Sales forecasting is the basis of budgeting too, which is an important tool for controlling the business affairs.

## ■ MEANING OF FORECASTING

Forecasting is a systematic attempt to make an assessment of the future by inference from known facts.

## ■ MEANING OF SALES FORECASTING

Sales forecasting means estimating the future sales either in terms of value or in terms of units

## ■ DEFINITION OF SALES FORECASTING

According to American Marketing Association, sales forecasting is an "estimate of sales in dollars or physical units for a specified future period under a proposed marketing plan or programme and under an assumed set of economic and other forces outside the unit for which the forecast is made". In the words of Phillip Kotler, "The sales forecast of any company is expected level of sales based on a chosen marketing plan and assumed environmental conditions." According to Cundiff and Still, "Sales forecast is an estimate of sales during a specified future period which is tied to a proposed marketing plan and which assumes a particular set of uncontrollable and competitive force."

## ■ IMPORTANCE OF SALES FORECASTING

The data of sales forecasting is very essential for an industrial enterprise. This is highlighted under the following points:

1. **A guiding factor for a firm:** Sales forecasting enables an organisation to produce right quantity in right quality at the right time and at the reasonable price. It is based on sales forecasting so that the organisation plans its resources, i.e. raw materials, labours, etc. Forecasting enables the firm to manufacture according to the likely demand of the product. This enables us to reduce inventory, production and distribution cost.
2. **The basis of formulating policies:** Sales forecasting is the basis for formulating production policies, such as quantity of production, method of production, etc. and personnel policies, such as recruitment, promotion, wage fixation, etc. The financial policies, such as short-term working capital and fixed capital is also based on sales forecasting. Other policies, such as marketing policies, is also based on sales forecasting.
3. **Taking correct decisions:** It enables the management to decide whether to take up production manually or mechanically, sale of scrap or utilise the material in the organisation, shut down or continue operation, continue or discontinue the existing product, introduce new line of product and so on.
4. **Setting goal for sales department:** Sales forecast sets the goals to be achieved by the sales department. If these goals are achieved, it reflects the efficiency of the sales department.

### Objects of sales forecasting

The objects of sales forecasting depends upon the types of forecasting. Accordingly, there are two types of forecasting, viz. (1) short-run forecasting, and (2) long-run forecasting.

### 1. Short-run forecasting

A short-run forecasting is one which is undertaken maximum for a period of one year. The objectives of short-run sales forecasting are as follows:

(a) **Formulation of production policy:** Based on sales forecasting, it is possible to avoid over-production and under production of goods. When goods are over-produced, it involves more investment. When goods are under and produced it amounts to loss of sales.

(b) **Ensuring regular supply of raw materials:** If raw materials are bought in excess quantities than required, it involves storage problems and more investment on it. If materials are under stocked it leads to stoppage of production. Sales forecasting helps in the purchase of required quantities of materials only thus avoiding the problems associated with over stock and under stocking of the same.

(c) **Proper utilisation of machines:** Maximum utilisation of machines is yet another object of sales forecasting. In times of increased production, the production capacity must be utilised fully and in times of decrease in demand the machine should not remain idle.

(d) **Determination of price policy:** Sales forecasting has an important bearing on pricing policy of an organisation. During the period of depression the price should not be increased and during inflation, the price must not be decreased.

(e) **Regular supply of labour:** Sales forecasting also facilitates regular supply of skilled and semi-skilled workers to an organisation. During peak period, the organisation should not face the problem of shortage of labour and during slack season there should not be idle resources of labour.

(f) **Facilitates preparation of short-term financial plan:** The financial requirements of an organisation depends on the level of sales and volume of production. Sales forecasting enables the organisation to arrange funds according to its needs on reasonable terms and well in advance. It will minimise the cost of borrowing.

(g) **Setting the sales target and to control over-sales:** It sets the sales targets for different market segments on the basis of which control can be exercised on the people concerned with production work. It is possible to introduce incentives for implementing the programmes and to achieve sales target.

### 2. Long-run forecasting

Forecasting of sales for more than one year is known as long run forecasting. The objectives of long-term forecasting are as follows:

(a) **Estimating long-term financial requirement:** Long-term financial requirement is predicted on the basis of long-term sales forecast. Cash inflow can be estimated by determining cash and credit sales ratio. It also helps in planning credit policy of an organisation. The long-term requirement of working and fixed capital is estimated by means of sales forecasting.

(b) **Planning plant capacity:** If the sales forecasts reveal that the plant capacity will fall short of the future demand, a decision to install a new plant or to increase the capacity of the existing one can be taken.

(c) **To facilitate budgetary control:** Sales forecast facilitates the preparation of various budgets. Budgetary control can be exercised by comparing actuals with budgets to set right adverse variance.

(d) **Dividend and reserve policy:** Sales forecasting can also forecast the profit of the firm on the basis of gross profit ratio on sale. Profitability has an influence over many managerial decisions. The rate of dividend and creation of reserve also depends upon the profit earning capacity of the business.

## ■ TECHNIQUES OF SALES FORECASTING

The important techniques of sales forecasting are as unders:

### 1. User's expectation method

Under this technique the actual users of the product of the organisation are contacted and they are questioned about the intention of buying the articles for a given period, usually for a year. On the basis of the reply given by the customers the total forecast of sales is assessed.

**Advantages**

1. There is reliability factor under this technique because actual data furnished by the customers constitute the basis for sale forecast.
2. Based on the reply of users it is possible to develop a new product.
3. This technique is best suited where previous record is not available.
4. This technique is more suitable for short-run forecasting.

**Disadvantages**

1. This technique is difficult to adopt where customers are numerous.
2. The technique is based on intention and expectations of customers which may change subsequently.
3. The technique is not useful for long-term forecasting.

## 2. Collective opinion or sales force composite method

Under this technique the information is gathered from salesmen, branch manager, area manager, and for the different segment of the market. As salesmen are close to the customers, they will estimate the expected sale in their respective territories. These views of all salesmen are then consolidated to get total sales forecast. By taking into consideration the likely changes in product design, advertisement competition price, etc. they are finally taken as the actual sales forecasts.

**Advantages**

1. As first hand information is obtained from salesmen and other managers, the sales forecast is more reliable.
2. This technique infuses greater confidence among sales force.
3. It fixes responsibility on sales personnel.
4. Market segmentation can be undertaken on the basis of product, territory, customer, etc.

**Disadvantages**

1. Salesmen know that the sales quota is fixed on the basis of information furnished by them. So, they deliberately underestimate the sale.
2. This technique is not suitable for long-term forecast.
3. The information furnished by salesmen and other managers may not be accurate as they are sometimes over optimistic or under optimistic.

## 3. Executive judgment method

This is a process under which opinions expressed by various executives, such as marketing manager, finance manager, production manager, etc. are averaged or evaluated by some means. Sales forecasts are then prepared based on average or combining the opinions of the concerned executives.

**Advantages**

1. It is a speedier technique of sales forecast compared to other techniques.
2. Difficulty involved in collecting data is not experienced in this technique.
3. Where adequate data is not available this is the only means of forecast.

**Disadvanages**

1. It is not based on actual facts.
2. The forecast may not be accurate.
3. Precious time of executives is wasted on this sales forecast technique.

## 4. Experts opinion

Under this technique, the organisation will collect information from experts or specialists who are external to the organisation. Some specialists whose opinions that are relied upon are: (a) authors who express their opinions in journals and magazines, (b) wholesalers and distributors of company's products, (c) professional experts such as chamber of commerce, etc. By analysing these opinions and views of experts, deduction is made for the company's sales and accordingly sales forecasts are made.

**Advantages**

1. As different opinions experts are considered, it is possible to evaluate them before forecasting the sales.
2. This technique is suitable where person's records are not available.
3. This method is economical as no data is collected. The expenses involved in seeking expert's opinion is lesser than the expenses of actual survey.

**Disadvantages**

1. The opinions of experts need not reflect the opinions of neutral users.
2. It is not possible to segment the market on the basis of product, territory or customers.

## 5. Market test method

Under this technique, the manufacturer sells his product on a trial basis in some part of the market and makes an assessment of sales for the full market on the basis of results of test sales. This method is suitable under the following conditions.

(a) Where new products are involved.
(b) Where good estimators are not available.
(c) Where buyers do not prepare purchase plans.

**Advantages**

1. This technique is most suitable in case of new product.
2. If there is any defect in the product it can be set right immediately to make the product more successful in the market.
3. Sales forecast is more reliable, as it is based on actual result.

**Disadvantages**

1. It takes more time to test the product in the market.
2. The entire market is not covered for testing the product in the market.

### 6. Trend projection method

Under this technique, the sales data is collected over a period of time. Such a data is generally referred to as time series. The change in values of sales is found out. The study may show that the sales sometimes are increasing and sometimes decreasing, but a general trend in the long run will be either upward or downward. The trend is called secular trend. Under this technique, sales forecast is made on the assumption that the same trend will continue in the future.

The method which is generally used in fitting the trend is known as the method of least squares or straight line trend method. With this method, a straight line trend is obtained. This line is called the 'line of best fit'. By using the formula of regression equation of Y on X, the future sales are projected.

### Calculation of trend

The trend can be calculated by the least square method as follows:

(a) Find out time deviations ($X$) of each period from a certain period and then find the sum of time deviation ($\Sigma X$).

(b) Square the time deviations of each period ($x^2$) and then find the sum of squares of each period ($\Sigma X^2$).

(c) Multiply the time deviation with the sales of each period individually ($XY$) and then add the product of the column to find ($\Sigma XY$).

(d) To find out the trend ($Y$) which is equal to $a + bx$. The value of $a$ and $b$ may be determined by either of the following two ways.

***(i) Direct method***

This method is applicable only when $\Sigma X = 0$. To make $\Sigma X = 0$, it is necessary that the time deviations should be calculated exactly from mid-point of the series. Then the values of a and b will be calculated as follows:

$$a = \text{average} = \frac{\Sigma Y}{N}$$

$$b = \text{(rate of growth)} = \frac{\Sigma XY}{\Sigma X^2}$$

***(ii) Indirect method***

The method is difficult compared to the direct method. This method can be applied in cases where $\Sigma$ has any positive or negative values or $\Sigma$ is not equal to zero. The values of $a$ and $b$ are calculated by solving the following two equations

$$\Sigma Y = Na + b\Sigma X$$
$$\Sigma XY = a\,\Sigma X + b\Sigma X^2$$

By solving the above equations, the values of $a$ and $b$ can be obtained. Using the formula $Y = a + bX$ it is possible to forecast the sales.

**Advantages**

1. This technique is less expensive because no survey is conducted nor customers are contacted.
2. This is a mathematical method and as such there is no possibility of subjectiveness.

3. Because it is a mathematical method it is more accurate.
4. Trend values can be obtained for all the given time period in the series.

**Disadvantages**

1. This method is more tedious and involves more calculations.
2. Forecasting is based only on long-term variation i.e., trend and the impact of short-term variations are ignored.
3. This technique relies largely on statistics but not on personal skill and experience.

## 7. Moving average method

When a trend is to be determined by the method of moving averages, the average value for a number of years is secured. This average is taken as the normal or trend value for the unit of time falling at the middle of the period covered in the calculation of the average.

The following steps will be taken into account while calculating the trend with the moving average method.

1. The years of the moving average can be even like 2, 4, 6 etc. or odd like 3, 5, 7 etc. depending upon the length of cycle.
2. Suppose, if it is the case of 3 years moving average, the values for the first 3 years are added and the total is put corresponding to the middle year. Similarly, first year is ignored and the values of next three years are added and the total is put corresponding to the middle year. This process will continue till the value of the last year's value is taken into account. In the case of even number of years, the total is put corresponding to the mid of the middle two years, and rest of the process remains the same as in the case of odd number of years.
3. In order to get the averages, the totals will be divided by the number of years. These averages are "Trend values". In the case of even number of years, the averages will not be corresponding to the particular years. Therefore, the averages are re-done by taking the averages of the two averages. This process is known as centring.

In order to get "short-term variations", we subtract trend values from the actual data.

**Advantages**

1. This method is simple when compared to the method of least squares.
2. It is a flexible method of measuring trend for the reason that if a few more figures are added to the data, all the calculations are not changed, we only get some more trend values.
3. If the period of moving average happens to coincide with the period of cyclical fluctuations in the data, such fluctuations are automatically eliminated.
4. It is particularly effective if the trend of a series is very irregular.

**Disadvantages**

1. Trend values cannot be computed for all the years. The longer the period of moving average, the greater the number of years for which trend values cannot be obtained for the first and last year, in a five-yearly moving average for the first two years and the last two years, and so on.

2. Since moving averages are not represented by a mathematical function, this method cannot be used in forecasting which is one of the main objectives of trend analysis.
3. When the trend situation is not linear (a straight line), the moving average lies either above or below the true sweep of the data. Consequently, the moving average is appropriate for trend computations only when
   (a) The purpose of investigation does not call for current analysis or forecasting.
   (b) The trend is linear.

Unfortunately, these conditions are encountered quite infrequently.

## ■ APPROACH TO SALES FORECASTING

Sales forecasting involves the following steps:

1. **Determining the objectives:** The first step involved in the forecasting process is to determine the purpose of forecasting. This is, in turn, based on certain other factors such as duration of forecasting (viz. short-term or long-term forecasting), area of sales forecasting (whole country or a specific area), and unit of sale for forecasting (value or quantity). Besides these factors, money, time and labour involved in sales forecasting is also to be considered.

2. **Sub-dividing the task:** Secondly, the task is to be sub-divided into homogeneous group according to area, customer, and product. The data of sales forecasting shall be the sum total of the sales forecasts of all the groups.

3. **Identifying the factors:** Having subdivided the task of forecasting, the various factors affecting the sales should be identified in order to give weights to these factors.

4. **Selecting the technique:** The next step is to choose the appropriate technique of sales forecasting, as discussed earlier. The technique to be selected is, in turn, affected by the situation prevailing in the organisation, the authority who selects the technique, the convenience of the technique the purpose of the sales forecasting and the desired accuracy.

5. **Collection and analysis of data:** This step involves collection, analysis and interpretation of data. Statistical techniques help us in this connection. After interpretation, necessary decisions are arrived out.

6. **Forecast and sales promotion:** In order to know the effectiveness of sales promotion on actual sales, it is necessary to establish the correlation between the two. If there is a positive correlation between the two, it is worth undertaking sales promotion measures in future too.

7. **Effect of competition:** Actual sales of a business is affected by competitors. Therefore, it is necessary to study the policies, strategies, price, programmes of competitors before finalising the sales forecast. If need be, our polices and programmes can be adjusted accordingly.

8. **Preparing final sales forecasts:** The data collected before preparing sales forecast has to be reviewed by taking into account the sales promotion plans and competitor's attitude. The final sales forecast is then prepared.

9. **Evaluation and adjustment:** The sales forecast figures becomes the basis of operation for the next year. The actual sales performance of next year should be reviewed and evaluated on a regular basis. Based on the difficulties of the past year, the sales forecast is to be revised. Similarly, based on the actual sales performance, the sales forecast for the subsequent years should also be revised.

## ■ LIMITATIONS FOR SALES FORECASTING

Sales forecasting is subject to the following limitations:

1. **Customer's tastes, habits, preferences:** The tastes, habits, and preferences of customers, vary from time to time. Further, the fashions, the standard of living of customers also keep changing from time to time. In the fast changing environment, it is very difficult to prepare an accurate sales forecasts.

2. **Lack of past data:** In case of new products, it is very difficult to prepare sales forecast as data relating to earlier years are not available. It is based on guess work which will not always be true.

3. **Lack of anticipatory growth:** It is difficult to maintain the steady rate of growth. The future demand of customers vary. Increase in population, rise in income, etc. also affect the demand for goods and services. Unless these additional demand of customers are taken into account, a good sales forecast cannot be prepared.

4. **Psychological factors:** It is difficult to make out the psychology of customers. If they apprehend a scarcity of goods or a price rise they want to buy in bulk and even stock for the future. On the other hand, if they come to know of a better product, or there is likely fall in prices of goods, it may result in the decline in demand.

## QUESTIONS

### A. Very short answer type

1. What do you mean by sales forecasting?
2. Define sales forecasting.
3. List out the various techniques of sales forecasting.
4. State the limitations of sales forecasting.

### B. Short answer type

1. Explain the importance of sales forecasting.
2. Explain the objectives of forecasting.
3. Explain the steps involved in sales forecasting.

### C. Long answer type

1. Discuss the various techniques of sales forecasting.

Chapter 5

# PLANT LOCATION

## ■ INTRODUCTION

Plant location refers to area where the plant will operate to produce goods or services. The choice of a suitable location is the first item that a factory owner has to consider. When plant location is decided upon, a suitable site must be selected for the factory building. Thus, plant location comprises of (1) a selection of larger general area, such as a state, district or a town, where production and distribution activities are carried on, and (2) a selection of site which is a smaller area within the general area for putting up a factory. The site to be selected may be an urban site, suburban site or a country site depending upon their comparative merits and demerits. The ideal location is one that permits the lowest unit cost in the production and distribution of a product or service.

## ■ MEANING OF PLANT LOCATION

Plant location means deciding a suitable location, area or place where the plant will start functioning.

### Definition

1. R.C. Davis in his book "*Industrial Organisation and Management*" defines plant location as "the function of determining where the plant should be located for maximum operating economy and effectiveness."
2. Bethel, Smith and Atwater in their book "Industrial Organisation and Management" have defined plant location as "that spot where, in consideration of the business as a whole, the total cost of production and delivering goods to all the consumers is the lowest."

## ■ NEED FOR PLANT LOCATION

The need for plant location arises under the following circumstances:

1. When a new plant is to be established.
2. In case of established plants, the need for plant location arises when expansion, decentralisation and diversification is undertaken to meet the increased demand for its products.
3. Whenever the existing factory is not in a position to obtain renewal of lease.
4. When an undesirable location is to be abandoned.
5. When the tendency of shifting the market, depletion of raw materials, changes in transportation facilities, new processes requiring a different location are observed in a factory.
6. When a new branch or branches are to be opened for increasing the volume of production or distribution or both.

## ■ IMPORTANCE OF PLANT LOCATION

The selection of an appropriate location enables the factory to operate smoothly, efficiently, and with minimum cost. It is estimated that manufacturing and distribution costs may vary to an extent of 10 per cent simply by virtue of the choice of plant location. Wrong location leads to wastage in efforts and talents of the promoters with consequent uncertainty in results. The location of plant has a great effect on the success or failure of the operation of that plant. If the selection of the site is not proper, all the money invested on factory building, machinery and their installation, etc. will go waste and the owner of the factory has to suffer a great loss. Further, the cost of transferring it from one location to another would prove a very costly affair and pose problems which cannot be easily solved. Therefore, while selecting a site, the owner must consider technical, commercial and financial aspects and then to select a suitable site that may provide maximum advantage.

## ■ STEPS IN PLANT LOCATION

According to Bethel, Atwater and Smith, plant location involves three main steps. They are:

(1) Selection of the region or general area, (2) Selection of the particular community, and (3) Selection of the exact plant site.

If the above steps are applied for the selection of a locality by an entrepreneur in India, first of all, he has to select one of the four regions, viz., Southern, Northern, Eastern or Western regions. If the entrepreneur wants to select southern region, then selecting a particular community, viz., Andhra, Karnataka, Kerala and Tamil Nadu is to be decided upon. Finally, having selected one of the community the selection of an urban, suburban or country site is to be decided upon in that community. The application of each step in plant location are, in turn, determined by a number of factors. These are explained below.

## ■ FACTORS AFFECTING PLANT LOCATION

The location of plant is determined by a number of factors. This is represented in the following chart:

**Factors Affecting Plant Location**

**Selection of Region**

1. Availability of raw materials
2. Fuel and power
3. Transport
4. Market
5. Meteorological conditions and topography

**Selection of Community**

1. Labour
2. Supplementary and complementary industries
3. Banking and credit institutions
4. Local taxes and insurance
5. Water
6. Momentum of early start
7. Personal factors
8. Historical factors
9. Political stability
10. State assistance

**Selection of Exact Plant Site**

1. Price of land
2. Type of soil
3. Waste disposal
4. Expansion potential
5. Commercial services
6. Communication
7. Availability of amenities
8. Health of the locality
9. Statutory consideration
10. Flood and drought conditions
11. Right and title of the land
12. Good scenery
13. Attitude of local people
14. Technological know-how
15. Religious and social institutions

## ■ SELECTION OF REGION

Selection of a region calls for information more of a general nature. Information about the locality is of a general nature which may be obtained from the following sources:

1. Ministry of industrial development
2. National Council of Applied Economic Research
3. Indian Federation of Chamber of Commerce,
4. Department of Industry in State Governments.

The following factors determine the selection of a region.

1. **Availability of raw materials:** Raw materials for the purpose of plant location can be broadly classified into two categories, namely (1) ubiquities, i.e., existing everywhere, like clay, water, etc., and (2) localised materials, such as minerals, timber, coal, sugarcane, etc., which are available only in certain places. Localised materials can be further sub-divided into pure material and gross materials. Pure materials add to the weight of the finished product and, therefore, factories using pure materials are located near markets. Some examples of pure materials are: cotton, raw wool, raw silk, etc. Gross materials are those which lose their weight in the process of their transformation into finished goods. Examples of gross materials are sugarcane, iron ore, lime stone, etc. Factories requiring gross materials are located near the sources of raw materials. This is because bulky raw materials would be expensive to be carried to distant areas. Thus, this is the main reason why early localisation of most of iron and steel industries in Orissa and Bihar, sugar factories in U.P. and textile mills in Maharashtra were undertaken. Further location of factories near the source of raw materials ensures the continuity of production.

Nearness to raw materials is especially important in the case of heavy and bulky materials of small value as in the case of coal. In the words of Spiegel and Lansburgh, "Nearness to the source of raw materials is of special importance when the material is bulky in relation to its value and when the volume and weight are greatly reduced during the processing."

Again, if the raw materials are perishable, proximity to supply of raw materials is an advantage. Examples of such factories are fruit canning, fish canning, etc.

In case of imported materials, it is necessary to locate factories near the ports to take advantage of low cost of raw materials due to cheaper sea transport charges. In U.S.A, steel plants are mostly situated near the costal areas.

2. **Nearness to fuel and power:** Nearness to cheap fuel and power is second decisive factor in plant location. In olden days, coal for generating steam, oil, and natural gas constituted as chief sources of power. Therefore, during the 19th century, most of the factories were located near the coal mines where coal could be taken cheaply and conveniently. But in 20th century, electricity has assumed great importance as a source of power. This is because of its relative cheapness, ease in handling, cleanliness, flexibility and easier to transmit over long distances. Still, it is necessary to ensure that the phase, voltage, frequency, rates, regularity, special discounts allowed are suitable to the factory. Availability of electricity has been one of the reasons for the development of many new industries in sub-urban and rural areas. In India, we have four types of power sources: (1) Thermal power, (2) Hydroelectric power, (3) Nuclear power, and (4) Solar power. Technologists are exploring the possibility of obtaining power from wind and sea waves.

3. **Transport:** Transport as a factor will influence plant location in following ways. *First*, transport facility is necessary for getting raw materials to the place of manufacture. *Secondly*, for transporting

finished goods to the place of consumption. *Thirdly*, transportation facilities are essential for carrying employees and sales representatives of the factory.

According to James Lundy, the ideal plant from the point of view of transportation is one which is centrally located and directly connected by water, rail, road and air facilities. For a factory which has to distribute large volume of goods, water transport is suitable as it is a cheap mode of transport. Rail transport is economical for long distances. Road transport, which includes trucks is suitable for transportation of goods over short distance. Airways is useful for emergency distribution of spare parts, for products of relatively high value and if the product is of perishable in nature.

The factors to be considered in choosing a particular mode of transport are cost, dependability, time required to transport finished goods, prompt availability, shift in the market and speed.

4. **Market:** Technically, market denotes a place where particular products are sold. The location of plant near the market are influenced by the following factors:

(a) It reduces the cost of transporting finished goods and also advertisement expenses. So goods can be sold at cheaper rates.

(b) Nearness of market enables us to study the whims and fancies, tastes and habits, likes and dislikes of customers and thus adjust production according to the demand of the customers.

(c) It enables us to render prompt and quick service to customers.

(d) It enables us to provide after sale services to customer who complain about the product.

(e) It is possible to execute replacement orders without delay.

(f) When goods manufactured are of perishable type or susceptible to spoilage, it is desirable that plant is established adjacent to market to enable quick delivery of such products.

(g) In case of production of fragile goods, such as glass and ceramics, nearness of the plant to market will reduce costs due to breakage.

5. **Meteorological conditions and topography:** Meteorological conditions are an additional factor influencing the plant location. Before locating a plant, an idea should be made about rainfall, heat, cold, fog, humidity, etc. in the locality. It will facilitate in determining the influence of these elements on the processes to be carried out in the factory. Some industries require special climatic conditions, as for example, the cotton textiles favouring a humid climate, dry climate for flour mill industries, etc. Therefore, such industries are located in areas like Pune, which do not have damp climate. Climate partly determines the cost of erecting suitable building and providing heating and air-conditioning. Climate affects the efficiency of workers to a considerable extent. In the words of Kimball and Kimball, "The effect of climate upon the efficiency in case of working force required to work outdoors, as in the case of quarries, constructional industries, etc. cannot be minimised. A cool climate develops the best of industrial worker."

Topography also exercises an important influence on location. A hilly and rocky region is unsuited for agro-based industries. Further, topography of a particular region affects the cost of transportation which, in turn, influences the cost of production.

## ■ SELECTION OF COMMUNITY

Once the general area has been determined, the search for a plant site leads to the second step, the selection of the particular locality. The selection of a community in the chosen region depends upon the following factors:

1. **Labour:** As the labour cost is an important component of total cost of production, priority should be given to that locality which is in the vicinity of adequate supply of labour. Depending upon the type of labour required, a factory will be located near a place of supply of the particular type of labour. If only skilled labourers are required, the factories are located near the urban areas with the existence of such labour. On the other hand, if semi-skilled and unskilled labourers are needed, a factory will be located in the rural area where such labourers are largely available. A factory which employs both male and female labourers seeks a place for locating the factory where such type of labour is available without much difficulty. The characteristics of labour supply are: (a) Stable labour force, (b) Right type of labour, (c) Adequate number of employees, (d) Reasonable wage rates, (e) Proper attitude towards work and (f) Reliability of labour supply. As Kimball and Kimball wrote, "The need of adequate supply of labour is obvious, but a number of considerations, such as cost of living and the character of labour available as to both skill and temperament, should be taken into account." The purpose of management is to face less boycotts, strikes, or lockouts and to achieve lower labour cost per unit of production.

The employment of labour is also governed by labour laws and state legislation. The recruitment of child labour, fixation of minimum wages, workmen's compensation, trade unions are all affected by state legislation. These laws vary considerably from State to State. So, the selection of a locality must be such that, where the labour laws and State legislations do not pose big problems.

2. **Supplementary and complementary industries:** The existence of supplementary and complementary factories have led to concentration of industries in particular region. For instance, in Mumbai, simultaneous to the existence of the cotton textile mills, there are a number of chemical and dye stuffs manufacturing units which produce the chemicals and dyes needed by the textile industry. Similarly, in USA, some chemical plants have been started where they are inter-connected by means of pipe lines so that the output of one factory constitutes the input of another factory. The location of plant near subsidiary industries will enjoy certain benefits. These advantages have been summarised by D. Jones in his book "Administration of Industrial Enterprise" are as follows:

(a) An industrial unit can secure materials to better advantage that anyone can do singly. Concentration of similar establishments helps to increase the variety of materials that can be offered by suppliers.

(b) The concentration of establishments of identical industries improves the labour market both for the employer and the employee.

(c) In specialised centres, banks become familiar with the requirements of the industry. The banks can gather full information about each and every industrial establishment and this will enable them to discount the commercial papers readily and more safely.

(d) A group of plants will attract a variety of repair plants such as foundries, machine shops, tool makers, factory store suppliers, etc. Along with these, other supply houses will also establish themselves near the industrial area.

(e) A group of similar manufacturers established in one place serves to perfect the local markets — reputation of each firm. It should also be noted that a firm enjoys prestige from the mere fact of location in the noted place.

(f) Lastly, division of labour is possible. The principle of division of labour may reach a high perfection, particularly the new enterprises should find no difficulty in getting skilled or specialised labour.

3. **Banking and credit institutions:** For any industrial enterprise the need for finance cannot be underestimated. As and when a factory grows in size, it requires funds to meet capital expenditure and revenue expenditure. The possibility of raising finance in a locality certainly exerts locational pull. Therefore, the existence of banking institutions will exert influence over the location of plant. Further, locality, which is inhabited by the people motivated with savings and investment habits, also enables the factory to raise finance through issue of shares, debentures, public deposits, etc.

4. **Local taxes and insurance:** The locality for the setting up a new factory must be such that the taxes levied are reasonable. The common taxes collected from factories are octroi and license fee. Similarly, income tax, sales tax and property tax must be considered, as they vary in each area. Among insurance costs, fire insurance is the most important. Fire insurance premium depends on the availability of quality of protection and prevention services. Similarly, employee accident insurance premium must be considered. In case the taxes and insurance costs are high, factories must be located in other places, where the taxes and duties are comparatively low.

5. **Water:** Water is used for processing the products, for drinking purpose, for sanitary purpose, for cooling, for waste disposal, for sprinkler system in case of fire. Depending upon the nature of plant, water should be available in adequate quantity and should be of proper quality, i.e., clean and pure. The other factors to be considered in this connection are stability in the supply of water, problems leading to water pollution, mineral content of the water, and lastly of the transportation of water if it is not readily available in the locality.

6. **Momentum of early start:** This, as one of the factors of plant location, is responsible for the selection of an area, where other successful factories thrive. As and when the factories start in an industrial community, we come across various facilities extended to such area. Some of these facilities are transport facility, banking facilities, repair services, communication system, shops and restaurants, etc. All these factors give momentum to the growth of new industries in such an area.

7. **Personal factors:** Factory owners are not always guided by purely economic considerations in deciding location of their factories. Personal preference and prejudices of these persons are equally important. It is well known that Ford started to manufacture motor cars in Detroit because it was his home town. Lord Nuffield selected Cowley because the school in which his father was educated happened to be for sale.

8. **Historical factors:** Sometimes, locations of plants are the result of historical events. Kanpur is an example of such locality, which has developed as the 'premier textile centre of northern India' but has hardly any advantage. It grew largely because Europeans chose Kanpur as the centre of their cotton dealings. Similarly, the existence of certain historical towns are responsible for the location of industries in such places. Some of the examples are: Banaras and Kanjiwaram where silk industries are located.

9. **Political stability:** The political situation in potential locations should be considered while selecting a locality for establishing a factory. Even if other considerations demand a particular locality, knowledge of the political situations and local prejudices can assist in taking decision. At present, the political situation is not so good in West Bengal and Punjab for setting up industries.

10. **State assistance:** Assistance of the Government to start industries in particular areas is one of the significant factors reckoned in plant location. In Karnataka State, the following incentives are offered to encourage the setting up of industries, tap the local resources, provide employment opportunities and to develop backward regions: (1) feasibility study subsidy, (2) investment subsidy, (3) concession

on term loans, (4) concession on processing fee, (5) concession on working capital loan, (6) sales tax exemptions to some extent, (7) subsidy on electricity tariff, (8) stamp duty exemption. The other incentives offered are: (1) allotment of land and sheds to entrepreneurs, (2) Technical guidance, (3) raw materials, and (4) marketing facilities.

## SELECTION OF EXACT PLANT SITE

The step involves the question of determining the exact site where the new plant has to be established within the selected locality. The following factors must be considered in selecting the exact site.

1. **Price of land:** The price of land, to a great extent, determines the selection of a particular site. If the price of land is unduly high it involves investment of much of fixed capital. Where there is no adequate capital available for the purchase of land, it can be acquired on lease basis. But this again involves payment of rent rates and taxes which may prove to be expensive and consequently reduce the profits of the factory.

2. **Type of soil:** Before deciding upon a site, the sub soil condition especially, its load bearing condition, should be properly determined. Analysis of the soil at different strata below the surface at various points on the proposed location should be carried out. This is necessary because sandy or soft soil may demand deep foundation involving extra costs which, more often, outweigh initial cheapness.

3. **Waste disposal:** It is one of the inherent features of all factories to generate waste and its disposal is essential as it endangers human and animal life. In certain factories, its waste products are utilised by other factories. In such cases, the factories utilising the waste products can be located near the source of such (waste) products. Industrial waste can take three different forms: (i) solid waste (ii) liquid waste, and (iii) gaseous waste. Solid waste requires acquisition of additional land space, as the waste can be deposited on such land. Liquid waste should be disposed through sewerage connections in the factory areas. Gaseous waste must be led into high altitudes in the atmosphere by means of tall chimney pipes after treating them specialy so as to render them harmless before final disposal.

4. **Expansion potential:** While selecting a site for a factory one should look into the future and ascertain the chances of a possible expansion of the factory. It is advantageous to choose a site adjacent to which land is bought for factory building in anticipation of expansion of factory in future. Often, the additional land can be obtained and sublet for a short period.

5. **Availability of commercial services:** Commercial services of every kind, such as warehousing, repair workshops, insurance, legal services, accounting and audit services must be available near the site selected for plant location. Security services, such as police stations, fire stations, are also equally important factors of plant location.

6. **Communication:** It is necessary to check the availability of postal and telephonic communication facilities in the site selected for plant location.

7. **Availability of amenities:** A location which provides good amenities outside the factory – hospitals, schools, clubs, cinema theatres, restaurants, community halls, shopping centres – are often much more attractive to staff than an one which is more remote.

8. **Health of the locality:** It should be enquired into if any disease is conspicuous near the proposed site of a factory. It is also fruitful to determine its causes. If the disease is due to local conditions, water, heat, rain, insects, etc., and they are uncontrollable; then it is advisable to abandon the site.

9. **Statutory consideration:** Although a good plant site may be available to start a factory, yet sometimes government may not allow the formation of factories in some areas under Competition Act, and FEMA.

10. **Flood and drought conditions:** If the proposed site to be selected is on a river bank it would be worthwhile to enquire whether or not the land was ever under floods, and to what height the flood water rose. If the enquiries reveal that the land was frequently flooded to a high depth, the site should be abandoned. In the case of low floods, the plinth of the building and foundations of machinery are to be raised above flood level in order to save them from flood damage. Similarly, the drought conditions should be carefully studied. The factory is to be assured of its water requirement even in the year of drought. In case of any doubt, the site is to be abandoned.

11. **Right and title of the land:** The right and title of the land should be thoroughly looked into by competent person. No laxity should be shown in this respect. Any defect in the right and title of land can drag the factory into prolonged and costly litigation. Unless clean and clear title of land without encumbrance is available the site and location of a factory should not be determined.

12. **Good scenery:** The land selected should be in the midst of a good scenery. Ebenezer Howard was dismayed at the ugliness and shocking state of industrial towns. In his book "Garden Cities of Tomorrow", he suggested that new towns should be built of limited sizes, each having enough industries to provide employment to the inhabitants. A good park with beautiful garden in and around the factory attracts the attention of public at large.

13. **Attitude of local people:** Success of a factory depends very much on the attitude of the local people. Generally speaking, the attitude of people must be cooperative and sympathetic. They must patronize the products manufactured by the factory.

14. **Technological know-how:** The knowledge of various techniques should be available in nearby sources, to avoid any delay in repair if there is any breakdown in the plant. The factory should also be located near a consultation organisation so that future expansion problems and present difficulties can be discussed more often for a continuous run of factory.

15. **Existence of religious and social institutions:** The presence of religious and social institutions enable the employees of a factory to lead a value-based life. This contributes a lot to industrial peace and avoids labour unrest in a factory.

From the foregoing observations, it is clear that the plant location is not a simple job. The plant location depends on a number of factors which are to be investigated thoroughly and extensively. But rarely we come across the availability of all factors at one particular place. So, a balance is to be struck among all these factors. The plant must be so located as to derive maximum benefits from all these factors. All things being equal, one needs unbiased scrutiny of the results of the investigation, thoroughness in calculation, judicious reasoning, and courage of conviction to enable one to make the right decision.

## ■ SELECTION OF MOST ECONOMIC SITE

According to Kimball and Kimball in *Principles of Industrial Organization*, the "Most advantageous location is that at which the cost of gathering material and fabricating it plus the cost of distributing the finished product to the customer will be a minimum." This statement can better be explained with the help of the following diagram:

Let 'A' and 'B' represent the two sources of supply of materials. Let 'C' stand for the market place; and let 'D' represents the site of the factory. If the site of the factory is located at the market place 'C', then only transportation cost of raw materials will have to be paid. Instead, if the factory site is located either at 'A' or 'B', only distribution cost of finished goods are to be incurred. If the

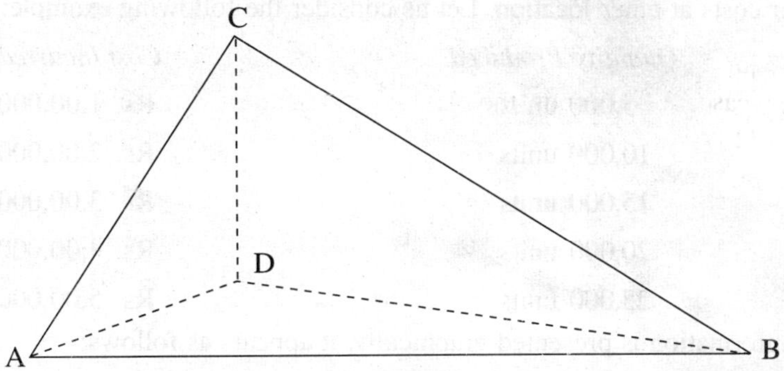


site is located at an intermediate point 'D', then transportation cost on incoming raw materials and outgoing finished goods will have to be paid. In order to arrive at the final decision for the most economic site, a comparative statement of total cost is to be prepared for alternative site. This is illustrated below:

**SELECTION OF ACTUAL SITE**

| ITEMS OF COST | Cost per unit at site | | |
|---|---|---|---|
| | SITE–A | SITE–B | SITE–C |
| ***Fixed capital*** | | | |
| 1. Land acquisition cost | | | |
| 2. Building construction cost | | | |
| 3. Equipment installation cost | | | |
| Total of Fixed cost | | | |
| ***Cost of production and distribution*** | | | |
| 1. Materials cost: | | | |
| (a) Direct Materials | | | |
| (b) Indirect Materials | | | |
| 2. Labour cost: | | | |
| (a) Direct labour cost | | | |
| (b) Indirect labour cost | | | |
| 3. Overheads: | | | |
| (a) Factory insurance | | | |
| (b) Factory taxes | | | |
| (c) Factory depreciation | | | |
| (d) Office salaries | | | |
| (e) Selling overheads | | | |
| (f) Distribution overheads | | | |
| | | | |

## ■ SELECTION OF LOCATION GIVEN COST OF PRODUCTION AND QUANTITY PRODUCED

It is a common observation that some of the items of expenses will be higher in one location when compared to similar costs at other location. Let us consider the following example:

| *Quantity Produced* | *Cost Incurred* |
|---|---|
| 5,000 units | Rs. 1,00,000 |
| 10,000 units | Rs. 2,00,000 |
| 15,000 units | Rs. 3,00,000 |
| 20,000 units | Rs. 4,00,000 |
| 25,000 units | Rs. 5,00,000 |

If the above information is presented graphically, it appears as follows:

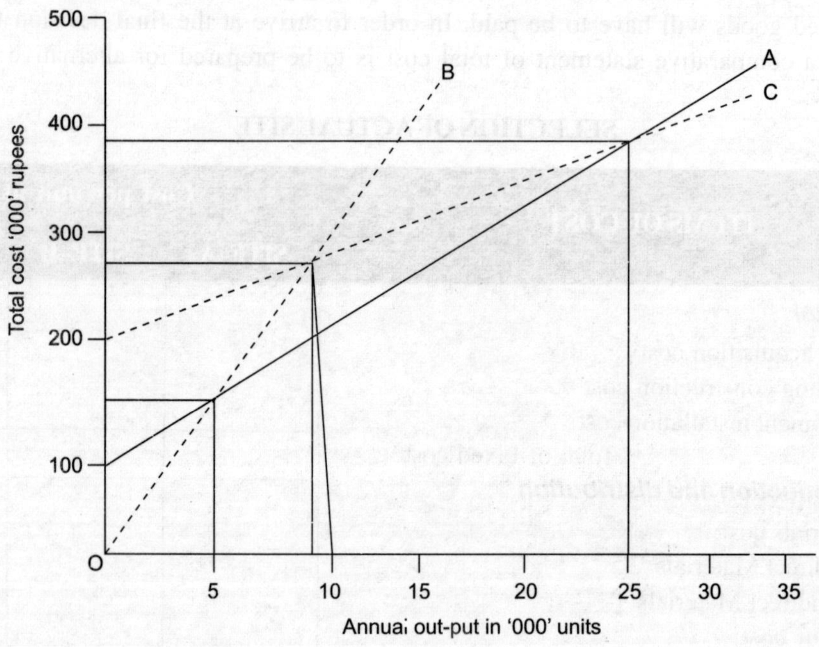


If cost minimisation is desired, it can be seen from the graph that site-B is preferable for output up to 5,000 units. Site-A is preferable for output from 5,000 to 25,000 units and site-C is preferable for output above 25,000 units.

The location that offers the lowest cost of production and distribution will be given prime consideration. If the units costs of production in the various locations are more or less the same then the location that requires the least fixed capital outlay will be preferred. However, the final selection depends not only upon the immediate investment and cost of production, but also upon the possible future trends, such as expansion potential, changes in market, changes in technology, tax rates, wage rates and the government's attitude towards industrialisation.

**Illustration:** From the following particulars select the most advantageous location for setting up a factory.

| | *Bangalore* Rs. | *Mysore* Rs. | *Hubli* Rs. |
|---|---|---|---|
| Total initial investment | 40,000 | 40,000 | 40,000 |
| Total expected sales for the period | 50,000 | 60,000 | 50,000 |
| Raw material cost of | 14,000 | 16,000 | 18,000 |
| Power supply cost of | 8,000 | 6,000 | 4,000 |
| Wages and salaries | 4,000 | 5,000 | 4,000 |
| Distribution expenses | 8,000 | 8,000 | 15,000 |
| Other expenses | 5,000 | 8,000 | 6,000 |

**Solution:**

Total expenses of Bangalore site = Rs. 39,000

Total expenses of Mysore site = Rs. 43,000

Total expenses of Hubli site = Rs. 47,000

$$\text{Rate of return} = \frac{\text{Total sales} - \text{Total expenses}}{\text{Total investment}} \times 100$$

$$\text{Rate of return of Bangalore site} = \frac{50{,}000 - 39{,}000}{40{,}000} \times 100$$

$$= \frac{11{,}000}{40{,}000} \times 100 = 27.5\%$$

$$\text{Rate of return of Mysore site} = \frac{60{,}000 - 43{,}000}{40{,}000} \times 100$$

$$= \frac{17{,}000}{40{,}000} \times 100 = 42.5\%$$

$$\text{Rate of return of Hubli site} = \frac{50{,}000 - 47{,}000}{40{,}000} \times 100$$

$$= \frac{3{,}000}{40{,}000} \times 100 = 7.5\%$$

As the rate of return is highest at Mysore site, it is more advantageous site to locate the plant in Mysore.

## ■ RECENT TRENDS IN PLANT LOCATION

Seven most important trends have come to fore with regard to plant location. These trends are:

I. To locate plants away from cities
II. The development of industrial estates
III. Competition among states to develop industries
IV. Trend towards decentralisation
V. Pollution control

VI. Location of industries leading to balanced regional development

VII. Growth of multinational firms thereby transcending the geographical area of the country.

## I. Location of plants away from cities

Originally, most of the factories were located near the big cities. But, now a days, there is a trend to locate the factories near the suburban and even sometimes in rural areas. The comparative merits and demerits of such location are listed below:

**Merits of plant location in suburban areas**

1. Labour supply of required quantity and quality are available.
2. It is possible to establish close contact with suppliers and obtain the raw materials at the right time and at the right price.
3. Repairs and maintenance facilities are available.
4. Quick transport facilities are available as the suburban areas are connected with roadways and railways.
5. In a suburban area, multistorey operation can be carried on in a small plant site.
6. Municipal services, such as supply of power, water, gas, drainage, health, education and recreational facilities are available.
7. Technical and commercial services, such as repair workshops, training facilities, warehousing, banking and insurance are available.
8. It has the advantage of proximity to allied industries.
9. Ready market is available near suburban areas.
10. Locating a plant in suburban areas has better advertising value.
11. Security in the form of police protection, fire fighting facilities are available.

**Demerits of plant location in suburban areas**

1. The price of land is generally high.
2. Often, sites are limited in area and are much congested. This leads to poor lighting and ventilation and hence climate is not healthy.
3. Expansion of factory is hampered on account of limited space.
4. Property tax, water tax etc. are high.
5. Higher wages are to be paid to employees because of higher standard of living.
6. There will be frequent labour unrest on account of organised trade unions.
7. Suburban areas over a period of time grow into big cities and leads to overcrowding and its evils.

**Merits of rural site**

1. Compared to city site the price of land is considerably low in rural areas.
2. Labour is available at cheaper rates as the standard of living is not so high as in cities.
3. Ample scope for expanding the factories are available.
4. Local taxes are lower in rural areas.
5. There is less labour trouble and there are generally no organised trade unions in rural areas.

6. Rural areas have the advantage of healthy surroundings and pleasant atmosphere.
7. As more land space is available, it is possible to have spacious layout providing adequate space for car parking, gardening etc.
8. Waste disposal becomes easy.
9. Government gives inducements as it wants to develop the underdeveloped areas.
10. Pure water is available in abundant quantities.

**Demerits of rural site**

1. It is not always possible to get skilled labourers in rural areas.
2. Rural sites pose difficulties in respect of proper supply of power.
3. Rural sites suffer from lack of transportation and communication facilities.
4. Rural sites will not have the facilities of technical education for employees.
5. Rural sites are always distant from market.
6. Contact with suppliers are not close. So, materials have to be bought in large volume. This blocks the capital in factories.
7. Repairs and service stations are not available in rural areas.
8. Recreational facilities, colleges, hospital are not available.
9. Housing difficulties should pose a problem in rural areas.

## II. Swing towards industrial estates

The second trend in plant location is to set up factories in industrial estates. An industrial estate is a group of factories constructed on an economical scale in suitable sites with various facilities. The United Nations has defined an industrial estate as "a planned clustering of industrial enterprises offering standard factory building, erected in advance of demand and variety of services and facilities to the occupants". Thus, it is a tract of land which is subdivided and developed according to a comprehensive plan for the use of community of industrial enterprises.

In India, there are three categories of industrial estates. They are: (1) conventional or diversified industrial estates consisting of units manufacturing different types of unrelated products, (2) Functional industrial estates dedicated to a particular discipline like ceramic leather or electronics, and (3) ancillary estates feeding components and sub-assemblies to a large industrial undertaking. India has undertaken the largest programme of establishment of industrial estates among the developing countries. By the end of March, 31, 1975, there were about 700 industrial estates established in the country, housing 12,830 small units.

The establishment of industrial estate provides several advantages. These are:

1. As a large area is taken up for development, economies in the use of land and its development are possible.
2. Construction of factories and provision for facilities like water and power can also be undertaken economically.
3. The factories in the estate are built as per factory laws with facilities of lighting, ventilation, in attractive and spacious surroundings with green lawns, and are let out on reasonable rents.
4. The industrial estates provide commercial services, such as bank, post office, health services, recreational facilities, transport facilities, etc.

5. Plant and machinery are made available on hire purchase basis.
6. The establishment of industrial estates enable the facility of inter-trading and inter-service activity.

## III. Competition among states to develop industries

A third trend relates to the growing competition for industries among states. There is a competition among various states to establish as many factories as possible by offering various concessions, within their states. Given below are the concessions and other facilities offered by the Government of Karnataka and Tamil Nadu (two states from South India) for establishing factories. This shows the competition among these two states to encourage setting up of many industries.

### Incentives offered by Government of Karnataka

| Incentives offered | Small scale industries | Medium and large scale industries |
|---|---|---|
| (1) Feasibility study subsidy | Subsidy to a ceiling of 75% of the cost of preparing the report up to a maximum of Rs. 5,000 | Loan of 75% of cost of preparing feasibility report up to a maximum of Rs. 50,000. |
| (2) Investment subsidy | 10% of value of fixed assets subject to a ceiling of Rs. 5 lakhs | 10% of the value of the fixed assets subject to a ceiling of Rs. 10 lakhs |
| (3) Development loan | Overall ceiling of 25% of the value of fixed assets | For Zone II – 10% of the value of fixed assets to a maximum of Rs. 50 lakhs and for Zone – III & IV 15% of the value of fixed assets subject to a maximum of Rs. 50 lakhs. |
| (4) Working capital loan | Interest free loan offered subject to a ceiling of 25% of the value of fixed assets or the development loan taken whichever is less | Interest free loan subject to maximum of Rs. 50 lakhs |
| (5) Procurement of know-how | It shall be reimbursed in full subject to a maximum of Rs. 25,000 | 50% of fees paid by new units for procurement of know-how shall be subsidized up to a ceiling of Rs. 1 lakh |
| (6) Stamp duty exemption and reduction in registration fee | Exemption on stamp duty for executing agreement with KSFC. There is also reduction in registration fee of Re. 1 per Rs. 1,000 for registering the agreement deeds | Same as in the case of small scale industries |
| (7) Subsidy on housing | Subsidy at the rate of Rs. 1,500/- per house of built up area of not less than 300 sq ft shall be offered for the new units, who have plans to build the houses for the employees | Same as in the case of small scale industries. |

## Incentives offered by government of Tamil Nadu

1. **Interest-free sales-tax loan:** Medium and major units set up in certain specified areas are eligible for interest free sales tax loans.

2. **State investment subsidy:** Under this scheme, 32 notified backward *taluks* and new industrial complexes to be set up in Tuticorin and Cuddalore are eligible for state subsidy equivalent to 15% of the fixed capital investment or Rs. 15 lakhs, whichever is less.

3. **Subsidy scheme for selected categories of industries:** This is a unique scheme in the whole country introduced by the Government of Tamil Nadu. In order to encourage certain specified categories of industries, the State government has a special scheme to grant subsidies to selected categories of industries set up anywhere in Tamil Nadu not covered by the State or Central Cash Subsidy Scheme. The subsidy will be 10% value of the fixed assets to be created or at the rate of Rs. 20,000 per every regularly employed worker, whichever is lower, subject to the ceiling of Rs.10 lakhs.

4. **Subsidy for project reports:** Project reports providing critical, important and necessary information on various projects are made available by State Industrial Promotion Corporation of Tamil Nadu Ltd. (SIPCOT) to prospective entrepreneurs to help them to take investment decisions and implement their projects. This is obtained on payment of 10% cost incurred by SIPCOT when the project gets implemented, 40% of the cost of the report will be converted into loan recoverable and the balance 50% will be treated as subsidy grant from SIPCOT.

5. **Concessional power tariff:** New industries set up anywhere in Tamil Nadu are charged concessional power tariff for the first five years of the working on graded scale. This concession will be higher for new industries set up in any other selected backward *taluks* of the State.

6. **Concessions in water royalties:** This form of permitting new units to draw water from public sources is on payment of a fixed amount of Rs. 200 per annum as water royalty, irrespective of the quantity of water drawn for an initial period of six years.

In addition, SIPCOT offers other concessions like stamp duty exemption and special concessions to schedule castes and schedule tribes entrepreneurs.

## IV. Decentralisation movement

The fourth recent trend in plant location is towards decentralisation. This means spreading out plants of particular industry into new locations. The large plant, when it outgrows in size, will pose the following problems:

(a) It becomes unwieldy, difficult to manage and becomes static in nature.

(b) A large plant is difficult to control. The control of such plant by top executives becomes ineffective,

(c) It leads to difficulties in servicing and maintenance,

(d) It leads to inefficient and socially undesirable city structures.

(e) Transport problems on account of narrow streets, numerous intersections and on-the-street parking, and

(f) Lack of space for expansion. Because of these problems, the decentralisation movement is largely observed today.

Decentralisation may be accomplished by two methods, viz., (1) Horizontal method and (2) Vertical method. Under horizontal method, each branch plant is set up to manufacture a complete product starting from raw materials to finished products. Under vertical type of decentralisation, plants and sub-assemblies are manufactured in subsidiary or complementary plants and are brought to the main plant for final assembly operations on the products.

The decentralisation of industries have many advantages to the employer and employee.

**Advantages of decentralisation to the employer**

1. It leads to better quality of work.
2. It involves low overhead charges.
3. It develops goodwill and reputation of employer.
4. It involves less loss of time in production.
5. Labour turnover in decentralised plants are small.
6. It gives rise to facility in changing and improving methods.
7. It leads to closer relationship between labour and management.

**Advantages of decentralization to the employees**

1. There is a probability of steady work undertaken by employees.
2. It gives rise to opportunities to develop individual aptitudes.
3. It enables employees to lead a more comfortable tempo of life.

## V. Pollution control

Pollution refers essentially to a process by which a resource (natural or man-made) is rendered unfit for use due to physical, chemical or biological factors. The pollution control with respect to factories relate to the following areas: (1) water, (2) air, (3) noise and (4) solid waste pollution.

1. **Water pollution:** Water pollution is defined to mean such "contamination of water or such alteration of the physical chemical, or biological properties of water or such discharge of any sewerage or trade effluent or any other liquid, gaseous or solid substances into water that is likely to create a nuisance by way of physical appearance, odour, or taste or render such water harmful and injurious to public health, for the purpose of domestic, commercial, industrial, agricultural or other legitimate use to the health of animals and aquatic life."*

A recent survey conducted by the National Environmental Engineering Research Institute, Nagpur and the All India Institute of Hygiene and Public Health, Kolkata, has described the 225 km Asansol-Durgapur-Kolkata stretch of the Damodar river as 'one of the most polluted rivers' containing toxic chemicals. It has been estimated that nearby 159 industries along both sides pour their toxic wastes into the river belt of Hooghly.

In the 120 km path from one end of greater Kolkata to the other, there were almost 270 outlets of untreated water discharged into the Hooghly river mainly from jute mills, rayon industries and other distilleries. The Damodar river, while flowing through the coal belt area in Bihar and West Bengal, present serious problems because of discharge of industrial effluents, while the Yamuna river is choked by DDT factory wastes.

The Government of India, having realised the importance of water pollution control, enacted a law on the March 23, 1974, known as Water Prevention and Control of Pollution Act. This Act provides

*"Report of the committee for recommending legislative measures and administrative machinery to ensure environmental protection." Department of Science and Technology, Government of India, September 15, 1980.

that there should be a vigorous campaign by the central and State governments to prevent, to control and eliminate water pollution in a most judicious manner.

2. **Air pollution:** Air pollution creates problems of high proportion including health effects, damage to vegetation and agricultural crops, effects on weather, climate and atmospheric processes. The metallurgical industries liberate sulphur dioxide, the chemical industries, hydrochloric acid and host of other poisonous fumes. Certain large industrial units have been identified in India for polluting air. Some among them are: Trombay unit of Rashtriya Chemicals and Fertilizers Corporation and Bombay Gas Company in Mumbai, Indraprastha Thermal Power Plant in Delhi, Mathura Refinery near Agra, Textile Mills of Ahmedabad, Distilleries, Iron and Steel industry, and Paper and Pulp factories in various parts of India. In order to control air pollution, in modern days tall pipes are constructed in factories so as to allow the gases of various types to flow out to a higher altitude. Sometimes the poison contents of such gases are treated at the source of their liberation.

3. **Noise pollution:** In our industrial society, mechanically-generated noise has increased dramatically in the past few decades. Medical experts say that constant exposure to loud noise, say above 90 decibels, is known to cause insomnia, fatigue, decreased work efficiency, hypertension, cardiac conditions, deafness and some form of allergy, etc. Industrial noise in India is a great hazard. It is common to feel a kind of deafness after coming out of a noisy factory or power station. Workers in several factories all over the country complain of numbness around their ears. There is growing evidence to point out that an industrial worker is losing a part of his hearing ability because of a continuous assault on the ear. In a study undertaken in four factories, viz., textile, automobile, oil and fertiliser and chemical in Coimbatore, it has been revealed that the noise level was somewhat above what was prescribed by the US Occupational Safety and Health Administration.

S. Purushothman of the Central Labour Institute, Mysore, has, in an article on 'Industrial Noise Control', suggested methods to diminish noise at the planning stage of industry, at its source and at the receivers end. Installation of machinery that can act as a barrier for sound and use of mufflers or silencers are strongly advocated by him. Further, periodic medical checkup is suggested to study and control the effect of factory noise on workers.

4. **Solid waste pollution:** The generation and disposal of solid waste products represents another significant pollution problem in our country. The components of solid waste are paper, grass, leaves, etc., garbage, sewage solids (in a dry state) metal, glass, plastic and others. Industries produce a significant amount of solid waste. Traditionally, two methods were followed to dispose it of, viz., (a) through incineration of the combustible materials, and (b) open dumping. Whereas incineration contributes to air pollution, the problem with open dumping is that it is unsanitary, unsightly and is increasingly taking up space.

## VI. Location of industries leading to balanced regional development

The concept of regional development of industries has assumed great significance in current economic thinking and planning. The objectives of regional distribution of industries may be enumerated as follows:

(a) It aims at an even development of the local resources of the country as a whole

(b) It involves an optimum industrial activity based on broader economic, social and strategical considerations,

(c) It seeks the objective of conservation of limited and exhaustible resources for the benefit of posterity,

(d) It leads to an equitable distribution of employment opportunities which remain no more confined to a few states, and

(e) It also helps in the attainment of certain social objectives like avoidance of emigration of labour, prevention of the occurrence of depressed areas, and equalization of the per capita income in different parts of the country.

The Industrial Policy Resolution of 1956 stressed the fact that disparities in the levels of development between different regions should be progressively reduced. Only by securing a balanced and co-ordinate development of the industrial and the agricultural economy in each region can the entire country attain higher standards of living. The resolution also emphasised the establishment of industrial estates which were likely to help in the dispersal of industrial activity.

The principal measures for giving effects to the approach of balanced regional development were:

(a) Provision of facilities, such as power, water supply, transport and communication, training institutions, etc. in areas which were lagging behind industrially.

(b) programmes to be undertaken for expanding small industries.

(c) Consideration to be given to the need for developing balanced economy for different parts of the country in the location of new enterprises, whether public or private.

The Planning Commission had set up two committees to consider the problem of industrial backwardness between states. They are: (1) Pandey Committee, and (2) Wanchoo Committee. Both these committees submitted their reports in early 1969. While the former committee suggested selection of backward districts only in industrial, backward states for special treatment and incentives, the latter committee suggested various incentives to be offered for the establishment of industries in such selected backward areas.

## VII. Growth of multinational firms

As and when the factory expands its size, it becomes extremely difficult to maintain it with the existing capital structure and technical know-how. However, in recent times, some of the large industries are started with foreign collaboration with a view to take advantage of increased capital, technical know-how, better management and to market the products in different markets of the world. Under such circumstances, the factory establishment is no longer confined to the boundaries of a particular country but spread out in different parts of the world. When this is followed, the location of plant is no longer affected by the factors which were discussed earlier. Such factories, which are set up in different countries, are governed by multinational corporations. Franklin R. Root defines, multinational corporation in his book "International Trade and Investment: theory, Policy, Enterprise" as "denoting headquarters of parent company that engages in foreign production and other activities through its own affiliates located in different countries; exercise direct control over the policies of those affiliates; strives to design and implement business strategies in production, marketing, finance, and other functions that transcend national boundaries, becoming thereby progressively more geocentric in outlook". There are more than 10,000 multinational corporations throughout the world, some having affiliates in as many as 20 countries. The United Nations Commission on Transnational Corporations estimates that the multinational corporations control more than 50,000 affiliates. This only shows the increased number of industries which are set up in different countries, thereby not paying any attention to the localities available within the country.

## SUMMARY

The location of a factory has to be carefully selected. A wrong choice sometimes proves fatal for the factory. The selection of a suitable locality depends upon a number of factors. Further, each factor is influenced by some other factors. So, a thorough analysis of the location to be selected is to be undertaken by the entrepreneur before he selects a particular area. The following check list prepared by the United States Department of Commerce will help in the appraisal of basic location factors.

## ■ CHECK LIST FOR CONSIDERING BASIC INDUSTRIAL LOCATION FACTORS

### I. Location for the production raw materials

A. What production materials exist in the area?

B. In what volume are the production materials available?

C. What is the quality of each production material?

D. How accessible are the available material?

Does nature of such production materials (quantity, bulk, perishability, etc.) or any unusual advantage attendant thereto definitely favour plant location at or near site or source?

### II. Labour

A. What is the labour force of the area?

B. What is the quality of the available labour force?

C. What is the character of the labour force?

D. What quantity of labour is seasonably available?

1. Is a large supply necessary?
2. Are special skills required?

### III. Sites

A. How much land is available for industrial expansion?

B. What are soil and topographic features?

C. At what cost and terms can land be purchased or leased?

D. What facilities are now or will be available?

E. What industrial floor space is or will be available in existing structures?

1. Is a large area needed?
2. Most of the sites have special features, such as topographic soil conditions, transportation facilities, low cost, etc.

### IV. Industrial fuel

A. What industrial fuel is available for additional industry?

B. How dependable is the supply?

C. At what cost is the fuel available?

1. Is low cost heat a major factor in processing?
2. Is a particular fuel required?

### V. Transportation facilities

A. What transportation facilities are available?

B. What is the rate situation?

1. Do materials and/or product require prompt and/or low cost movement?
2. Does product or raw material require a special type of transportation?

### VI. Market

A. Which trading area is generally served by this location?

B. What is general quality of this market?

1. Are time and distance vital matters to reach the market?
2. Is price or quality a vital market factor?

### VII. Distribution facilities

A. What agencies and services are available?

1. Are there channels for marketing complex and do they require special financing, inspection, warehousing, storage or terminal facilities?

### VIII. Power

A. What kind of industrial power is available?

B. How dependable is the power supply?

C. At what cost is the power available?

1. Is power a significant factor?
2. Is sufficient surplus power available?

### IX. Water

A. How much water is available for additional industry?

B. What is the quality of the water supply?

1. Is significant quality of low cost water required in processing?
2. Whether required quantity is available?

### X. Living conditions

A. Are adequate facilities available for education, recreation, shopping, religious and social life, health and professional services?

B. Is sufficient housing available?

- Will the industry employ enough people to make housing and environment significant factors?

### XI. Laws and Regulations

A. What laws and regulations exist in relation to prospective industries?

- Is the industry subject to special local and/or state regulation?

## XII. Tax structure

A. How favourable is the tax structure to industry?

- Is the capital investment at some level can attract tax rate or assessment policy?

## XIII. Climate

A. What are the climate characteristics of the area?

1. Do processes require special natural atmosphere conditions?
2. Does climate have a major influence on living conditions, transportation facilities, water, storage or accessibility of materials?

The selection of a most economic site is possible where an entrepreneur prepares a comparative cost statement taking into account the availability different sites. Certain recent trends in plant location are now discernible. These are: (1) To locate plant away from cities, (2) the development of industrial estates, (3) competition among states to develop industries, (4) trend towards decentralisation, (5) pollution control, (6) location of industries leading to balanced regional development, and (7) growth of multinational firms thereby transcending the geographical area of country.

# QUESTIONS

## A. Objective type

### I. Fill in the blanks:

(a) Selection of .................... is the first step involved in plant location.

(b) Selection of .................... is the second step involved in plant location.

(c) Selection of .................... is the final step involved in plant location.

(d) Service oriented industries are located near .................... .

### II. Write *True* or *False* for the following sentences:

(a) A decision regarding location once taken is final and need not be reviewed later.

(b) For a given factory, there is usually a unique location that is clearly superior to all others.

(c) The choice of moving or staying in an area usually does not come under consideration until expansion is contemplated.

(d) Many of the intangible factors in plant locations can have an effect on long-run costs.

(e) All location factors should receive equal consideration while selecting a location for a factory.

(f) If various locations have comparable unit cost of production and distribution, the location requiring the least investment should ordinarily be chosen.

(g) An 'Industrial Estate' usually offers the advantages of low property taxes

(h) Urban location of factory allow fuller and more profitable utilisation than rural location.

(i) In modern days, the location of factories are largely influenced by the government policy.

(j) Location of factories in urban areas enjoy more advantages than its disadvantages.

(k) The recent trend in the factory location is to move away from cities to rural areas.

(l) Decentralisation of location is always the best policy for an expanding factory.

**III. Choose the correct answer from the following alternatives:**

(i) The main criterion for site selection of the factories processing cement is
- (a) finance factor.
- (b) labour factor.
- (c) proximity to raw material.
- (d) power factor.

(ii) In the case of factories using gross materials, location will be near
- (a) source of raw material.
- (b) source of labour.
- (c) market.
- (d) transportation.

(iii) Materials which do not exercise any influence on location are
- (a) pure material.
- (b) gross material.
- (c) ubiquitous material.
- (d) localized materials.

(iv) Vertical integration of processes
- (a) increases size.
- (b) decreases size.
- (c) will have no influence on size.
- (d) none of the above.

(v) Which of the following does not constitute among the recent trends in factory location?
- (a) Pollution control.
- (b) Centralisation.
- (c) Decentralization.
- (d) Formation of industrial estates.

## B. Very short answer type

1. What is meant by plant location?
2. What is an industrial estate?
3. What do you mean by the term "Decentralisation?"
4. Define an ideal plant location.

## C. Short answer type

1. Explain the need for plant location.
2. Explain how the raw materials influence plant location.
3. Explain the market problems in plant location.
4. Explain how special inducements cements influence plant location.
5. Explain how the power supply factors affect plant location.
6. Name the factors that influence the choice of a local site.
7. Discuss the influence of climate on plant location.
8. State the merits and demerits of a plant location in a city.
9. Examine the relative advantages and disadvantages of locating is plant in a rural area.

## D. Long answer type

1. Explain the various factors that influence plant location.
2. Explain the recent trends in plant location.

## ANSWERS TO OBJECTIVE TYPE QUESTIONS

**I. Fill in the blanks:**

(a) region (b) locality or community

(c) site (d) market

**II. True or False:**

(a) F (b) T (c) T (d) T (e) F (f) T (g) T

(h) T (i) T (j) T (k) T (l) F.

**III. Choose the correct answer:**

(i) (c) (ii) (a) (iii) (c) (iv) (a) (v) (c).

# Chapter 6

# PLANT LAYOUT

## ■ INTRODUCTION

The term 'plant layout' is used in a broad sense to include factory layout and machine layout. Plant layout is a plan or the act of planning to obtain an optimum arrangement of industrial facilities, including personnel, operating equipments, storage space, material handling equipments and all other supporting services along with the design of the best structure to contain these facilities.

The layout of a plant is of major importance, as it affects the flow of materials and processes, efficiency of labour, supervision and control, use of equipment, use of space, expansion possibilities and plant appearance. When plant layout is properly implemented, it prevents waste of time, waste of money and waste of efforts on account of useless movement and travel of work in process. It increases the efficiency of workers, as it enables them to prevent from taking unnecessary steps and making needless motions. Thus, it permits them to direct their energy into productive efforts. A systematic arrangement of plants and equipments increases the speed of production process, in meeting delivery schedules, in maintaining the quality of products and thus in establishing better relationships with customers. It keeps capital investments low by means of preventing the unnecessary duplication of machinery and equipment. It saves floor space, thereby reducing the investment in plant and increasing the efficiency of operation. A good layout of plant provides for expansion and contraction of production depending upon fluctuation in demand for its products. Last but not the least, a good plant layout provides for an orderly arrangement which is attractive to look at and a safe and pleasant place to work.

## ■ DEFINITION OF PLANT LAYOUT

According to K.G. Lockyer*, "The disposition of the various parts of a plant, along with all the equipment used therein, is known as the plant layout, which should be designed to enable the plant to function most effectively".

Mallick and Gaudreau, in their book "Plant Layout-planning and Practice" have defined plant layout as, "a floor plant for determining and arranging the desired machinery and equipment of plant, in one best place, to permit the quickest flow of materials at the lowest cost and with the least amount of handling in processing the product from the receipt of raw materials to the shipment of finished products".

*Factory Management, p. 54.

Sansonetti and Mallick in their book, "Factory Management" define plant layout as "placing the right equipment, coupled with the right method, in the right place, to permit the processing of a product unit in the most effective manner, through the shortest possible distance and in the shortest possible time."

In the words of John, A. Shubin, "Plant layout is the arrangement and location of production machinery, work centres and auxiliary facilities and activities (inspection, handling of materials, storage and shipping) for the purpose of achieving efficiency in manufacturing products or supplying consumer services."

According to James, L. Lundy, plant layout ideally involves the allocation of space and the arrangement of equipment in such a manner that overall operating costs are minimised.

The above definitions bring forth the following essential features of plant layout:

1. Departmentation of factory into a number of units to facilitate smooth flow of production.
2. Arrangement of plant and machinery in a systematic and orderly way to quicken the process of production.
3. Placing the right equipments and tools in their appropriate places so that they are readily available when required.
4. To arrange the material handling equipment and other auxiliary services required in the course of manufacturing.

## NEED FOR PLANT LAYOUT

The need for plant layout, arises on account of the following factors:

1. When a new plant is set up to manufacture newly designed products.
2. When a new product line is introduced in the factory.
3. When additional space is required to meet increased demand for the products.
4. When frequent accidents occur in the factory.
5. When the existing facilities are to be rearranged due to changes in methods of production.
6. When the existing factory is shifted to a new area.
7. When the cost reduction programme is launched.
8. When improvements are to be made by incorporating scientific and technological innovations.

## OBJECTIVES OF PLANT LAYOUT

The objectives of a good plant layout, are explained below:

1. **To facilitate manufacturing process:** The first object of a good layout is to facilitate the complete manufacturing process, so that production can be carried out in an optimum manner. This objective is achieved by (1) arranging the equipments to secure greater utilisation, (2) minimising production delays and reducing congestion owing to better flow, and (3) increasing the output by shortening the manufacturing time which is possible in an improved layout.

2. **To minimise material handling:** In a good plant layout, the arrangement of plant and material handling equipments, such as belts, conveyors, lifts, hoists, chains, etc., will enable the material handling costs to be kept at minimum. Further, such an arrangement provides for a direct movement of raw materials and semifinished products without any back tracking.

3. **To maintain high turnover of semifinished goods process:** In factories, where production process involves more time, it is common to see the accumulation of semifinished products at various points. This increases not only the storage costs but also requires more space. Further, such accumulation of semifinished products hinders the easy flow of other materials. So, a good layout ensures a high turnover of such semifinished goods by proper arrangement of plant and machineries.

4. **Effective utilisation of space:** Arrangement of plants and equipments in an orderly way increases the effective utilisation of the floor space in production departments. Similarly, even in service departments, space can be saved if an arrangement of furniture and other equipments are properly undertaken.

5. **To provide comfort and job satisfaction to employees:** The layout of a plant involves provision of facilities, such as safety measures, reducing excessive noise, and better environment. Further, it involves taking such considerations as to heat, ventilation, light, removal of moisture and dirt which promotes worker's job satisfaction.

6. **To provide effective utilisation of labour:** The idle time which occurs in a factory can be minimised by adopting 'line balancing.'* Similarly, indirect labour can be utilised by proper design of handling equipment and aisles.

## PRINCIPLES OF PLANT LAYOUT

The foregoing discussion on objectives of plant layout leads to enunciation of principles of plant layout. The good plant layout can be designed by following certain principles of layout. Besides the application of these principles, a considerable amount of art and skill is required in order to develop a scientific approach for solving plant layout problems. Muther in his book, "Practical Plant Layout", has enunciated six principles of best layout. These are:

1. **Principle of overall integration:** An efficient layout should be capable of integrating the various ingredients of a factory, such as raw materials, men, machines, and other supporting activities in a logical and balanced manner. Before integrating, it is essential that these factors of production must be procured in right proportion and at the required time. The purpose is to put each and every factor of production to derive maximum benefit from them and to reduce the operating cost of production to the least.

2. **Principle of minimum distance:** According to this principle, in a factory the men and materials have to move the minimum required distance between operations. Of the two, it is the handling of materials which effects the production and is responsible for increased cost of production. This cost of material handling can be considerably reduced by proper plant layout.

3. **Principle of flow:** According to this principle, a good layout is one which arranges the work area for each operation in the same order or sequence of production. To ensure this, bottlenecks in the

*Line balancing refers to utilisation of all the machinery to full capacity so that production capacity might be maintained steadily.

flow process, congestion points and back tracking should be removed. For a proper flow of materials, the plant layout should provide for easy movement of raw materials to production departments and, finally, to packing department. The following factors are to be considered while designing a proper flow of materials: (a) frequency of flow between different production departments, (b) nature of operations in each production department, (c) volume of production in each department, and (d) total area of floor space available within each department.

4. **Principle of cubic space:** According to this principle, the best layout ensures the efficient use of available space, both vertically and horizontally. Apart from using the floor space of a room, if the ceiling height is also utilised, more materials can be stored in the same room. Further overhead material handling equipments save a lot of valuable floor space.

5. **Principle of satisfaction and safety:** A best layout must protect the employees from accidents. Workers must also be safeguarded from the occurrence of fire. As the satisfaction of employees is largely decided by environmental facilities, plant layout must provide for lighting, ventilation and prevention of hazardous conditions. Employees must be protected from excessive heat, dust, glare and fumes. All these lead to satisfaction amongst the workers in a factory.

6. **Principle of flexibility:** In the modern dynamic world the structure of factory will not always remain same. The expansion of factory with the change in scientific and technological developments necessitate a change in the plant layout. Under such circumstances, the rearrangement of existing pattern must be achieved at the least cost and with least disturbance.

## FACTORY LAYOUT

A factory layout is one of the components of plant layout, the other being machine layout. The layout of a factory means the position of the departments or shops in the factory, storage points in the working areas, including office and staff facilities relative to one another.

While designing the layout of a factory, the following rules are to be followed:

1. As far as possible all the 'machining departments' should be set up under one roof. In case of multistorey building, heavy machines must occupy ground floor, machine departments should be centrally situated near the location of the tool room, sub-stores and inspection department.
2. The assembly department should be set up near the despatch department.
3. The pattern shop should be adjacent to the foundry.
4. The storeroom should be located near transport avenues with provision for feeding the sub-stores.
5. "Obnoxious process" departments should be situated away from the machine shops.
6. Inspection department can have a principal office in the main office with inspection sections in each manufacturing departments.
7. The drawing office should occupy the top most floor.
8. The general office should be situated in front of the factory.

Considering the above rules, the layout of a typical medium-sized engineering factory is depicted below:

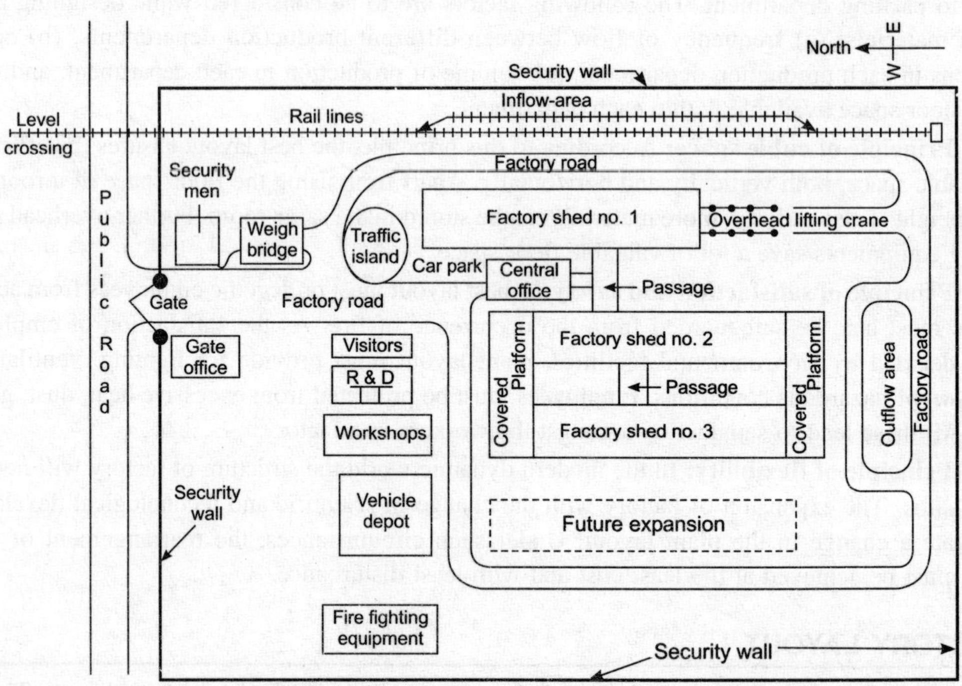


**Fig. 6.1** A typical layout of a factory building

## ■ MACHINE LAYOUT

In the strict sense, machine layout is another name of plant layout. While setting up the machine layout, the following rules should be kept in mind:

1. There must be enough space between two machines to enable workers to operate the machines easily.
2. Adequate allowances should be provided for the projections, overhangings or over travel of machine parts.
3. Adequate space for inserting and removing the raw materials of large size into and from machines is to be provided.
4. Adequate space must be provided for material handling equipments.
5. Adequate space must be provided for the storage of raw materials and semifinished or finished products near the machines.
6. Adequate space for keeping furniture of all kinds to store the tools and other equipments must be arranged near the machines.
7. Adequate space should be provided for keeping safety devices so that easy access is available in case of emergency.

## ■ FACTORS INFLUENCING PLANT LAYOUT

There are four important factors which affect the layout of the plant. They are:

1. Location of the factory
2. Manufacturing process
3. Type of product
4. Managerial policies.

### 1. Location of the factory

The pattern of plant layout that is to be designed is influenced by the general location and specific site of the factory. Certain localities will have more advantages by way of supply of labour, proximity to market, availability of raw materials and so on, than other localities. The size, shape and topography of the site will affect the construction of factory building, which, in turn, affects the location of various departments and the general layout of machines.

### 2. Manufacturing process

The manufacturing processes involved in a factory determines the type of plant layout that is to be designed. For a careful analysis of layout, manufacturing processes can be grouped into following:

(a) **Synthetic processes:** A synthetic process is one which combines various inputs, as in the case of cement, soap, medicines or assembling various component parts as in the case of refrigerator, TV, to manufacture a finished product.

(b) **Analytic processes:** An analytic process is one that starts with a basic raw material and splits it down into various constituent products. Oil refining which yields petrol, diesel, bitumen, kerosene, etc. is a good example for this process.

(c) **Intermittent process:** An intermittent process is one in which work is completed in various stages at various workshops in the factory. This process can be found in scooter, car and aeroplane manufacturing plants.

(d) **Repetitive processes:** Such processes are seen in plants manufacturing standard products which are manufactured on large scale basis in anticipation of demand from customers. The production process consists of operations which are to be repeated in the same way for getting the finished products. Examples of products involving such processes are drugs, soaps, etc.

(e) **Non-repetitive processes:** Non-repetitive processes are found in manufacturing non-standard products which are undertaken for production on receipt of an order from customers. The final product depends upon the specification of customer and, as such, the same sequence of operations are not used for all manufacturing order. Best examples of products involving non-repetitive processes are furniture, machineries, etc.

The above classification of manufacturing process should not be treated as standard one. In practice, we come across a combination of some of these processes.

The layout of plant differs in all the above cases. For example, in continuous manufacturing process the arrangement of plant and machineries is such that there is a definite *sequence in the flow of materials and semifinished* products from one machine to another. But this is not the case in intermittent production process.

### 3. Type of product

The physical and chemical constituents of the product, its design, its size, its form, etc., would decide the pattern of plant layout. Further, the simplicity or complexity of the product, in terms of production, whether it is a luxury or an ordinary product, whether it is costly or cheap; solid or liquid and the quantities of manufacture also determine the type of layout. Further, the products requiring similar process require different types of layout. For example, radios and cars require assembly processes, yet the layout is different in these two cases.

### 4. Managerial policies

The layout of plant often depends upon the policies of management. The policies, which govern the layout, are; the quality of products, the size of plant and the degree of its integration, the extent of flexibility of plans desired, plants for expansion, the amount of stock to be carried in storeroom, and the type of facilities to be provided to employees.

## ■ TYPES OF PLANT LAYOUT

There are four types of plant layout. They are:

1. Product or line layout
2. Process or functional layout
3. Combination of product and process layout
4. Fixed position layout or static product layout.

### 1. Product or line layout

In a product layout of machines, the focus is on the product. All the machines required in the processing of the product are brought together in the production department and are installed according to the sequence of operations. Product layout is intended to affect an orderly and logical arrangement of productive facilities that will be consistent with large production volume. Under this type of layout, the materials and semifinished products move in a predetermined channel of operation thus involving a lesser manufacturing cycle time. This layout permits the forward flow of materials to the fabrication of the component parts, to the finishing stage and then to despatching centre. Product layout can be arranged in any one of the following four types:

(a) Straight line type
(b) U-shaped type
(c) Circular type
(d) Odd angle type.

(a) **Straight line type of product layout:** Under this type of product layout, the machines are arranged in a straight line in the sequence of operations. These machines are installed as near as possible because the output of one machine becomes the input of next machine.

| | Machine (1) | Machine (2) | Machine (3) | Machine (4) | Machine (5) |
|---|---|---|---|---|---|
| Raw materials | → Drilling operation | → Welding operation | → Heat treatment operation | → Grinding operation | → Inspection |

**Fig. 6.2** Straight line type of layout

(b) **U-shaped product layout:** This is a more compact layout than straight line type. This type of layout economises floor space and allows closer supervision than the straight line type. This is illustrated below:

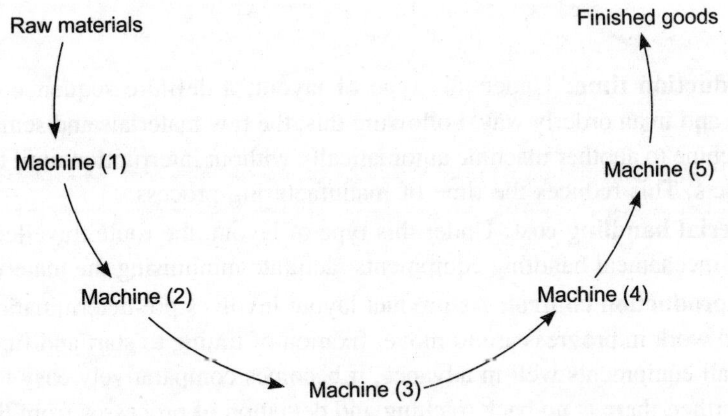


**Fig. 6.3**

(c) **Circular layout:** In this type of layout, machines are arranged in the form of a circle. The operations can be carried on inside or outside the circle. If production is carried on outside the circle, the inner portion of the circle can be used for storing the finished products.

(d) **Odd angle product layout:** In this type of layout, there is no fixed pattern of arranging the machines but it is designed to suit the available space. Nevertheless, the sequence of operation is strictly maintained under this type of layout. Considering three products this is illustrated below:

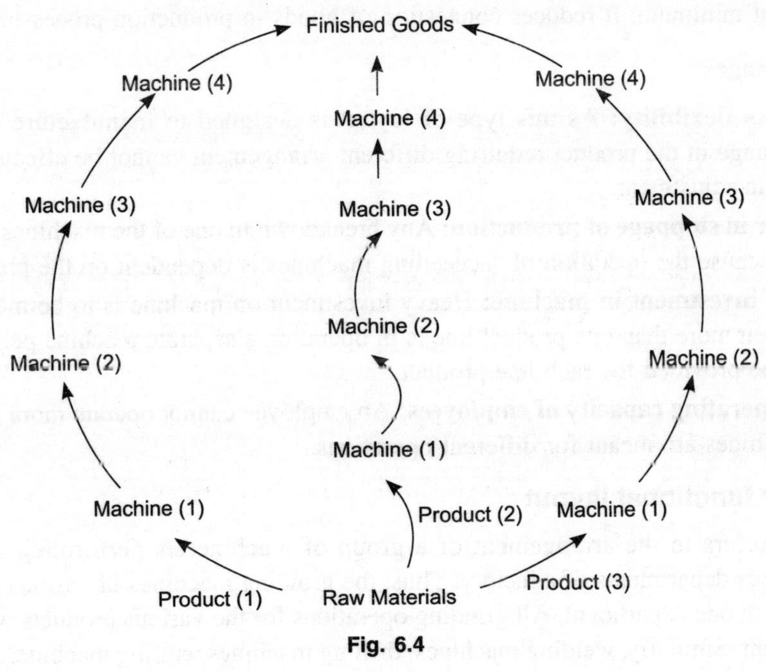


**Fig. 6.4**

Product layout is used when (a) large quantity of products are to be produced, (b) design of the product is more or less standardised, and (c) demand for the product is steady. This type of layout is adopted in continuous processing industries, such as cement, sugar, paper, etc. and in assembly type of industries, such as T.V., scooters, refrigerators, etc.

**Advantages**

(a) **Less production time:** Under this type of layout, a definite sequence of operations are planned in advance and in an orderly way. Following this, the raw materials and semifinished products move from one machine to another machine automatically without interruption until they are converted into finished products. This reduces the time of manufacturing process.

(b) **Less material handling cost:** Under this type of layout, the route travelled by the materials is short. The use of mechanical handling equipments facilitate minimising the material handling cost.

(c) **Effective production control:** As product layout involves pre-determination of routes along which materials and work in progress are to move, fixation of timing to start and finish the works and make provision of all equipments well in advance, it becomes comparatively easy to exercise control over production. Further, there is no back tracking and deviation of processes from the scheduled path and time.

(d) **Effective utilization of space:** Owing to systematic arrangement of plants and equipment, use of mechanical handling devices and quick flow of materials from one machine to another, the available space is effectively used by not crowding with all tools, materials and work in process.

(e) **Effective inspection:** As the goods produced are of standard type and as all the production processes are integrated, inspection work is reduced and efficiency of inspection increases on account of repetitive nature of work.

(f) **Less work in process:** Since the production is continuous and uninterrupted, work in progress is always kept at minimum. It reduces congestion of goods in production processing.

**Disadvantages**

(a) **It lacks flexibility:** As this type of layout is designed to manufacture only one type of product, any change in the product requiring different arrangement cannot be effected easily. Thus, it lacks flexibility in adjustment.

(b) **Danger in stoppage of production:** Any breakdown in one of the machines leads to stoppage in production because the operation of succeeding machines is dependent on the preceding machine.

(c) **Heavy investment in machine:** Heavy investment on machine is to be made on account of duplication. When more than one product line is in operation a separate machine performing the same operation is to be provided for each line product.

(d) **Less operating capacity of employees:** An employee cannot operate more than one machine as different machines are meant for different operations.

## 2. Process or functional layout

Process layout refers to the arrangement of a group of machineries performing the same type of function in various departments of a factory. Thus, the grinding machines of various types in a factory may be grouped in one department. All grinding operations for the various products will be undertaken by this department. Similarly, welding machines, drilling machines, cutting machines, etc. are arranged in different departments and the respective welding, drilling and cutting operations are performed in such departments. The areas assigned for each group are so arranged that it will be convenient for the majority of the products to follow the easiest path to flow. Whenever any operation (say cutting) is to be performed on a product, it will be allowed to move into that department. Later on, it will be transferred to next department where a second operation (say drilling) is to be carried out. In this way, the product will pass from one department to another until all the operations on it are carried out.

This type of arrangement is shown in the following diagram:

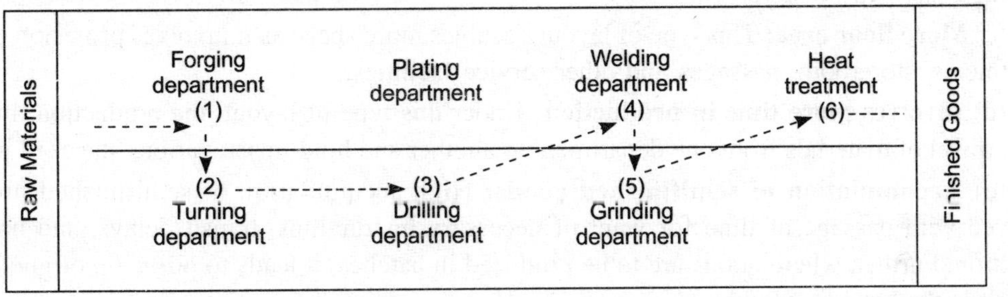


**Fig. 6.5** Diagram showing process layout

This type of layout is used under the following circumstances:

(a) When the goods to be manufactured depends upon customers' specification as in the case of furniture making,

(b) Where a variety of products are manufactured,

(c) Where the manufacturing time varies from operation to operation,

(d) Where the demand for the products from customers are not regular, and

(e) In case of assembly type of industries.

**Advantages**

(a) **Lower capital investment:** The investment in capital equipment is lower because there is less duplication of equipment. When four machines working half the time are required in manufacturing four products in the product layout, two machines will be sufficient in process layout.

(b) **Greater flexibility:** Under this type of layout, frequent changes in operations and their order can be made without disturbing the existing layout. For example, six different products can flow in six different ways (as shown in the previous diagram) without causing inefficiency in other departments.

(c) **No disruption in work schedule:** As each department has number of related machines, the breakdown of one machine will not disrupt the production process. This is so because work from one machine can be transferred to other machines.

(d) **Scope for expansion:** It is possible for expanding the departments by installing the new machines for better operations.

(e) **Full utilisation of machines:** As a machine is not meant for manufacturing any particular product, there is greater degree of machine utilisation. Even if a particular product is not manufactured for any reason, still the machine can be kept engaged in manufacturing other products.

(f) **Better supervision:** The supervisor will acquire greater knowledge of the problem-solving technique connected with one type of process performed. Such a specialised knowledge is necessary when there is diversification of products manufactured in a factory.

**Disadvantages**

(a) **Difficulty in production control:** Since the production process is undertaken in different departments, it is difficult to lay down definite routing, scheduling and controlling techniques.

(b) **Difficulty in material handling:** As the routes travelled by products are longer, material handling costs will be more.

(c) **More floor area:** This type of layout occupies more space as it involves provision of different departments, storeroom, passages and other service facilities.

(d) **Involves more time in production:** Under this type of layout, the production time is more due to travel of materials from one department to another and hold-ups at various stages of production.

(e) **Accumulation of semifinished goods:** High accumulation of semifinished products are observed with passage of time for want of necessary instructions, transit delays, and hold-ups for inspection. Further, where goods are to be produced in batches, it leads to piling up of goods until the last unit in the batch is completed.

## ■ DIFFERENCES BETWEEN A PRODUCT LAYOUT AND PROCESS LAYOUT

1. **Duplication of equipment:** There is more duplication of plant and equipments in product layout when compared to process layout.

2. **Production control:** Production control becomes more effective in product layout, because of preplanning and establishing definite sequence of operation. In process layout, production control becomes difficult as production is carried out in a number of departments.

3. **Adaptability in case of breakdown of individual machine:** In product layout, the breakdown of one machine cannot be replaced by other machines. So, production comes to a halt, whereas in process layout the breakdown of one machine can be replaced by another one as they are related to each other.

4. **Material handling cost:** In product layout, material handling costs are less because of short routes over which materials flow. However, in process layout material handling costs are high because materials have to travel over long distance.

5. **Production time involved:** Production time involved is less in product layout and it is more in process layout.

6. **Accumulation of work in process:** The pile up of work-in-process is low in product layout whereas it is high in process layout.

7. **Floor area occupied:** Floor area occupied under product layout is less whereas it is more in process layout.

8. **Greater utilisation of machines:** Machine utilisation is less in product layout unless production is carried out throughout the day, whereas it is high in process layout because even in the absence of one particular product, operation can be carried out on other products.

9. **Flexibility:** Product layout cannot be changed frequently so as to meet the desirable change. Whereas process layout lends itself for any modification without disturbing the existing arrangement.

10. **Application:** Product layout is applied in industries which manufacture standard products and have repetitive process. Process layout, however, is adopted in non-repetitive process industries where goods are manufactured as per the requirements of the customers.

## Combination of product and process layout

In practice, the adoption of pure product layout or pure process layout is rarely seen, as it is not possible to adopt either of these in isolation. So, we come across a combination of product and process layout which are widely practiced, especially in factory which are engaged in repetitive process manufacturing standard products. This is on account of deriving the benefits accruing from both the products and process layouts thereby overcoming the disadvantages of these layouts. In the words of Keith and Cubellini in their book, 'Business Management.' 'Many business firms find it to their economic advantage to apply both the approaches as a solution to their production problem.' A combined layout is a compromise between product layout and process layout.

A combined layout is possible where an item is being made in different types and sizes. In such cases, machines are arranged in a process layout, and the process grouping (i.e., a number of machines performing related activities) is then arranged in a sequence to manufacture various types and sizes of products. This type of layout is shown in the following diagram:

| Department | Output of product (1) ↑ | Output of product (2) ↑ | Output of product (3) ↑ | Output of product (4) ↑ |
|---|---|---|---|---|
| (4) | Polishing machine (4) ↑ | Polishing machine (4) ↑ | Polishing machine (4) ↑ | Polishing machine (4) ↑ |
| (3) | Machine (3) welding ↑ | Machine (3) welding ↑ | Machine (3) welding ↑ | Machine (3) welding ↑ |
| (2) | Machine (2) drilling ↑ | Machine (2) drilling ↑ | Machine (2) drilling ↑ | Machine (2) drilling ↑ |
| (1) | Machine (1) cutting ↑ | Machine (1) cutting ↑ | Machine (1) cutting ↑ | Machine (1) cutting ↑ |
| Stores department | Raw materials for product (1) ↑ | Raw materials for product (2) ↑ | Raw materials for product (3) ↑ | Raw materials for product (4) ↑ |

**Fig. 6.6** Diagram showing combined product and process layout

In the above diagram, M1 type of machines is similar and perform the same operations, namely cutting operations. These machines constitute one production department. Similarly, machines M2, M3 and M4 representing the drilling department, welding department and polishing departments constitute three separate production departments. These departments are suitably integrated to constitute different product layout. The arrow marks indicate the sequence of production of the four different products.

## Fixed position layout or static product layout

In this type of layout, the materials and major components remain in a fixed location. The required tools, machineries, men and supporting equipments are brought to this location. This type of layout is laid because the production raw material is too heavy or too big and, as such, it is not economical and convenient to move it to a factory. Instead, the required men and machines are moved to the fixed work place where work is executed. This type of layout is used in manufacturing aircrafts, ships, heavy machines, etc.

**Advantages**

(a) Handling of heavy materials are reduced.

(b) Quality of output is ensured because the responsibility can be fixed on the group of employees who execute the work.

(c) Maximum flexibility is possible in this type of layout.

**Disadvantages**

(a) It involves movement of men and machines to the work place which may be time consuming.

## ■ TOOLS AND TECHNIQUES FOR PLANT LAYOUT

In order to ensure continued production in factories, it is necessary that plant and machineries are placed in their appropriate place. This ensures the flow of materials in the shortest time and at minimum cost. While planning for a plant layout it is desirable to devise certain tools and techniques for better arrangement of plant and machines. These tools and techniques are:

(A) **Tools**

(a) Process charts and flow diagrams

(b) Machine data cards.

(B) **Techniques**

(a) Templates

(b) Model of equipment

(c) Layout drawings

(d) Plot plans.

### A. Tools of plant layout

(a) **Process charts and flow diagrams:** The American Society of Mechanical Engineers Standards (ASMES) has defined the process chart as "a graphic representation of events and information pertaining thereto occuring during a series actions or operations." The process charts are prepared with a view to analyse the production processes and to simplify such processes. There are two types of process charts, namely, the operation process chart and flow process chart. According to ASME standard, "An operation process chart is a graphic representation of the points at which materials are introduced into the process and of the sequence of inspections and all operations except those involved in material handling. It includes information considered desirable for analysis such as time required and location." An operation process chart indicates the overall picture of the processes involved in a factory and it serves as a basis for location of plant, tools, etc. This chart is useful in improving the existing processes and location.

Flow process chart has been defined by ASME standard as "a graphic representation of the sequence of all operations, transportations, inspections, delays and storage occuring during a process or procedure, and includes information considered desirable for analysis, such as time required and distance moved". This chart is useful in making several improvements in the factory with respect to several aspects. For example, any static elements of storage indicate delays in production or even unnecessary transportation of materials. The inefficiencies disclosed by such a chart may require the need for rearranging production centres or may point out need for better transportation facilities. Similarly, the chart also discloses the sequence of the various elements in the process which can be rearranged to eliminate back tracking and unnecessary handling.

A flow diagram indicates the procedure of operation and guides in deciding upon economical sequence of plant operation and machine arrangements in the factory. This diagram helps in locating the points at which materials are unnecessarily held up. A study of flow diagram helps in economical flow of work from one stage of operation to another.

(b) **Machine data cards:** The machine data card contains illustrations about the equipments and the information necessary to layout such equipments. These information relates to capacity of output, space, power, material handling devices, etc.

## B. Techniques of plant layout

(a) **Templates:** A template is a drawing of a machine or equipment cut out on a thick paper. Before an actual plant layout is prepared it is always better to have its miniature form so that the actual layout can be designed based on the miniature form. A template shows the area taken up by a machine or other equipment, which is condensed to a small area (cut to scale) shown on a thick paper, or a plywood. Templates, which represents machines and operations, should be located on floor plan according to the sequence indicated on the operation process charts and in conformity with production plan. While drawing templates, sufficient floor space should be allowed around each machine to allow for the operation of the machine, the movement of work, the convenience of worker, the storage of goods which are in process, the installation of material handling equipments and maintenance and repair needs.

It can be said that template serve as a trial layout and, depending upon its success, necessary blue prints can be taken up for laying out a final layout.

(b) **Model of equipment:** A model equipment is a miniature of all the machineries and equipments which are used for production in a factory. This model of machines is prepared for designing plant layout, which is complex in nature. The model layout helps in determining the extent of space required by various equipments. The model of equipments can be made out of wood or any other material which should resemble exactly to the actual plant and machinery to be installed. This should enable the layout engineer to fully visualise plans and simplify the detection of weaknesses and the revision of plans. Different models have been developed by the American Society of Mechanical Engineers Plant Layout Standards Committee. Important among them are block template, two dimensional template and three dimensional models. Three-dimensional model is increasingly used now a days.

(c) **Layout drawings:** The layout drawings are a miniature of floor plan which shows appropriate space to be provided for walls, staircases, passages, storage areas, office areas, etc.

(d) **Plot plans:** This shows a miniature of the entire factory building containing various departments-production and service and other physical facilities to be provided in the factory.

## ■ LAYOUT PROCEDURE

The various steps involved in plant layout have been listed and explained below:

1. Collection of basic data,
2. Analysis and coordination of basic data,
3. Decide the type of machines required,
4. Decide material handling plan,
5. Sketch the plot for factory building,
6. Plan the general flow pattern,
7. Plan individual work station,
8. Calculate the storage space required,
9. Locate service departments,
10. Construct master plan,
11. Check the final layout,
12. Get official approval, and
13. Install the approved layout.

1. **Collection of basic data:** First of all, the product design must be considered by manufacturing department so as to eliminate costly and troublesome operations involved. An operation list indicating the operations involved, place of their performance, sequence and tools required is to be prepared. For the collection of data, such as volume of production, production capacity, hours of work involved becomes necessary.

2. **Analysis and coordination of basic data:** The analysis and coordination of basic data is undertaken with the help of "assembly chart" and "operation process chart". An assembly chart shows.

(a) The parts which make up the total assembly and sub-assemblies,

(b) The sequence in which parts are assembled

(c) The flow of parts and sub-assemblies into assembly. The operation process chart shows (a) an idea of complexity of production, (b) an overall picture of the desired flow pattern and all the necessary production operations.

3. **Deciding the type of machines required:** Number of machines required to meet a given production target can be calculated by knowing (a) the number of articles to be produced, (b) capacity of each equipment, and (c) time within which production can be completed.

4. **Deciding material handling plan:** It is estimated that material handling costs account for about 25% of total production cost and therefore it is essential to give more importance to this factory. The general material handling equipments used in a factory are overhead conveyors, roller conveyors, trucks, trolleys, belts and chains and so on. This type of material handling equipments depend upon the product to be moved, container in which it will be moved, distance of movement, frequency of movement and speed of movement.

5. **Sketching the plot for factory building or building layout:** The building layout is a prerequisite to machine layout. The building layout involves location of internal transport passages, external transport passages, service departments, parking place and storage place. The plan of building must be sketched to take the advantage of natural ventilation and lighting. The location or receiving department and

despatch department, when properly planned, enables us to move the raw materials and finished products into and outside the factory quickly.

6. **Planning of the general flow pattern:** The flow of materials through the plant is the core of the entire plant layout. The objective of flow pattern is to plan the movement of raw materials in as direct a path as possible through the plant. The flow pattern depends upon such factors as external transport facilities, number of parts to be handled, number of units to be processed and number of operations on each part. In case more than one line of product is undertaken for manufacturing it is desirable to prepare a *travel chart*, which shows an analysis of movements of materials to and from a number of locations. Travel charts are useful for shortening manufacturing cycle time, to reduce work in progress, to show inventory control and to make economical use of floor space. Based on the flow pattern one can design the plant layout into product, process, combined or fixed position layout.

**Types of flow pattern:** Flow patterns can be designed under two types: (a) Horizontal flow lines, and (b) Vertical flow lines.

(a) **Horizontal flow lines:** This type of flow pattern is used in single storey building where more space is available on the shop floor. Flow pattern under this type can take any of the following lines:

(i) **I or L flow:** Under this type, the raw materials are fed at one end and finished products are obtained at the other end. This is illustrated below:

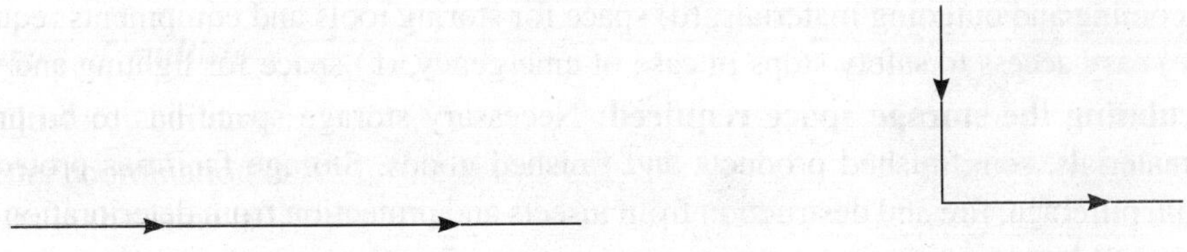


Fig. 6.7

(ii) **U-flow:** Under this type, the feeding and receiving take place at the same end. This is illustrated below:

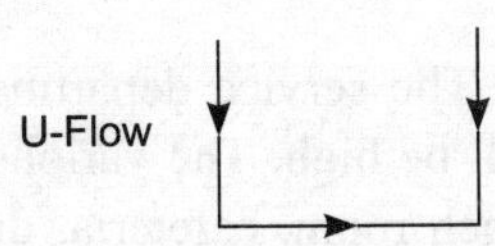


Fig. 6.8

(iii) **S-flow:** This type is used when the production process is undertaken at various stages. This type is used to utilise the available space efficiently. This is illustrated below:

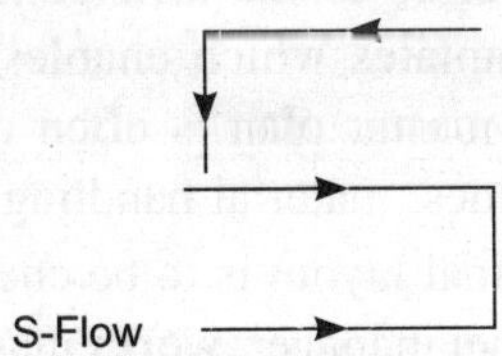


Fig. 6.9

(iv) **O-flow:** This type is used where the handling of materials is in circulation. This is illustrated below:

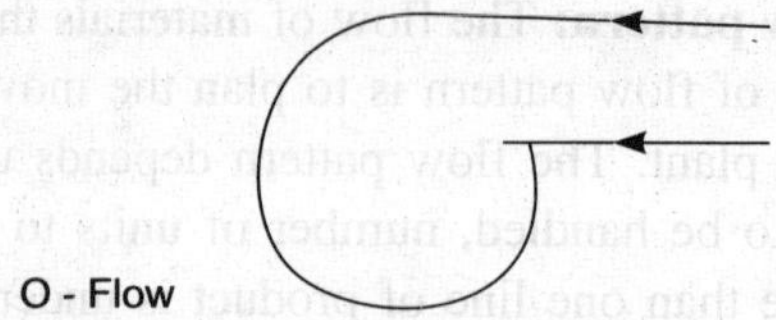


Fig. 6.10

(b) **Vertical flow line:** This type is used in multistorey buildings with a view to use the material handling system effectively. Under this type, the flow pattern can be taken the form of (i) downward or upward flow (ii) unidirectional or retractional flow, (iii) vertical or inclined flow.

7. **Plan individual work station:** The work station is the floor area occupied by the worker and the machines or group of machines which he operates. The work station design affects the production rates, efficiency and the accuracy of work. The work station design depends on such factors as (a) the space for the worker to sit, stand or move comfortably to operate machine, (b) space for the machine taking into consideration the projection or over travel of the machine part, (c) space for bins and racks for storing incoming and outgoing materials, (d) space for storing tools and equipments required by the employees, (e) easy access to safety stops in case of emergency, (f) space for lighting and ventilation.

8. **Calculating the storage space required:** Necessary storage space has to be provided for storing raw materials, semifinished products and finished goods. Storage facilities protect materials and goods from pilferage, fire and destruction from insects and protection from deterioration on account of temperature and humidity.

Solid materials are stored in boxes and bags, liquid materials are stored in barrels and bottles, and gases are kept in cylinders. Unless goods are properly stored, it may give rise to congestion thereby throwing out of gear the whole storage system. The storage space to be provided depends upon such factors as size and weight of raw materials, their quantities, frequency of usage, the size of plant and the type of storage materials used.

9. **Location of service departments:** The service departments must be located at convenient places, otherwise the operating expenses will be high. The various service departments that are to be located in a factory are offices, rest and lunch room, cafeteria, dispensary, tool room, power house, etc., whereas general office is to be located in a separate building. Factory office can be set up on balconies of the production department. Tool room should be located near production departments. The dispensary should be situated adjacent to personnel department. Cafeterias should be situated in a central place so as to minimise travel time of employees.

10. **Constructing master plan:** It refers to the arrangement of a final plan of plant layout incorporating the drawings, diagrams, templates which enables us to adopt the layout by making necessary improvements if desirable. The master plan is often drawn by using different colours to emphasise the present and proposed flow lines, material handling equipment, storage space, etc.

11. **Checking the final layout:** The final layout is to be checked by various persons concerned, viz., plant engineer, safety engineer, personnel manager, works manager, chief engineer so as to ensure: (a) safe and economical handling, (b) effective production control, (c) product design, (d) service areas, (e) employee safety and comfort, etc.

12. **Geting the official approval:** The final layout thus designed must ultimately be approved by the representatives of management from their point of view. The chief officials whose approval is to be obtained are: Managing Director, General Manager and Plant Layout Engineer.

13. **Installing the approved layout:** Where any improvement is made in the proposed plant layout, it shall be considered and this step involves the actual installation of plant and machinery, work apparatus, furniture, creation of service departments and storage room and path ways to carry the materials.

## ■ CHECK LIST TO KNOW THE EFFECTIVENESS OF A PLANT LAYOUT

The plant manager can ensure the effectiveness of the plant layout by adopting the check list given below.

### A. The product

(a) Is it bulky or light or hard to handle?

(b) Is the product hazardous, requiring isolation?

(c) Is it valuable or fragile?
What about quality control, volume, protection?

(d) Is secrecy required?

### B. Type of layout

(a) Is the factory meant for processing job orders or for mass production?

(b) The sequence of operations.

(c) Product or process layout.

### C. Space requirement

(a) Floor space, overhead clearance.

(b) Passage space.

(c) Space for material-handling equipment.

### D. Selecting the equipment

(a) General purpose or special purpose machines.

(b) How machines be driven: electric power, compressed air, or steam.

(c) Availability of tools.

### E. Productive capacity

(a) What is the probable productive capacity?

(b) Will the factory be run on single-shift or multi-shift basis?

(c) Does the layout have uniform flow?

(d) Have bottlenecks been eliminated?

### F. Flow

(a) Is there any optimum flow of materials through the plant?

(b) Effective flow, i.e., minimum movement of parts.

### G. Other considerations

(a) Has sufficient space been allocated for employees to work are, render service, wait during processing, inspection, etc.?
(b) Air-conditioning, lighting, ventilation to be provided to employees.
(c) Check hazardous processes including fire protection, theft, etc.

## ■ REVISION OF LAYOUT—RE-LAYOUT PROCEDURE

The need for revising the original layout arises on account of the following:

(a) Use of an unsuitable site or factory building
(b) Failure to make periodic work simplification surveys
(c) Rapid expansion of the factory
(d) Shifting the plant to other locality
(e) Introduction of new production line

Three steps are involved in the re-layout procedure:

1. Statement of the objectives and collection of data
2. Conducting a work-simplification survey
3. Development of an improved layout.

1. **Statement of objectives and collection of data:** The objectives of re-layout may relate to enlarging plant capacity, to modify facilities for the production of new plants, to improve the existing layout or to adopt latest technology in the factory.

For meeting any of the above purposes, it is necessary to collect data relating to floor-plan, and plot-plan drawings, together with original specification of the building. These must be checked to ensure efficiency in the re-layout procedure.

2. **Conducting a work-simplification survey:** A check list can be prepared to conduct a work-simplification survey for improving an original layout. In simplifying the work process, the following loopholes are to be guarded against (1) inefficiency in the over all process for example, uneven flow, illogical sequence, unnecessary operations and wasteful facilities, (2) uneconomical handling of materials, (3) wasteful allocation of floor space, (4) excessive production cycle time because of delays, (5) defective arrangement of service departments, (6) poor lighting, heating and ventilation, and (7) inadequate safety provisions.

3. **Development of an improved layout:** In order to develop an improved layout, it is necessary to use (a) flow diagram to analyse the effectiveness of the over-all arrangement of plant activities, the location of specific machinery and the allocation of space. The flow diagram will show how a more logical arrangement and economical flow of work can be devised through the elimination of long lines for handling, wasteful back tracking and criss crossing, congestion and confusion, (b) a flow process chart, the study of which points out the places where operations can be eliminated, rearranged, combined, simplified or subdivided for greater economy, (c) operation analysis, which can increase plant capacity with a minimum of investment and can eliminate bottlenecks at specific operations through the introduction of better methods, (d) analysis of floor space, which enables the acquisition of more floor space, by eliminating waste space and unnecessary racks and benches, reducing work in process, eliminating temporary storage areas, providing common passages for joint use of space by two different

activities. This additional space acquired can be used for installing new machines or to eliminate congested departments. These finally lead to installation of an improved layout. One point to be remembered in this connection is that the benefits derived by installing a new plant layout must be excess of the cost incurred in revising such a layout.

In modern days, the layout revisions are mostly undertaken with the help of computers. The arrangement of several parts of a factory building, including arrangement of machines, are easily evaluated in terms of cost. The analysis of cost factor and the impact on total cost of production is known through computers. Based on this cost analysis, re-layout designs are undertaken. In America, three layout planning programmes are available, based on computers. These are: (1) Computerised Relative Allocation of Facilities Technique (CRAFT), (2) Computerised Relationship Layout Planning (CORELAP) and Automated Layout Design Programme (ALDP).

## ■ ADVANTAGES OF PLANT LAYOUT

**Advantages to the workers**

(a) Efforts of workers are reduced by eliminating unnecessary movement of employees and materials.
(b) By cutting down the unnecessary movement and handling of machines, workers' efficiency is improved.
(c) It increases the specialisation of workers as, under product layout, employees concentrate on product, and, under process layout, they specialise in a particular operation.
(d) A good layout system improves the working conditions by reducing congestion.
(e) It provides the basis for better services for employee and this improves employer and employee relations.

**Advantages in minimising manufacturing cycle**

(a) A good layout reduces the length of travel of materials and semifinished products.
(b) It reduces manufacturing cycle by eliminating movement of workers and use of material handling equipments.

**Advantages in production control**

(a) A definite routing, scheduling and despatching and controlling system will ensure smooth flow of production.
(b) By enabling the materials and semifinished goods to flow in the laid out routes, the accumulation of work in process is reduced.
(c) It enables us to predict the production time by using despatching and scheduling programmes.
(d) It reduces cost of production control.
(e) Production control techniques ease the burden of supervision.

**Advantages in reducing cost**

(a) It reduces set up time of machines involved in factory.
(b) It decreases spoilage and scraps cost.

(c) It reduces the idle time cost.
(d) It decreases maintenance cost.

**Advantages in capital investment**

(a) As machines are arranged according to best requirements of the factory, it does not involve any further capital investment on account of unplanned and defective installation of layout.
(b) Any expansion in the layout can be conveniently undertaken without investing heavy capital expenditure in a planned layout.
(c) A good layout lends itself to adaptability.
(d) Good layout reduces investment in plant and machinery by increasing the volume of production, by utilising fully the available machines and providing for specialisation.
(e) It saves the floor space in building by careful arrangement of plant and equipment in various other departments.

## SUMMARY

The term plant layout is used in a wider sense so as to include the factory layout and machine layout. Factory layout refers to the location of various production and service departments so as to derive maximum benefits from them. Machine layout denotes a logical arrangement of machines in a factory so as to take the advantage of quick production at a reduced cost. The need for plant layout arises not only when a new factory is established but also in case of existing factories, especially when improvements are sought.

(a) To facilitate manufacturing process,
(b) To minimise material handling,
(c) To maintain a high turnover,
(d) Effective utilisation of space,
(e) To provide comfort and job satisfaction to the employees, and
(f) To provide effective utilisation of labour.

### Principles of layout

(1) Overall integration,
(2) Minimum distance,
(3) Flow,
(4) Cubic space,
(5) Satisfaction and safety, and
(6) Flexibility.

### Factors influencing plant layout

(1) Location of the factory,
(2) Manufacturing process,

(3) Type of product, and
(4) Managerial policies.

## Types of layout

(a) Product layout,
(b) Process layou,
(c) Combination of product and process layout, and
(d) Fixed position layout.

## Tools of plant location

(a) Process charts and flow diagram,
(b) Machine data cards.

## Techniques of plant layout

(a) Templates,
(b) Model equipments,
(c) Layout drawings, and
(d) Plot plan.

## Layout procedure

(a) Collection of basic data,
(b) Analysis and coordination of basic data,
(c) Deciding the type of machines required,
(d) Deciding material handling plan,
(e) Sketching the plot for factory building,
(f) Planning the general flow pattern,
(g) Planning individual work station,
(h) Calculating the storage space required,
(i) Locating service departments,
(j) Constructing the master plan,
(k) Checking the final layout,
(l) Geting the official approval, and
(m) Installing the approved layout.

## Re-layout procedure

(a) Statement of objectives and collection of data,
(b) Conduct of work-simplification surveys, and
(c) Development of an improved layout.

**Advantages of plant layout:** It has several advantages, both to employer and employees, in a factory.

## QUESTIONS

## A. Objective Type

### I. Fill in the blanks:

1. Factory .................. is to be planned in such a way as to utilise the available floor space to the maximum advantage.
2. In ...................... layout, the factory floor space can be efficiently utilised.
3. .................. type of layout is adopted in the manufacture of the bulky and heavy products, such as railways engines.
4. Arrangement of machines, according to the functions performed, is known as .................. layout.

### II. Write True or False for the following sentences:

1. Special purpose machines are used in process layout.
2. General purpose machines are used in product layout.
3. Production control can be exercised effectively in product layout.
4. Material handling costs can be considerably reduced in product layout.
5. Process layout always involves economy in manufacturing time.
6. Product layout involves a small investment on plant and machinery.
7. Although refrigerator and car manufacturing industries belong to assembly type, yet the layout differs in both these industries.
8. When the existing layout calls for changes, there is a need for re-layout.
9. Product layout requires more floor space than process layout.
10. Better supervision is possible in product layout than in process layout.
11. The flow process chart is a graphic tool useful only for the analysis of manufacturing process.
12. An "Operation analysis" is a disciplined procedure that subjects a machine or work place to a detailed improvement study.
13. It is best to select equipment in conjunction with the development of a plant layout plan.
14. The plant site and type of building should always be selected and acquired before a layout study is undertaken.
15. Process layouts are suited to job-order manufacture whereas product layouts are suited to repetitive manufacture.
16. In principle, plant layout achieves flexibility at the sacrifice of economical handling.
17. Product simplification, work simplification and plant layout often substantially increase output without any need for investment in plant.

### III. Choose the correct answer from the following alternatives:

1. Continuous manufacturing factories adopt
   (a) product layout
   (b) process layout
   (c) combined layout
   (d) fixed position layout

2. Intermittent type of factories adopt
   (a) product layout
   (b) process layout
   (c) combined layout
   (d) fixed position layout
3. An assembly type of factory adopts
   (a) product layout
   (b) process layout
   (c) combined layout
   (d) fixed position layout
4. In which of the following layouts, the line need not be balanced
   (a) process layout
   (b) fixed position layout
   (c) product layout
   (d) functional layout
5. Capital outlay in case of process layout, as compared to product layout is
   (a) more
   (b) equal
   (c) less
   (d) has no relation
6. Space needed for placing machines in case of product layout as compared to process layout is
   (a) less
   (b) more
   (c) equal
   (d) has no relation
7. An example of analytical process is
   (a) automobile assembly line
   (b) petroleum refining
   (c) plastic plant
   (d) extraction of iron from iron ore

## IV. Match the following:

| Column A | Column B |
|---|---|
| (a) synthetic industry | (1) separation of one element from the other |
| (b) analytical industry | (2) standardised production |
| (c) conditioning industry | (3) resolves a material into elements |
| (d) extractive industry | (4) a change in form or its physical properties |
| (e) continuous industry | (5) assembles the products |
| (f) product simplification | (6) movement of items on floor plan |
| (g) plot plan | (7) amount and variety of inventories |
| (h) flow process chart | (8) activities in manufacturing cycle |
| (i) flow diagram | (9) site utilisation |
| (j) operation analysis | (10) work place and machine station |
| (k) special purpose facilities | (11) mass production |
| (l) balanced capacity | (12) model change |
| (m) product diversification | (13) backlog |
| (n) job order manufacture | (14) elimination of bottle necks |
| (o) tooling up | (15) utilisation of idle capacity |

## B. Very short answer type

1. Define plant layout.
2. Define continuous industry.
3. Define job order industry.
4. Define a product layout.
5. Define a process layout.
6. What do you mean by fixed position layout?
7. What is a process chart?
8. Distinguish between a operation process chart and the flow process chart.
9. What is flow diagram?
10. What is an operation sheet? How is it used in plant layout?
11. What do you mean by template?
12. What is a model equipment?

## C. Short answer type

1. Explain the need for plant layout.
2. Explain the objectives of plant layout.
3. State the principles of plant layout.
4. State the rules which are to be considered while designing factory layout.
5. State the rules which are to be considered while designing machine layout.
6. Explain the factors which influence plant layout.
7. What is product layout? What are its merits and demerits?
8. Distinguish between product layout and process layout.
9. Explain the tools of plant layout.
10. Explain the techniques of plant layout.
11. Explain the procedure involved in a re-layout.

## D. Long answer type

1. Explain different types of plant layout with their merits and demerits.
2. Explain the procedure involved in setting up a new plant layout.
3. Explain the advantages of plant layout.

## ANSWERS TO OBJECTIVE TYPE QUESTIONS

I. 1. layout, 2. product,
3. fixed position, 4. process layout.

II.

| 1. F, | 2. F, | 3. T, | 4. T, | 5. F, |
|---|---|---|---|---|
| 6. F, | 7. T, | 8. T, | 9. F, | 10. T, |
| 11. F, | 12. T, | 13. T, | 14. F, | 15. T, |
| 16. T, | 17. T. | | | |

III.

| 1. (a), | 2. (b), | 3. (c), | 4. (c), | 5. (c), |
|---|---|---|---|---|
| 6. (a), | 7. (b). | | | |

IV.

| (a) – (5) | (f) – (7) | (k) – (11) |
|---|---|---|
| (b) – (3) | (g) – (9) | (l) – (14) |
| (c) – (4) | (h) – (8) | (m) – (15) |
| (d) – (1) | (i) – (6) | (n) – (13) |
| (e) – (2) | (j) – (10) | (o) – (12) |

Chapter 7

# FACTORY BUILDING

## ■ INTRODUCTION

After plant layout has been decided upon, the next step in factory planning is to construct factory building to house and protect employees, equipments, tools, machineries and materials. According to James Moore, a factory building is required to provide protection for men, machines, materials and products, including company secrets. In other words, factory buildings are necessary enclosures for production equipments and facilities. In the words of William Spiegel, "Factory building is the primary tool with which production is carried on and into which all other production tools and mechanisms must fit. Like all other tools, the factory building must be adapted to the operations to be performed if these operations are to be most effectively carried on." Factory building constitutes one of the fixed assets of the factory owner. It has a permanent effect on the operating cost of the factory. Therefore, the construction of factory building must receive all attention on the part of an architect to erect it so as to ensure a smooth production flow in the factory. An ideal factory building, according to James Lundy, is 'one which is built to house the most efficient layout that can be devised for the process involved, yet which is architecturally attractive and of such a standard shape and design as to be flexible in its use and inexpensive in its construction'.

## ■ DEFINITION OF FACTORY BUILDING

Factory building may be defined as any structure constructed for the purpose of undertaking manufacture of goods or services and includes foundation, plinth, walls, floor, chimneys, building services, fixed platforms, balcony, conic and outdoor display structures. Broadly speaking, factory building consists of three parts, viz., (a) foundation, (b) plinth. and (c) superstructure.

(a) **Foundation:** It is the lowest artificially prepared part, below the surface of the surrounding ground, which is in direct contact with sub-strata and transmits all the loads to sub-soil.

(b) **Plinth:** It is the middle part of the structure above the surface of the surrounding ground up to the surface of the floor.

(c) **Superstructure:** The part of structure constructed above the plinth level is termed as superstructure.

## ■ IMPORTANCE OF FACTORY BUILDING

The importance of good factory building are reflected in the following points:

1. It helps in performing different operations most effectively and continuously by decreasing work stoppages and interruptions.
2. It reduces material handling costs.
3. It offers protection to men, machines and materials from bad weather or theft.
4. It minimises production cycle time by reducing bottlenecks and interruptions.
5. It lowers down the maintenance and cost of repairs, plant and machinery by offering protection to machines.
6. It provides healthy and pleasant working conditions by the installation of lighting, ventilation and air-conditioning facilities.
7. It saves area of land through multistorey and mezzanine floor space. Thus, it enables reduction in storage cost.
8. It helps in simplifying production control techniques.
9. It increases flexibility in the use of factory building.
10. It increases the morale of the employees and thus reduces labour turnover.

## ■ DESIGN OF FACTORY BUILDING

The design of factory building must be such that:

1. It derives over-all economical operation of factory.
2. It should be conducive to future expansion of the factory.
3. It should involve least maintenance cost of building.
4. It should provide pleasant working conditions which will improve employee job satisfaction and morale.
5. It should provide flexibility so that it can be adapted to the changing production processes without incurring additional costs.
6. It must have an easy access to service departments.
7. It must be durable and not subjected to depreciation.
8. It must satisfy essential requirements of Factory Acts, related industrial enactments and local or municipal regulations.

The design of factory building depends on certain important factors. These factors are: (a) the type of plant layout, (b) the type of products to be manufactured, (c) the volume of production, and (d) the type of machines and equipments used. Effective design of building involves careful consideration of the location and size of the factory as well as the layout of plant. This is because the layout and value of site determine other aspects of the design of building, such as amount of floor space required, whether to construct single storey or multistorey building, carrying capacity of the floor, ceiling height, passages and so on.

Broadly speaking, the main points in the design of factory building are two, viz. (1) the floor space required, and (2) allocation of space among various departments. The floor space required can be known by taking into account the following:

(a) Space required for keeping various types of furniture and for installing plant and machinery.

(b) Space to be provided for each and every worker to enable him to operate the machines freely.

(c) Space required for storing raw materials, semifinished products and finished products.

(d) Space required for material handling equipments.

(e) In case of electricity and steam generation plants, space required for generators, boilers, heating plants, etc.

(f) Space required for office and administration department.

(g) Space required for parking, trucks, cars scooters, etc.

(h) Space for service departments, such as canteen, first aid room, recreation room.

(i) Space for future expansion.

The allocation of space among various departments depends upon the number of production and service departments and their relative importance in the factory.

## ■ FACTORS TO BE CONSIDERED WHILE DESIGNING FACTORY BUILDING

The following factors are to be considered while designing a new factory building:

1. Types of foundation.
2. Location of receiving and despatching departments.
3. Location of aisles.
4. Material handling plan.
5. Location of production departments.
6. Location of service departments.
7. Types of construction.
8. Types of buildings.
9. Flexibility and expandability.
10. Floor and roof model.
11. Ventilators, doors and windows.
12. Sanitary facility.
13. Damp prevention.
14. Security of building.
15. Good appearance.

1. **Type of foundation:** A foundation is the base of factory building which is in direct contact with the soil. It provides a level surface for building operations. Foundation should be designed in such a way that it is economical in its construction and does not involve much delay. The type of foundation to be laid mainly depends upon the type of building to be constructed and type of soil. However, the foundation of a factory building must be strong so as to prevent frequent repairs and possible collapse. Bed rock and gravel generally provide better foundation for the factory building.

While designing the foundation of the building, it must be considered that environmental factors have a strong impact on the foundation. Some of the environmental factors are: vibration and noise produced by machines, pumping and discharge of ground water, disposal of waste materials and the operation of heavy mechanical plant. Foundations must be durable to resist attack of harmful substance in the soil, rocks and in-ground water. They must also accommodate movement from external causes, such as seasonal moisture, changes in the soil, erosion and seepage, landslides, etc.

Foundations may be classified under two categories: shallow foundation and deep foundation. A foundation is said to be shallow if its depth is equal to or less than its width. In a deep foundation, its depth is greater than its width.

2. **Location of receipt and despatch departments:** The receipt department is the beginning point and the shipping department is the end point in almost all the factories. In between these two departments, the pattern of the flow of materials is to be decided. The receipt department is responsible for receiving the incoming materials, check the terms of quantity and quality and store them until need arises for production department. In the despatch department, goods are stored until they are transported to market areas.

The relative positions of receipt and despatch departments vary from factory to factory. In some cases, both these departments can be combined into one department while in other cases it can be adjacent to each other. This depends upon the availability of loading and unloading facilities in the factory.

3. **Location of aisles:** Aisles are pathways over which all men and materials move in factory. Necessary care must be taken to provide pathways so as to ensure smooth flow of materials and fullest use of these pathways. The aisles to be provided are of two types: (a) Main aisle and (b) Departmental aisle.

The main aisle can be denoted by highways and is provided for the movement of materials into and out of factories. The arrangement of aisles is important, as it enables quick flow of materials thus speeding up production. Generally, main aisles are decided first and then various departments are located so as to prevent difficulties in the movement of materials.

The departmental aisle can be denoted by by-ways and are provided for the movement of men and materials within the departments.

4. **Material handling plan:** The material handling equipments, to a large extent, determines the design and the type of building to be considered. The various materials handling equipments used on the surface of factories, such as tractors, trolleys and those mounted on working tables and benches, such as chains, belts and overhead conveyors, such, as cranes, pulleys, fork lifts, etc., have a decisive role to play in the construction of factory building.

The factors relating to materials handling, which affect the construction of buildings, are the width of aisles to be provided, location of loading and unloading centres, elivators, turning points, angle of inclinations, etc.

5. **Location of production departments:** The location of production departments is the core of factory building design. The number and type of production departments are based on the nature of products manufactured and size of the factory. Some of the types of production departments are cutting department, drilling department, welding department, assembly department, painting department and finishing department. The various production departments should be located so as to provide easy movement of materials and semifinished products from one department to another department. A detailed study of operations involved and product analysis will help in this regard.

6. **Location of service departments:** Service departments are auxiliary to production departments. The provision of certain services are obligatory as per the Indian Factories Act, 1948. These departments

must be positioned both in the interest of employer and employees. The service departments can be divided into two types: (i) those which render service to production departments, and (ii) those which offer welfare facilities to employees. The examples for former type of service departments are repair shops, power house, tool rooms, storeroom and examples for latter type of service departments are canteen, dispensary, recreation rooms, etc.

7. **Types of construction:** Factory buildings are constructed mainly with the help of steel frames, concrete, brick and mortar. Depending upon the type of materials used for construction, the factory buildings are classified into six classes. They are:

(a) ***Slow burning mill design*:** This is a brick and timber construction consisting of concrete foundation, brick walls and plank roof.[1]

(b) ***Fire retardant type*:** This is a brick and steel construction consisting of concrete foundation, exposed steel column.[2]

(c) ***Fire resistant type*:** This is a brick and steel construction as above, except that the steel columns and beams are encased with fire-resisting materials and the floors and roof are of concrete.

(d) ***Steel frame construction*:** These buildings are made up of a steel framework which supports all the loads. The columns, the beams and girders in these buildings are made of steel sections. They can be of two types: (a) 'fire retardant' type in which all the steel is exposed with brick or concrete walls and heavy plank roof, (b) 'fire resistant' type in which all the wall columns are embedded in brick plasters; the interior columns and beams are encased with concrete.

(e) ***Reinforced concrete type*:** This type of construction may be monolithic[3] or framed.[4]

(f) ***Miscellaneous construction*:** These are adopted for low cost or temporary buildings, using wood.

8. **Types of buildings:** Two types of buildings can be adopted by an architect: (a) single storey building, and (b) multistorey building. The type of building to be adopted depends on factors, such as the value of land, the requirements of the layout, the cost of construction, the type of product manufactured and the manufacturing process involved. Necessary care must be taken to decide the construction of particular type of buildings, because any mistake in the selection only involves wastage in resources and land.

**Advantages of single storey buildings**

1. It can be constructed at lower cost per square meter
2. It can be constructed quickly
3. It facilitates expansion through addition to the existing structure
4. Vibration of machinery operations are comparatively less because the machines will be set

---

[1] Long, flat piece of timber.

[2] Column is an isolated vertical load bearing member, the width of which is neither less than its thickness nor more than four times the thickness.

[3] Monolithic is built of a construction material requiring some form of support in the initial stages of construction such as earth walls, plain concrete walls.

[4] Frame structures are comprised of series of frames. These frames are formed of columns which are connected by means of beams at floor and roof levels. Within these frames, walls are constructed.

on prepared foundations in the workshop

5. It is convenient for consecutive operations
6. It lends itself for the flexibility in the layout of machines
7. It provides scope for the use of natural lighting and ventilation
8. Production control can be effectively implemented
9. Supervision becomes effective as production is spread over horizontally
10. Floor space can be effectively used as no stair cases or lifts for upper floors are needed
11. Less danger from fire because of lateral spread.

***Disadvantages of single storey buildings***

1. Single storey buildings involve high capital cost for the acquisition of large land area
2. It results in crowded state in the various departments
3. The advantage of lower transportation cost due to gravitational force is denied.

**Multistorey building:** Multistorey buildings are the outcome of the large scale industrialisation and prohibitive cost of land. A common concept of multistorey buildings in our country is a building having over 3 or 4 storeys.

***Advantages of multistorey building***

1. Multistorey building involve efficient and economical use of land space
2. Better coordination of plant operations is possible on account of vertical layout of production areas in the same building
3. It has the advantage of lower transportation cost due to gravitational force
4. The upper storeys are free from dirt, dust, noise and other odours
5. The multistorey allow lower cost air-conditioning and heating because there is less roof area for escape of cold or heat
6. Upper storeys may be utilised as office accommodation, thereby increasing the size of production floor on the ground floor.

***Disadvantages of multistorey building***

1. Material handling cost is high
2. Expansion beyond certain limit becomes difficult
3. Involves long time for the movement of material and so production is delayed
4. It is difficult to supervise in multistorey buildings
5. More the number of storeys, higher is the cost of foundation.

***Suitability of multistorey building***

Multistorey building is suitable under the following circumstances.

1. Where cost of ground area is high
2. Where the area of the site available is limited
3. Where goods produced are light in weight
4. Where the plant and machines to be installed are light in weight

5. Where both heavier and lighter operations are involved so that heavier operations can be carried out on the ground floor and lighter operations on the upper storeys.

9. **Flexibility and expandability:** The architect must consider the long run requirements in constructing a factory building. The changes brought about by modern technology has resulted in three key words, namely, flexibility, convertibility and expandability. Larger spaces make it possible to change processes and layouts with the minimum of obstruction. The expansion of factory building can be undertaken either horizontally, by adding wings to the single storey building or vertically, i.e., by adding more floors to the multistorey building. If horizontal expansion is expected, the side walls can be made non-load bearing to provide for easy removal and expansion. If vertical growth is contemplated, adequate foundations, supports and such other provisions can be incorporated in the original structure. In the past, factory buildings were constructed corresponding to alphabets, such as E, L, F, H, T, U, so as to lend themselves for easy expansion. Fig. 7.1 shows how each of the above letters give scope for expansion of the buildings in several directions from end walls.

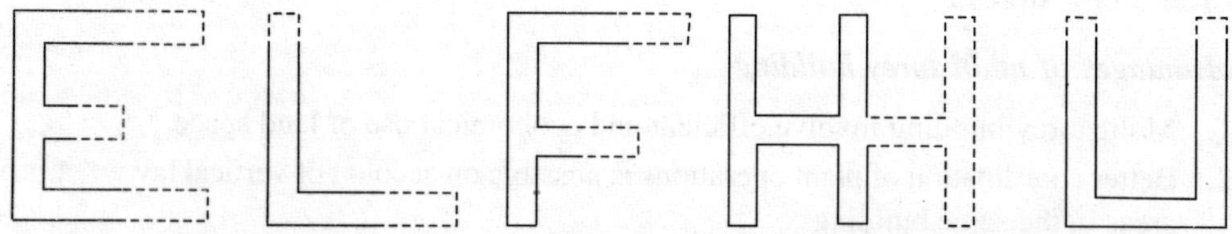

**Fig. 7.1**

The flexibility of a factory building can be increased by:

(a) Providing a large floor area unobstructed by pillars, walls, etc. so that layouts can be changed easily.

(b) Keeping adequate roof truss* strength and ceiling height so that new material handling equipments can be installed.

(c) Making heavy hard floors to accommodate even heavier machines.

10. **Floor and roof model:** Floors are the horizontal elements of building structure which divide a building into different levels for the purpose of creating more accommodation within a restricted space and provide support for the occupants, furniture and machines and equipments of a factory building. Floor can be laid on: (a) Ground floor, (b) Upper floor, and (c) Basement floor. The bottom floor, near the natural surrounding ground level, is termed as ground floor. A floor when provided for the accommodation below the natural ground level (i.e., a basement) is termed as a basement floor. All other floors above the ground floor, such as first floor, second floor and so on, are termed as upper floors.

The materials used in flooring the factory buildings influence the operational efficiency. A good floor must be durable, reduce vibration, it should be non-slippery, free from dust, easy to clean and repair, must bear good loading capacity, less costly and should not produce excessive noise when

*A roof truss is a framework of triangles designed to support the roof covering or ceiling over buildings.

people walk over it. A good floor must also reduce breakage of tools resulting from the dropping of tools. Concrete flooring or steel foundation with a wood is satisfactory type of floor for a factory. For chemical plant, cement flooring is damaged by contact with acids. Hence, vitreous[1] floor tiles with special jointing can be adopted. For electronic industries, marble tiles or use of linolium[2] fixed on cement floor can be adopted. For heavy machine shops, rough stone slabs are used.

Section 32 of Factories Act lays down that in every factory all floors, steps, stairs, passages and gangways shall be of sound construction and properly maintained.

Roof is the uppermost part of a building, which is supported on structural columns and is covered with roofing materials, whose main function is to enclose the space and to protect the same from weather effects, such as rain, wind, heat, snow, etc. As regards the type of roofing, a good roofing is that which is strong, light weight, durable, fire resistant and obtainable at a low cost. Nowadays, asbestos cement sheets are being used increasingly, although zinc sheets are equally popular. The material used must facilitate the flow of natural light and ventilation into the factory. Sometimes, R.C.C. roofs are also used, but it is expensive as compared to asbestos and zinc sheets.

Section 13(1) of the Factories Act lays down that the roofs shall be of such materials and so designed that the temperature shall exceed but kept as low as practicable so as to provide comforts to employees.

11. **Ventilators, doors and windows:** They are small windows either combined with a window or a door frame, or located near the ceiling of the room. They are mainly provided to have natural light and ventilation inside the building. They are generally mounted on a pivot (either horizontal or vertical) or hinged at the top.

A door is defined as a movable barrier secured in an opening, known as a doorway, through a building wall or partition for the purpose of providing an access to the inside of a building. A window is defined as an opening in a wall of a building to serve one or more of the functions, namely, natural light, natural ventilation.

The designer of factory building should observe the following rules while deciding the location of doors and windows:

(a) The number of doors should be kept minimum for each room because the larger number causes obstruction and decreases utility of the accommodation. The location and the size of door should be based on its functional requirements.

(b) From the purpose of utility of the accommodation, doors should preferably be located near the corner of a room.

(c) For good ventilation and free air circulation inside the room, the doors should be located in opposite walls facing each other.

(d) The location, number and size of the windows are decided considering various factors, namely, desired daylight, desired outside vision, natural ventilation.

(e) For ventilation, the windows should be located opposite to each other whenever possible.

(f) From viewpoint of maximum daylight, windows in a room should be located on the northern side.

---

[1]It is hard and brittle.

[2]Strong floor covering of canvas treated with powdered cork and oil.

12. **Sanitary facility:** For improving the efficiency of workers it is necessary to provide toilets and washing facilities to employees according to their status. Necessary drainage must be provided to the outflow of liquid waste by means of sewer pipes. A detailed study about the provision of sanitation facilities in factories is discussed separately.

13. **Damp prevention:** The term dampness indicates the entry or presence of moisture in buildings due to several causes such as rain water penetration, rise of ground water, improper drainage, use of defective materials, etc. Dampness is highly undesirable as it deteriorates the structural strength, stability and durability of building on one hand and creates unhygienic conditions for the employees on the other. Dampness in buildings is generally due to design of structure or faulty construction or use of poor materials in construction. The term 'damp prevention' is used to check the entry of water in different components of a building such as walls, floors, roofs, etc. by way of damp-proofing materials and techniques.

The following precautions should be taken to prevent the dampness in factory buildings:

(a) The site should be located on a high ground and well drained soil to safeguard against foundation dampness.

(b) All the walls shall be of sufficient thickness to safeguard against rain penetration.

(c) Bricks of superior quality which are free from defects such as cracks should be used.

(d) Good quality cement mortar should be used to produce a definite pattern throughout construction work.

(e) Hollow or cavity walls are more reliable than solid walls in preventing dampness and hence the cavity wall construction should be adopted wherever possible.

For prevention of dampness on flooring, bituminous layers below it or concrete base is essential. For protection of outer walls, a layer of Cuddapah stone slabs over plinth level is adequate.

14. **Plant protection (security of building):** Protection of the factory property from theft and fire is one of the important factors which must be considered while designing layout of factory building. It is common to observe construction of boundary walls all around the factory, which, in turn, is covered by broken glass pieces. Where it is not possible to construct compound walls, it is desirable to cover the area by means of fencing. The entrance of the factory must be provided with security rooms with guards so as to prevent unauthorised persons from entering the factory.

More important than the protection from theft is protection from fire. The damage caused by fire to factory buildings involve both direct and indirect losses. In USA, the direct losses arising out of fires in factory building is estimated at 250 million dollars each year. The amount of indirect losses in production and wages being estimated at double the direct losses. The occurrence of fire in the factories not only destroys the buildings which require huge fixed capital to renovate, but is also responsible for the deaths of workers.

It is said that fire prevention is more important than fire combating. Therefore, it is necessary that the factory buildings are built with fire resisting materials. In this regard, following points should be considered while constructing factory building:

(a) Arrangement of physical conditions of factory to prevent possibility of fire occurrence.

(b) Proper arrangements to detect and extinguish the fire.

(c) Arrangement of area in such a way that fire does not spread to other areas.

(d) Arrangement for the exit of the employees from the building on the occurrence of fire.

It is always better to construct fire proof factory buildings. According to James Lundy, a fire proof building is not one in which a fire cannot occur, but one which will remain structurally sound for four hours under severe fire conditions. Fire proof buildings will have walls and floors resistant to heat transmission, columns and beams which will be capable of carrying loads under fire conditions.

15. **Good appearance:** As huge amount of capital is invested in factory buildings, its appearance must be elegant so as to create a good image in the minds of public. This can be ensured by a good building finish using painting, whitewashing, colour washing, varnishing, distempering, etc. Such buildings will have lasting impression in the minds of employees and psychologically they feel like working in the same factory, thus reducing labour turnover.

## BUILDING MATERIALS

1. **Building stones:** These are cut from natural rocks into different sizes for masonry construction. These stones are used for laying foundations, floors and in constructing walls.

2. **Bricks:** This is a product of clay which is obtained by moulding clay in rectangular blocks of uniform size which measures 19 cm × 9 cm × 9 cm. When it is burnt in clay kilns it assumes hardness which is used in the construction of walls.

3. **Cement:** It is a very important building material which is artificially produced by grinding a mixture of clay, limestone, and gypsum.

4. **Mortar:** It is a mixture of binding material (such as cement), fine aggregate (such as sand) and water. This is used to bind masonry or other structural unit.

5. **Concrete:** This is a mixture of stone chips, sand and cement in proportion of 4:2:1 and it resembles stone when set. To increase its strength, it is reinforced with steel rods. Then it is called reinforced concrete.

6. **Steel:** It is an alloy of iron and carbon and is used for laying beams, roof trusses, columns, etc.

7. **Wood:** Wood used in building construction can be classified into two types. (1) Hard wood, and (2) Soft wood. Hard wood, such as teak, sal, etc. is used largely in the construction of building. It is immune from attacks of white ants and other insects. Soft wood, such as mango, pine, etc. are often used for preparing window frame. Use of wood in building construction is not common as it is least to fire resistant.

8. **Glass:** It is an amorphous, transparent or translucent material which is obtained by melting at a high temperature a mixture of pure sand, soda and chalk. Different kinds of glass are being used for various purposes, such as walls and cellings of hollow glass blocks, windows, furniture, etc.

## RECENT TRENDS IN FACTORY BUILDINGS

1. The first trend in the construction of the factory building is the use of automation which makes use of Computer Numerical Control (CNC) devices reducing utilisation of very skilled labour. Thus, it has replaced the services of even expert engineers. By feeding various data in the computers, we get solutions for various problems relating to the length, breadth, dimension of building construction implementation of air-conditioning, dust proofing, etc.

2. Expansion and diversification of end products in some factories demanding a new structure of factory building is second prevalent trend. An example in this regard is Brook Bond Ltd., which, in the

beginning, started with tea, then introduced coffee and extended it further to include sona spices and has recently added motorcycles. A new structure may be simply an addition to the existing building or it may involve construction of entirely new buildings. Although the problems of the two are not identical, their solutions are such that many basic considerations are applicable to both.

3. The third current trend in factory building is the construction of single storey buildings. As single storey buildings require more space, the sites for factory buildings are selected near suburban and rural areas. The factors which support single storey buildings are: need for flexibility in plant layout, location of production departments adjacent to each other, lower material handling equipments, and effective production control.

4. The fourth trend in factory building construction is the use of mezzanine floor. It is an additional intermediate floor between two floors above ground level with area of mezzanine restricted to 1/3 of the area of that floor and with a minimum height of 2.2 m. Mezzanine floors are largely used for packing goods, as a warehouse, for servicing equipments, such as fans, heater, and air-conditioning units. Sometimes, it is used for assembling the component parts, for erecting light machines which can be used for performing light work.

5. Fifthly, the basement for factory buildings are mostly constructed with marble stones and mosaic flooring as against the traditional flooring, such as concrete flooring. Further floor covering, which provides a clean, smooth, durable dust proof and wear-resisting surface, are also increasingly used. The basement of the factory buildings are so constructed as to use it for storing raw materials, for providing facilities to employees, such as toilets and washrooms, canteens and dispensary, etc.

6. Sixthly, prefabricated constructions are increasingly used in factory buildings. These are manufactured parts which are assembled while constructing the buildings.

7. Seventhly, novel designs in factory building are observed everywhere nowadays. Some of the factory buildings are cylindrical in shape while others are square type. The cylindrical buildings require comparatively less space for stair cases, elevators, etc. The square type of building allow maximum utilisation of floor space, its maintenance cost is low and it is more flexible for future expansion.

8. Eighthly, to derive maximum natural lighting and ventilation, large sized windows are made use of. To suit the controlled environment, automatic opening and closing doors are used. Provisions are made within the factory buildings for fire alarm, fire protecting equipments.

9. Ninthly, enough space is provided around the factory for parking vehicles, for gardening, for outdoor games, swimming pools and other recreational facilities for employees.

10. Tenthly, necessary precautions for controlling the pollutants, which are ejected by the factory, are given utmost importance while constructing factory buildings. This takes the form of tall pipes to let off poisonous gases to a higher altitude and drainage system to dispose liquid waste.

11. Lasty, the appearance of factory building is given an anaesthetic look. This has the value of self-advertisement. To attract the attention of strangers, suppliers, prospective investors, the office building is equipped with a replica of the factory in its miniature form along with the photographs of the founders and some national leaders. Similarly the progress made by the factory together with certain important achievements are displayed through attractive pictures, diagrams, charts. Use of slogans are also commonly seen in various parts of factory buildings. This helps in projecting image of the factory among the people.

## SUMMARY

A factory building provides shelter to materials, men, machines and finished products. The need for and importance of factory building is reflected in the following points: (a) for performing manufacturing operations more effectively, (b) for reducing material handling cost, (c) for minimising production time, (d) for providing safety to equipments and employees. The design of factory building depends upon: (a) the type of product to be manufactured, (b) the layout of the plant, (c) production capacity, and (d) types of machines and equipments used. The two main points which determines the design of factory building are: (1) space required and, (2) allocation of space to various departments. Before constructing a building, the following factors must be considered: (a) type of foundation (b) location of receiving and despatching department, (c) location of aisles, (d) material handling plan, (e) location of production department, (f) location of service department, (g) type of construction, (h) types of building, (i) flexbility and expandability, (j) type of floor and roof, (k) ventilation facility (l) sanitary facility, (m) damp prevention, (n) protection of building, and (o) good appearance.

The building materials used in factory building are wood, bricks, cement, concrete, steel and asbestos sheet.

A modern factory no longer resembles its ancient counterpart. The recent trend in the factory building layout are: (1) use of automation for its designing, (2) use of new structures for meeting the needs of diversified products, (3) use of single storey buildings to a large extent, (4) use of mezzanine floors, (5) use of basements, (6) prefabricated construction, (7) novel designs in factory building, (8) provision of more windows and automatic doors with fire protection devices, (9) provision of employee services, (10) control of pollutants, and (11) beautification of buildings.

## QUESTIONS

### A. Objective Type

**I. Fill in the blanks:**

(a) ......... type of building is more suitable for maximum utilisation of operating floor space available.

(b) Future expansion can be undertaken easily in ......... type of building.

(c) Factories manufacturing heavy products require ..... type of building.

(d) Better supervision can be exercised in ........... type of building.

(e) Production control can be effectively implemented in ...... type of building.

**II. Write True or False for the following sentences:**

(a) The only justification for multistorey factory building is the possible use of gravity handling of materials.

(b) A single storey building is generally more adaptable than a multistorey building for layout purpose.

(c) The recent trend in the factory building construction is towards single storey building.

(d) In planning a new factory, first comes the layout and then factory building.

(e) The design of the factory building depends upon the shape of site available.

## III. Choose the correct answer from the following alternatives:

1. Which of the following type of building construction is more popular in factories now-a-days?
   (a) Wood construction (c) Steel frame construction
   (b) Slow burning construction (d) R.C.C. construction
2. Under which of the following circumstances single storey building is preferable over multistorey building?
   (a) When materials can be handled by gravity feed
   (b) When the material handling is difficult because the product is heavy
   (c) When the acquisition of land becomes difficult and expensive
   (d) When the floor space is less
3. Under which of the following circumstances multistorey building is preferable to a single storey building?
   (a) In manufacturing light products using light materials
   (b) Where natural light is desired
   (c) Where the construction is to be completed within a short time
   (d) Where frequent changes in layout is anticipated
4. Which of the following type of constructing factory building are largely used in modern days?
   (a) Slow burning type (b) Fire retardant type
   (c) Steel framed type (d) Reinforced concrete type
5. Which one of the following is not the current trend in factory building layout?
   (a) Prefabricated construction (b) Provision of mezzanine floor
   (c) Single storey building (d) Multistorey building

## IV. Match the following:

| Column A | Column B |
|---|---|
| (a) Wood frame construction | (1) Fit for multistorey construction |
| (b) Brick construction | (2) Built with spaces between columns |
| (c) Slow burning construction | (3) Cheap |
| (d) Steel frame construction | (4) Constructed quickly and easily |
| (e) RCC construction | (5) Rarely used nowadays |

## B. Short answer type

1. What is an ideal factory building?
2. What do you mean by prefabricated construction?
3. Distinguish between 'fire retarding' and 'fire resisting' construction.
4. State the factors which determine the multistorey building.
5. List out various building materials used in modern factories.

### C. Short answer type

1. Bring out the importance of factory building.
2. "A factory building is the primary tool for production". Explain.
3. State the merits and demerits of single storey building.
4. State the merits and demerits of multistorey building.
5. Explain the recent trends in factory building layout.
6. Explain the various types of constructing factory building.

### D. Long answer question

Explain the various factors that are to be considered in a factory building layout.

## ANSWERS TO OBJECTIVE TYPE QUESTIONS

| | | | | | |
|---|---|---|---|---|---|
| I. | (a) Multistorey, | (b) single storey, | (c) single storey, | (d) single storey, | (e) single storey. |
| II. | (a) F, | (b) T, | (c) T, | (d) T, | (e) F. |
| III. | 1. (a), | 2. (b), | 3. (c), | 4. (d), | 5. (e) |
| IV. | (a) 4, | (b) 3, | (c) 5, | (d) 2, | (e) 1. |

# Chapter 8

# FACTORY LIGHTING

## ■ INTRODUCTION

Provision of adequate light is the most important environmental factor in factories as it increases productivity and adds to employee satisfaction. No person, either in a factory or in an office, can work efficiently where lighting arrangements are not satisfactory. A good light refers to economical provision of right quantity and right quality of light in the right place. The quantity of light required in a factory depends upon the type of work to be performed. Although there is no upper limit to the intensity of light, it is always essential to determine the minimum intensity of light required to perform different operations in a factory. Lighting with 20 foot candles has been considered adequate in factories. The quality of light to be supplied is as important as the quantity of light. The quality of light includes its colour, direction, diffusion, streadiness and the glare it produces. Any deviation from the above will impair the vision and add fatigue to employees. In the words of John A. Shubin, an efficient lighting system in a plant or office reduces fatigue of the eye, helps in preventing accidents, and improves morale. It decreases spoilage, raises the quality of workmanship, and increases production.

The provision of adequate lighting facilities in factories is governed by statute in India. Section 17 of the Factories Act lays down the following:

1. In every part of the factory, where workers are working or passing, there shall be provided and maintained sufficient and suitable iighting, natural or artificial or both [Sec. 17(1)].
2. All glazed windows and skylights used for lighting of the workroom shall be kept clean on both inner and outer surfaces and free from obstruction [Sec. 17(2)].
3. Effective provision shall also, as far as practicable, be made for the prevention of:
    (a) glare, either directly from a source of light or by reflection from a smooth or polished surface.
    (b) the formation of shadows to such an extent as to cause eyestrain or the risk of accident to any workers [Sec. 17(3)].

## ■ FEATURES OF GOOD LIGHTING

The following are the characteristic features of good lighting:

1. Supply of adequate light
2. Proper intensity
3. Proper diffusion

4. Elimination of glare
5. Right direction and reliability
6. Economical and less maintenance cost
7. Elimination of abrupt contrast
8. No dazzling light
9. It should be cool
10. It should be steady
11. Colour combination.

1. **Supply of adequate light:** The supply of light must be adequate so as to enable the employees to increase the ability to see the objects clearly. Adequate light on small articles acts as a magnifier which makes small details more visible. The supply of light must be such that the details of the objects can be seen in a shortest possible time. The importance of time in seeing is even more important when the object is moving.

2. **Proper intensity:** The unit used to measure the intensity of light is known as lumen, one lumen per square foot being equal to a foot candle.* As the intensity of light varies from department to department and operation to operation, it is better to classify all departments and work areas according to the number of foot candles necessary for optimum lighting condition. Work that requires more fineness, accuracy and discrimination needs more light.

The required intensity of light for different types of work and work places are given below:

| | Type of work and work areas | Intensity of light in foot candles |
|---|---|---|
| 1. | Machine shops-ordinary work area | 100 |
| 2. | Inspection | 50 |
| 3. | Office areas | 100 |
| 4. | Receiving and despatching areas | 20 |
| 5. | Sense areas | 10 |
| 6. | Sheet metal work area | 50 |
| 7. | Minute and precision work | 1000 |

Fig. 8.1

3. **Proper diffusion:** It means an even spread of light over the working place. When the light is not properly diffused, the reflected light falling on eyes from a glass, working tables or any other equipment will result in poor visibility. Proper diffusion of light is necessary as eyes cannot adjust each

*A foot candle is the intensity of the light emitted from a standard candle at a distance of one foot.

time when brightness varies. For uniform distribution of light the spacing between light units should not exceed their mounting light above the level of the work area.

4. **Elimination of glare:** The brightness or brilliance produced by light will have certain adverse effects over employees, such as discomfort, interference with vision, high fatigue, headache and nervous effect. One of the features of good lighting system is the avoidance of surface glare completely. There are two types of glare which are observed in lighting system, namely, direct glare and reflected glare. Direct glare, which results from sunlight or ceiling light can be eliminated by mechanical devices and appropriate light fixtures. Reflected glare is caused by light striking on highly polished surfaces. Reflected glare can be eliminated by relocating the work and source of light to prevent reflections towards the worker.

5. **Right direction and reliability:** Light must come from correct direction so as to prevent falling shadow on the objects. The supply of light must also be reliable. We can overcome frequent power cuts resulting in disruption of lighting facility by installing generators.

6. **Economical and less maintenance cost:** The cost of operating and maintenance cost of lighting equipments must be less.

7. **Elimination of abrupt contrast:** In order to see a particular part of an object properly that part should differ in brightness compared to other parts of the object and its surrounding background. This contrast between an object and its immediate background should be made as high as possible but it should not produce abrupt contrast.

The contrast of light between two surfaces can be measured in terms of foot-lambert.* When the contrast between two surfaces is excessive, eye fatigue results from the frequent expansion and contraction of pupils of the eyes. An acceptable range form contrast of light is a three to one ratio. This means that the brightness of the surface on which a task is being performed should be no greater than three times the brightness of the background. Therefore, if a task is being performed on a surface reflecting 60 foot-lamberts, the background of the surface must have a brightness of approximately 20 foot-lamberts if the three to one ratio is to be obtained.

8. **No dazzling light:** As far as possible the dazzling light should be avoided in factories because the eyes cannot perceive brightness beyond a certain limit. Otherwise, it may lead to problems of eyesight to employees.

9. **Cool light:** The heat emitted by light often makes employees tiresome and this reduces their efficiency. Therefore, the light must not produce excess heat in factories.

10. **Steady flow of light:** Often, there is flicking in light due to objects passing through the source of light or due to sudden change in load. This produces undue eye strain to employees and so the steady flow of light is essential.

11. **Colour combination:** The use of colour increases illumination and helps in comfortable seeing. According to Bethel and others, "Light and paint are the Siamese twins of illumination. Together, they form a team which can banish darkness; one without the other will only half do the job."

## ■ NEED FOR AND IMPORTANCE OF LIGHTING

The importance of lighting in factories is felt on account of the fact that 85% of the working movements are controlled by sight. Further, the need for plant lighting has increased due to the fact that the

*Foot-lambert is a unit used to measure brightness of light.

factories are run in different shifts and during the night shifts the illumination problem is of major importance. According to W. Sprigel and Lansberg, "Defective lighting may cause defective work, increased accidents, reduced output, excess eye strain, fatigue, increased absenteeism, increased labour turnover and, at times, unrest bordering on low morale." In the words of Caudex. S. George in *Management for Business and Industry*, good lighting helps in providing a safe working place, aids in the performance of operations and helps conserve vision and energy. The need for plant lighting arises on account of the following:

1. Increases quantity and quality of goods
2. Reduces spoilage and wastages in production
3. Enables effective utilisation of space
4. Reduces fatigue and eyestrain
5. Reduces accident
6. Effective supervision
7. Reduces absenteeism and labour turnover
8. Good house keeping
9. Better human relations.

1. **Increase in quantity and quality of goods:** Adequate supply of light enables the workers to increase their efficiency. This is responsible for increasing the speed of production which, in turn, increases the quantity of goods to be produced. Provision of good light increases the skill and accuracy of workmanship. This results in improved quality of goods.

2. **Reduction in spoilage and wastages in production:** A good light enable the workers to view clearly the machines, materials and tools in the course of production. Any defect in machines, materials or equipment can be easily detected and thereby avoids spoilage and wastage in production.

3. **Saving of floor space:** Floor space is completely utilised in workshops, storeroom, godown, because of satisfactory visibility and proper arrangement of materials, tools, and equipments and finished goods.

4. **Reduction in accidents:** There is a close relationship between lighting arrangement and industrial accidents. It has been estimated that approximately 70% of industrial accidents are due to poor lighting. By providing proper lighting facilities the losses arising out of industrial accidents such as payment of compensation, loss of man hours, disturbances in production and suffering can be eliminated.

5. **Protects health of employees:** A good lighting system, first of all, reduces the eyestrain of employees. Secondly, it minimises the fatigue of employees. Thirdly, it helps the older employees from poor eyesight. Fourthly, it reduces headache caused by poor light. Thus, it is responsible for maintaining health of employees.

6. **Effective supervision:** When adequate lighting facility is provided, effective supervision is possible as a supervisor can exercise better control in the presence of good light.

7. **Reduces absenteeism and labour turnover:** Provision of good lighting enables the workers to work in a good working conditions. This reduces excess absenteeism and labour turnover.

8. **Better house keeping:** Good lighting helps in maintaining neatness and cleanliness, which is quite important in factories.

9. **Better human relations:** Provision of good light increases the morale of employees as it has psychological effect over the mind of employees. This results in a good relationship between the employer and employees.

## ■ SOURCES OF LIGHT

There are two sources of light: (1) Natural or daylight, and (2) Artificial source.

### 1. Natural light

Light, which is obtained from sun through factory roofs, doors, and window openings, are referred to as natural lighting. It has the following advantages:

(a) Its supply is plentiful

(b) It is available free of cost.

(c) It requires no maintenance.

(d) It is always available regularly.

(e) Its distribution is uniform.

But natural light suffers from certain disadvantages. They are:

(a) It varies from season to season, day to day and sometimes even hour to hour.

(b) It varies with the size and positions of windows and roofs.

(c) Its intensity cannot be altered.

(d) It is not available during night shift work.

When it is desired to get daylight in any factory, it involves careful designing of windows and type of roofing. More windows and transparent materials are used for roofing, more is the availability of light in factories. Moreover, it also depends upon the frequent cleaning of windows and roofing materials so as to get maximum supply of light.

**Lighting facility through windows**

The flow of light and its intensity through windows many factory are summarised as under:

(a) **Entry of light when only side windows are provided:** The light transmitted into a factory building through side windows is expected to be 10 foot candles for a distance which is about twice the height of the windows. This is shown in the following figure.

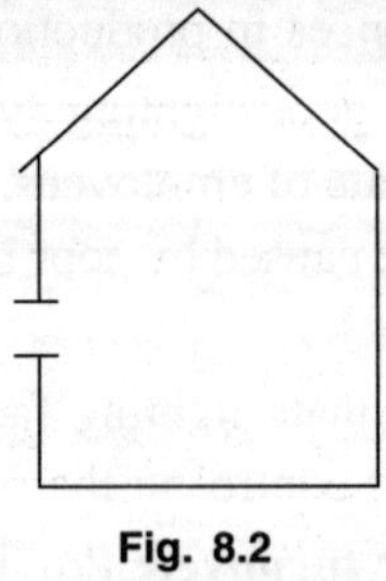

**Fig. 8.2**

(b) **Entry of light when opposite side windows are provided:** The light transmitted into a factory building through two opposite windows is expected to be 10 foot candles for a distance which is about three times the height of windows. This is shown on the next page.

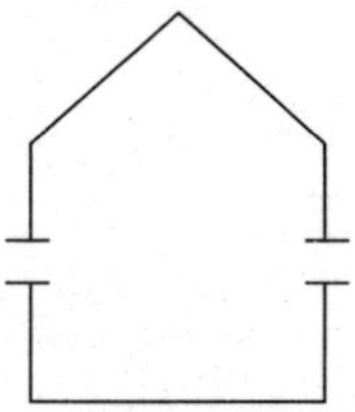

Fig. 8.3

(c) **Entry of light through side and monitor windows:** Monitors of the buildings may have windows either on sloping side or on vertical side. But best light is obtained when windows are provided on vertical side. Along with monitor windows, the provision of side windows enable the transmission of more light into factory building. This is shown in the following diagrams.

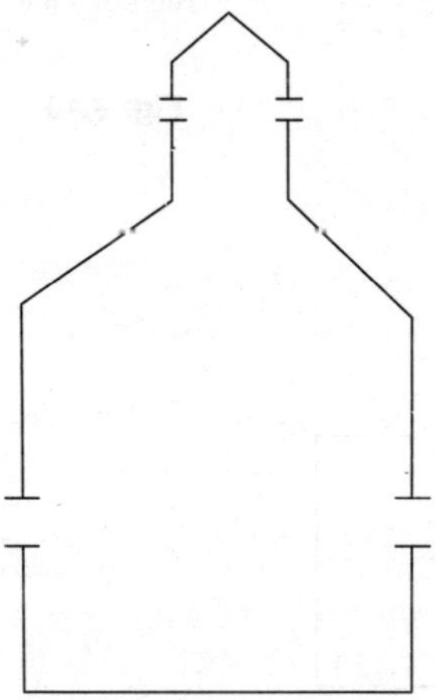

Fig. 8.4

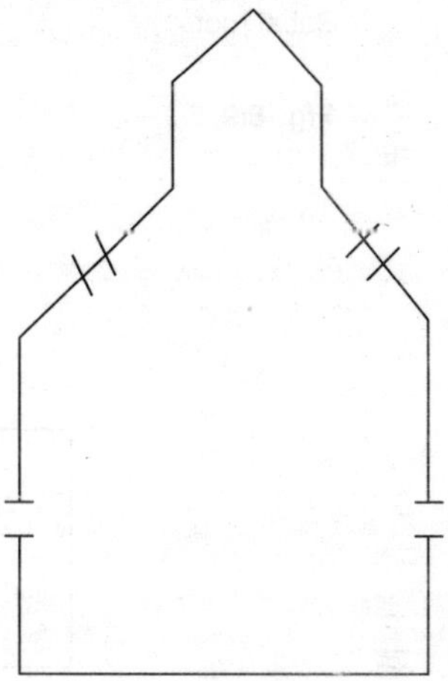

Fig. 8.5

**Lighting facility through roofs**

Three points must be considered while designing the roofing structure for obtaining maximum light. First, the type of roofing materials, to a large extent, determines the extent of flow of light into factories. The transparent materials are best suited in this regard. Second is the model of roof to be used in constructing the factory building. Below are given a few models of roofing used in factory building which allow the free transmission of light. Third is the height of ceilings which also enables the admission of more light into the factory.

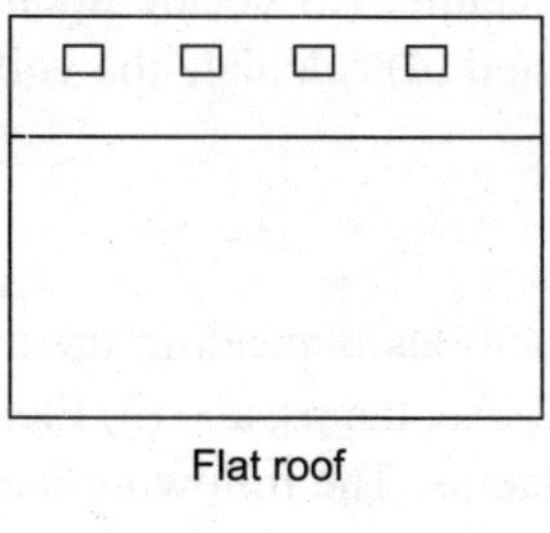

Flat roof

Fig. 8.6

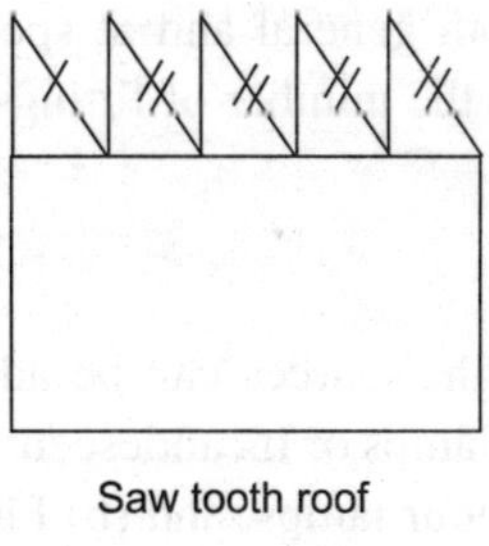

Saw tooth roof

Fig. 8.7

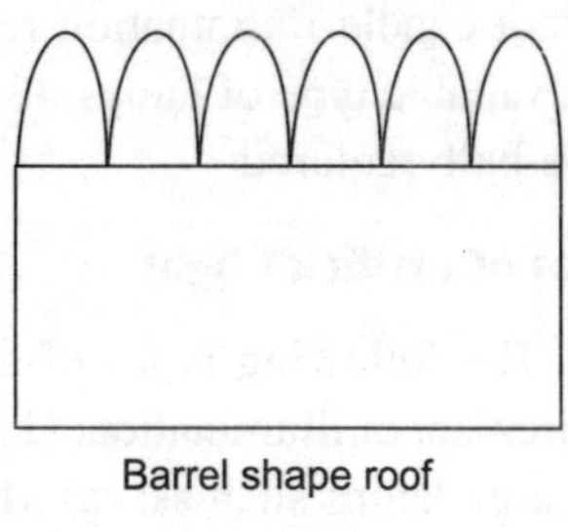

Barrel shape roof

Fig. 8.8

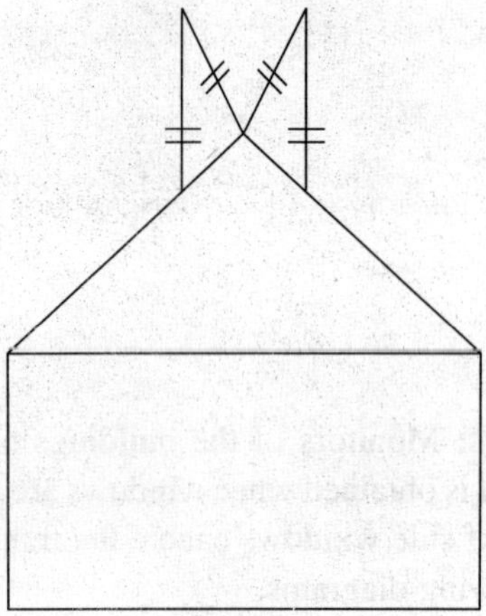

Gabel roof

Fig. 8.9

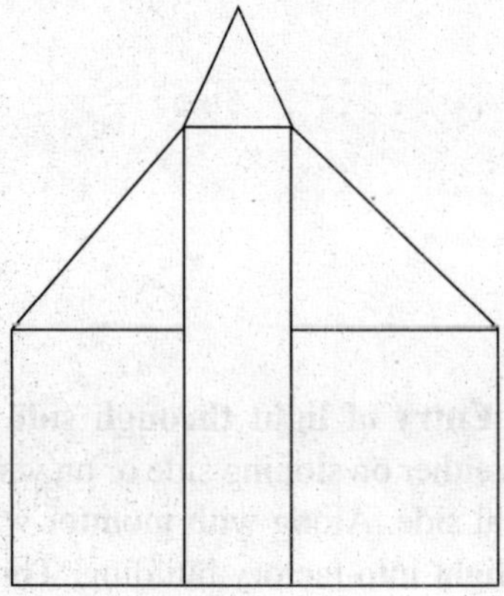

High bay mill

Fig. 8.10

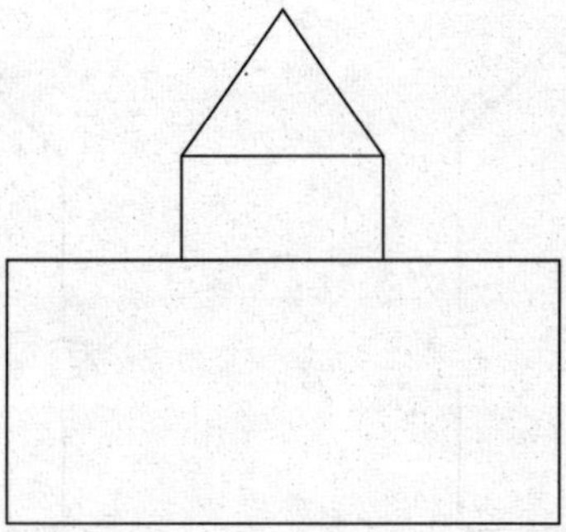

Flat with monitor roof

Fig. 8.11

## 2. Artificial light

While natural light is useful for performing operations during day shifts, artificial lighting is essential during night shifts. Further, the intensity of day light is less during cloudy days which is to be supplemented with artificial lighting. Again, even during the normal days, when day light varies with the passage of time, it is necessary to use artificial light, because poor light results in mental and physical strain of employees. The following steps are to be taken in designing an artificial lighting system: (1) ascertain the foot candle illumination required, both general and at specific work centre, (2) decide upon the most suitable type of lamps, (3) calculate the number of fittings required, and (4) calculate the voltage of the bulb required.

### Types of artificial light

The following types of artificial light sources can be adopted in factories depending upon the requirement of illumination: (1) Filament lamps or Incandescent lighting, (2) Arc lamps, and (3) Electric discharge lamps such as: (a) Mercury vapour lamps, and (b) Fluorescent lamps. The following factors are to be considered while selecting a suitable type of lamp (1) Initial outlay, (2) Cost of renewal, (3) Current consumption, and (4) Suitability and efficiency.

1. **Filament or incandescent lamps:** This type of light is produced by filament bulbs. These lamps involve less initial investment. They burn instantaneously when switched. They require less maintenance and have longer life. But the intensity of light is insufficient for industrial work. They produce excess heat and do not possess ordinary daylight colour. Still they are used in toilets, wash rooms, cafeteria, etc.

The filament temperature determines the life and efficiency of filament lamps. If the temperature of filament is high, the efficiency of light will also be high. But the life of the filament bulb will be short with a high temperature. But by using different voltage of bulbs, it is possible to regulate the output and efficiency under different circumstances.

2. **Arc lamps:** These are suitable where high power illumination is required.

3. **Mercury vapour lamps:** This is a form of electric discharge lamp which emits a greenish blue light of high intensity. These are usually used as exterior light to illumine dark passages, exterior work, such as loading and unloading of materials and finished goods during nights and to help security staff to locate trespassers at night. It can be easily maintained and it has a long operating life. But, it has no daylight colour which is unnatural to look at, but by a combination of 80 per cent mercury and 20 per cent fluorescent light it can give better natural light.

4. **Fluorescent lamps:** These are used in machine shops and storerooms. The advantages of this type of light is (a) they consume less power, (b) they do not provide shadow and glare, (c) they do not produce excess heat, (d) the light is distributed uniformly, (e) it has daylight colour, and (f) it has long life. But it has two disadvantages, namely, (a) its initial investment is high, and (b) its maintenance charges are high.

From the point of efficiency and output, filament lamp is the least efficient. It produces only 13.9 lumens per watt when a 60 watt bulb is used. As against this, the mercury vapour lamp produces about 40 to 55 lumens per watt. The most efficient lamp is the fluorescent lamp, as it produces about 74 lumens per watt.

### Advantages of artificial lighting

1. Artificial light is available both during day shifts and night shifts.
2. Its intensity can be altered by using different voltage of bulbs.
3. Its facility can be extended to any corner of the factory including the interior portions of the factory building.

### Disadvantages of artificial lighting

1. The initial investments are high in case of artificial lighting system.
2. Its maintenance and replacement costs are also high.
3. Cost of electricity consumed is an additional expenditure under this system.
4. To some extent, it is also not a reliable system as during power cuts imposed by state governments, it results in darkness.

## ■ DIFFERENCES BETWEEN NATURAL LIGHT AND ARTIFICIAL LIGHT

| Points of differences | Natural light | Artificial light |
|---|---|---|
| 1. Availability of light | It is available only during day shift | It is available both during day and night shifts |
| 2. Initial investment | It requires no investment as it is available free of cost, being the gift of nature | It requires initial investment for its installation |
| 3. Cost of operation and maintenance | It does not require maintenance cost and no power cost need be incurred for its operation | It requires maintenance and consumes power. So, its operating cost is high |
| 4. Quantity of supply | Its supply is in abundance | Its supply is limited |
| 5. Regularity | It is available throughout the year. But the intensity varies from season to season. | Its availability depends upon electricity supply and during period of power generators or inverters are to be made operational to get light |
| 6. Alteration of intensity | Its intensity cannot be altered | Its intensity can be altered by using bulbs of different voltages |
| 7. Suitability | It is suitable during day shift | It is suitable during in case of any need |
| 8. Colour | It has natural day light colour | The colour varies depending upon the vapour contents of the bulb |
| 9. Utility | It is used only at spots where light spreads | It can be extended to interior places where natural light is restricted |
| 10. Uniformity | Natural light is distributed uniformly | Artificial light is unevenly distributed |

### Types of lighting installation

The artificial light required in a factory can be installed in the following ways: (a) General lighting, (b) Supplementary lighting, and (c) Local lighting.

(a) **General lighting:** General lighting is fixed either by means of fixture or grid system usually 10 feet above the work places. Light fixtures should be fixed at uniform height and should be spaced in such a way so as to get adequate diffusion and intensity of light. This type of installation is useful when there is frequent change in the machine layout.

(b) **Supplementary lighting:** As the name itself suggests, this type of installation is provided to derive additional light required by employees to meet their particular requirements. The supplementary lights are installed on working tables or mounted on machines which can be adjusted by the employees depending on its need. But care to be taken to prevent the shadows created by supplementary light over general lighting in the work and surrounding areas.

(c) **General lighting combined with local lighting:** Whenever high intensity of light is required to do work requiring precision or more accuracy, this type is made use of and local lighting supplements the general lighting. When local lighting is applied, abrupt contrasts with the remainder of the room should be avoided to prevent eye strain.

## TYPES OF LIGHTING SYSTEMS

Lighting system consists of the following types:

(a) Direct lighting,

(b) Semi-direct lighting,

(c) Indirect lighting,

(d) Semi-indirect lighting, and

(e) General diffuse lighting.

(a) **Direct lighting:** Under this system, approximately 90 to 100 per cent of the lighting is directed downward to the working surface. This results in excessive glare and very little light is diffused. This is responsible for creation of shadows. So, unless light fixtures are closely arranged, a uniform light may not be obtained.

(b) **Semi-direct lighting:** Under this system, about 60 to 90 per cent of the light is directed downward, the remainder being directed outward. This system eliminates the shadows that are characteristic of direct lighting.

(c) **Indirect lighting:** Under this system, about 90 to 100 per cent of the light is first directed upwards to the ceiling. The light then becomes diffused and is reflected downward to the working area. As the light is diffused before it reaches the working surface, shadows and glares are eliminated under this system.

(d) **Semi-indirect lighting:** Under this system, about 60 to 90 per cent of the light is directed towards ceiling and is then reflected downwards. The balance 10 to 40 per cent of light is immediately directed downward. This system of light produces more glare and shadows.

(e) **General diffuse lighting:** Under this system about 40 to 60 per cent of light is directed to the working surface. The remainding of light is reflected from ceiling. This system of lighting produces more light for the same wattage when compared to semi-indirect system. But the shadow and glare produced is more when compared to semi-indirect light.

### Procedure for attaining good lighting

The following steps are to be followed for achieving good light in factories:

1. Provision for getting maximum natural lighting
2. Provision for effective use of artificial lighting
3. Proper painting or colour combination for the interior walls
4. Good maintenance.

1. **Provision for getting maximum natural lighting:** In order to get maximum advantage of natural light, the factory building must be designed with provisions to get the required intensity of light. The usual means through which natural light is derived are windows and roofs. Adequate number of windows must be provided in factories. The use of transparent materials for roofing makes possible

the scattering of light farther into the room. The use of certain types of glass also helps to keep interior parts of the room cool by absorbing sun heat, eliminate the need for painting windows and reduce glare. The use of monitor windows and saw-tooth roofs supplement window light. A saw-tooth roof facing north provides a uniform distribution of light for the centre of the building.

2. **Provision for effective use of artificial lighting:** Depending upon the extent of illumination required, lighting equipment is to be located and arranged to provide general lighting, supplementary lighting and local lighting. Reflectors producing direct and indirect lighting are better suited for industrial purposes. Different types of bulbs can be used in different rooms for getting maximum efficiency of light.

3. **Proper painting or colour combination for the interior walls:** The use of a suitable combination of colour on the interior walls will increase the intensity of illumination. Intensity can be increased by repainting in lighter colours, since light colours reflect rays. Glare can be reduced by using a flat paint finish instead of bright finish. Vision can be improved by avoiding monotonous effect of a uniformly coloured surrounding area. Floors should be painted in bright colours to gain greater reflection.

4. **Good maintenance:** Maintenance of lighting system improves the efficiency and output of light. It is estimated that 50 per cent of light is lost due to dust and dirt covered on the windows. Deterioration of bulbs and dirt on reflectors also reduce effective illumination. The proper maintenance of lighting system calls for washing windows, repainting walls, cleaning lamps and reflectors and replacing bulbs when the output of light falls below standard. It has been estimated that group replacement of bulbs has advantages over individual replacement. In group replacement, bulbs are systematically replaced on the basis of areas or group of bulbs, irrespective of the fact that they are operational out or not. This group replacement saves labour cost of fixing new ones and also helps in improving overall lighting. Other advantages of group replacement are that it helps in estimating the actual amount required for investing on bulbs. It requires less storage space, less work interruption and less spoilage of starters which results in longer fixture life. Ford Motar Company in U.S.A. follows this type of group replacement of bulbs.

## ■ EFFECT OF USE OF COLOUR ON LIGHTING

The use of appropriate colour in factories on the interior walls, floor space, and ceilings is closely related to illumination. The dark painting always creates a dull impression and the use of light colours produce better illumination as it increases the light reflection. The use of colour combination along with good lighting system increases the visibility, and provides pleasant working conditions in the factory. The illumination in plant can be maximized by use of appropriate colours even without changing the fixtures and wattage of bulbs. This means better illumination is possible through colours without incurring extra cost.

Different colours are used in different work places not only to improve illumination but also to ensure safety and to provide a good working environment. Generally, a light green colour is used for walls where workers are engaged in production. Light grey colour is used on the floor assembling section because it improves visibility on all sides of assembly work. Yellow colour is used on moving objects such as trucks, cranes, conveyors, etc. as yellow colour resembles daylight. Green colour is used on articles, such as racks, receptacles, tool boxes so as to distinguish them from moving objects. White colour is used in storerooms and traffic area. Red colour is used in places where danger is apprehended. Certain colours, such as blue, violet, and green are used at the work places where high temperature prevails, as they psychologically offset hot working areas. Similarly other colours, such as red and orange psychologically offset the cool work place.

Colours are also used to differentiate various pipes in factories, whenever pipes enter or leave the factory. For example, red colour is used for sprinkler system, which is used for fire fighting, yellow colour is used for pipes containing dangerous materials, such as steam acids, etc. This is to prevent workers from opening taps of pipes to wash their hands but which might contain, hydrochloric acid or steam which cause burning on the hands.

## SUMMARY

Among the various factors required to improve the working conditions in a factory, lighting facility is the most important. Illumination of the working areas improves the vision of employees and thus increases the productivity of the factory. In India, provision of adequate light in factories is obligatory.

Section 17, Sec. 17(2) and Sec. 17(3) of the Factories Act deal with the provision of lighting in factories. A good light must possess certain characteristics. These are: (1) Proper intensity, (2) Proper diffraction, (3) Elimination of glare, (4) Light must come from right direction and it must be reliable in its supply, (5) It must be economical in installation and maintenance, (6) It must eliminate abrupt contrast, (7) It should not produce dazzling light, (8) It should be cool, (9) It should be steady, (10) It must make use of colour combination to improve intensity.

The importance of lighting is felt in factories because of the following reasons: (1) It increases quantity and quality of goods, (2) It reduces spoilage and wastages in production, (3) It enables effective utilisation of space, (4) It reduces accident, (5) It reduces fatigue and eye strain, (6) It facilitates effective supervision, (7) It reduces absenteeism and labour turnover, (8) It helps in good house keeping, (9) It establishes better relations between employer and employee.

Broadly speaking, there are two sources of light, viz. (1) natural light, and (2) artificial light. Natural light is obtained by making appropriate provisions in the factory building. Natural light depends upon type of roof structure, roofing materials and height of ceiling. Artificial light is obtained by fixing bulbs of various intensities. The various types of bulbs used in a factory are: (1) filament lamps, (2) arc lamps, (3) mercury vapour lamps, and (4) fluorescent lamps. There are three types of lighting installation. They are: (a) general lighting, (b) supplementary lighting, and (c) general lighting combined with local lighting.

The following steps are to be followed for achieving good light in factories: (1) provision for getting maximum natural lighting, (2) provision for an effective use of artificial lighting, (3) use of proper colour combination for the interior walls, and (4) provision for continual maintenance. Factory lighting can be best illumined by the use of colour combination.

# QUESTIONS

## A. Objective type

### I. Fill in the blanks:

(a) Fluorescent lighting is a form of .................. lighting.

(b) The unit used to measure the intensity of light is known as .................. .

(c) Frequent power cuts resulting in disruption of lighting facility can be over come by .................. .

(d) Best light is obtained when monitor windows are provided as .................. side.

(e) .................. source of light is available in abundance.

(f) Initial investment is less in case of .................. lamps.

(g) .................. source of light is available both during day and night.

(h) The intensity of light can be altered by using different .................. of bulbs.

### II. Write *True* or *False* for the following sentences:

(a) Good lighting achieves equal and uniform illumination of all work areas irrespective of the type of operation performed.

(b) Repainting of plant with a proper combination of colours can increases intensity of illumination and reduce glare but cannot improve perceptive seeing.

(c) Lighting in production department is as important as light in office.

(d) Quality of light can be sacrificed in return for quantity of light in factories.

(e) A foot candle is the intensity of light emitted from a standard candle at a distance of one foot.

(f) The unit used to measure the intensity of light is known as foot candle.

(g) Dazzling light leads to problems of eyesight to employees.

(h) Light and paint are the siamese twins of illumination.

(i) Artificial lighting is preferred to natural lighting in factories.

(j) The intensity of natural light can be altered.

(k) The distribution in natural light is more uniform than artificial light.

(l) The supply of natural light in factories depend upon the size and positions of windows.

(m) The type of roofing material used in the construction of building to a large extent determine the admission of light.

(n) Artificial lighting serves as a supplementary source to natural lighting.

(o) The initial investment are always high in case of artificial lighting.

(p) Artificial source of light is a reliable source of light.

(q) Excessive and unscientific lighting affects efficiency of employees.

### III. Choose correct answer from the following alternatives:

1. Which one of the following is not an essential requirement of good lighting in a factory?

   (a) Light should be cool
   (b) Light should eliminate abrupt contrast
   (c) Economical in operating
   (d) Should produce glare

2. Which one of the following is not a point of importance of good light?
   (a) Reduces accidents (b) Saves floor space
   (c) Increases spoilage and wastages (d) Increases quantity of output
3. Which one of the following is not a feature of natural light?
   (a) It is available in abundance (b) It is available at all times
   (c) It requires no maintenance cost (d) Its distribution is uniform
4. Which one of the following types of lamp is used to derive high power illumination in factories?
   (a) Arc lamps (b) Mercury-vapour lamps
   (c) Fluorescent lamps (d) Incandescent lamps
5. Current consumption is less in case of
   (a) Filament lamps (b) Fluorescent lamps
   (c) Arc lamps (d) Mercury-vapour lamps
6. Which one of the following types of lamps are not used very popularly in factories?
   (a) Filament lamps (b) Fluorescent lamps
   (c) Arc lamps (d) Mercury-vapour lamps
7. Which one of the following is not a type of electric discharge lamps?
   (a) Arc lamp (b) Mercury-vapour lamps
   (c) Fluorescent lamps (d) Incandescent lamp
8. Which one of the following types of lamp are mostly used to illumine dark passages in factories?
   (a) Filament lamps (b) Fluorescent lamps
   (c) Mercury-vapour lamps (d) Arc lamps

### B. Very short answer type

1. Mention the various effects of poor lighting in a factory.
2. Distinguish between a foot candle and a lumen.
3. State the provisions of Factories Act relating to the provision of lighting in factories.
4. State the merits and demerits of natural lighting.
5. State the merits and demerits of artificial lighting.

### 3. Short answer type

1. Explain briefly the features of good light.
2. Explain the importance of lighting in factories.
3. What provisions are to be made in a factory building to ensure sufficient natural lighting.
4. Briefly explain the types of lighting installations in a factory.
5. Explain the procedure involved in attaining good lighting.
6. Explain the effect of use of colour on lighting.

### 4. Long answer type

Explain with merits and demerits the sources of lighting in a factory. Explain the need for lighting in a factory.

## ANSWERS TO OBJECTIVE TYPE QUESTIONS

**I.**

| | | | | | |
|---|---|---|---|---|---|
| (a) False | (b) False | (c) True | (d) False | (e) True | (f) False |
| (g) True | (h) True | (i) True | (j) False | (k) True | (l) True |
| (m) True | (n) True | (o) True | (p) False | (q) False | |

**II.**

| | | |
|---|---|---|
| (a) artificial | (b) lumen | (c) generators |
| (d) sloping side | (e) natural | (f) filament |
| (g) artificial | (h) voltage | |

**III.**

| | | |
|---|---|---|
| 1. (d) | 2. (b) | 3. (b) |
| 4. (a) | 5. (b) | 6. (a) |
| 7. (a) | 8. (c) | |

Chapter 9

# VENTILATION IN FACTORIES

## ■ INTRODUCTION

The term ventilation in relation to factories is used in narrow and broad sense. In its narrow sense, ventilation is basically the removal of stale air in a factory building by fresh air. Inadequate ventilation results in discomfort and fatigue as the concentration of carbon dioxide, humidity and temperature will rise in the working areas of the factory. To ensure a comfortable and healthy working atmosphere it is necessary to provide a definite circulation of air throughout the factory. As a rule, the ventilation is considered satisfactory where ventilation arrangements provide a change of air four to six times per hour. To prevent overcrowding, it is stipulated that 500 cubic feet of air must be provided per worker in the workrooms, height above 14 feet from the floor being not considered for the calculation of cubic air space. The rate of ventilation in factory buildings depends on the number of workers, nature of manufacturing process involved, and type of products manufactured. But it is estimated that a supply of 10 cubic feet per minute for each person is desirable in factories.

In its broad sense, the term ventilation is used to create controlled environment which include control of (a) ventilation, (b) temperature, and (c) humidity as one integrated system.

(a) **Control of ventilation:** Control of ventilation is necessary not only to remove vitiated air in a factory building but also to eliminate the excess heat and the poisonous gasses liberated by manufacturing process, otherwise this will cause ill-health to the workers and reduces both quality and volume of production.

(b) **Control of temperature:** Comfortable temperature in work places would be conducive to good quality and increased productivity. This is achieved by (a) effective ventilation, (b) constructing thick walls, (c) construction of building with high ceiling or double ceiling with air gap, (d) insulation of hot portions, and (e) isolation of departments producing excessive heat in its process.

(c) **Control of humidity:** The humidity in the air has a definite effect on the mental and physical comfort of workers. Humidity varies as the temperature of the room rises or falls. Too high of humidity creates depression, while too low makes the air too dry for bodily comfort. The proper level of humidity not only induces comfort but increases physical working efficiency, keeps the brain more alert and widens the favourable attitude towards work with less fatigue. The accepted figure for the year-round comfort is between 40 and 60 per cent which can be maintained by heating or cooling the room temperature.

Provision for adequate ventilation by circulation of fresh air and removal of dust and fumes is a statutory obligation of the employer.

Section 13 of the Factories Act 1948 deals with ventilation in Factory buildings. It lays down that effective and suitable provisions shall be made in every factory for securing and maintaining in every work room.

(a) adequate ventilation by the circulation of fresh air, and

(b) such a temperature as will secure to workers therein reasonable conditions for comfort and prevent injury to health.

Section 13 (2) provides that "the state government may prescribe a standard of adequate ventilation and reasonable temperature for any factory and direct that a thermometer shall be provided and maintained in such place and position as may be specified."

## ■ DEFINITION OF VENTILATION

Ventilation can be defined as the process of removing or supplying air by natural or mechanical means to and from a factory building.

According to Hemeon, Factory Ventilation is concerned largely with engineering techniques for controlling air currents within the plant and for introducing outdoor air in a pattern and on a scale that is just adequate to maintain satisfactory air purity.

The following features of ventilation emerge out from the above definitions:

1. It creates air movement, so as to remove the vitiated air by fresh air.
2. It is undertaken either by natural or mechanical means.
3. It involves designing the factory building so as to allow required inflow and outflow of air currents.
4. The technique of providing facility for ventilation facility is predetermined so that adequate air purity is maintained throughout.

## ■ IMPORTANCE OF VENTILATION

The importance of adequate ventilation has been realised as an outcome of the blackout conditions which were enforced during the war times. One of the major problems in the older buildings has been 'draughts' which often gives rise to unrest, poor morale and a sense of grievance by employee when nothing is done by the management to remove these unsatisfactory conditions. The importance of factory ventilation is reflected in the following points:

(a) Provision of adequate supply of fresh air,

(b) Reduction of odours, impurities and injurious gases,

(c) Reduction of dust and other suspended particles and bacteria,

(d) Prevention of excess heat produced in factories, and

(e) Provision of required humidity in factories.

(a) **Provision of adequate supply of fresh air:** Whenever workers assemble in an enclosed space, the air becomes stale. Unless the stale air is replaced by fresh air, it leads to nausea, sleepiness, laziness and fatigue. It is not only enough to make adequate provision for the proper supply of fresh air but it is also important to provide for distribution of air properly throughout the factory building.

(b) **Reduction of odours, impurities and injurious gases:** Manufacturing processes in factories release large amount of poisonous gases, fumes, and other impurities which will contaminate the air. The inhaling of these toxic gases and fumes for a long time leads to lung disease, breath problems and other ailments. To eliminate such gases, fumes, and vapours it is necessary to provide good ventilation in factories.

(c) **Reduction of dust and other suspended particles and bacteria:** In Factories where trimming and cutting operations are largely involved, it produces too much of dust. In food processing industries, it is common to observe bacteria on a large scale. This can lead not only to health hazard but is also responsible for the deterioration of quality of products. Ventilation eliminates such dust and bacteria in factories.

(d) **Prevention of excess heat produced in factories:** Industrial operations are always characterised by the generation of excessive heat, especially in power station, boiler houses, furnaces, heat treatment departments, etc. Moreover, the heat produced by sun rays during summer also intensify the warmth in factories. This is responsible for causing headache and fatigue for the employees. Provision of fresh air alone can solve this problem.

(e) **Provision of required humidity in factories:** Research has shown that the effect of high humidity can reduce mental alertness and increase physical fatigue to a great extent. This leads the employees to spend their time for taking rest. Generally speaking, it is desirable to keep the relative humidity below 50%.

## ■ ESSENTIAL REQUIREMENTS OF VENTILATION

In order to provide better working conditions and comfort to employees ventilation system should meet the following requirements:

1. Rate of supply of fresh air
2. Air movements or air changes
3. Temperature of air
4. Humidity
5. Purity of air.

1. **Rate of supply of fresh air:** The rate of supply of air in factory buildings depends on the size of production departments, the number of employees occupying the departments, type of work performed, period of working, etc. The minimum rate of fresh air in the working rooms of factories is estimated at 23 $m^3$ per person per hour. A ventilating system should be designed so as to provide inflow of minimum air inside the factory building and flow of vitiated air from the factory building.

2. **Air movements or air changes:** For effective working of ventilation system, it is estimated that 5 or 6 air changes per hour is sufficient. Air change per hour is the volume of outside air allowed into a room in onc hour compared with the volume of the room. The air movements must be uniform and should not be stagnant at any spot of the work. The free movement of air is secured by providing cross-ventilation in naturally ventilated building. In mechanically ventilated building, air movement is achieved by means of fans. Air movement should be ensured not only in terms of velocity but also in direction.

3. **Temperature of air:** The incoming air in a factory building through ventilation system should be cool in summer and warm in winter. This implies that effective temperature should be maintained

with respect to comfortable conditions for different seasons of the year. Investigations undertaken in regard to temperature of air reveals that 20 – 22°C of temperature is to be maintained during summer and winter respectively in factory buildings. However, the value of effective temperature depends upon the type of work to be done, geographical conditions, etc.

4. **Humidity:** Ventilation system must fulfill the humidity requirement when work is to be performed at a higher temperature.

5. **Purity of air:** The ventilation system must provide for pure air which is free from impurities such as bad odours, dust and fumes, such as carbon dioxide sulphur dioxide, etc. To get pure ventilated air, it is necessary that ventilators should not be located near chimneys, latrins and such other places.

## SOURCES OF VENTILATION

Supply of air ventilation in factories can be provided from two sources, viz. (1) Natural source and (2) Artificial source.

### 1. Natural source

This is considered to be the best source of ventilation in factories as it involves no investment and maintenance cost. However, it is not always a reliable source, because blow of wind varies from season to season. In order to derive the maximum ventilation into a factory, it is necessary to make adequate provisions in the factory building, such as provision of required number of windows, constructing the building giving importance to the height of the building, and using building materials, such as hollow blocks, which permit inflow of air into factory building.

The rate of ventilation by natural source depends upon the following effects:

(a) **Wind effect:** Under this effect, the ventilation is caused by the direction of wind blow, the velocity of wind, size and position of the opening of the factory building. Whenever wind blows, against a factory building, a positive pressure is created windward side. This positive pressure creates suction on the leeward side. If openings are provided on leeward side, wind enters into the building through the openings. This is illustrated below.

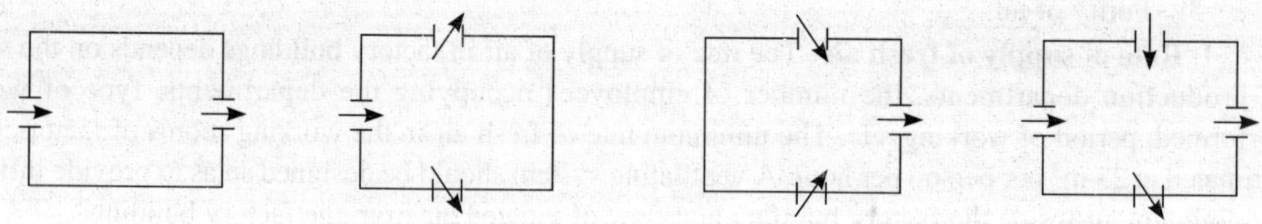

**Fig. 9.1** Movement of wind through buildings

The rate of air flow depends upon the pressure difference of the inside and outside air. The pressure difference inturn depends upon the speed of wind. Higher is the speed, greater will be the pressure and rate of air flow occur quickly and vice versa.

(b) **Stack effect:** Under this effect, the ventilation is caused by convection effects which arise from a temperature difference or vapour pressure difference or differences of both which is present inside and outside the factory building. Whenever air inside the factory becomes warm on account of heat produced by machines the warmer air rises and pass through the ventilators provided on the upper part of the factory building. Simultaneously, the incoming cool air from outside replaces it through windows and doors. This effect also depends upon the difference in height of inlet and outlet openings and the ratio between the areas of two openings. This is illustrated below.

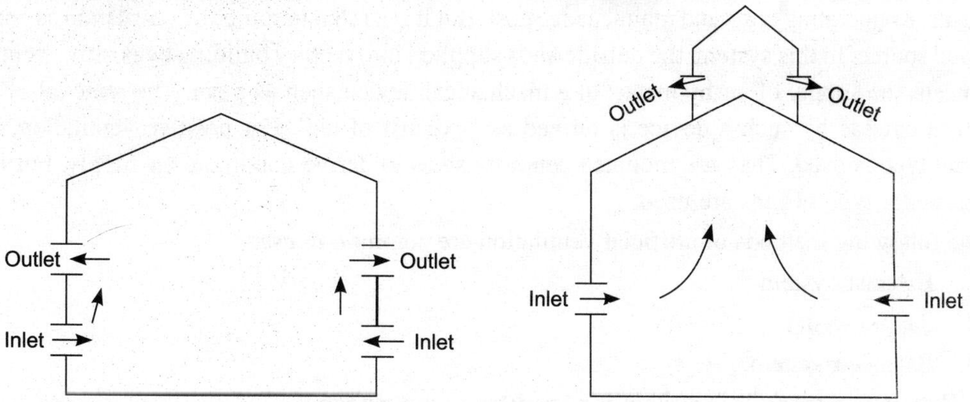


**Fig. 9.2** Ventilation due to stack effect

1. The inlet openings should be located on the windward side at a low level. Outlet openings should be located on the leeward side near the roof.
2. For greater air flow, the size of inlet and outlet openings should of equal.
3. The ventilators and other openings should be provided on all sides where wind direction is variable.
4. Care should be taken to see that inlet openings are not obstructed by adjoining building, trees, signboards, etc.
5. The ceiling of the building must be kept high to derive better ventilation due to stake effect.
6. In order to eliminate the warm air through stake effect it is desirable to provide ventilators as close to the ceiling as possible.
7. Ventilation through windows can be improved by using them (windows) in combination with a radiator, deflector and exhaust duct as shown below.

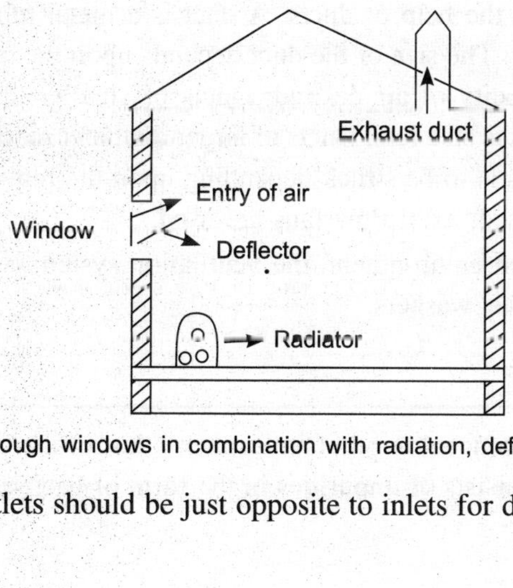


**Fig. 9.3** Ventilation through windows in combination with radiation, deflector and exhaust duct

8. The position of outlets should be just opposite to inlets for deriving cross-ventilation.

## 2. Artificial source

This source of ventilation involves the use of mechanical arrangement for providing enough ventilation in factory building. This source of ventilation is expensive, as it involves initial investment on mechanical equipments, its operating costs and maintenance cost. But it is a reliable source of ventilation as compared to artificial source. In this system, the outside air is supplied into factory building by positive ventilation, which means the supply of air by means of a mechanical device such as a fan. The removal of air and its disposal outside by such a device is termed as "exhaust of air". For positive ventilation, fans of centrifugal type is used. They are mounted centrally so as to derive maximum air supply. For exhaust of air, propeller type of fans are used.

The following methods of artificial ventilation are common in use:

1. Exhaust system
2. Supply system
3. Balanced system.

1. **Exhaust system:** This system is useful for removing smoke, odours, fumes, dust, etc. from factories. In this system, a partial vacuum is created inside the working departments by means of removal of the vitiated air through propeller fans. This exhaustion of air from within the factory building permits the flow of fresh air in the building.

2. **Supply system:** Under this system, the arrangement involves the supply of air by means of a fan, but no special provision is made to remove it. Ventilation under this system, may be downward or upward. In downward ventilation, the incoming air is allowed to enter at the ceiling height and it flows outside through outlet situated at floor level. In upward ventilation, the incoming air is allowed to flow through the inlets situated at floor level and the vitiated air flows out through the outlet provided at the ceiling height.

3. **Balanced system:** This is a combination of exhaust system and supply system of ventilation. Under this system, fans are used to supply and extract air into and from the factories. This system ensures full control over the air movement and meets the requirements of complete ventilation system.

Sometimes, ventilation systems involves the extension of ventilation facilities to other rooms of factory. This is undertaken with the help of ducts. A duct is a metal tube which is intended for the outlet of air into factory building. The size of the duct depends upon the quantity of air required in the factory per minute and the velocity of air desired. Ducts of smaller diameter will produce higher velocity and its initial investment is also less. Ducts of larger diameter require higher initial investment. A balance between the two sides is to be struck depending upon the requirement of ventilation in the factories. Where duct work is used, axial flow fans are used.

In order to create controlled environment, the ventilation system is to be combined, with other devices, such as air filters, and air washers.

## ■ AIR FILTERS

Air filters are used to reduce the concentration of atmospheric dust of incoming air to make it harmless. Usually, the atmospheric dust consists of impurities in the form of bacteria, chemicals, soot and small particles such as air sand etc. The filter used to accomplish this purpose must have the following features:

1. The filters must work under a wide range of velocities.
2. The filters must have low frictional resistance to the flow of air.
3. The filters must have the capability of holding a moderate dust on its surface without affecting the working efficiency.
4. The filters must be capable of cleaning either manually or mechanically.
5. The filtering medium must be of any fibrous material, such as porus paper, cloth, etc. so that dust particles adhere to it.

Based on principle of working, the air filters can be classified into following types:

1. Viscous filters
   (a) Automatic type
   (b) Unit type
2. Dry filters
3. Electric precipitators.

1. **Viscous filters:** Under this type, materials such as fibre mats, or screen of split wire is used on which non-drying viscous oil is coated. The dust during its passage through viscous filters gets stuck on this material. These viscous filters can be of two types: (a) automatic type and (b) unit type.

Viscous *automatic filters* are mechanically operated in a continuous cycle consisting of mechanism to clean the air, remove air pollution particles, replace the viscous filter medium, and place the refreshed area of filters into air system for further utilisation.

*Unit type filters* are replaced when they become useless. They can be washed and coated with viscous oil again for reuse.

2. **Dry filters:** Under this type, materials, such as flannel, felt, cellulose, etc. are used. When the air passes through filters, the dust particles are trapped on these materials. These materials are discarded when they finally become useless.

3. **Electric precipitators:** This type of filter is latest of all, filters. Its initial investment is high. Under this type, dust particles get charged and are attracted by negative electrodes when subject to strong electric field. The negative electrode falls down when large amount of dust particles are deposited on it.

## AIR WASHERS

Air washers are used for cleaning the air. Under this devise, air is forced through water which comes out as sprays. The dust and fumes are removed by the drops of water. It is estimated that air washers can remove about 65% of the dust from air. The cleaning process largely depends upon the type of dust particles and the period of time it is in contact with the spray.

**Distinction between natural ventilation and artificial ventilation**

| Natural Ventilation | Artificial Ventilation |
|---|---|
| 1. It is obtained by making appropriate provisions in factory buildings | 1. It is obtained by using mechanical equipments, chiefly fans |
| 2. It requires no initial investment, as air is free gift of nature | 2. It requires initial investment |
| 3. It involves neither cost of operation nor the maintenance cost | 3. It involves cost of operation as well as maintenance |
| 4. Its supply is uncertain as it depends upon the type of climate prevailing in an area | 4. Its supply is certain except during period of power cut imposed by State Government |
| 5. It is not amenable for providing controlled environment | 5. It is amenable for providing controlled environment |
| 6. Natural ventilation is not available for the interior rooms of factory | 6. It can be extended even to interior rooms |

## SUMMARY

Factory ventilation is used in narrow and broad sense. In its narrow sense, it means provision of adequate air so as to eliminate stale air. In its broad sense, it is used to provide controlled environment which include control of ventilation, heating and humidification. Provision of good ventilation system, apart from improving the productivity, also maintains quality of products. The provision of adequate ventilation facilities in factories are governed by Section 13 and Section 15 of Factories Act. Factory ventilation must meet the following requirements in order to call it as good ventilation system. (1) Provision of adequate supply of fresh air (2) Reduction of odours, impurities and poisonous gases (3) Removal of dust and bacteria (4) Maintaining proper temperature (5) Maintaining proper humidity (6) Maintaining proper velocity of air.

Ventilation can be provided either from natural source or artificial source. Natural source of ventilation is obtained from windows and root openings. Artificial ventilation is obtained by mechanical devices, such as fans. Ventilation system to be complete must be supplemented by air ducts, air filters and air washers.

## QUESTIONS

### A. Objective type

**I. Fill in the blanks:**

(a) A supply of .................. cubic feet per minute for each person is desirable in factories.

(b) Ventilation in broad sense refers to creation of .................. environment in factories.

(c) Section .................. of the Factories Act deals with ventilation of factories.

(d) For effective ventilation system, air change of .................. times per hour is required.

(e) .................. source of ventilation is a reliable source.
(f) Under .................. effect ventilation is caused by convection effect.
(g) .................. is used to reduce the concentration of atmospheric dust of incoming air.
(h) .................. is used for cleaning air in factories.
(i) .................. ventilation requires appropriate provisions to be made in factories.
(j) The facility of .................. ventilation is not available for the interior rooms of factory.

**II. Write *True* or *False* for the following sentences:**

If the statement is false, underline the word or words which makes it false.

(a) Inadequate ventilation affect the efficiency of factory employees.
(b) Control of ventilation is necessary only to eliminate vitiated air in the factory.
(c) Under the wind effect ventilation is caused by the direction of wind blow, the velocity of wind, and size and position of the inlet.
(d) Artificial ventilation is expensive when compared to natural ventilation.
(e) For achieving positive ventilation, propeller fans are used.
(f) Balanced system of ventilation meets the requirements of complete ventilation.
(g) Axial flow fans are used when ventilation is provided through ducts.

**III. Choose the correct answer from the following alternatives:**

1. Which one of the following does not fall under the broad meaning of ventilation?
   (a) Control of air movement
   (b) Control of temperature
   (c) Control of humidity
   (d) Control of purity of air
2. Under which of the following circumstance, natural ventilation is most suitable.
   (a) Where it is not available regularly
   (b) Where heavy investments are involved
   (c) Where controlled environment is possible
   (d) Where it can be extended to interior rooms
3. Which one of the following is a disadvantage of artificial ventilation?
   (a) Cost of operation and maintenance is high
   (b) It is not amenable for providing controlled environment
   (c) Its supply is uncertain
   (d) It cannot be extended to interior rooms

## B. Very short answer type

1. Define ventilation.
2. State the provisions of Factories Act relating to factory ventilation.
3. What do you mean by ventilation in its broad sense?
4. What is exhaust system of ventilation?
5. What is supply system of ventilation?
6. What do you mean by balanced system of ventilation?
7. What are air filters? What purpose do they serve?

### C. Short answer type

1. Explain the importance of ventilation in factories.
2. Explain the essential requirements of factory ventilation.
3. Distinguish between wind effect and stake effect in natural ventilation.
4. Explain the methods of artificial ventilation.
5. Distinguish between natural and artificial ventilation.

### D. Long answer type

Explain the various sources of factory ventilation.

## ANSWERS TO OBJECTIVE TYPE QUESTIONS

| | | | | | |
|---|---|---|---|---|---|
| I. | (a) ten, | (b) controlled | (c) 13, | (d) five, | (e) artificial, |
| | (f) stake, | (g) air filters, | (h) air washers, | (i) natural, | (j) natural. |
| II. | (a) T, | (b) F, | (c) T, | (d) T, | (e) F, |
| | (f) F, | (g) T. | | | |
| III. | (1) d, | (2) b, | (3) a. | | |

Chapter 10

# INDUSTRIAL AIR-CONDITIONING

## ■ INTRODUCTION

Man, in quest for his comfort, has been evolving various devises from time to time. In the beginning, to protect himself, he built cottages and houses. Thereafter, to safeguard against the odd weather conditions he has been going to hill-stations or near sea-shores to be exposed to favourable temperature. Even for undertaking industrial processes requiring controlled environment, in the earlier years, man has been trying to use natural resources at the available points. For example, the breweries requiring controlled temperature conditions suitable for fermentation were located at hill stations as cold and hot temperature were arranged from snow melting or sun's rays. This was so because in the ancient days the resources were limited and technology was not so highly developed. In modern days, in order to have a better localised control of climate, air-conditioning system has been developed.

Air-conditioning is generally regarded as a development of 1930's. But very few people realised that air-conditioning was not used extensively and exclusively in factories until 1925. The credit for installation of air-conditioning goes to S.W. Cramer, who presented a paper in humidity control in textile mills before the National Cotton Manufactures Association in 1907. At that time, the term "yarn conditioning" was in common usage and "air-conditioning" seemed to be a logical expression for the process of controlling the atmospheric conditions. In India, where man-power is plenty and resources limited, the use of air-conditioning for human comfort is not being encouraged. But it is used mostly for process control, preservation of finished goods and in office and administration departments of factories.

## ■ MEANING OF AIR-CONDITIONING

By popular usage, the term "air-conditioning" is often used to describe system which provides cooling of the atmosphere within a building structure. Technically speaking, air-conditioning refers to simultaneous control of air, temperature, humidity, motion, distribution, pressure and purity including such factors as dust, odours, bacteria and toxic gases. A true air-conditioning system must be able to provide control over these factors both during summer and winter season.

## ■ DEFINITION OF AIR-CONDITIONING

1. According to the *New Business Encyclopedia*, air-conditioning has been defined as "the process by which simultaneously the temperature, moisture content, movement, and quality of air in enclosed space intended for human occupancy may be maintained within required

limits". On the basis of recent developments, this might be amended to read ". . . . . spaces intended for human occupancy or for certain industrial process . . . . . ." This definition covers both the cooling and heating aspects of air-conditioning, as found in a year-round installation.

2. According to Riggs, Bethel, et al, "Industrial air-conditioning in its broadest sense requires control over temperature, humidity, dust, motion, purity and odours."
3. In the words of Jordon and Priester (*Refrigeration and Air-conditioning*, p.444), "Air-conditioning is the simultaneous control of temperature, humidity, motion and purity of atmosphere in a confined space."

From a close observation of the above definitions, it is clear that an air-conditioning system controls the circulation, temperature, and humidity of air and removes the foreign substances in an enclosed area. To ensure good atmospheric conditions inside the factory, it may be necessary to install a complete air-conditioning system for simultaneous circulation, heating or cooling, humidifying or dehumidifying and clearing of air.

**Difference between air-conditioning and ventilation**

| Air-conditioning | Ventilation |
|---|---|
| 1. It conditions the air by heating or cooling. | 1. It does not condition the air. |
| 2. It is concerned with regulating only inflow of air from outside the factory. | 2. It is concerned with regulating both inflow and outflow of air in the factory. |
| 3. It is very expensive as it involves investment on plant, power consumption, land maintenance expenses. | 3. It is not so expensive in terms of investment. |
| 4. In factories, it is secondary and important. It is luxury to derive comfort. | 4. It is primary in importance, because it is indispensable in factories. |
| 5. It is obtained only by artificial source. | 5. It is obtained both by natural and artificial source. |
| 6. It exercises simultaneous control over the composition of air, such as temperature, humidity, dust, etc. | 6. It is not possible to exercise a simultaneous control over these composition of air. |
| 7. The techniques of air-conditioning is of recent origin. | 7. It was known even in earlier days. |
| 8. It requires maintenance cost. | 8. It does not require maintenance cost. |

## ■ IMPORTANCE OF AIR-CONDITIONING IN FACTORIES

The importance of air-conditioning in factories is discussed under the following points:

1. To provide comfort to employees
2. To safeguard health of employees
3. To improve the efficiency of employees
4. To maintain quality of products
5. To maintain quality of finished product

6. To undertake production throughout the year
7. To enable proper storage of raw materials
8. To protect costlier equipments
9. To undertake research and development
10. To keep production cost low
11. To improve good relation between employer and employees.

### 1. To provide comfort to employees

Whenever air-conditioning is installed, it creates a healthy atmosphere and provides a feeling of comfort to employees. Investigation has shown that temperature range, which is known as "comfortable zone" is suitable for workers working in factories. This comfortable zone is different for summer and winter season. The effective temperature zones for summer and winter range between 20°C to 23°C and 18°C to 22°C respectively. This effective temperature range is the measure of comfort of human body under most of the conditions of humidity and air circulation. This is provided by air-conditioning.

### 2. To safeguard health of employees

Air-conditioning is essential to protect the health of employees from toxic by-products, poisonous gases and harmful substances, such as soot, bacteria, etc. Unless the contaminated air is purified it leads to different types of ailments.

### 3. To improve the efficiency of employees

Research has indicated that worker's efficiency and morale as well as productivity improve with the use of proper air-conditioning, a comfortable environment to work in a factories.

### 4. To maintain quality of the products during manufacturing stage

Air-conditioning system is suitable to maintain the quality of products while in manufacturing stage. The best examples for such products are watches, plastics and rayon, colour printing, pharmaceuticals, photographic materials, matches, textiles, electrical equipments and hygroscopic products. Secondly, air-conditioning is essential in the manufacturing process to increase workability and to maintain quality of the product. For example, in a textile mill, if the humidity is too low, the yarn becomes dry and breaks during weaving. If the humidity is too high, the working conditions are intolerable. Similarly, in a tobacco factory if the air is dry the leaves become too brittle for handling without breakage. If the air is excessively humid, the leaves will be spoilt.

### 5. To maintain quality of finished product

The maintenance of the quality of certain products, such as ice-cream, drugs, etc. essentially require the air-conditioning facility. Otherwise, they deteriorate very soon in quality which cannot be acceptable to the customers.

### 6. To undertake production throughout the year

Factories dealing in confectionery, and manufacturing units often are required to stop operations during certain seasons of the year. Cooling becomes necessary on account of the heat generated from power driven equipments. This can be met by air-conditioning the plant.

### 7. To enable proper storage of raw materials

In certain factories, such as paper mills, paper received during cool weather should be warmed to storage-room temperature before the package is opened. After it is opened, it should be conditioned immediately for press work, if it is not already in the proper state. This is also the case in food processing industries, fruit canning industries and dairy industries. The following table presents the storage life of various perishable products used in various industries.

**Storage life of perishable products under air-conditioning and refrigeration**

| Name of product | Storage temperature in °C | Storage life |
|---|---|---|
| Pasteurised milk | 1 | 7 days |
| Butter | 0–4 | 2 months |
| Apples | (– 1)–(0) | 2–4 months |
| Mango | 12 | 2–3 weeks |
| Fish | 1–3 | 5–15 days |
| Ice-cream | (–26) | Several months |
| Dried fruits | 0 | 9–12 months |

### 8. To protect costlier equipments

The operations of certain machines and equipments are to be protected against the excessive heat, dust and smoke. Such machines perform work of high precision and unless they are protected against high temperature, they are succeptible to damages which demand frequent repairs. The electronic industry, for instance, produces many microscopic parts in which close tolerances are essential. Temperature and humidity must be closely controlled not only in the manufacture of these parts but in the operation of the machines of which they become a part.

### 9. To undertake research and development

Many small laboratory rooms and cabinets require closely controlled air-conditions for testing or production work. Often the exact conditions desired may vary over a wide range of temperature and humidities requiring special equipment. Control may be obtained first by over-cooling and dehumidifying, then by reheating and rehumidifying.

### 10. To keep production cost low

The provision of good working condition by air-conditioning system increases the production thereby reducing the cost of production. The United State government made a closely controlled study of two groups of workers during identical work in identical surroundings, one group working in air-conditioned comfort and the other without this advantage. The group in air-conditioned place performed more than 9 per cent efficiently as compared to the other. Again, a survey of 75 industrial plants in the New York area showed that the average plant without air-conditioning lost the equivalent of US$ 108 in wages for each employee in one year because of hot weather shutdowns.

### 11. To improve relations between employer and employees

The provision of good working condition by air-conditioning system psychologically improves the morale of employees. This reduces excess of absenteeism and labour turnover. Whenever incentives are allowed for higher productivity of employees, this system enables us to increase the efficiency and produce more units of products, thus enabling workers to earn better wages. This improved facilitates relationship between employer and employees.

## ■ TYPES OF AIR-CONDITIONING

Air-conditioning can be broadly classified on the basis of functions performed by it and on the basis of air-conditioning process. This is shown below.

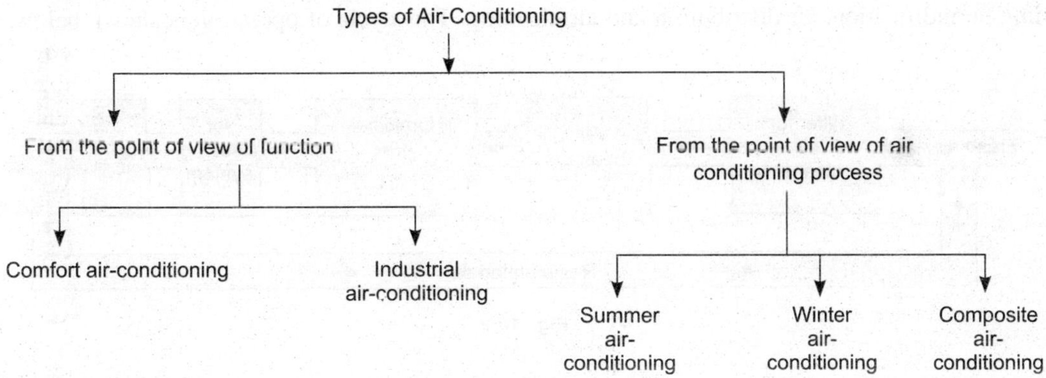


From functional point of view, the air-conditioning is of two types.

### 1. Comfort air-conditioning

Under this type, the air-conditioning process is undertaken with a view to provide comforts to the occupants of an enclosed space. This is commonly observed in factory office, and administration buildings mainly to ensure comforts to the office and administrative staff.

### 2. Industrial air-conditioning

Under this type, air-conditioning is undertaken mainly to create, maintain and control the atmospheric condition with a view to assist material processing, manufacturing and storage of finished goods in its proper condition.

From the point of view of air-conditioning process, involving various stages, it is classified into (1) summer air-coditioning, (2) winter air-conditioning and (3) composite air-conditioning.

#### *1. Summer air-conditioning*

In this type of air-conditioning, the main intention is to provide coolness to employees and the products manufactured. In summer season, the outside temperature is high and hence the cycle of operation in this type of air-conditioning involves air-cooling, dehumidifying, air distribution and air cleaning. This cycle of operation is shown on the next page.

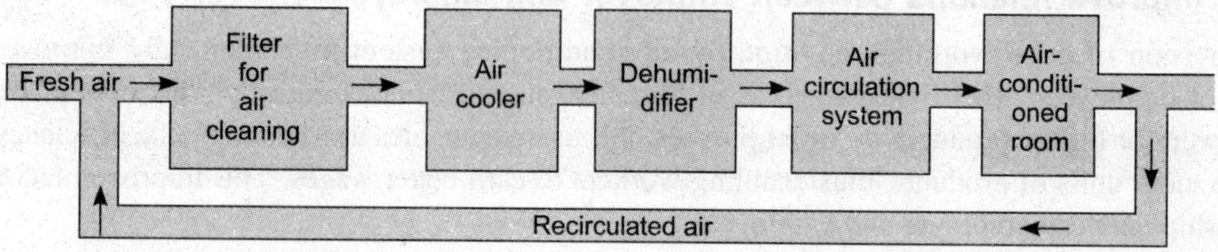


**Fig. 10.1** Showing cycle of operation in summer air-conditioning

### *2. Winter air-conditioning*

In this type of air-conditioning, the main intention is to provide warmth to employees. In winter season, the temperature is low and hence the cycle of operations in this type of air-conditioning involves air heating, humidification, air distribution and air cleaning. This cycle of operation is shown below.

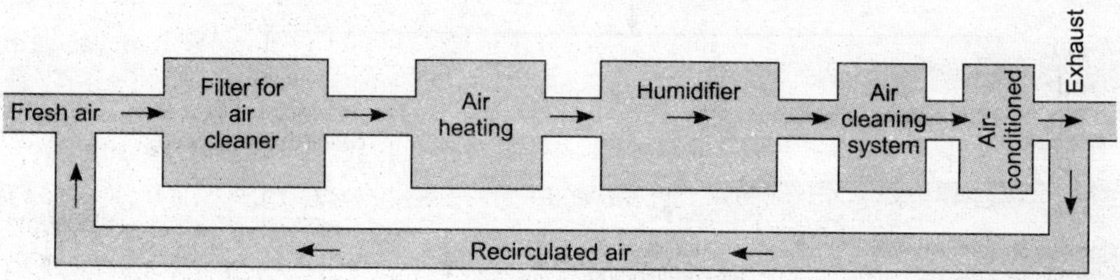


**Fig. 10.2**

### *3. Composite air-conditioning*

In this system, air-conditioning is meant both for cooling and warming the temperature which is required for the whole year. In other words, it is meant for providing year round facility of heating and cooling in the factory building. Hence, the cycle of operation involves both humidifying and dehumidifying with air distribution and air purity.

## ■ SYSTEMS OF AIR-CONDITIONING

On the basis of location of air-conditioning equipment, the system of air-conditioning can be classified into three systems. These are:

1. Central system,
2. Self-contained or unitary system, and
3. Semi-contained or unitary-central system.

Whatever maybe the system of air-conditioning, the principles involved are same. These principles are:

(a) Sucking of air through air filters.
(b) Cooling of air during summer and heating it during winter.
(c) Humidifying the air, if it is to be heated and dehumidifying if it is to be cooled.
(d) Circulating the conditioned air into the rooms through grills for proper distribution.
(e) Collection of used air with outside fresh air and sucked again through air filters thus completing the cycle.

Adopting the above principles the various systems of air-conditioning is explained below.

### 1. Central system

Under this system, the air-conditioning equipment is installed in one central point instead of providing separate units of air-conditioning for every room. Then the conditioned air is distributed to all the rooms by ducts. This system of air-conditioning requires less space for installation, its maintenance is easy and it is also economical.

### 2. Self-contained or unitary system

Under this system, an attractive portable air-conditioning plant is placed inside the room near the ceiling or window. This air-conditioning plant is self-contained in all respects and conditioned air formed inside the unit itself. This conditioned air is circulated into the room without the help of any ducts.

### 3. Semi-contained or unitary-central system

Under this system, air-conditioning plant is installed in each and every room. But the supply of conditioned air is supplied from central system. For supplying the conditioned air to a number of air-conditioning plant it requires small sized ducts. Alternatively, conditioned air may be supplied from a central plant but the heating or cooling may be carried in the room itself.

## ■ ESSENTIALS OF AIR-CONDITIONING SYSTEM

The essential requirements of an air-conditioning system are as follows:

1. Air filters
2. Heating
3. Cooling
4. Humidification
5. Dehumidification
6. Air distribution.

### 1. Air filters

This is a devise which is used for purifying the incoming air which contains harmful ingredients such as dust, chemicals, bacteria and other microscopic organisms. The various types of air filters used in creating a controlled environment is already discussed in 'plant ventilation' chapter.

### 2. Heating

During winter season, it becomes necessary to supply heated air into factory building. This heating of air is carried out by means of warm air furnaces or coils around which steam is surrounded. The incoming air is allowed to pass over the furnace of coils. When the air comes into contact with heated coils or furnace, it gets heated.

### 3. Cooling

Cooling of air becomes essential during summer season. The cooling can be carried out by the following methods: (1) surface cooling, (2) spray cooling, and (3) evaporative cooling.

In surface cooling, the incoming air is allowed to pass over coils on which volatile refrigerants are circulated. The volatile refrigerants may be of inflammable type such as chloroform or methyl chloride or non-inflammable type such as carbon dioxide or sulphur dioxide. Such coil absorb heat from the incoming air thus letting in cool air.

In spray cooling, water is cooled by ice and incoming air is allowed to pass through spray of water. Later on, this water is allowed to escape in the form of small drops. The cooled air enters into the factory building.

In evaporative cooling, the incoming air is passed through a spray of air and the air gets cooled. There are different methods for evaporative cooling methods. One such method is to circulate the incoming air around coils containing cold water. The coil absorbs the heat from the air and makes it cool.

### 4. Humidification

The process of adding moisture to the air is known as humidification. In winter season, the outside air has low humidity because of low temperature. Hence, the required amount of moisture is added to the air to get the desired humidity. This is accomplished under any one of the following processes: (a) passing the incoming air over wet cloth strips, (b) allowing a direct spray of water into the room, and (c) a combination of both the processes.

### 5. Dehumidification

The process of removing moisture content from the air is known as dehumidification. In summer season, the outside air will have a high humidity because of high temperature. This air is dehumidified before it is allowed to enter into rooms. There are two ways of dehumidifying the air: (1) condensation and (2) desiccation. Under condensation method, first of all the temperature of air is brought down below the dew point. Secondly, the moisture from the air is condensed to the extent desired. Finally, the air is reheated up to the desired temperature. Under desiccation method, absorbers are used to dehumidify the air. These absorbers, such as salt solution or ammonia, have the capacity to absorb moisture from air. These absorbing solutions are spread over glass wool after heating it to a certain temperature. The air which is to be dehumidified is passed over such materials, where the salt solution absorbs the moisture from the air.

### 6. Air Distribution

The distribution of conditioned air in rooms is one of the most essential requirements of air-conditioning system. As per the I.S.I. code of practice, minimum fresh air requirement in factories is 0.21 $m^3$ per minute per person as against the recommended volume of 0.28 $m^3$ per minute per person. The air distribution can be carried out by the following devices: (a) air pumps, (b) air delivery system, and (c) air distribution system.

#### *(a) Air pumps*

In an air-conditioning system, two types of air pumps are used: (a) propeller fan type, and (b) radial flow type.

The propeller type fan has about eight blades of various grades and thickness. They are used to produce air relatively at lower pressure. Its initial cost is low and it is economical in operation. But they produce excessive noise.

The radial flow type of fan may consist of different types of blades, such as straight blade, forward curved blade and backward curved blade. The forward curved multi-blade fan is very suitable as it possesses low speed and quiet operation.

### *(b) Air delivery system*

This system consists of ducts for supplying and returning the air dampers and duct insulation. The supply ducts carry conditioned air to various rooms, while the returning ducts carry the recirculating air. The dampers are placed in the ducts for controlling the direction, velocity and volume of air. Duct insulation enables the prevention of possible heat loss in the air distribution process.

### *(c) Air distribution system*

Air distribution system consists of outlets and inlets in the form of grills. The outlets distributes the conditioned air all over the room. The outlet can be positioned in the ceiling or near the high wall. Inlets are meant for removing foul air from individual rooms and are kept at the receiving end of the return air duct.

## ■ FACTORS INFLUENCING THE CHOICE OF AIR-CONDITIONING SYSTEM

The selection of a particular system of air-conditioning depends upon the following:

### (a) Purpose

The system of air-conditioning depends upon the purpose for which it is installed. As discussed earlier, the purpose of industrial air-conditioning can be to create favourable working conditioning, or to facilitate production process or to protect the equipments and machines. The need for air-conditioning is felt more in some plants where all these purposes are to be met than other plants.

### (b) Climate

Climate affects all factories and the air-conditioning is largely felt in areas of hot climate and humidity.

### (c) Nature of manufacturing process

Certain manufacturing processes are characterised by the letting off of obnoxious gases including dust and dangerous fumes. Such factories require the facility of air-conditioning than factories where such gases are not liberated.

### (d) Comfort of workers

Employees with different cultural and climatic background prefer different types of climate. So, this factor determines the system of air-conditioning.

## SUMMARY

Earlier, for want of resources and technology, controlled environment was created with the help of natural resources. Air-conditioning was invented in 20th century. The term air-conditioning, in its strict sense, is taken as a devise to provide comfort to people. But when it is applied to industry, apart from comfort to employees it controls temperature, humidity, purity and distribution of air. Air-conditioning basically differs from ventilation in the sense that the former controls the air whereas the latter does not. The need for air-conditioning in factories arises to (1) provide comfort to employees, (2) safeguard health of employees, (3) improve the efficiency of employees, (4) maintain quality of product, (5) ensure production throughout the year, (6) enable proper storage of raw materials, (7) protects costlier equipment, (8) undertake research and development, (9) keep production cost low, and (10) improves good relation between employer and employee.

Air-conditioning can be of two types. From the point of view of its functioning, it is classified as (1) comfort air-conditioning, and (2) industrial air-conditioning. For air-conditioning process, it is classified as (1) summer air-conditioning, (2) winter air-conditioning, and (3) composite air-coditioning. Depending upon the location of air-conditioning plant, it can be classified into three systems: (1) central system, (2) unitary system, and (3) unitary-central system.

Air-conditioning system should have the following essentials: (1) air filters, (2) heating, (3) cooling, (4) humidification, (5) dehumidification, and (6) air distribution. Air-conditioning system depends upon (a) the purpose, (b) climate, (c) nature of manufacturing process, and comfort of workers.

## QUESTIONS

### A. Objective type

**I. Fill in the blanks:**

(a) ................ type of air-conditioning is installed in office and administrative buildings of the factories.

(b) ................ type of air-conditioning is installed in factories to create, maintain and control the atmospheric condition to assist manufacturing process.

(c) Under ................ system of air-conditioning, unit air-conditioning is installed at several rooms.

(d) Under ................ system of air-conditioning, portable air-conditioning equipment is fixed in each and every room.

(e) ................ is a devise which is used to purify air in air-conditioning plant.

**II. Write *True* or *False* for the following sentences:**

(a) Composite air-conditioning is installed for providing year round facility of heating and cooling.

(b) Air-conditioning is required only for providing comfort but not for industrial operations.

(c) Under central system of air-conditioning a number of air-conditioning plants are installed for every room.

(d) Under unitary system of air-conditioning, separate air-conditioning equipments are installed in each and every room.

### B. Very short answer type

1. Define air-conditioning.
2. Distinguish between summer air-conditioning and winter air-conditioning.
3. Distinguish between comfort air-conditioning and industrial air-conditioning.
4. Mention the principles involved in air-conditioning.
5. What do you mean by central system of air-conditioning?
6. What do you mean by unitary system of air-conditioning?
7. What do you mean by unitary-central system of air-conditioning?
8. Mention the factors which influence the choice of air-conditioning system.

### C. Short answer type

1. Distinguish between ventilation and air-conditioning.
2. Explain the importance of air-conditioning in factories.
3. Explain different types of air-conditioning.
4. Explain different systems of air-conditioning.
5. Explain the essentials of air-conditioning system.

## ANSWERS TO OBJECTIVE TYPE QUESTIONS

I. (a) comfort, (b) industrial, (c) central, (d) unit, (e) Air filters.

II. (a) True, (b) False, (c) False, (d) True.

# Chapter 11

# INDUSTRIAL SANITATION

## ■ INTRODUCTION

Industrial sanitation refers to maintenance of cleanliness to make it dust free or else dirt that might cause disease. In other words, industrial sanitation is concerned with the protection of health of employee in a factory. The protection of health of the employees has gained more importance in recent times on account of the following six factors.

1. The quality of the work performed by an employee is intimately related to his physical and mental health. This fact has been clearly established by the experience of industry and by scientific research.
2. Management and labour are both affected by health conditions that prevail in an industry. In this connection, it is to be remembered that health programme in industry is not merely a step to improve the living conditions of ordinary employees. The mental illness of an executive may have tremendous impact on hundreds of other employees. Similarly, the loss, arising out of health reason, of an engineer may make the difference between success or failure of a factory.
3. Each kind of work has its special health hazards. This point assumes greater importance from legal point of view. Careful analysis should be made to study the implication of health hazard on different types of jobs. Analysis of each type of work can reveal the factors that reduce the efficiency of the employee or that produce serious impairment of his health. Payment of compensation to employees for health hazards can be minimised by the analysis of work.
4. Much of the illness of workers is caused by factors which are unrelated to occupation of employee. This calls for health education on the part of employees.
5. Industrial hygiene programme is a profitable investment in factories, as it is based on real need and is carefully implemented. Neither management nor employees stand to loose by a properly conducted programme of industrial hygiene.
6. The industrial health programme is to be extended to the family and community where the worker lives.

The management of every factory is committed to protect and improve the health of the employees. The following reasons can be attributed for the growing attention of management towards health of employees.

1. The management has to comply with the legislation framed by the Government to meet the minimum requirements of working environment of the factory.
2. The moral and social responsibility on the part of the management to reduce disease of employees, is a prominent reason for protecting the health of their workers.
3. Management has realised the financial advantages which accrue from the efficiency of workers in their factories.

## ■ ELEMENTS OF INDUSTRIAL SANITATION

The health of a worker, to a large extent, depends upon the physical environment in which he works. The physical environment in a factory is often surrounded by variety of hazards. So, while conducting any investigation about work environment, more attention must be given to the following elements.

1. Water supply
2. Waste disposal
3. Personal service rooms
4. Supply of hygienic food
5. Good housekeeping and storage
6. Sanitation
7. Noise control
8. Illumination
9. Building construction and maintenance
10. The adequacy of tools and mechanical equipment.

The above facilities when provided to the workers can ensure congenial working environment in a factory. Thus, industrial sanitation, in its broad sense, includes the provision of environmental health services to employees in industrial undertakings. Such important elements of industrial sanitation are discussed in the following paragraphs:

### 1. Provision of adequate water

There are four separate water systems that are necessary for industrial establishments. They are:

(1) Potable water for drinking purpose,

(2) Water for fire fighting equipment, preferably with high-pressure,

(3) Process water for cooling the air-conditioning, and

(4) Pure and clean water for washing and cleaning purposes.

Adequate supply of water is very essential in factories. Water for factory use can be drawn from the supply provided by Municipality through water pipes. Where Municipal Supply is inadequate, borewells can be installed in the factory premises. In the event of inadequate supply from this source, also, it can be resorted to wells, lakes or river. But care must be taken to see that only soft water is obtained but not hard water. It is also very essential to treat water before it is used, so as to kill any harmful bacteria in it; water can be chlorinated and dechlorinated before it is actually used, especially when it is drawn from tank.

Water for drinking purpose must be free from all contamination. Provision of drinking water in factories is a statutory requirement in India. The Factories Act, 1948 lays down that:

1. In every factory, effective arrangements shall be made to provide and maintain at suitable points conveniently situated for all workers employed therein a sufficient supply of wholesome drinking water [Section 18(1)]. All such points shall be legibly marked 'drinking water' in a language understood by a majority of the workers employed in the factory. Such points shall be situated beyond 20 feet of any washing place, urinal or latrine, unless a shorter distance is approved in writing by the Chief Inspector [Sec. 18(2)].
2. In every factory, where more than 250 workers are ordinarily employed, provisions shall be made for cooling of drinking water during hot weather by effective means and for distribution thereof [Sec. 18(3)].

In industries, such as breweries, pharmaceuticals, food processing and beverages, water constitutes part and parcel of the finished product. Under such circumstances, extraordinary precautions must be taken for the supply of pure water. Otherwise, it contaminates the whole output which, when consumed, leads to harmful consequences.

## 2. Waste disposal

Manufacturing processes in factories are always characterised by the discharge of wastes which can take different forms. These wastes pose constant threat to the health of employees. Appropriate measures must be taken to dispose of these wastages so as to make working environment congenial. The disposal of industrial waste is also governed by factory legislation. Section 12 of the Factories Act, 1948 lays down that effective arrangements shall be made in every factory for the treatment of wastes and effluents due to the manufacturing process carried on therein, so as to render them innocuous, and for their disposal.

Industrial wastages can take four different forms: (a) solid waste, (b) liquid waste, (c) gaseous waste, and (d) radiation waste.

### *(a) Solid waste*

Solid waste chiefly consists of garbage, waste paper, packing materials and rejects from manufacturing. These are scattered in different places in factories which needs to be collected and disposed of.

The problem of solid waste can be divided into two major areas

1. **Collection:** Including storage, transfer and transport.
2. **Disposal:** Including any accompanying treatment.

The collection operation can be a subdivided into two unit operations, viz., collection and haul. The collection operation consists of removing solid waste from the storage point. The haul operation includes the total round trip travel time (for the vehicle) from the collection route to the (waste) disposal site.

The planning of solid waste disposal involves an assessment of many complex interactions among transport system, pattern of land use, urban growth and development, and public health considerations. The following methods are generally used for disposal of the solid waste matter.

**Sanitary landfill:** This is an acceptable disposal method which is an improvement over the undesirable open dump of solid waste. It is a method of disposing the solid waste on land in such a manner that no nuisance nor health hazards are created. This involves reducing the waste matter to the smallest volume through compacting. This is covered with a layer of soil following daily operation and covering of the final landfill site with additional compacted soil.

**Advantages**

1. This is the most economical method presently available for the disposal of solid waste.
2. Requires less skilled manpower when compared to most alternative disposal method.
3. This method does not give rise to air pollution.
4. Low initial investment is required as compared to other disposal methods.
5. All types of solid waste, irrespective of the volume, may be disposed of.

**Disadvantages**

1. There is difficulty in location of acceptable sites within a reasonable transportation distance and with adequate accessibility.
2. Difficulty of gaining public acceptance in the vicinity of the site.
3. Wet weather may cause operational difficulties and pollution of surface water.
4. An improperly designed and operated sanitary landfill may become a nuisance and health hazard by way of generation of gases, fire and living place for rats.

**Incineration:** Under this method, the solid waste is reduced to ashes by burning it. The resulting inert residue is usually between 5 to 25 per cent of the initial weight of the solid waste. Proper incineration also eliminates the health hazard present in solid waste by reducing the rottening matter to inert ash.

**Advantages**

1. This method requires small land.
2. This method does not pose any nuisance when compared to the first method, as the inert ash contains negligible amount of organic materials.
3. Modern incineration can burn all kinds of solid waste.
4. Incinerators are not adversely affected by weather conditions.
5. Revenue may be obtained from the generated heat, viz. steam or power.

**Disadvantages**

1. Large initial capital investment in plant and equipment.
2. High operation and maintenance cost.
3. Requires skilled personnel.
4. Future air pollution laws could make incineration impossible.
5. Secondary disposal of the residue, ranging from 5 to 25 per cent, must still to be undertaken.

### *Mechanical composting*

Mechanical composting is a conversion process of solid waste material into an organic soil conditioner. Composting is accomplished by manual or mechanical process. Mechanical composting takes time 3 to 6 days and about one month for manual processing. The compost material may be treated to increase the nitrogen content, and then can be sold as fertilizer.

**Advantages**

1. Waste is converted into a usable product.

2. Revenue may be obtained from the product which is not normal with most of the other disposal methods.
3. Compost improves physical properties of most of the soil and makes the soil easier to till. This also helps the soil to absorb moisture which reduces soil erosion.

**Disadvantages**

1. Composting costs may be equal or it may exceed the incineration costs, depending on the method and volume being treated.
2. There is no present indication of the livelihood of development of large compost market in our country.
3. When manual method of composting is used, it leads to odour problem.

### *Recycling*

Recycling of wastage may be accomplished by the separation of the components of solid waste which is economical. The method involves the following steps:

1. Receiving the raw industrial waste and conveying it to a salvage separation area.
2. Separating the salvageable materials from waste material to be further processed.
3. Unsalvaged waste residue is conveyed to the main pulverizer unit.
4. Composting system is employed to compact the pulverized residue for disposal.

The following diagram shows the Recycling of Industrial Waste:

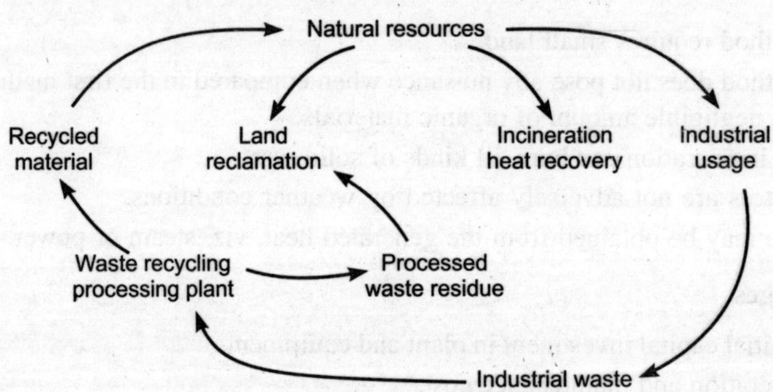


**Fig. 11.1** Recycling industrial waste

**Advantages**

1. It results in added revenue.
2. It involves less waste to be disposed of.
3. It involves less transportation costs.
4. Processed residue waste is put into a form which makes it suitable for land reclamation.

### *(b) Liquid waste*

Liquid waste in industries mainly arises on account of pollutants such as: (1) chemical which includes organic and inorganic, (2) physical, which includes colour, turbidity (thickness) temperature, suspended solids foam, (3) physiological which includes undesirable taste and odour present in water, (4) biological, which includes harmful bacteria.

Before the liquid waste is disposed of, it is to be treated for eliminating all objectionable materials from it. The various phases of waste treatment are as follows:

1. **Pre-treatment:** It includes processes to remove larger aggregate of floating and suspended solid material and also much of the oil and grease content.

2. **Primary treatment:** It consists of the pre-treatment process and stabilisation of water in the absence of free oxygen in a sedimentation tank. Under this treatment, solid particles are separated out.

3. **Secondary treatment:** It resembles the filtration process through which microorganisms are separated.

After giving the above treatment, it may be allowed to flow into a tank or river.

#### (c) Gaseous waste

Gaseous waste in industries are generated as a result of industrial operations. Gaseous waste includes smoke, soot, fly ash, dusts, and fumes. Individuals, who breath such substances into their lungs, will suffer from respiratory diseases. Several devices are used to control the pollutants of gases before they are disposed of. Important among them are (1) mechanical collectors, which use gravitational force to remove air pollutants, (2) electrostatic precipitators which attracts and collects dust from the gases, (3) wet scrubbers, which can handle hot gases and sticky particles, and (4) absorbers which removes all odour, moisture, solvents or other pollutants from the gas. Later on, this can be allowed to flow outside the factory through tall pipes.

#### (d) Radiation waste

With increased utility of energy and the traditional sources of energy being depleted, nuclear generators are seen as the most feasible solution. But there are general potential hazards of nuclear energy which are of public concern. Firstly, the release of radio activity waste during the normal operation of power station is responsible for cancer and birth defects. Secondly, the disposal of radioactive waste poses the problems of retrieval, transportation and storage. This is because many of the radioactive elements in this waste have a prolonged effect.

### 3. Provision of personal service rooms

In all factories, workers after working for long hours continuously, would like to relax themselves for regaining the comforts. Under such circumstances, it is very essential on the part of management to provide separate rooms for washing, cleaning and for easing. Provision of such personal service rooms is compulsory in all factories as per the provisions of Factories Act, 1948. Some of these personal service rooms are:

#### (A) Latrines and urinals

1. According to Section 19 (1) in every factory,
   (a) Sufficient latrine and urinal accommodation of prescribed types shall be provided to be situated conveniently and accessible to workers at all times while they are in the factory.
   (b) Separate enclosed accommodation shall be provided for male and female workers.
   (c) Such accommodation shall be adequately lighted and ventilated.
   (d) All such accommodation shall be maintained in a clean and sanitary condition at all times.

(e) Sweepers shall be employed whose primary duty would be to clean latrines, urinals and washing places.

2. In every factory wherein more than 250 workers are ordinarily employed:
   (a) All latrine and urinal accommodations shall be of prescribed sanitary types.
   (b) The floors, and internal walls up to a height of 3 feet of the latrines and urinals and the sanitary blocks shall be laid in glazed tiles.
   (c) The floors portions of the walls and block so laid or finished and the sanitary blocks of latrines and urinals shall be thoroughly washed and cleaned at least once in every seven days with suitable detergent or disinfectants or both.

***(B) Spittoons***

Section 20 of the Factories Act lays down that

1. In every factory there shall be provided a sufficient number of spittoons in convenient places and they shall be maintained in a clean hygienic condition.
2. No person shall spit within the premises of a factory except in the spittoons provided for the purpose and a notice containing this provision and the penalty for its violation shall be prominently displayed at suitable places in the premises.

***(C) Washing facilities***

According to Section 41 of Factories Act, in every factory:

1. Adequate and suitable facilities for washing shall be provided and maintained for the use of the workers
2. Separate and adequately screened facilities shall be provided for the use of male and female workers.
3. Such facilities shall be conveniently accessible and shall be kept clean.

***(D) Facilities for storing and drying clothing***

According to Section 43 of the Factories Act, the State Government may, in respect of any factory, make rules requiring the provision therein of suitable places for keeping clothing not worn during working hours and for the drying of wet clothings.

***(E) Facilities for sitting***

According to Section 45 of the Factories Act, in every factory:

1. Suitable arrangements for sitting shall be provided and maintained for all workers obliged to work in a standing position in order that they may take advantage of any opportunity for rest which may occur in the course of their work.
2. If in the opinion of the Chief Inspector the workers in any factory engaged in a particular manufacturing process or working in a particular room are able to do their work efficiently in a sitting position, he may, by order, in writing, require the occupier of the factory to provide before a specified date such seating arrangements as may be practicable for all workers so engaged.

***(F) Shelters, rest rooms and lunch rooms***

According to Section 47 of the Factories Act:

1. In every factory, wherein more than 150 workers are ordinarily employed, there shall be a provision for shelters, rest rooms and a suitable lunch room where workers can eat meals

brought by them with provision for drinking water. Where a lunch room exists no worker shall eat any food in the work room.

2. The shelters or rest rooms or lunch rooms shall be sufficiently lighted and ventilated shall be maintained in a cool and clean condition.

## 4. Supply of hygienic food

The efficiency of employees in factories, to a large extent, depends upon the supply of wholesome and nutritious food. While providing food to employees in a factory, the following guidelines may be adopted.

(a) The food to be served must be conveniently available to all workers and at the prices which the workers can afford to pay.

(b) Any regular supply of meal in the factory should contribute at least one third of the daily food requirements of the worker.

(c) It is desirable to serve beverages and snacks in between two meals. Milk or fruit juice is preferable over cool drinks or beverages.

(d) The choice of food served in factory canteen should be determined by a trained dietition.

(e) Studies of workers' diets should be made in order to plan menu to overcome nutritions deficiencies.

(f) The use of specific nutritional measures to prevent disease in certain occupations is advisable.

(g) An adequate amount of time should be allowed for lunch. Any duration of 30 minutes or less is not sufficient.

(h) Adequate facilities for lunch rooms should be provided for workers.

For ensuring the supply of pure and clean food the following precautions are to be taken in factories.

1. As far as possible all the vessels and utensile used for cooking and serving must be cleaned before they are used.
2. The vessels and utensils in which food is cooked and served must be properly tinned from time to time.
3. Care must be taken to clean the food articles, such as rice and vegetables, before they are cooked.
4. Proper precautions must be taken to store the cooked food. They should not be accessible to lizards, cockroaches, etc.
5. The cook and the servers must also be clean while cooking and serving food.
6. Stale food should never be served to employees.
7. Refrigeration and air-conditioner may be resorted to for storing perishable commodities.

A general educational programme in nutrition should become part of health education. The programme should be non-technical and should emphasize the practical selection of food. The average employee can be reasonably sure of securing a well balanced diet, if he is well informed in the general field of nutrition.

## 5. Good plant housekeeping

The term 'house keeping' is borrowed from the maintenance of domestic properties in the house and is now liberally applied to the maintenance of both cleanliness and order in all kinds of business establishments including factories. Cleanliness is a condition wherein buildings, work and rest areas, machinery, equipment and tools are kept free from dirt, dust, filth, etc. Orderliness implies a place for everything and everything in its place.

**Necessity of good housekeeping:** Good plant housekeeping is necessary in order: (1) to maintain clean, neat and orderly factory work area and its surroundings, (2) to improve the morale of employees, by making work areas look pleasant and more satisfying, (3) to minimize injury and accidents, (4) to conserve space, improve material handling system, (5) to facilitate inspection, maintenance and production control function.

The following steps are involved in a good housekeeping procedure:

(a) Carefully planning of the programme of housekeeping. It is better to take the cooperation of workers in this regard.

(b) Dividing factory into different cleaning zones and make a person responsible for each zone.

(c) Undertaking a periodical inspection of housekeeping.

The following check list may help in carrying out inspection properly:

**(a) Machinery and equipment**

| | | |
|---|---|---|
| (i) | General cleanliness | Yes/No |
| (ii) | Containers for waste material | Yes/No |
| (iii) | Machine guards on operating machines | Yes/No |
| (iv) | Portable equipments—Do they hamper personnel and material movements | Yes/No |

**(b) Materials and storage**

| | | |
|---|---|---|
| (i) | Filing and stacking | Yes/No |
| (ii) | Materials projecting out of racks, bins, benches, etc. | Yes/No |

**(c) Building**

| | | |
|---|---|---|
| (i) | Windows clean and unbroken | Yes/No |
| (ii) | Painting and upkeep | Yes/No |
| (iii) | Fire extinguishers and sprinklers in working condition | Yes/No |

**(d) Floors**

| | | |
|---|---|---|
| (i) | Slippery, wet or oily | Yes/No |
| (ii) | Badly worn and rutted | Yes/No |
| (iii) | Garbage, dirt or debris | Yes/No |

**(e) Facilities for employees**

| | | |
|---|---|---|
| (i) | Drinking taps clean | Yes/No |
| (ii) | Toilet and locker rooms clean | Yes/No |
| (iii) | Soap and towels available | Yes/No |

**(f) Other aspects**

| | | |
|---|---|---|
| (i) | Lamps and lamp reflectors, clean | Yes/No |
| (ii) | Bulletin Boards and safety signs, clean | Yes/No |
| (iii) | Protective equipment in good condition | Yes/No |
| (iv) | Electrical motors, clean | Yes/No |
| (v) | Ventilation unobstructed. | Yes/No |

## 6. Sanitation

This refers to maintenance of cleanliness in factories through proper measures. Maintenance of cleanliness is obligatory in all factories as per the requirements of Factories Act Section 11 of the said Act provides that

1. Every factory shall be kept clean and free from effluvia emanating from any drain, privy or other nuisance, and in particular.
   (a) Accumulation of dirt and refuse shall be removed daily by sweeping or by any other effective method from the floors and benches or workrooms and from staircases and passages and disposed of in a suitable manner.
   (b) The floor of every work room shall be cleaned at least once in every week by washing, using disinfectant, where necessary, or by some other effective method.
   (c) Where a floor is liable to become wet in the course of any manufacturing process to such extent as capable of being drained, effective means of drainage shall be provided.
   (d) All inside walls and partitions, all ceilings sides and tops of packages and staircase shall,
      (i) where they are painted or varnished be repainted or revarnished at least once in every period of five years.
      (ii) where they are painted or varnished or where they have smooth impervious surfaces, be cleaned at least once in every 14 months by such methods as may be prescribed.
      (iii) in any other case, the premises be kept white washed, or colour washed and it shall be carried out at least once in every period of fourteen months.
   (e) The dates on which the provisions as per clause(d) above are required to be carried out shall be entered in the prescribed register.

## 7. Noise control

This is separately dealt within the next chapter.

## 8. Illumination

This has already been discussed in Chapter 8.

## 9. Building construction and maintenance

This has already been discussed in the earlier Chapter 7.

## 10. Maintenance of tools and mechanical equipments

This is being discussed in a separate chapter later on.

## SUMMARY

Industrial employee's health has assumed considerable importance now a days. This refers to the maintenance of a healthy environment in the plant conducive to healthy working conditions for the benefit of the employees. This is because unhealthy working conditions lead to diseases of various types, including occupational diseases ultimately affecting productivity of the factory. Maintenance of health of employees include provision of pure drinking water, waste disposal, and personal service rooms. Supply of hygienic food, cleanliness and sanitary facilities, noise control, illumination, maintenance of building, maintenance of tools and mechanical equipments and, last but not the least, good industrial housekeeping.

## QUESTIONS

### A. Objective type

**I. Fill in the blanks:**

(a) Industrial sanitation refers to maintenance of .................. in factories.

(b) The provision of personal services room to employees is a .................. obligation.

(c) Industrial sanitation is concerned with the protection of .................. of the health of employees in a factory.

(d) According to Factories Act, cool water must be provided in a factory which employees .................. number of workers.

(e) Sanitary landfill involves reducing the waste matter to the smallest volume through .................. .

(f) .................. is a conversion process of solid waste into an organic soil conditioner.

(g) Section 11 of the Factories Act deals with provision of .................. facilities to employees in a factory.

**II. Write *True* or *False* for the following sentences:**

(a) It is easy to dispose of solid waste when compared to liquid waste in industries.

(b) It is easy to dispose of gaseous waste in factories than the disposal of liquid waste.

(c) 'Sanitary landfill' method of disposing the solid waste is superior to 'open dump' of solid waste.

(d) Sanitary landfill is the most economical method of disposing of waste when compared to any other method.

(e) Under 'composting method' of waste disposal, waste is converted into a usable product.

(f) Increased revenue is obtained from the process of recycling wastages.

(g) Section 20 of the Factories Act deals with the provision of spittoons.

**III. Choose the correct answer from the following alternatives:**

1. Good housekeeping is an important quality factor in a factory, because
   (a) it promotes good working conditions
   (b) it minimises fire hazards
   (c) it enhances safer operations
   (d) it reflects favourably on the efficiency of the management of the factory.

2. Section 12 of the Factories Act deals with
   (a) provision of adequate water
   (b) waste disposal
   (c) supply of nutritious food
   (d) personal Service rooms.

### B. Very short answer type

1. Define industrial sanitation.
2. List out the factors which has led to the growing importance of industrial sanitation.
3. List out the elements of industrial sanitation.
4. Mention the purposes which is served by the water in factories.
5. Mention different forms of industrial waste.
6. What factor are to be considered while disposing of solid waste in industries?
7. What is sanitary landfill?
8. Distinguish between sanitary landfill and incineration.
9. What do you mean by mechanical composting?
10. What do you mean by plant housekeeping?
11. What is the need for maintaining good plant housekeeping?

### C. Short answer type

1. Explain the need for sanitation in factories.
2. Account for the increased importance of adequate supply of water in factories.
3. Explain briefly the different methods of disposing of solid waste in industries.
4. State the merits and demerits of the different methods of disposing of solid waste.
5. Explain some of the personal service rooms to be provided as per the Factories Act 1948.
6. State the guidelines and precautions to be taken while providing food to employees.

### D. Long answer type

1. Define sanitation. Explain the various elements of industrial sanitation.

## ANSWERS TO OBJECTIVE TYPE QUESTIONS

I. (a) cleanliness (b) statutory (c) health (d) 250
   (e) compacting (f) composting (g) cleaning.

II. (a) F; (b) T; (c) T; (d) T;
    (e) T; (f) T; (g) F.

III. (1) d; (2) b.

# Chapter 12

# NOISE CONTROL

## ■ INTRODUCTION

In olden days, industrial noise was considered as an evidence of progress and prosperity of industries. In those days, noise meant operating a machines to its full capacity, performance of more jobs, payment of better wages and higher standard of living. Today, noise from industry is regarded as a nuisance and a hazard. Noise is a form of air pollution and like other forms of pollution it affects efficiency of workers in factories. A system of noise control results in increased work performance, improvement in the quality of products, a reduction of accidents, and payment of less compensation to employees involved in 'industrial deafness.' Therefore, utmost importance is given for noise control in industrially advanced countries.

## ■ DEFINITION OF NOISE

Noise is defined as unwanted sound. But this definition cannot be an acceptable one because for a person who does not want to listen to a musical sound becomes a noise. So, a better definition of noise would be "a sound that does not have an agreeable quality". A more useful definition of noise is offered by Burrows. According to him, "noise is that auditory stimulous or stimuli, bearing no informal relationship to the presence or completion of the immediate task." (Adopted from E.J. Mc-Cormick, *Human Factors in Engineering and Design*, McGraw Hill, New York 1976, p. 327.)

Noise or sound is the sensation of hearing which results from the stimulation of the auditory nerves and auditory centers of the brain. This sensation is transmitted through a medium, such as air. Sound travels in air at a speed of approximately 330 meters per second. When the pressure waves meet the human ear, they cause a sensation which we call noise or sound.

## ■ TYPES OF NOISE

Industrial noise can be classified under two categories on the basis of their origin and analysis of sound insulation problem. This classification is shown in the following chart.

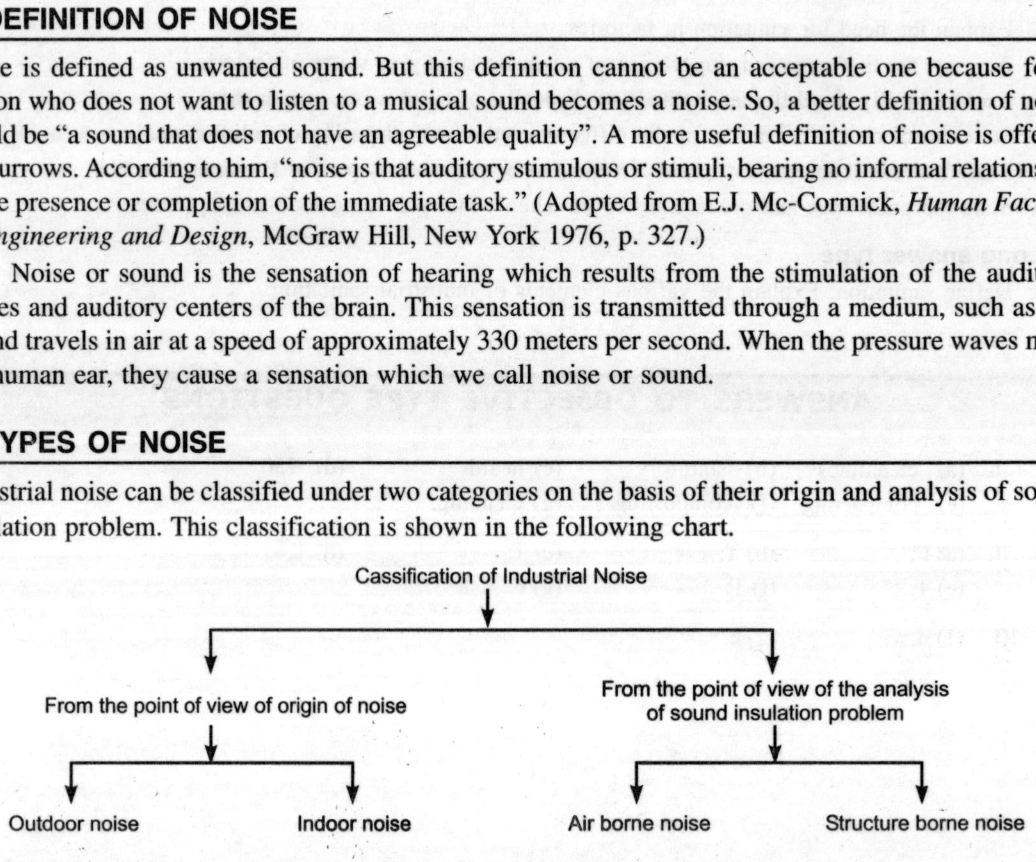

1. **Outdoor noise:** Such a noise has its source of origin from outside the building, such as lifts, sirens, moving machines, from the adjacent building.
2. **Indoor noise:** This noise has its source of origin from inside the building, such as sound of machine operations, typewriters, etc.
3. **Air borne noise:** Air borne noise is one which is generated in the air by outdoor source, such as road traffic or from indoor source through building openings. This type of sound travels from one point of the building to another or from outside the building to the inside, through openings such as doors, windows, ventilators, etc. or through small gaps around door and windows or by vibrating the partition walls or doors.
4. **Structure borne noise or impact noise:** Structure borne noise is originates and progresses in the building structure. This noise may be caused due to structural vibration caused by any activity at around, above, or below the structure. The most common source of this type of sound is from moving of furniture, dropping of tools on the floor, hammering, drilling operations, etc.

**Method of measuring noise level:** The unit of measurement used for sound is a decibel, which is one tenth of a bel. The decibel is defined as "the smallest change which the ear can detect in the level of sound." The decibel scale is a logarithmic scale, on which a difference of intensity level of I decibel corresponds to a ratio of intensities whose logarithm is 0.1. A noisy factory room is rated at about 85 to 90 decibels, as against a whisper which is rated at about 20 decibels and an ordinary speech at 60 decibels. The range running on the scale as a decibel (i.e., unit of measurement) is about 130 decibels.

The relative intensity of sound above does not account for quality and the irregularity in the production of sound, which causes a tiring effect. Most of the factories work in between 40 and 90 decibels. Mr Hunt, in his standard *Handbook for Mechanical Engineers* lists the data as typical sound levels for illustrative purposes, as shown below.

| Intensity of Sound | Decibels | Source of noise |
|---|---|---|
| Deafening | 110<br>100 | Near by riveter<br>Bioler factory |
| Very loud | 90<br>80 | Noise factory<br>Noise office |
| Loud | 70 | Average factory |
| Moderate | 50<br>40 | Average office<br>Private office |
| Faint | 30<br>20 | Quiet conversation<br>Whisper |
| Very faint | 10 | Sound proof room |

It is agreed by most of the engineers that no damage will occur for the employees of a factory, if the noise is below 85 decibels. Between 90 and 95 decibels, it is assented that loss of hearing can be expected by the employees. At high levels, such as 125 to 130 decibels, pain and hearing loss are almost certain, especially at the early stage of exposure. It can be said that any exposure to levels of industrial noise, as high as 150 decibels, could have disastrous effects.

**Objectives and importance of noise control:** The objectives of noise control may be discussed under the following points:

1. To improve the efficiency of workers.
2. To protect the loss of hearing capacity of workers.
3. To facilitate oral communication.
4. To protect the mental health of employees.
5. To check excess payment of compensation to workers on health grounds.
6. To make signals and warning work effectively.
7. To improve community relations.
8. To improve productivity.

1. **To improve the efficiency of workers:** Excess noise in factories results in degradation of work performance. Ample evidence is available to show that noise affects performance under those circumstances where sustained performance is required on jobs which are not challenging. The characteristics of noise that reduce the efficiency of workers are high intensity, high frequency, intermittency and reverberation effects.

2. **To protect the loss of hearing capacity of workers:** Continuous and extensive exposure to noise level above 85 decibels is generally considered to cause say hearing loss. Impact noise, from drop forges and impulsive noise, and from gun blasts generally bring about hearing loss more quickly than exposure to continuous noise.

A study made by a sub-committee of United States of America Standard Institute relating to hearing loss of continuous exposure to noise over prolonged period revealed three implications. They are: (a) hearing loss is related to level of noise to which it is exposed, i.e., the greater the intensity of exposure, the greater the loss of hearing, (b) hearing loss is related to the exposure time, i.e., hearing loss is higher for high exposure intensity and limited degree for low intensity exposure, and (c) hearing loss in usually greater in the 4000 HZ range than in the levels of 1000 to 2000 HZ range.

3. **To facilitate oral communication:** Very often high level of noise is responsible for poor and ineffective communications, as oral communication goes unheard. Any interruption in oral communication will affect the quality of the product, reduction in the volume of output, more scraps and rejections, and delay in manufacturing process.

4. **To protect the mental health of the employees:** Continuous exposure to high noise levels affects one's health, nervous disorders, and frequent headaches. It also causes irritable sensation and fatigue to employees.

5. **To check excess payment of compensation to workers on health grounds:** The amount of compensation paid to employees owing the damage caused to them by excess noise produced in factories is one of the factors which makes industrialists more conscious about noise control. In modern days, courts are sanctioning substantial amount of damages to be paid to employees by the employers. At present in USA, industrialists are spending around 60 million dollars annually in the form of compensation.

6. **To make signals and warning work effectively:** An excess noise produced in industries makes alarms less audible and danger signals in operating machines may go undetected. Therefore, controlling noise is a positive step for safe working conditions.

7. **To improve community relations:** Controlling outside factory noise also results in improved community relations. This type of problem is posed particularly by automobile industries, especially aircraft engine factories which test jet engines. In order to make community a better place to live and work, some industries are taking steps to control noise.

8. **To improve productivity:** The effects of noise control on employees and their productivity is best indicated by a National Office Management Association Survey of 1974 of American companies. According to the survey, 43 per cent of the companies experienced an improvement in morale as a result of noise reduction, 29 per cent reported an increase in accuracy, 16 per cent an increase in quality of work, 4 per cent lost time, and 4 per cent resulted in a decrease in turnover.

## ■ PLANNING FOR NOISE CONTROL

The construction of new factories provide an ideal planning situation for noise control. By considering the potential noise problem at an earlier stage of designing, the factory building provides an opportunity to control the noise. Unfortunately, this fact is forgotton until much of the layout of factory is designed. Noise problem arising in a factory can be anticipated based on data obtained from machines installed in other plants. Geographical planning should be included in any plant survey, since the location of the plant itself can contribute to the noise control problem. Landscaping, such as trees and shrubs, have a psychological effect on residents since they hide the factory from sight and make the noise less disturbing.

## ■ METHODS OF NOISE CONTROL

Noise control in factories can be exercised under the following methods:

1. Noise control at source.
2. Noise control along the path of sound.
3. Noise control at the receiver.
4. Noise control through relayout of plant.
5. Noise control through acoustic treatment.
6. Noise control by isolating noise producing equipment.

1. **Noise control at source:** There are two ways of controlling noise at source. Firstly, by proper maintenance and lubrication of machines. Secondly, by enclosing the noise producing elements by appropriate enclosures. Sometimes, to avoid excess vibrations, machines can be installed firmly on concrete floors.

2. **Noise control along the path of sound:** Once the sound has left its source, it must travel some distance before reaching the place at which the noise nuisance will occur. Common paths for noise are air-borne paths, such as ducts and corridors, and it is usual to include walls that break up air-borne sound paths. To control noise along the path in a factory the following may be employed.

(a) **Noise barriers:** This involves frequency dependent diffraction effects which is based on the size of the barrier. Noise barriers do not eliminate sound, but merely reflect it somewhere else.

(b) **Enclosures:** The inside part of the building is fixed with sound absorbing material, such as fiber glass.

(c) **Noise screen:** Noise screen limit the spread of noise and provides quiet place at sendentary work.

3. **Noise control at the receiver:** In many industrial situations, it is not practical or economical to reduce noise to levels that are not dangerous. In such cases, personal ear protectors are of great value and, as such, it is recommended. Ear protectors are capable of reducing noise levels at the ear by 10 to 45 decibels depending on their make and frequency content of the noise. Ear protectors are generally divided into four categories, according to their position, relative to the ear, viz. earplugs, semi inserts, earmuffs and helmets.

Ear plugs are inserted in the ear and they usually remain there without any additional support. Ear plugs generally provide high noise attenuation, are unobstructive and do not interfere with head covers or any other devices worn on the head. They can be carried in pocket and are less expensive when compared with other types of ear protectors.

Semi inserts close the entrance to the ear canal without being inserted into it and are supplied by a head band. They are usually used as a part of an earphone system. It can provide high sound attenuation and a satisfactory fit for almost any person.

Earmuffs cover the entire outer ear in much the same way as an earphone mounted on an earphone socket. Almost anyone can fit it satisfactorily with little difficulty. But average noise attenuation of earmuffs for frequencies under 1000 HZ is usually lower than that of earplugs. An earmuff costs about Rs. 150 to Rs. 250 and its price is high when compared to earplug.

Helmets cover most of the head surface. They are not commonly used for ear protection. They are usually used to protect the head against injury. They act as support for earphones or earmuffs. Helmets are most expensive of all ear protectors.

4. **Noise control through relayout of plant:** Under this method, necessary arrangements are made to spread out a noisy battery of machines, or enclose the noise source with sound resisting materials.

5. **Noise control through acoustic treatment:** Acoustics is the science of sound which includes the study of the origin, propagation and sensation of sound. Noise control through acoustic treatment can be achieved by considering three broad aspects, namely: (a) Adequate planning of buildings with respect to their surroundings, (b) Acoustical design, and (c) Insulation of machines.

The first aspect, viz., adequate planning of buildings, was dealt in the chapter on factory building.

The second aspect, viz., acoustical design of building involves the study of principles of acoustics for the design and construction of buildings which are free from disturbing noise. The construction and application of sound absorbents and sound reflective materials will provide the optimum conditions for the steady distribution of sound in a building.

The third aspect, viz., insulation of machine, involves insulating the machines by resting them on resilient supports or mounting them on steel springs, rubber corks, etc.

6. **Noise control by isolating noise producing equipment:** The noise producing equipment may be isolated by mounting on rubber spring or felt pads.

There is no therapy or surgery or medicine for hearing loss due to noise exposure. Prevention of exposure to noise is the best available cure. This requires noise level monitoring, regular hearing testing, employee education and training at least annually regarding the effects of noise, the use and fitting of hearing protection devices. Employers must keep a record of duration of noise exposure and results of hearing evaluation. It will help both employee and employer to take correct preventive measures at the right time. So, cooperation of the employee as well as employer is important in any noise control programme.

## SUMMARY

Noise is a form of air pollution and, if it is uncontrolled, it will have disastrous effect over the employees. The unit of measurement used for sound is a decibel. Most factories work in between 40 and 90 decibels. Any increae in noise about 90 decibels is said to cause deafness to the employees. So, it is very essential to exercise control over excess noise produced in industries.

The objectives of noise control are: (1) to improve the efficiency of workers, (2) to protect the loss of hearing capacity of workers, (3) to facilitate oral communication more effective, (4) to protect the mental health of employees, (5) to check excess payment of compensation to workers on health grounds, (6) to make signals and warning work effectively, (7) to improve community relations, and (8) to improve productivity.

Planning of noise control must take place at the time of designing the layout of the building and also at the time of location of factory site.

Noise control is exercised (1) at source of noise, (2) along the path of the sound, (3) at the receiver, (4) through relayout of plant, (5) through acoustics treatment, and (6) by isolating noise producing equipment.

## QUESTIONS

### A. Objective type

**I. Fill in the blanks:**

1. Noise is a form of .................. pollution.
2. The unit of measurement used for sound is .................. .
3. .................. is sound of science which study the origin, propagation and sensation of sound.

**II. Write *True* or *False* for the following sentences:**

1. Noise in a factory can be completely controlled.
2. There is no remedy available for curing hearing loss due to noise exposure.

### B. Very short answer type

1. Define noise.
2. What is a decibel?
3. Mention any four objectives of noise control.
4. Mention any four methods of noise control.
5. Distinguish between indoor and outdoor noise.
6. What is air borne noise?
7. What is structure borne noise?

### C. Short answer type

1. Define noise. Explain the importance of noise control in industries.
2. Review the importance of planning of noise control.

### D. Long answer type

Explain the need for and methods of noise control in factories.

## ANSWERS TO OBJECTIVE TYPE QUESTIONS

I. (a) air
   (b) decibel
   (c) Acoustics.

II. (a) false
   (b) true.

Chapter 13

# INDUSTRIAL SECURITY

## INTRODUCTION

The term "Industrial Security" refers to the measures taken to safeguard and protect the property and personnel of a factory against theft, sabotage and other losses. As setting up of a factory involves heavy investments for construction of its building, installation of machineries, purchase of raw materials and other component, it is essential that all these properties are properly secured. Any damage or loss caused to the factory property involves not only dislocation in the production process but also additional investment to set right the damaged property. According to Kenneth T. Derr, Director and Vice-President of Standard Oil Company of California, USA, "Management of an organization is most often aware of breaches of security, events that result in reported losses for the company. It is impossible to estimate the losses that don't occur, thanks to effective security. But those prevented losses, and events that never happened, do get reported in one sense. They show up in the bottom like a part of the profits that any business earns."

Over the years, crimes against business have grown alarmingly in complexity and in the value of losses. According to estimates of the Chamber of Commerce of USA, in 1982 "crimes against business have grown to represent an annual 40 billion dollars bite out of business profits". In our country, in the absence of such a study either by the government or by the Chamber of Commerce, no estimate is possible. But the situation seems to be alarming.

## IMPORTANCE OF INDUSTRIAL SECURITY

The security function is often relegated to a very insignificant position. There is a wide gap between security and other management functions. The blame for this lies equally with the management as well with security professionals. On the one hand management feels that security is an unproductive activity, and on the other security officers have their background in watertight compartments either in the police or defence, finding themselves in completely new atmosphere overnight. In the absence of proper training, security officers find themselves at sea till they learn by themselves. But it is a time consuming affair and may not help majority of them to fit into an organization as quickly as they should.

Security is a specialized function, details of which are unfamiliar to most of the people. It is the only function in a company, other than the chief executives, that can affect, at one time or the other, every person, operation, product, service and financial procedure. The security department does not just fit neatly into an organization chart. This uniqueness makes it imperative that the security officers constantly strive to sell management security.

The connection between security and profitability is asuming importance year after year. It used to be that industrial security meant guards and gate, lights and locks after a retired defence or police official, as a security chief, standing at the gates just to salute the bosses as they come in or go out. But the industry is becoming gradually conscious of the need for a new breed of highly trained professionals who can develop new concepts of security. The days of simply locking up company property are over. Now, it means a systematic approach to protect all forms of corporate assets, including those intangible but precious assets, the company's reputation and ethics. Industrial espionage is now worrying many corporate bodies, as how to do with the new vulnerabilities of automation technology. Computers have opened up new opportunities for criminals today.

### Requisites of security personnel

For successful working, the security personnel must satisfy the following requisites:

1. The industrial security staff should set an example of good behaviour and, on their part, should maintain their own character and dignity in the organization.
2. The industrial security staff should properly keep themselves alert and properly armed. They should not allow unauthorized persons to enter the factory premises. They should organize a fool-proof system of entry passes for all kinds of visitors.
3. They should be well-trained in fire-fighting.
4. They should be in proper uniform for easy identification from other persons.
5. The industrial security men must be regular, punctual and must posses integrity, loyalty and honesty. They should be careful while taking and handing over charge of their duties.
6. They should be ready to do their duty at all times as their duties come under the essential category of services.
7. They should be gentle and tactful in all their dealings with others.
8. They should keep contact with pro-management and right thinking persons in all parts of the organization, so that they can get information on any negative action well in time so that timely remedial steps can be taken.
9. Industrial security officers should have good relations with police and other officers of the government machinery.
10. Industrial security officers should have good relations with neighbouring industries as labour trouble in the neighbourhood affects industrial relations in other industries.

### Qualities of security staff

The security staff should inculcate the following qualities in order to accept them as a part of the management team.

1. **Competency:** The success of security function, to a large extent, depends upon the ability and capacity of the security staff. Competence in the field of security can be derived from both experience and knowledge. Therefore, a security officer must keep abreast with the latest techniques and developments that combine those with tried and proven methods.

2. **Good judgement:** This is a learned attribute. It involves pansing to reflect on the possible outcome of a decision, weighing all available data and doing the right thing at the right time. All this can be learnet from others who display such qualities.

3. **Personality fit:** Every factory has a personality/philosophy of its own. A successful manager strives to discover that personality and then adopt his own style to fit into the organisational chart.

4. **Communication skill:** Communication skill go a long way in being understood properly for reporting cases to the concerned authorities, both internal and external. Good communication skill avoid misunderstanding of security problems.

## Development of security professionalism

The methods and techniques of security functioning can be developed through the following four educational processes:

1. **Security and safety causes:** Various courses on security and safety can be organized by professional bodies, universities and industrial enterprises. The Indian Institute of Security Management is the leading institute in this country, especially in the field of security and fire safety.

2. **In-company training:** Instead of allowing the security personnel to equip themselves in the field of security management necessary training facilities can be offered within the company itself. Seminars, expert lectures, symposia, etc. can be organized frequently in the company premises.

3. **Security survey:** Since a survey can be conducted in almost every facet of the organization, this opportunity to learn a great deal about the company is unique. Security survey is also an excellent method of continuous business education.

4. **Self study:** A self-introspection or appraisal of one's position in the security department will enable the security person to know where exactly he stands. This is a continuous process and requires management skills and security expertise in presenting facts and figures impressively and achieve tangible results.

## Types of industrial security

Industrial security can be classified under two categories, viz. (1) external security, and (2) internal, security.

1. **External security:** External security of industry implies the protection to be provided to the tangible properties and persons of the industry. The main functions of external security in industries are as follows:

(a) To protect the personnel of the industry against gheraos and other forms of violence.
(b) To arrange fire-fighting and maintenance of fire-fighting appliances.
(c) To control the movement of workers and visitors.
(d) To check all incoming and outgoing goods and vehicles.
(e) To assist management in case of strikes and labour unrest.
(f) To investigate accidents and thefts.
(g) To assist management in case of threats, intimidation, etc.
(h) To give timely information to the management about the negative plans of certain misguiding elements in the factory.
(i) To conduct search of the personnel of the organization while getting out of the factory.
(j) To get theft cases registered with the police station and pursue them at the court level.
(k) To check tresspassing.
(l) To provide timely help to workmen, when they are in trouble, e.g., providing conveyance for taking injured to hospital presenting the managements care properly when any case goes for litigation.

(m) To use sirens and signals to serve as precautionary measures to the adjorning industries.

(2) **Internal security:** It refers to safeguarding the intangible assets of the factory. The secrets of factory operations are considered to be an intangible asset. The business secrets in factories may relate to accumulating experience, research in production process, conducting experiments over various years, information contained in product design specifications, quality control reports, routing sheets, the names of factories, suppliers and customers, machine productivity records, manufacturing problems, new product development plans, maintenance schedules, future plans for expansion. Thus, knowledge should be used exclusively for the benefit of factories but not to be exposed to competitors.

## Types of information

Broadly speaking, information in factories can be classified into two types: (1) open information, and (2) confidential information.

1. **Open information:** Open information refers to information which is meant for advertising purposes that enables employees to perform their jobs. Examples of open information are financial statements to be advertised to meet legal requirements, advertisements about the financial prospects to build the factory's image, information necessary to order materials and information required on the skill and knowledge of prospective employees the factory is seeking to recruit.

2. **Confidential information:** This type of information is deemed it necessary to withhold from being released to unauthorized persons, e.g., confidential information relating to new technology, changes in the use of technology, equipments and processes employed, costs incurred, operating methods, productivity records, sources of procuring new materials and organizational problems. Confidential information may be sub-divided into three classes: (1) information that is likely to damage the factory's competitive position, if revealed, (2) information which would adversely affect the firm's public image, and (3) information that would weaken the firm's position when dealing with unions, customers and suppliers.

## Security aspects of industrial information

The main purpose of information relating to industrial security is to prevent the leakage of confidential information to unauthorized persons. There are four ways by which factory information is lost. They are: (1) physical security, (2) personal security, (3) communications security, and (4) technological security.

1. **Physical security:** This is concerned with the safeguard of property of factory's, such as equipments, materials, etc. and preventing them from being stolen, damaged or destroyed by the sneakers in order to achieve their own objects. Physical security functions through impediments such as fences, locks and lights. Physical security can be achieved by means of guards, locked doors, identification badges and inspection procedures. Visitors and suppliers should not be allowed access to confidential rooms and should not be allowed to take photographs without prior permission from the management. Other areas where models are presented and research is undertaken should be isolated by using screens or partition walls.

2. **Personnel security:** This is concerned with employees who come in contact with outsiders such as suppliers, customers, government inspectors and union leaders. The information is passed on either deliberately or unconsciously out of ignorance or for personal gain by persons having access to it. The information which the sneakers are interested in are about individual habits, character, traits motivations, associations, past employment and personal obligations. This information is generally obtained by the factory personnel or the security department.

3. **Communications security:** This is concerned with safeguarding information which is communicated either orally or in writing. This can be controlled by means of restricting the duplication of information and strict supervision of written documents.

4. **Technological security:** This aims at protecting information from individuals who use more sophisticated means for listening to conversation and other sound related communications. The areas of information sought through these means are availability of resources, initiative and ingenuity.

## Educational Safeguards

One way of controlling the dessimination of information through employees is to educate the employees. Employees can be educated on the following topics:

1. The importance of proprietary information about the factory's ability to compete successfully, provide employment and funds for expansion.
2. The need for an employee to avoid discussing proprietary and confidential topics at technical and professional meetings.
3. Employees, responsibilities for maintaining control over documents entrusted to them and for ensuring that these documents are returned for destruction when they are no longer required.
4. The employees to refrain from discussing factory matters on telephone and personal conversation with outsiders and other employees who have no connection with such matters.
5. The need for employees to recognize that when factory information is discussed with any one, "the need to know" criterion must be followed.
6. The need for employees to avoid leaving confidential papers and documents unguarded where they might be seen, copied, or acquired by others.

## QUESTIONS

### A. Very short answer type

1. Define industrial security.
2. Mention four qualities of security staff.
3. Mention four methods of developing security profession.
4. Distinguish between external security and internal security.
5. Distinguish between open information and confidential information.
6. Mention the four ways by which factory information is lost.

### B. Short answer type

1. Define industrial security. Discuss its importance.
2. State the essential requisites of security personnel.
3. Briefly explain the functions of the external security department in factories.
4. Explain the various security aspects of industrial information.
5. What are those areas in where employees are to be educated to control information security?

### C. Long answer type

Explain the functions of external and internal security department in a factory.

# Chapter 14

# PLANT MAINTENANCE

## ■ INTRODUCTION

The word "maintenance" historically brings to one's mind the picture of a person in a grease-stained clothes carrying an oil-can and a piece of cotton waste, followed by a helper holding a tool box. To many people, the maintenance implies a job meant either for oiling a machine, tightening a bolt or dismantling a machine. The philosophy of maintenance has come a long way from the crisis to activities of repair. As in the field of medicine, where parameters like temperatures, pulse-rates, heart-beat and blood pressure equipment's are measured and monitored to decide on the patient's state of health, and the line of treatment to be adopted, maintenance these days use special instrument devised to keep track of indicators of equipment's health like temperature, noise, vibration and shock pulse. The emphasis is on the the use of sophisticated instruments which have the ability to measure and forewarn the trend of the equipment's condition. The task of plant maintenance is to ensure the availability, reliability and safety of equipment at an optimum cost. This has become an essential job particularly in the developing countries, which are investing heavily in sophisticated plant and equipment to catch up with the advanced technology.

## ■ DEFINITION OF PLANT MAINTENANCE

According to Alford and Beatty, "Maintenance in an industrial plant is the upkeep, repair, renewal and replacement of worn-out, damaged or obsolete parts of buildings, machinery and equipment."

The principle of plant and equipment maintenance, which follows the engineering phrasing of the proverb, "A stitch in time saves nine", is anticipating repairs, renewals and replacements. It prevents interruption of operation due to poor condition of buildings or broken-down machinery and equipment.

## ■ NEED FOR PLANT MAINTENANCE

The need for plant maintenance arises on account of the following:

1. For preventing accidents.
2. For preventing breakdown of machines.
3. For preventing excess repairs of machines.
4. For preventing undue wear and tear of machines.
5. For preventing excessive vibration of machines.
6. For facilitating proper inspection of machines.
7. For proper lubricating the machines.
8. For designing proper layout of machines.

## ■ IMPORTANCE OF PLANT MAINTENANCE

The importance of plant maintenance is discussed as under:

1. **To ensure continuity in production:** It is a well known fact that continuity in production depends upon the running conditions of the machines. Frequent repairs, renewals, overhauls, and breakdown of machines interrupts production. This may lead to cumulative loss arising from the profit which would have been earned, had the production continued without any stoppage. For want of maintenance, the management of the Edison Company closed down its nuclear electric generating power plants for about 4 months because of the failure of one of the systems' cooling unit. The cost of repair was estimated to be US$ 10 millions, but the bigger loss to the company was from the loss of electric generating capacity which was valued at $80,000 per day.

2. **To ensure efficiency in production:** In order to ensure efficiency in production it is necessary to have a maintenance department with the maintenance staff. Owing to increased importance of maintenance function some industries have increased the number and ratio of maintenance employees to production workers. In 1945, General Motors in USA employee one maintenance employee for every eight employees in assembly-line. Today, the ratio is one maintenance employee for every six employees in assembly-line. This ratio is likely be 1:1 by the year 2000. The managerial functions, such as planning, organizing, controlling, coordinating and directing have been recognised as important, in maintenance because of the increased importance given to maintenance these days.

3. **To ensure productivity:** Plant maintenance plays a prominent role in improving productivity in manufacturing. Maintenance of plant and machinery avoids loss in production time, leads to minimum rescheduling of production, prevents overtime work, and eliminates temporary work shortages owing to workers seeking alternative work.

4. **To deliver goods on promised date:** Plant maintenance ensures production according to schedule. The possibility of delayed production owing to breakdown of machines is also quite remote, as all plants and machineries are repaired on a continuous basis. Thus, production is complete on time and goods are delivered on promised dates. This increases the prestige and goodwill of the factories.

5. **To minimise excess scraps and wastages:** One of the factors responsible for excess scraps and wastages in factories is defects in the working of machineries. So, unless the plant and machineries are set right properly from time to time, it results in excess wastages and scraps. Plant maintenance by continuous check-up sets right the defects in machines result in ensuring the quality of goods.

6. **To increase the lifetime of machines:** In developing country like ours, the capital is a scarce resource. For this reason, it is expected that the capital goods, like plant and machineries are maintained in a better way to ensure the durability of machines. Besides, the natural conditions like tropical climate, extremely high or low humidity in our country calls for special care of machines. Because of inadequate maintenance, factories in our country suffer from an unduly high rate of depletion of capital assets and a chronic waste of production capacity.

7. **To avoid losses due to poor maintenance:** Poor maintenance of plant and other assets results in four types of losses. They are:

(a) ***Destruction of equipment*:** The most important loss due to poor maintenance is the premature deterioration of valuables assets. This happens mainly because of allowing machines to deteriorate beyond repair.

(b) ***Production loss***: Deterioration or destruction of equipment leads to losses in production. Production loss can be of two types: (1) disruption of the production process, and (2) deterioration in the quality of products. The former loss results in payment of idle time wages and capital cost per idle equipment. The latter type of loss involves additional expenses in converting a defective unit into good unit.

(c) ***Induced losses***: Frequent breakdown of machineries, which reduces the output of an industry or leads to irregular deliveries, affects the whole lot of small industries which depend on other industries for their supplies. In order to reduce their dependency on unreliable suppliers and to keep their production flow uninterrupted, most of the industries keep high stocks of components which is unnecessary. This is an uneconomical locking up of scarce capital and hence an induced loss. The other induced losses that occur is because of bottlenecks in the supply of spare parts. As a result, many factories try to hold large stock of spare parts.

(d) ***Disguised loss***: It is now a well known fact that in many factories the installed capacities are under-utilized. But it is less known that excess capacity quite often disguises inadequate maintenance. A switch over to idle equipment is an ideal practice in the event of breakdown of an ill-kept machine, so that production process is not disrupted. In such a situation if the practice of poor maintenance and incompetent repair is continued over a longer period of time, deterioration and frequent breakdown of the whole set of equipment will become apparent.

8. **To ensure good housekeeping:** The maintenance of building and equipments of a factory in an orderly fashion is always considered to be safe. One of the principles of factory administration is that good housekeeping provides better quality, lower costs and contentment among workers. To ensure good housekeeping the responsibility should be fixed and it must be supervised frequently. Good housekeeping committees have been effective in improving attitudes and in securing the desired results.

## ■ FUNCTIONS OF PLANT MAINTENANCE

Among other things, plant maintenance include the following functions:

1. Make emergency repairs.
2. Inspect buildings and fixed equipments at such intervals as will ensure detection of deterioration and the need for repairs.
3. Inspect machinery and equipment at such intervals as will ensure detection of misadjustment, wear and tear or impending breakdown.
4. Make such repairs, renewals or replacements as inspection shows to be necessary.
5. Keep systematic record of inspections and the repairs to be made.
6. Suggest and assist in developing changes and improvements in the design of machinery and equipments to decrease liability of breakdown, reduce the necessity for frequent adjustments or repairs and prolong the service life of the machinery.
7. Put in effect changes and improvement developed under point 6 above.
8. Operate such service activities as may be assigned to the maintenance department, e.g., aiding in new equipment installation and acting as liaison for outside building contract works.
9. Maintain an adequate written work order system.

10. Maintain control procedure to ensure future inspection, lubrications and so on.
11. Maintain adequate trained minimum size work force.
12. Plan all work at least one day in advance.
13. Establish and maintain an adequate store of maintenance materials with minimum investment, consistent with the needs.

## ■ SCOPE OF PLANT MAINTENANCE FUNCTION

The scope of plant maintenance can be outlined under the following points:

1. Building construction and maintenance.
2. Mechanical equipment maintenance.
3. Electrical equipment maintenance.
4. Plant safety, fire and theft protection.
5. Yard and ground maintenance.

### 1. Building construction and maintenance

The maintenance of factory building includes the following:

(a) Masonry, which includes foundations, wall, permanent partitions, plastering, etc.
(b) Steel work which includes—columns, beams, stairways, windows, etc.
(c) Floor.
(d) Service, which includes—water, gas, and steam.
(e) Heating, ventilating and air-conditioning.
(f) Carpentry and wood construction.
(g) Painting.
(h) Plumbing.
(i) Roofing.
(j) Inspection of construction done by outside contractors.

### 2. Maintenance of mechanical equipment

The maintenance of mechanical equipments includes the following steps:

(a) Heat treatment and furnace equipment.
(b) Machine and operating equipment installation and repairs.
(c) Lubrication of machinery and equipment.
(d) Materials handling equipment.
(e) Factory layout.
(f) Mechanical meters, recording devices and instruments.

### 3. Electrical equipment maintenance

The maintenance of electrical equipments includes the following, steps:

(a) Electrical power plant equipment, transformers, etc.
(b) Wiring, switch boards, power outlets, etc.

(c) Electric lighting.
(d) Motors rewinding, repairs, etc.
(e) Alarm signaling.
(f) Private telephone systems.
(g) Electrical equipment, tools, furnaces, etc.
(h) Lighting protection devices.
(i) Electric meters.
(j) Battery charging.

### 4. Plant safety, fire and theft protection

This step includes the following:

(a) Safety installation.
(b) Floor marking in plant and road marking.
(c) Warning signals.
(d) Roadway crossing protection.
(e) Watchmen's service-fire, burglary.
(f) Fire-fighting equipment.

### 5. Yard and ground maintenance

This step includes the following:

(a) Sheds and other yard structures.
(b) Poles for cables, wiring, etc.
(c) Fences.
(d) Outdoor signs.
(e) Outdoor storage areas.
(f) Landscaping and gardening.
(g) Parking facilities.
(h) Collection and disposal of waste.

## ■ ORGANISATION OF MAINTENANCE DEPARTMENT

The organisation of maintenance department depends upon the size of the factory and the functions to be performed in a factory. Maintenance department can be organized under either of the following:

1. Centralisation by trade.
2. Maintenance coverage by area.
3. A combination of central and area administration.

1. **Centralisation by trade:** Under this organization, the various maintenance skills are segregated and the supervisor responsible for each skill is usually designated as a master craftsman of that trade. The following diagram depicts this type of organization.

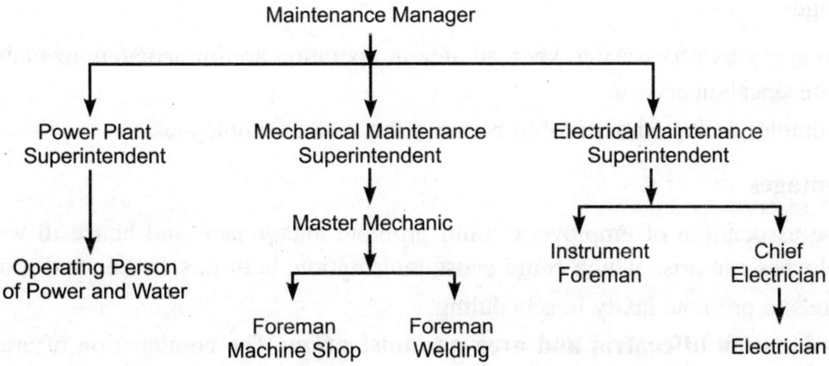


**Fig. 14.1** Centralisation by trade maintenance organisation

### Advantages

1. A direct responsibility is fixed on qualified person for the performance of each job.
2. Since the supervisor is a master craftsman of the job, he is competent to instruct his subordinates and in maintaining the efficiency of the job.
3. When recruiting new employees, the central trade supervisor is in a better position to select the best qualified people for the job.

### Disadvantages

1. There is a tendency towards overstaffing.
2. A central maintenance requires more accuracy in scheduling when compared to the other methods of organization.

2. **Maintenance coverage by area:** A maintenance organization which has more than one craft reporting to one supervisor is termed as area maintenance. This is illustrated in the diagram given below:

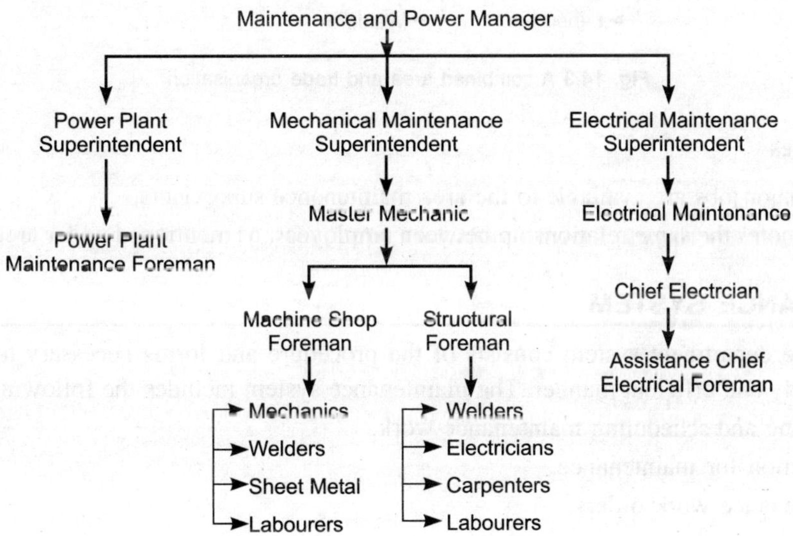


**Fig. 14.2** Organisation based on area maintenance

**Advantages**

1. All major jobs necessary to keep an area in operation are immediately available to the area maintenance supervisor.
2. It promotes a closer relationship between the various employees.

**Disadvantages**

1. Close association of employees could promote antagonism and hence ill-will among the employees can arise which could cause interruption, both in schedule and production.
2. It tends to promote laxity in scheduling.

3. **A combination of central and area administration:** The combination of area and central administration is the most orderly organisation and is used most widely in all types of industries. This organization structure affords more latitute than the others with the advantages of both area and central. This type of organisation is shown in a diagram given below.

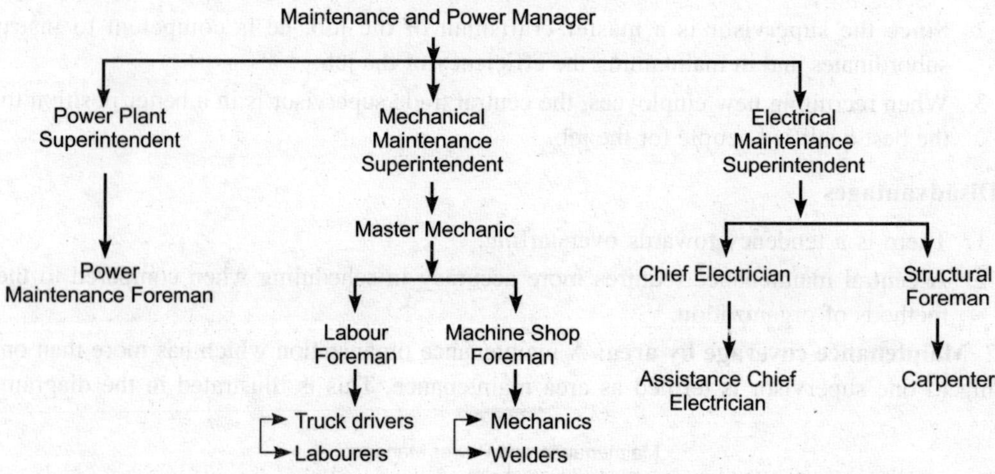


**Fig. 14.3** A combined area and trade organisation

**Advantages**

1. The major jobs are available to the area maintenance supervisors.
2. It promotes the same relationship between employees, as mentioned under area maintenance.

## ■ MAINTENANCE SYSTEM

The maintenance department system consists of the procedure and forms necessary to get the work done in an orderly and efficient manner. The maintenance system includes the following:

1. Planning and scheduling maintenance work.
2. Inspection for maintenance.
3. Maintenance work orders.
4. Building and equipment records.

1. **Planning and scheduling maintenance work:** This involves planning the maintenance work so as to utilize the employees of maintenance department to the maximum extent. The need for maintenance work is determined from maintenance inspection reports. The planned maintenance work together with current request for repairs and improvements is then built into a maintenance programme. The required number of maintenance employees are estimated so that a schedule indicating the time of commencement and completion of each job can be prepared. This is undertaken in order to avoid interruption in production. Purchase requisitions are prepared to draw materials and tools for undertaking maintenance work.

2. **Inspection for maintenance:** The purpose of inspection for maintenance is to discover and anticipate needs for repairs, renewals and replacement and to arrange for their completion before a breakdown occurs. By this procedure, the cost of repairs is minimized and losses from interruptions to production are averted. The frequency of inspection is determined by judgement and experience.

3. **Maintenance work orders:** Maintenance work order is a document which authorises maintenance work to be undertaken. Maintenance work orders originate in the following:

(a) From inspection reports on which are indicated the need for repairs and replacement.

(b) From heads of the operating departments for maintenance work.

(c) From the plant engineer for the purchase of new equipment owing to changes in the process of manufacturing.

The requests for maintenance work is received by plant engineer. He issues maintenance work orders authorising each division of the maintenance organization to take up its part of the required work.

Usually, maintenance repairs are classified into three categories on the basis of priority of repairs. They are emergency repairs, major repairs and minor repairs. While no hard and fast rules are laid down for undertaking the above types of repairs, they are dictated by good judgement and circumstances under which they arise.

4. **Building and equipment records:** In addition to the forms discussed earlier, the maintenance department system also includes permanent records of all tangible assets. The record contains location of every tangible asset. They include the following:

(a) Plans and blue prints of factory building.

(b) Machine layouts.

(c) Layout of transport system.

(d) Stock of machinery and equipment.

(e) Summary of records of repairs, replacements and costs.

## ■ TYPES OF MAINTENANCE

Maintenance work may be classified into following categories:

1. Corrective or breakdown maintenance.
2. Scheduled maintenance.
3. Preventive maintenance.
4. Predictive maintenance.

1. **Corrective or breakdown maintenance:** This type of maintenance implies that repairs are made only when the equipment goes out of order and it cannot perform its normal function any longer. It is known as breakdown maintenance because repairs are undertaken after the breakdown. Some of the typical causes of machine breakdown are as follows:

(a) Failure to replace worn out parts.
(b) Lack of lubrication.
(c) Neglected cooling system.
(d) External factors, such as too low or too high level of voltage, wrong fuel, etc.
(e) Indifference towards equipment vibrations, unusual sounds coming from the rotating machinery, getting too much heated up, etc.

**Disadvantages of breakdown maintenance**

This type of maintenance hampers production process especially in continuous manufacturing concerns, where the output of one machine becomes the input of other machine's.

It results in delayed repairs if tools and accessories and maintenance personnel are not readily available.

It involves payment of idle time wages for so many number of hours during which no production is obtained. This increases the cost of production.

Often, failure of machines may cause accidents to industrial workers. There will be excessive spoilage of finished goods.

2. **Scheduled maintenance:** It is planned or predetermined procedure which aims at avoiding frequent breakdown of machines. Scheduled maintenance system incorporates in it inspection, lubrication, repair and overhaul of certain equipments which, if neglected, can result in breakdown. This type of maintenance is commonly followed for overhauling machines, cleaning of water tanks, white-washing of building, etc.

3. **Preventive maintenance:** Preventive maintenance is defined as periodic inspection or checking of facilities to uncover conditions that may lead to breakdown in production or harmful depreciation and the correction of these conditions while they are still in a minor stage. Before an effective preventive maintenance plan is made, the following data should be obtained.

(a) Length of time the equipment has been in operation.
(b) Length of time needed to repair the equipment.
(c) Detailed description of work to be done.
(d) Total time spent from the failure to the beginning of work.

The aim of ideal preventive maintenance is to make repairs and renewals before the failure of equipment and remedy minor defects before they lead to major crisis by the way of major repairs. The major source of physical deterioration are:

(a) Vibration, which can be eliminated by design.
(b) Corrosion, which may be prevented by using more resistant material or by applying a protective coating.
(c) Wear and tear, which may be controlled through proper design of velocity and area factors, the careful selection of materials, the use of lubricants etc.

(d) Constant training in the proper use of equipment is one method by which damaging treatment of apparatus can be reduced.

**Advantages of preventive maintenance**

(a) It results in minimum breakdown of machines because of periodic inspection. The maintenance work can be scheduled systematically so as to utilize the services of the maintenance staff to the fullest extent.

(b) It does not require frequent repairs of machines and hence involves less maintenance and repair cost.

(c) It results in better quality of products and rejection of few products.

(d) It increases lifetime of machines.

(e) It ensures continuity in production.

## Functions of preventive maintenance

1. **Classification of equipments:** For undertaking preventive maintenance, machines are classified into three types:

(a) Machines whose failure results in high mechanical expenses.

(b) Machines, whose failures result in costly investment.

(c) Machines, whose failures leads to no interference in the general production schedule.

Of the above types of machines, the first type of machines mentioned above are given more attention for preventive maintenance to avoid a unexcepted shutdown.

2. **Provision of stand-by equipments:** In order to ensure continuity in production, very often duplicate equipments are also installed so that if the original equipment fails the duplicate can be operated upon. But, where it is not possible to install duplicate equipment, spare parts are kept ready for quick substitution as and when a part fails or shows a sign of failure.
3. **Setting up preventive maintenance programme:** This refers to a schedule which is prepared according to the nature of the item to be serviced.
4. **Setting up organization for preventive maintenance:** Organisation of preventive maintenance becomes necessary in large sized factories with the coordinated efforts of a number of employees. But in small factories, it is undertaken by one or two trained persons.
5. **Carrying out maintenance operation and repairing:** Repairs are carried out as per the detailed maintenance programme.
6. **Maintenance of records:** Statistical records are maintained to ensure whether preventive maintenance programme has really become effective.
7. **Providing a follow-up system:** This is to check up whether preventive maintenance programme is being actually followed.

4. **Predictive maintenance:** It is comparatively a newer maintenance technique. It makes use of human or other sensitive instruments, such as audio gauges, vibration analysers, amplitude meters, pressure, temperature and resistance strain gauges, etc. to predict troubles before the equipment fails. In predictive maintenance, equipment conditions are measured periodically or on a continuous basis and this enables maintenance men to take a timely action, such as equipment adjustment, repair or overhaul. Predictive maintenance extends the service of life of an equipment without fear of failure.

### Recent trends in plant maintenance

In recent years, there has been a tendency to use a variety of management techniques for plant maintenance. These techniques have led to (a) an increase in maintenance efficiency, (b) reduced maintenance cost, and (c) improved services. Some of these are mentioned below:

1. **Use of computers:** Many factories in USA are now using computers to manage their maintenance. Computers have proved their usefulness to large factories in a great way. Computers in the field of preventive maintenance results in (a) reduced overtime caused by emergency repairs, (b) eliminates premature parts replacement, (c) reduces cost of equipment record keeping, and (d) eliminates human errors in preparing work orders and other records.
2. **PERT techniques:** PERT (Programme Evaluation Review Technique) methods have been used effectively in planning major maintenance projects. The projects on which PERT can be used are: additions to existing facilities, new buildings, etc. Some factories in USA have reported that there is a saving to the extent of 25% by using PERT.

## ■ GENERAL PURPOSE AND SPECIAL PURPOSE MACHINES

General purpose machines are meant for a wider range of jobs while special purpose machines are meant for particular or limited jobs. The special purpose machines are used in mass production because of their very high productivity within limited range.

### Differences between general purpose and special purpose machines

1. A general purpose machine is meant for a wider range of jobs whereas the special purpose machines are meant for a specific type of job.
2. A general purpose machine is used in job production industries whereas the special purpose machines are used in mass production industries.
3. The initial cost of general purpose machine is less whereas the initial cost special purpose machine in high.
4. The general purpose machine has utility throughout its life whereas the special purpose machine can be used only when there is sufficient work.
5. A general purpose machine can be bought at a short notice whereas a special purpose machine takes a long time to be delivered to the factory.
6. It is possible to repair general purpose machines whereas it is not easy to repair the special purpose machines.
7. Spare parts of the general purpose machines are easily available whereas it is not easy to get spare parts of the special purpose machines.
8. Maintenance cost of general purpose machine is low whereas the maintenance cost of special purpose machines is very high.
9. The risk of obsolescence in general purpose machines is low whereas in the special purpose machine the risk of obsolescence is very high.

## SUMMARY

Plant maintenance is a task which is concerned with repairs and renewals of machineries in factories. It is usual in factories, when machines are constantly operated for a long time they are subject to breakdown which need to be repaired for continuation of production. The importance of plant maintenance is reflected under the following points:

(a) It ensures continuity in production.
(b) It ensures efficiency in production.
(c) It ensures productivity.
(d) It ensures prompt delivery of goods.
(e) It minimizes excess scraps and wastages.
(f) It increases the lifetime of machines.
(g) It avoids various losses due to poor maintenance.
(h) It ensures good housekeeping.

The functions of plant maintenance varies from emergency repairs to maintenance of plant and machinery up to date. The scope of maintenance function covers:

1. Maintenance of building,
2. Maintenance of mechanical equipment,
3. Maintenance of electrical equipment,
4. Plant safety, and
5. Maintenance of ground.

The organisation of the maintenance department depends upon the size of the factory. Maintenance department can be organized on the following basis:

(a) Centralisation by trade,
(b) Maintenance coverage by area,
(c) A combination of central and area type of administration.

The maintenance system includes the following:

1. Planning and scheduling maintenance,
2. Inspection for maintenance,
3. Maintenance work order, and
4. Building and equipment records.

Maintenance work are of four types, viz.,

(a) Breakdown maintenance,
(b) Scheduled or planned maintenance,
(c) Preventive maintenance, and
(d) Predictive maintenance.

The recent trend in plant maintenance is towards the increased use of computers and PERT techniques.

# QUESTIONS

## A. Objective type

### I. Fill in the blanks:

.................... maintenance is designed to bring down breakdown to a ........................ .

### II. Write *True* or *False* for the following sentences:

(a) Since machine failures cannot be avoided, there is little that management can do to assure continuity in production.

(b) Breakdown maintenance can be programmed accurately.

## B. Very short answer type

1. Define plant maintenance.
2. State the principle of plant and equipment maintenance.
3. How do maintenance work order originate?
4. Mention four points which support the need for plant maintenance.
5. Distinguish between "Induced Loss" and "Disguised Loss" in plant maintenance.
6. State the elements of maintenance system.
7. Mention four types of maintenance work.
8. What are the recent trends in plant maintenance?
9. What do you mean by breakdown maintenance?
10. What do you mean by scheduled maintenance?
11. What do you mean by preventive maintenance?
12. What do you mean by general purpose machines?
13. What do you mean by special purpose machines?
14. List out four important functions of preventive maintenance.
15. List out any four advantages of preventive maintenance.

## C. Short answer type

1. Explain the importance of plant maintenance.
2. Explain the functions of plant maintenance.
3. Outline the scope of plant maintenance.
4. Explain how maintenance department is organized in factories.
5. Describe the maintenance system in a factory.
6. Distinguish between general purpose machines and special purpose machines.

## D. Long answer type

Explain advantages and disadvantages of the various types of plant maintenance.

# ANSWERS TO OBJECTIVE TYPE QUESTIONS

I. Preventive, minimum

II. (a) False (b) False

Chapter 15

# MATERIALS MANAGEMENT—PURCHASE CONTROL

## ■ INTRODUCTION

Materials Management is concerned with controlling the kind, amount, location, movement and timing of the various commodities used and produced by industrial enterprise. Cost of materials constitute a substantial portion of the capital invested in factories and thus demand a continuing and considerable attention from its management. Failures of many factories are the direct outgrowth of excessive inventories. Too much materials cause idle funds, storage, obsolescence problems and marketing difficulties. On the other hand, if the materials are not adequate to meet the needs of the operating and distribution segments of the enterprise, efficiency suffers, costs sky-rocket, manufacturing delays are frequent go up considerably and broken delivery promises inevitable. Materials Management is a continuous struggle between too much and too often the delaly in the availability of materials.

## ■ DEFINITION AND SCOPE

The American Production and Inventory Control Society defines Materials Management as the grouping of management functions related to the complete cycle of material flow, from the purchase and internal control of production materials to the planning and control of work in process to the warehousing, shipping and distribution of the finished product. The grouping of all functions concerned with the flow of materials from planning for its procurement to ultimate delivery to customer is shown in the following figure:

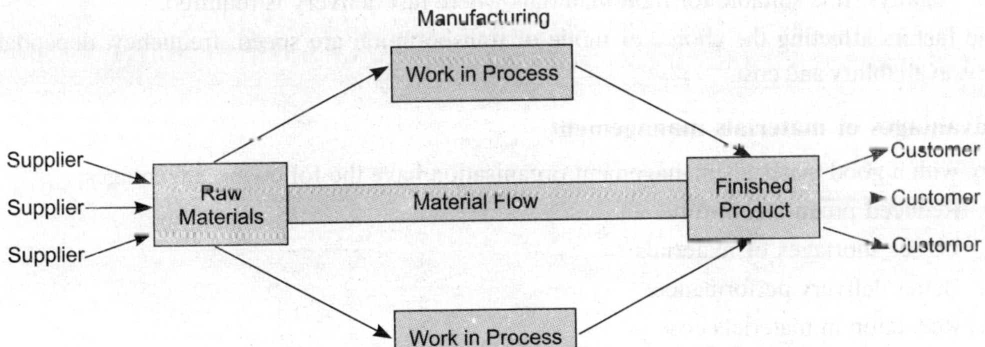


**Fig. 15.1** The concept of materials management

## Scope

Materials Management embraces the following functions:

(a) Planning: This function deals with the type, quantity, quality and time of purchasing the materials.

(b) Procurement: This function deals with the timely procurement of raw materials and component parts, on time from various sources.

(c) Control: This function deals with follow-up to ensure that the plan and schedules are adhered to. It also includes expediting, record-keeping, data collection and feed back of information.

(d) Storing: This function deals with receiving, inspection, storing an issuing of raw materials required by the production departments.

(e) Handling: This function deals with movement, packaging, transfer, and delivery materials from the time they are received until they are issued.

(f) Distribution: This function deals with the distribution of finished goods, warehousing, packing and shipping to customers.

(g) Transportation and traffic control: The external transportation of materials involves:

1. Shipping: Arrangement of goods for delivery to the customer.
2. Traffic: Transportation of both outgoing and incoming items.
3. Receiving: Acceptance of incoming articles.

The above functions are the responsibility of the traffic manager. The everyday activities of a traffic department generally include preparation of goods for shipment, selection of carriers, handling of all matters pertaining to shipping, tarriff and rates, weighing, marking, documenting and loading goods for shipment, inspecting goods received and processing claims for damaged goods.

There are several modes of transportation. The common and frequently used ones are:

(a) Water transport: It provides slow but inexpensive means of shipping large quantities of bulk material.

(b) Railways: It provides best means of handling heavy or bulky goods through long distances.

(c) Motor truck: A good way of transporting over short distances, where door to door delivery may be required.

(d) Airways: It is suitable for light materials where fast delivery is required.

The factors affecting the choice of mode of transportation are speed, frequency, dependability, capability, availability and cost.

### Advantages of materials management

A factory with a good materials management organisation have the following advantages:

1. Reduced procurement time
2. Lesser shortages of materials
3. Better delivery performance
4. Reduction in materials cost
5. Prevention of excess loss of materials
6. Strict and efficient control of materials

7. Increase in labour utilisation
8. Better coordination and cooperation of personnel working in purchase, production, storeroom, distribution and traffic department.

## TYPES OF MATERIALS

Materials used in factories can be divided into the following classes:

1. Raw materials: Raw materials comprise such items which are to be purchased for converting them into finished goods. Sometimes the finished product of one factory becomes the raw materials of another factory. Some of the examples of raw materials used in factories are metal bars, leather and hides, cotton, chemicals, etc.
2. Purchased parts: Items used in the assembly of the product, which are obtained from outside sources. Some of the examples of purchased parts are: bolts, nuts, screws, bearings and gear.
3. In-process material: Materials used in the product upon which work has been performed to change its form, size, or physical or chemical characteristics is known as in process material. Here, value in terms of processing labour or other materials are added to what originally was a raw material. E.g. sand blasted and painted casting.
4. Finished products: Goods completely manufactured, inspected and ready for sale to a customer are known as finished products.
5. Supplies: Consumable materials used in the manufacturing process, which do not become a part of the product, is known as supplies. Examples of supplies are: Sand paper, oils, cotton waste.
6. Equipment items: These are expendable parts of machines and other physical facilities. Examples of equipment items are: fixtures, fittings, valves, fuses, lamps, etc.

## DEFINITION AND IMPORTANCE

### Definition

Purchasing may be defined as the procurement of materials, supplies, machines, tools and services, required for the maintenance and operation of a manufacturing plant. The objective of scientific purchasing is to procure materials at

(a) Right price
(b) Right quality.
(c) Right contractual terms.
(d) Right time.
(e) Right source.
(f) Right materials.
(g) Right place.
(h) Right mode of transportation.
(i) Right quantity.
(j) Right attitude.

### Importance

The importance of purchasing may be summarised under the following:

1. Purchasing is a primary function and, as such, it directly influences the total cost of production. The increased or decreased amount of profit earned in a factory is determined by efficient purchasing.
2. The purchase department ensures receipt of proper materials, in sufficient quantities, when needed to maintain production. It checks unnecessary or excessive investment of capital on purchase of materials.
3. It is possible to discover new materials which may be used as a substitute for existing material. This is ensured by the purchase department by coming into close contact with other factories.
4. By discovering new substitute of materials, it enables us to introduce new lines of products.
5. It helps in framing plans and policies relating to marketing, scheduling of production, etc.

## ■ ORGANISATION OF PURCHASE DEPARTMENT

The organisational structure of a purchase department depends upon the size, the relative importance of procurement and the availability of the personnel. But purchase function is common in all factories. In large factories, an assistant purchase manager will direct the activities of his subordinates who might specialise in a particular line, such as chemicals, equipments, etc. In small factories, all the purchase functions are performed by a single individual. A typical organisation chart of purchasing department is shown below:

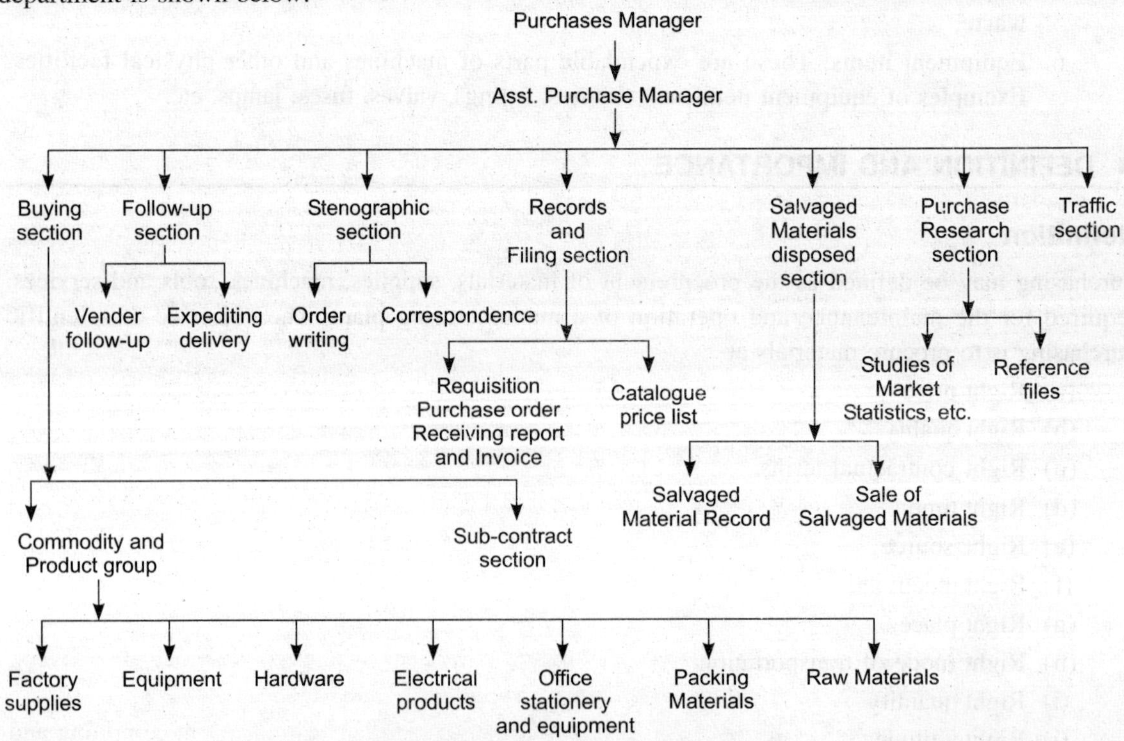


**Fig. 15.2** Purchase organisation chart

From the above chart, it is clear that purchase organisation includes the following sections:

1. Buying section: The buying section is responsible for purchasing all types of materials required by the factory. But where the factory is very large, to assist the purchase manager, there can be assistant purchase managers.
2. Follow-up section: This section is established to ensure quick supply of materials by the supplier. This is established as a separate section in large factories, but in small factories the purchase manager does the work or directs it to be done by his subordinate.
3. Invoice section: Invoices are checked by invoice clerks in large factories and by the purchase manager in a small factory. Sometime, this work is done in the accounting department.
4. Stenographic section: In large factories work can be pooled to minimise the number of stenographers. But in a small factory, a single stenographer will do follow-up, invoice checking, stenographic work and filing.
5. Records and filing section: Records and filing section is found only in large factories, in a small factory, the stenographer will do this work.
6. Salvaged materials disposal section: In large factories, records and sales of salvaged materials are under the direction of the purchase department. The Purchase Manager will sell all the surplus and salvaged materials of the factory through this section.
7. Purchase research section: This is rarely found in factories but it can be set-up in very big factories.
8. Traffic section: Where incoming materials are larger than outgoing goods, this section is set-up under purchase department. But when the outgoing goods are more than incoming goods, it is set-up under sales department.

## ■ CENTRALISATION AND DECENTRALISATION OF PURCHASE DEPARTMENT

The organisation of purchase department may be based on any of the following three systems:

### 1. Centralisation of Purchases

Centralisation of purchases refers to purchase of materials under one purchase manager. If the company has only one plant, it has to invariably follow centralisation of purchase. Where a company has many factories, certain factors are to be considered before centralising the purchases. These factors are: geographical location of factories, similarity of products manufactured, types of materials, the quantity of materials, the location of suppliers, and other conditions peculiar to industry. According to National Association of Purchasing Management, a company having several plants in the same country manufacturing similar products, requiring the same general types of materials, should have centralised purchasing.

**Advantages of centralised purchasing**

1. The principle of undivided responsibility: It means the sole purchase manager can be held responsible for inefficient purchasing.
2. It helps to maintain consistent buying policies, such as terms of payment (payment on delivery, cash on delivery, cash with order) terms of packing, marking, etc.
3. It results in economy of purchase records. Further, it facilitates simplicity in compiling and consulting the records.

4. It tends to reduce the inventories that must be carried and thus helps in low-capital investment on materials.
5. Bulk purchasing results in reduced price of materials on account of trade discount, cash discount facilities.
6. Free home delivery facility is available under centralised system owing to bulk purchases.
7. It relieves the departmental heads of the responsibility of procuring variety of materials.
8. Specialised and expert knowledge on the purchasing problems connected with specific items of materials can be made available to all the units.

**Disadvantages of centralised purchases**

1. The benefits arising out of local purchase cannot be availed of.
2. This system of purchases leads to communication difficulties between centralised purchasing office and the plants.
3. Emergency purchases cannot be made under this system.
4. Delay in receiving checking and approving the invoices, as central purchasing offices has to receive all the reports and invoices from all the plants.

## 2. Decentralised purchasing

Under decentralised purchasing system, a separate purchase department is established to make purchases independently. Decentralised purchasing is applicable to those manufacturing concerns which operates several plants in different localities, manufacturing different products, and each plant requiring different types of materials. Each purchase department will have a purchase authority who enjoys the freedom of making purchases of materials required for his department. The purchasing authority in each department reports to the chief purchase officer, who establishes the general purchase policies and coordinates the purchasing functions in all plants.

**Advantages of decentralised purchases**

1. Greater flexibility: If a centralised buyer is purchasing for a number of plants he will find it difficult to react rapidly to changes in the requirements of individual plant. But under centralisation system, the buyer can buy the required quantity and quality and at the time when materials are required.
2. Close liaison: A local buyer will be in close contact with his own manufacturing unit. Therefore, he is in a position to make scientific purchase of all kinds of materials.
3. Quick procurement of materials: The delay is involved in centralised purchasing system where all the purchase requisitions are to be pooled for placing the order and then supply of materials to each and every plant is avoided under this system.

## 3. Centralised-decentralised system

Companies which have more than one plant located in and around adopt this system of purchasing. Though such factories produce different products, there are some materials which are common to all plants. Under such circumstances, it is desirable to partially centralise and partially decentralise the purchase function. Under this system, it is necessary to make clear which type of materials are to be bought by the centralised buying officer and which type of materials by departmental buying officer.

For the successful operation of this system of buying, the following requirements are essential:

(a) The centralised purchase manager has to establish policies, procedures, record-keeping methods and exercise central control, and restrict the authority and range of buying under each decentralised purchase officer.
(b) All decentralised purchases must be reported immediately to the central office.
(c) The decentralised buying officer must buy the materials for his plant only within the budgeted amount.
(d) Approval of the central office must be obtained by the decentralised buying officer for special purchase and excess quantity purchases.
(e) The plan should be kept flexible so that specific buying authorities can be reassigned, as conditions change.

## ■ QUALIFICATIONS OR REQUISITES OF PURCHASE MANAGER

1. He must have considerable experience in buying and be conversant with the purchasing techniques.
2. He must possess technical ability to decide upon the most suitable source and the required quality of materials.
3. He must know how to negotiate with the suppliers.
4. He should acquaint himself closely with current quotations and sources of supply.
5. He should have practical knowledge of finance and business methods.
6. He should have knowledge of the materials which he is required to purchase and their specification, quality and quantity.
7. He should be honest and reliable.
8. He should be aware of the policy of management and financial resource of factory and its impact on purchases.
9. He should have an up-to-date knowledge of government policies regarding import and export restrictions and various duties and taxes on materials.
10. He should be well conversant with economic principles of demand and supply, price etc.
11. He should have a working knowledge of laws relating to Contracts and Sale of Goods Act and such other statutes which have a bearing on the purchase of goods.
12. He should be aware of the market conditions and should have a complete knowledge of the market, sources of supply, price and purchase formalities.
13. He should maintain proper records and documents like catalogues, price lists, trade magazines, journals to assist him in locating the best market.

## ■ DUTIES AND RESPONSIBILITIES OF PURCHASE MANAGER

The purchase department is headed by a competent authority, generally designated as purchase manager. He occupies the position of upper middle management group and is directly responsible to general manager. The purchase manager must possess good personality, versatility and breadth of vision. He must be capable of making prompt decision, having balanced judgment and clear foresight.

### Duties of purchase manager

1. To establish purchasing policies for his department to execute.
2. To locate and select the best source of supply for materials and services required.
3. To receive purchase requisitions from all the departments and know the exact quantity of material requirements of the factory.
4. To purchase the required quantity of materials at the lowest price and at the best possible terms.
5. To place purchase orders with the supplier.
6. To follow-up suppliers so that delivery of materials can be obtained at the proper time.
7. To make sure that materials received from suppliers conform to the orders placed.
8. To verify and check invoices and approve them for payment.
9. To secure adjustment on claims for goods received which are not in accordance with quality or quantity or which have been damaged.
10. To maintain proper records for efficient operation of the purchase department.
11. To keep constant touch with market conditions and try to secure new goods which are improvement over the existing materials.
12. To analyse the effects of changes in general business and trends upon purchase plans.
13. To advise on prices for materials to be used in new or modified designs.
14. To prepare and present all reports regarding the purchase of materials to the general manager.
15. To take part in inter-departmental conferences for planning formulation of policies or other purposes.

### Responsibilities of the purchasing manager

1. The purchase manager is responsible for purchasing the required quality of materials so that the finished product becomes more acceptable to customers.
2. Organising and directing the purchase department.
3. Judicious utilisation of funds while purchasing various types of materials.
4. Timely purchase of materials to ensure that the production process is not interrupted.
5. Maintaining the factory's reputation for integrity and fair dealing.
6. Preparing the purchase budgets.
7. Engaging in research on new materials, new tools, etc.
8. Final check on all goods requisitioned, questioning need, quantity and quality specification.

## ■ PURCHASING POLICIES

Purchase policy refers to guideiines along which the purchase manager will carry out his duties. The formulation of purchase policies reduces the complex decisions to be made by the purchase manager and ensures a reasonably uniformity of action. The number and details of purchase policies varies with the organisational philosophy of management. Some of the areas covered by the purchase policy are:

1. Price: As regards the selection of the supplies the purchase manager can select that supplier who has given the lowest quotation price for the supply of materials.

2. Firm bidding: Under this policy, the quotation price once submitted by a supplier is taken as final. But owing to increase in the price, it should not be acceptable by the purchase manager. If a policy of firm bidding is not followed, suppliers knowing that they will have an opportunity to revise their original bids, tend to bid at higher amount.
3. Reciprocity: This is a mutual agreement between two factory managers wherein the goods of one factory is bought in return for the sale of goods to the other factory. This creates goodwill among both the two factories.
4. Employee purchases: Under this policy, the factory will buy goods to be resold to its employees at less than retail price.
5. Acceptance of gifts: It is natural in modern days that in order to increase the volume of sales, the suppliers offer gifts to the purchase manager. As one of the purchase policy, accepting of such gifts by purchase managers may be restricted. Such expensive gift might create a condition wherein the purchase manager may place order for substandard materials.
6. Cancellation: Sometimes it becomes necessary for a purchasing manager to cancel an order previously submitted. Under such circumstances, the supplier must be compensated for all the expenses incurred in fulfilment of the contract.
7. Cooperative purchasing: Factory producing similar products and established in the same locality may buy their material in cooperation with other buying firms. Such a policy results in reduction in purchase cost, free home delivery services.
8. Speculative purchases: Speculative purchases are resorted to when the prices of materials fall down to a great extent. So, to take the advantage of fall in prices, materials may be purchased in bulk quantities. However, while following this policy, the cost of carrying such inventory must also be considered.
9. Bulk quantity purchase: One of the purchase policy that is practised by most of purchase managers is bulk purchase as against small quantity. This is to take the benefit of cash discount, trade discount and quantity discount, free home delivery services, credit facilities, after sale service, exchange of defective materials with good ones, etc.
10. Multiple sources: It is not desirable to rely upon one source of supply as it is risky to 'put all eggs in one basket'. Where large quantities are involved, a good purchase policy is to resort to more than one sources of supply.

## ■ PURCHASE BUDGET

A purchase budget is an estimate of the cost of material purchases for a specific period of time. The purchase budget is based upon (a) the forecast of future materials requirement, (b) records of materials, (c) prediction of market conditions and price trends, and (d) delivery schedules. When the purchase budget is approved, it becomes the plan for the guidance of the purchase manager. The main advantages of a purchase budget are:

1. Better judgment can be exercised when making long-term buying commitments.
2. Better control can be exercised over costs as it serves as measuring rod by which performance of purchase department can be judged.
3. It helps in procuring material at scheduled period and thus ensures continuous production.
4. It helps to avoid over stocking and under stocking of materials.

## PURCHASING METHODS

The important methods of purchasing materials are:

1. Purchasing strictly by requirement
2. Purchasing for a specified future period
3. Market purchasing
4. Speculative purchasing
5. Contract purchasing
6. Purchasing small items in group
7. Scheduled purchasing
8. Hand-to-mouth purchases
9. Zero stock purchases
10. Local purchases.

### 1. Purchasing strictly by requirement

This method of purchases is followed in job order industries where the goods to be manufactured strictly depends upon the customers' specification. This method of purchase is resorted to only on receiving an order from a customer. Therefore, it follows that the materials that are to bought under this method is not for storing for a long period of time but for immediate consumption in production process. In other words, no materials are purchased under this method until the need arises. The quantity of materials to be bought depends upon the requirements of the materials. Other industries (other than job order industries) adopt this method for purchasing special type of materials. However, the purchase manager has to keep a contact with various suppliers from whom such materials can be promptly purchased.

### 2. Purchasing for a specified future period

This method of purchase is adopted where (a) the materials are used regularly, (b) in small quantities, and (c) prices of such materials do not fluctuate widely. This is the most common method of purchases followed by most of the factories. The period for which materials are to be purchased depends upon the rate of consumption of materials and the time taken by the supplier to supply the materials on placing the order. Sometimes, past record serves as the basis for deciding the period for which materials are to be purchased. Sometimes, the cost of carrying the inventory as also the benefits derived front the suppliers for the purchase of bulk materials also determine the period for which materials are purchased. One point that is to be remembered under this method is no fixed period should be set for the purchase of all types of materials. Instead, a separate period should be set for each item of materials.

### 3. Market purchasing

When purchases are made in accordance with the conditions of the market to take advantage of price fluctuations, the method is known as market purchasing. By constant study of market conditions and factors that affect prices, it will be possible to forecast the trend of the market prices and buy the materials to take full advantage. When the study indicates that prices are falling and that they are likely to increase in the near future the purchase manager will adopt this method to buy relatively large quantities of materials even for the future period. The chief advantages of this method are:

(a) Material prices are very low and thus it is possible to save considerable amount of investment on materials.

(b) The amount of profit earned on sale of finished product is high, as the price fluctuations of finished products are lesser than raw materials.

(c) When small purchase orders are consolidated, it results in economy in the purchase.

However, this method suffers from the following disadvantages:

1. It requires more storage space and consequently increase in cost of carrying inventory.
2. Chances of obsolescence is high, especially when drastic change in material specifications take place.
3. The method leads to considerable amount of losses if wrong judgement is made about market trends.

### 4. Speculative purchasing

Under this method, the raw materials are purchased in excess quantities than is actually required at lesser prices with a view to sell, the surplus materials in near future at a higher price. Thus, under this method we come across an element of speculation with a view to make quick profit. This method differs from market purchasing in the sense that price fluctuation is given primary importance and materials are bought in excess of production schedule. In other words, speculative purchasing is not based upon the requirement of materials by the factory but on the possibility of savings in market price. This method is mostly used where raw materials cost constitute a very important component of total cost. For example, in cotton textile mills, cost of raw cotton outweighs all other elements of cost in producing cotton cloth. Here, savings of a few rupees a kilogram on raw cotton offers a huge profit when compared to other functions of cotton textile mill. The purchase manager can adopt this method only when he is authorised by the chief executive. The only advantage of this method of purchasing is the possibility of earning huge amount of profit. However, this method suffers from the following disadvantages:

(a) Heavy investment of capital is required on materials,

(b) It requires large storage space, and

(c) There is a risk of obsolescence owing to change in the specification of product.

### 5. Contract purchasing

The term 'contract purchasing' is applied to that type of contract where delivery of material is spread over a period of time. Under this method, a contract is entered into for the purchase of materials at the prevailing prices but whose delivery is required at a future period. Thus, the benefit of low prices of materials are derived without actually taking the physical possession which go to add to the cost of carrying the stock of materials. This method is adopted in such a situation where the production programme is known but its timing is not definite. Contract purchasing also serves as a means of continuous supply as the supplier has to supply the materials as per the contracts entered into by him.

### 6. Purchasing small items in group

This method of purchasing is followed to purchase small items of materials. Purchase of tiny and miscellaneous types of materials often pose problems to purchase manager in following a round about purchase procedure. Purchasing of such small items in groups enables quick and inexpensive purchases. Usually, the purchase manager prepares a list of all such materials and places an order with a single supplier who is known to have stock of all such materials. Such items of materials for which a single purchase order is prepared are pipe fittings, general hardware, electrical suppliers, stationery and so on. When a single supplier has no stock of all such materials, they can be bought by inviting tenders and placing order with the most competitive supplier. A considerable saving in clerical and purchasing expense is achieved by this method of purchases.

### 7. Scheduled purchasing

This method of purchasing is also known as 'programmed purchases'. Under this method, the quantity of materials required for a specific period is anticipated in advance and accordingly the suppliers are also informed so that they can keep all such materials for timely delivery to the factories. The main objective of this method are keeping inventory at minimum, ensuring good quality of materials, timely deliveries, and low cost. Good quality can be obtained by giving suppliers enough time to produce or acquire. Timely arrival of materials can be assured by informing in advance a definite material requirement. Low cost results on advance intimation to suppliers who can produce materials in the most economical manner.

### 8. Hand-to-mouth purchases

This method of purchase is followed where it is not possible to stock the materials or where the materials are of perishable nature. Food processing industries offer the best example, where fresh fruits can be bought directly from the orchards instead of buying them in bulk and allowing them to rot. In certain other cases, where more capital cannot be invested on purchases, materials can be purchased in extremely small quantities, but cost of acquisition on a daily basis proves to be costlier. The main disadvantage of this method is that there is danger in the stoppage of production if there is any interruption in the supply of materials.

### 9. Zero stock purchases

Some factories try to operate on the basis of zero stock and the supplier holds the stock for these factories. Usually, the buying and selling factories are close to each other so that the finished product of one factory constitutes the raw material of another factory. The system could work well if the seller holds inventories and if both the parties work in close coordination. In this method, the buyer need not lock up the capital and so the purchasing routine is minimised. This also significantly reduces obsolescence of inventory, lead time and clerical efforts in paper work.

### 10. Local purchases

To take advantages, such as reduction in transport cost, facility of inspection of materials, exchange of materials and reduction in the cost of materials, often local purchases are resorted to under this method, the elaborate purchase procedure which is commonly followed can be simplified. It also saves considerable period of time as materials are immediately delivered.

## ■ PURCHASING PROCEDURE

The main steps involved in the procedure for purchase are:

1. Receiving purchase requisitions.
2. Decision regarding what, when and how much to buy.
3. Determining the source of supply.

4. Selecting the supplier by issuing tenders.
5. Preparing and placing purchase orders.
6. Follow-up of purchase orders.
7. Receiving of materials.
8. Inspection of materials.
9. Checking invoices and settling the accounts.

## 1. Receiving purchase requisitions

The purchase requisition is a formal request made to the purchase manager to arrange for the purchase of materials described in the purchase requisition. It is a statement, which contains a list of materials and a request to purchase them. It serves as a basis for purchasing the materials when it is signed and approved by authorised person. The purchase requisition should give clearly and completely all the information that is required for initiation of the purchase procedure. The particulars ensure that the purchases can be made with speed and accuracy. It must contain the following essential information:

(a) Name and exact description of materials wanted.
(b) Quantity required.
(c) Date on which materials are needed.
(d) Statement of need, or record of use that justifies requisition.
(e) The place of delivery within the factory after passing through receiving and inspection or directly in case of machinery which should be unloaded as close to the point of use as possible.
(f) Vendor's name, in certain special cases as in repair parts for equipment.
(g) Signature of the authority initiating the purchase requisition.
(h) A space for use of the purchase department to add supplier's name, price, terms.

The above particulars are presented to show a typical purchase requisition hereunder:

**Purchase Requisition**

To,
The Purchase Manager,
.................................

Department.....................
Requisition No. ................
Date of Initiating ..............
Purchase Requisition .........
Required on .....................

Dear Sir,
Please purchase the following items in accordance with the below mentioned specifications.

| Sl. No. | Quantity | Description | Material in hand | Average consumption | Remark |
|---|---|---|---|---|---|
| | | | | | |

Requested by.....................
Special instructions:...........
Ordered from....................
Date ordered....................
Purpose............................

Approved by..................
Purchase order No..........
Approved by..................
Checked by ....................

**Fig. 15.3** Purchase requisition form

The purchase requisition form may originate from

(a) Storekeeper for the purchase of raw materials which have reached reorder level.

(b) Production control department for special type of materials.

(c) Head of the concerned department for buying equipments, such as almirah, filing cabinet, etc.

(d) Plant engineer for the purchase of plant and machineries and other tools and equipments.

(e) Office manager for purchase of office stationery.

Whenever a purchase requisition is received, it is reviewed to see whether the items are available in the storeroom or whether the request for some materials could be replaced by a standard item which is readily obtained at a lesser price.

## 2. Decision regarding what, when and how much to buy

The purchase manager, before proceeding further in purchasing the materials, has to decide the quality, quantity, price and time at which materials are to be purchased.

### *(a) Buying the proper quality of purchase specification*

A specification is an accurate description of material to be purchased.

Buying proper quality of materials depends upon (i) the accurate specification of materials required, (ii) placing the order with a reliable supplier, and (iii) checking materials against specification. Definiteness in the specification of materials always tend to minimise cost of materials. The form of specification may be indicated by trade name or brand name, blueprint, physical characteristics or chemical analysis, detail of materials, description of purpose or use, supplier's sample, buyer's sample.

### *(b) Buying the proper quantity*

As a rule, the quantity of a material to be purchased is specified in the purchase requisition. The quantity is often changed to take advantage of market or speculative purchasing. Quanity of materials required are determined by taking the following factors into consideration: (i) sales forecast, (ii) customer's orders, (iii) production authorisation, (iv) transfers from other departments, and (v) time taken to supply the materials by the suppliers.

### *(c) Buying at proper price*

In order to purchase materials at reasonable price, the purchase manager must obtain and record the price. Material prices may be classified into (i) prices obtained from market reports and newspapers, (ii) price listed in catalogues, and (iii) price quoted by the suppliers when tenders are issued.

The duty of purchase manager is to compare the prices quoted by most of the suppliers and buy the materials from that supplier who can sell them at the cheapest possible price.

## 3. Determining the source of supply

After determining the quality and quantity of materials to be bought, the sources of supply are to be tapped. The following sources are important to identify suppliers of materials.

(i) Trade directories

(ii) Telephone directories

(iii) Periodicals

(iv) Newspapers and commerce magazines

(v) Catalogues and blueprints
(vi) Suppliers index files
(vii) Exhibition and trade shows
(viii) Market survey
(ix) Quotations
(x) Experience of purchase manager.

While considering a suitable source of supply, it should be kept in view whether to purchase from a single supplier or from multiple suppliers.

**Advantages of a single source**

1. The purchase manager should place order for all items of materials with a single supplier to get largest possible discount.
2. There is less administration work in the purchase department.
3. A good relation will prevail between buyers and suppliers, wherein the supplier offers all facilities to the buyer, such as credit facilities, after sales service, exchange facilities, free transport facility, giving of first preference to the buyer over other buyers.

**Advantage of multiple source**

Many factories avoid relying on a single source for all their requirements. They try to have at least two suppliers for each item of materials. The main advantages of multiple sources are:

1. With several sources, there is less risk of interruption of supply. If one supplier fails, the other supplier can take up the supply of materials.
2. With two or more suppliers for one item a healthy competitive spirit can develop in which each vies to improve methods and reduce costs in order to get greater share of the business.
3. Whether to purchase from the local sources or from some distance place.
4. Whether to purchase directly from the manufacturer or through a wholesaler.

## 4. Selecting the supplier by issuing tenders

When there are more than one supplier dealing with materials, the purchase manager has to select the best supplier who can be relied upon for the quality of materials, ability to deliver the materials promptly, and sell at the cheapest price, and can offer better terms of sale. The selection of such a supplier is decided by issuing tenders. A tender is a written letter or an advertisement given in newspaper inviting the prospective suppliers to quote their lowest price and other terms and conditions of sale. The request for quotation should give the following information:

(i) quantity to be ordered.
(ii) name and full specification of materials.
(iii) place where materials are to be delivered.
(iv) other terms and conditions of sale which the supplier wishes to make.

## Types of tender

1. Single tender: Such a tender is issued where an item is of a proprietary nature or where the materials are dealt with by a single supplier.

2. Limited tender: When the value of the tender is moderate, limited tenders are issued. Here tenders are invited only from those suppliers who are on the approved list of suppliers. The merits of this method are:

(a) being regular suppliers they submit realistic quotations.

(b) they are fully conversant with the materials.

(c) the chances of selecting the supplier is better.

3. Open tender: This type of tender is issued when the sources are many and the value is large. Anybody who deals with such material and who is willing to supply the material can quote his prices in response to this tender.

4. Global tender: This type of tender is issued for the suppliers located beyond the boundaries of the country. This tender is mostly used when the factory is under the collaboration of foreign government.

## Earnest money

Earnest money is demanded from the supplier to discourage unreliable suppliers. This is also insisted upon so that the prospective supplier later on does not back out from the rate he has quoted for supplying the materials.

A specimen of tender form is given below:

### Request for quotation

From, Date..................

........................ Quotation Number..................

........................

To,

........................

........................

Dear Sir,

Please submit your quotation for the materials listed below so as to reach the office of the undersigned on or before.................... at .................... Please send full details, specifications and other literature if any along with the quotation. Please note the terms and conditions mentioned below:

1. Please mention on the top of the envelop Enquiry No............ Date on which due............
2. Submit quotations in duplicate.
3. Preferably quote in the same order as in the equiry letter.
4. Price each item separately and the prices quoted should be for destination...............
5. If your are unable to furnish materials as per our descriptions and wish to offer a substitute, please give details.
6. Quotation should be valid for at least one month from the date of opening.
7. Quotation should be tact in sealed covers.
8. Taxes should be mentioned for each item.
9. The right is reserved to accept or reject quotations on each item separately or as a whole.

The quotations will be opened on .............. at .............. in the office of the undersigned.

| Sl. No. | Description | Quantity | Unit | Price | Discount | Total price |
|---|---|---|---|---|---|---|
| | | | | | | |

Yours faithfully

Sd/

Purchase Manager

**Fig. 15.4** Tender form

The sealed quotations are opened on the last date on which it is to be submitted by all competitive suppliers. The Purchase Manager will then prepare a comparative tender statement to know the lowest quotation price and best terms and conditions of sale offered. Thus, the supplier is chosen with whom the purchase order is to be placed. A specimen form of comparative tender statement is given below:

Dated ..............

Section..............
Tender No.............. Dated ..............
Date of Opening Quotations ..............
Comparative Statement prepared by ..............
Checked by ..............

| Sl. No. | Description of materials | Quantity to be purchased | Supplier 1 | Supplier 2 | Supplier 3 |
|---|---|---|---|---|---|
| | | | | | |

Terms and Conditions

Delivery date
Place of Delivery
Terms of Payment
Taxes
Packaging and Forwarding Charges

**Fig. 15.5** Comparative tender statement

Once the supplier is selected, he is asked to make a security deposit so that in case he fails to furnish materials properly and in time, the deposit can be forfeited.

### 5. Preparing and placing purchase orders

A purchase order is a contractual document which authorises the supplier to supply the materials. Once the purchase order is issued to a supplier, it is obligatory on the part of Purchase Manager to take delivery of materials and arrange for the payment of invoice. The purchase order must be carefully drafted by including precisely all the essential elements of purchases to be made. It must be prepared in such a manner so as to avoid future misunderstanding and minimise the necessity of correspondence. The purchase order should include the following particulars.

(a) Purchase order number: Purchase order number helps in identifying the transaction in future correspondence. It also helps the supplier in preparing the invoice and in despatching the materials.

(b) Quantity ordered: The quantity ordered is expressed in different units depending upon the type of materials.

(c) Description: The full description of materials enable the supplier to supply the right quality of materials. It also helps the receiver to inspect the materials on its receipt.

(d) Delivery instructions: This relate to the date on which the materials are to be delivered. It also includes the place of delivery, packing, marking, insurance and mode of transportation.

(e) Terms of payment: The terms of payment, i.e. cash basis, credit basis, F.O.B., F.O.R., C.W.O, C.B.O., C.O.D. can be made clear under this head.

(f) Price: The unit rate and the total amount of materials purchased are to be included.
(g) Name and address of the buying company.
(h) Name and address of supplier.
(i) Date of placing purchase order.
(j) Signature of purchase manager.

A specimen form of purchase order is given below:

ABC Co. Ltd.
6, Harrington Road
Bangalore - 560001

Purchase Order Form

Telephone No..............
Telex..........................

Order No. ............
Date.................

To,

...........................
...........................

Dear Sir,

Please supply us the following items of materials as per the terms and conditions specified below:

| Sl. No. | Quantity | Description | Unit | Unit Rate | Total |
|---|---|---|---|---|---|
| | | | | | |

Terms of payment within 30 days from the date of receipt of stores.
Price F.O.B. ..............
Mode of Delivery
Special instruction

Sd/
for ABC Co. Ltd.

**Fig. 15.6** Purchase order

## 6. Follow-up of purchase orders

The continuation of production process, to a large extent, depends upon the regular and ready delivery of materials. While placing purchase order, the date on which materials are to be delivered must be clearly mentioned. It is the duty of the follow-up section to see that this date is kept. Where it is not possible to get delivery of material on the promised date, the follow-up section can take necessary steps to prevent crippling the production process due to lack of materials.

The following letter may be adopted to take follow-up action:

ABC Co. Ltd.
6, Harrington Road
Bangalore - 560001

Ref. No. .............

Date....................

To,

M/s..........................
..........................

Dear Sir,

We had placed our Purchase Order No. ............... dated ............. which had been confirmed by you on ............ In this connection, kindly refer the following.

The delivery of material was due on ........... but till date the despatch has not been made by you. Kindly do the needful without further loss of time and despatch the material on top priority basis.

Thanking you,

Yours faithfully
Sd/
for ABC. Co.

To avoid late deliveries of materials, the following points must be remembered:

1. Use clear and complete specifications.
2. Keep demands for 'Rush' delivery to minimum.
3. Keep records of the delivery performance of suppliers.
4. Try to find good alternative suppliers to those whose delivery performances are consistently bad.
5. Keep abreast the supplier's current range of delivery times.
6. Know supplier's policy regarding stock of raw material.
7. Visit suppliers regularly.
8. Pay suppliers promptly.

## 7. Receiving of materials

Before materials are taken delivery of, it is very essential to receive and inspect materials so as to ensure that the supplier has supplied the exact quantity and quality of materials. In large factories, a separate receiving and inspection department is set-up and receiving clerks are in charge of receiving the materials. To facilitate the receiving clerk to receive and inspect the materials a copy of purchase order without filling up the quantity of materials can be supplied. This serves as the basis for recording the entries by the receiving clerks. The duties of receiving department are as follows:

(a) To check the incoming materials to know whether all items of materials in terms of quantities conform to the purchase order.
(b) To record the receipt of the materials.
(c) To inform the storekeeper about the receipt of materials.
(d) To inform the purchase manager the fact which require an adjustment to be made with supplier in respect of shortage or defective materials.
(e) To deliver the material either to the department where it is required or to the storeroom.

Having received and checked the materials, the receiving clerk will prepare a Material Received Report. A material received report is also useful for checking the supplier's invoice. The material received report shows:

(a) Date of receipt.
(b) Supplier's name and address.
(c) Types of materials received.
(d) Quantity of materials received.

(e) Condition in which materials are received.
(f) Type of container.
(g) Mode of transportation.

A specimen of Materials Received Note is given below:

ABC COMPANY LIMITED
6, Harrington Road
Bangalore - 560001

MRN No. ..............
Date........................

To,

..................... (Department)
..................... (Department)
..................... (Department)

Please note that consignment containing the following materials has been received today. It will be inspected and sent to storeroom shortly.

| Sl. No. | Description | Quantity | Purchase Order Number and date | Condition of goods |
|---|---|---|---|---|
| | | | | |

Receiving Clerk's Signature

**Fig. 15.7** Materials received note

## 8. Inspection of materials

The next step involved in the purchase procedure is inspection of materials received. Inspection refers to comparison or checking of quality, size of materials, and quantity of materials. The quality of material is ensured if the properties, such as shape, colour, dimension and weight, composition, strength, etc. of the required standard are present in the material. Sometimes, materials, such as chemicals, are taken to laboratory and tested to know their quality.

### *Importance of inspection of materials*

(a) Materials received are in strict specification of purchase order. In other words only those materials that were ordered have been received.
(b) The quantity of materials confirm the quantity of materials ordered.
(c) The quality of materials are those specified in purchase order.
(d) No damage is caused to material during transit.

Inspection of materials in a large factory is usually undertaken by inspection officer. In small factories, inspection function is performed by the receiving clerk or by storekeeper himself.

The duties and responsibilities of Inspection officer are:

1. To sort out defective raw material, if received.
2. To report the management about the quality of materials received.
3. To check the quantity of materials received.
4. To suggest action regarding rejected materials, i.e. whether they are to be returned to the supplier or sell as scrap or deducted from the supplier's invoice.
5. To prepare and sign the certificate of inspection.
6. To use various inspection devices, such as steel rules, callipers, micrometers, electric instruments for the purpose of inspection.

### 9. Checking the invoices and settling the accounts

This is the last step in the purchase procedure. The invoice is checked with the purchase order and the materials received. The prices and terms of invoice are compared with those of purchase order. Similarly, the quantity received must tally with the quantity ordered. If there is any discrepancy or defective material, the purchase manager must correspond with the supplier. If everything is in order, the invoice is approved by the purchase manager and forwarded to the accounting section for payment. For availing cash discount, it is desirable to make the payment within the time allowed by the supplier.

## ■ VALUE ANALYSIS

Value analysis is an important technique of materials management. This technique was first developed by Lawrence. D. Miles of General Electric Company, USA. In a broad sense, it is a study of character-wise cost of an item, such as quality, design, methods of manufacture, etc., with a view to reduce the ultimate cost of the product. Value analysis also means the determination of the value of items proposed to be bought with a view to examine the worth of money spent in buying these items. Value analysis is based upon quality of materials in relation to its functional value and price. Value analysis helps in deciding what is actually required and what should be paid so as to derive the maximum benefit. This reduces the cost of purchase and enhances the profit of the factory. Value analysis is carried for the following purposes:

(a) Elimination of an item altogether, if possible.
(b) Examination of all the features of an item.
(c) Examination of materials of cheaper quality for their advantageous use in the factory.
(d) Examination of costlier quality in relation to its functional value and life and to give up purchase of specified cheaper quality materials.
(e) Examination of alternative source and price in relation to the money to be spent and realisation of its worth in due course.

### Recent trends in materials management

In order to know the recent trends, it is desirable to evaluate the factors related to factories. One such factor is advanced technology and increased automation which has led to introduction of new line of products. With the increasing complexity of industrial processes, the necessity of orienting materials management has been greatly felt so as to cope with increasing technological demands. Secondly, now-a-days, all the three functions of materials management, namely, purchasing, storage and distribution, have been combined. This has called for a scientific system of materials management in factories. Thirdly, in some factories, function, such as materials planning, has been included in the discipline of materials management. This has increased the scope of materials management. Fourthly, the inclusion of electronic data processing, which was added along with other sophisticated controlling system, has made materials management to assume more significance. The recent trends in materials management can be best presented in the following table.

**Table 15.1** Table showing trends in materials management

| Discipline | Yesterday | Today | Tomorrow |
|---|---|---|---|
| Planning and Coordination | — | Medium range planning | Long range planning |
| Purchasing | Manual process | Semi-automatic process | Fully automatic process |
| Storing | Manual process | Semi-automatic process | Highly mechanised operation |
| Inventory | Manual control | Semi-mechanised with computers | Highly mechanised |
| Shipping | — | Manual control | Computer control |
| Distribution | Unsystematic | Systematic based on information | Computer based |

## SUMMARY

Materials management is that branch of management which deals with acquisition, storage and usage of materials in factories. The types of materials used in a factory are commonly classified as:

(a) Raw materials

(b) Purchased parts

(c) In-Process materials

(d) Supplies

(e) Equipment items.

Scientific purchasing of materials involve purchasing the right quantity of materials, in right quality at the right price, from the right supplier and at the right time. Purchase Department can be organised under centralisation or decentralisation system. The purchase department is headed by a competent person known as purchase manager. He must possess certain qualities and qualifications to discharge his duties. His duties and responsibilities depend upon the size of the factory. Before purchasing the materials a definite policy must be decided upon. The policies relate to

(a) price
(b) firm bidding
(c) reciprocity
(d) employee purchases
(e) acceptance of gifts
(f) cancellation of orders
(g) cooperative purchasing
(h) speculative purchase
(i) bulk quantity purchase
(j) multiple source.

Purchase budget is an estimate of cost of material to be purchased for a given period of time. There are different methods of purchases that are practised by factories. They are:

(a) purchasing strictly by requirement
(b) purchasing for a specified future period
(c) market purchasing
(d) speculative purchasing
(e) contract purchasing
(f) purchasing small items in group
(g) schedule purchasing
(h) hand-to-mouth purchases
(i) zero-stock purchases
(j) local purchases.

The purchase procedure include the following steps:

(a) Receiving purchase requisition
(b) Deciding what, when and how much to buy
(c) Determining the source of supply
(d) Selecting the supplier by issuing tender
(e) Preparing and placing purchase order
(f) Follow-up purchase order
(g) Receiving of materials
(h) Inspection of materials
(i) Checking and approving the invoice.

Value analysis is a technique which offers a means of analysing in great detail all the material aspects that contribute to material cost, with the object of minimising these costs for a satisfactory level of product performance.

# QUESTIONS

## A. Objective type

### I. Write *True* or *False* for the following sentences:

(a) The purchasing manager should have the authority to decide 'what', 'where' and 'when' to buy.

(b) "Hand-to-mouth" purchasing should always be employed during the upswing period of the business cycle.

(c) The purchasing department in an organisation does not carry much importance.

(d) The duties and responsibilities of the purchasing department differ from factory to factory.

(e) Contract purchasing is purchasing under contract usually of needed materials, the delivery of which frequently spreads over a period of time.

(f) Centralised purchasing should not be used for any concern operating a single plant.

(g) Specification of materials means the material standards which are established by the factory to define its major materials requirement.

(h) Tenders are invited when time permits and money involved is in large amount.

(i) Once a tender or quotation has been received, no alteration or modification is allowed.

(j) Follow-up of purchase order is of vital importance.

### II. Match the following:

| Column A | Column B |
|---|---|
| 1. Raw materials | (a) Materials that are used in production but do not become part of the product. |
| 2. In-process materials | (b) Materials used directly in the product but have not undergone a major change. |
| 3. Finished products | (c) Products ready to be packaged and shipped. |
| 4. Supplies | (d) Machine parts that are used in manufacturing. |
| 5. Equipment items | (e) Materials used in the product whose form has changed as a result of the production process. |

## B. Very short answer type

1. Define material management.
2. List any four advantages of materials management.
3. Mention the different types of materials used in factories.
4. Define purchasing.
5. What do you mean by centralisation of purchases?
6. Mention four advantages of centralisation of purchases.
7. What do you mean by decentralisation of purchases?
8. What do you mean by purchase budget? What purpose does it serve?
9. What do you mean by value analysis?

### C. Short answer type

1. Discuss the scope of materials management.
2. Explain the various sections of a purchase department.
3. Explain with merits and demerits the centralisation and decentralisation of purchases.
4. State the qualifications of a purchase manager.
5. Outline the duties and responsibilities of a purchase manager.
6. What do you mean by purchase policy? What are the areas covered by it?
7. "The best purchasing policy is to buy from the cheapest source". Comment.

### D. Long answer type

1. Explain the various methods of purchasing materials.
2. Explain the procedure involved in purchasing materials.

## ANSWERS TO OBJECTIVE TYPE QUESTIONS

I. (a) T, (b) F, (c) F, (d) T, (e) T,
(f) F, (g) T, (h) T, (i) T, (j) T.

II. 1. (e), 2. (b), 3. (c), 4. (a), 5. (d).

# Chapter 16

## STOREKEEPING AND ISSUE OF MATERIALS

### ■ INTRODUCTION

Storekeeping is that aspect of Materials Management which is concerned with the physical storage of materials. The term 'stores' is often used to denote materials which are kept for use in storeroom. However, the term 'stores' is used in a broad sense to include not only raw materials but also sundry supplies and finished products. The chief objective of storekeeping is to protect all types of materials in the storeroom.

### ■ OBJECTIVES AND IMPORTANCE OF STOREKEEPING

As storekeeping is essentially a service function, it should aim at providing this service efficiently and effectively at a minimum cost. The main objectives of storekeeping are:

#### 1. Easy identification of materials

Identification of materials become very difficult, especially when varieties of materials are bought in bulk quantities. Unless they are sorted out and stored properly, identifying the materials becomes very difficult. Production is delayed to the extent of identification and its issue.

#### 2. To prepare purchase requisitions

By seeing the quantity of materials reaching the reorder level, it is possible to replace the exhausting materials by requesting the purchase manager to arrange for the purchase of materials. So, the danger in the stoppage of materials can be overcome by timely purchase of materials.

#### 3. Storage

To keep all materials in proper place so that they remain safe while in storage. Systematic placement of materials facilitate quick issue of materials to various departments.

#### 4. Store records

The objects of maintaining store records is to know the quantity of materials on hand, slow moving and fast moving materials, dormant materials, absolete materials, so that prompt action can be taken in respect of each of this material.

#### 5. Coordination with other departments

Coordination of stores and departments is necessary to know the exact requirement of materials and their specification so that only the required quantity and quality of materials could be procured.

### 6. Store verification

To exercise control over materials, stock verification is necessary.

***Importance of storekeeping***

1. Proper maintenance of stores helps the storekeeper to know the actual quantity of materials available in the storeroom. On the other hand, if the materials are not properly stored, it does not help in assessing the exact requirements. Whereas those materials, which are already available, are initiated for purchasing again and again, the one which must be bought may go unnoticed by the storekeeper.
2. Systematic arrangement of stores helps in easy location of materials. They can be issued immediately without wasting the time on searching. In fact, a store item 'misplaced' is a store item 'lost' for all purposes.
3. A good storekeeping with continuous stock verification provides useful data, such as the quantity of materials, fast moving materials, slow moving materials, dormant materials, obsolete materials which serves as a basis for formulating the policy by the management.
4. Disorderly maintained store may lead to losses due to breakage of materials.
5. Chances of theft are high in case of unorganised storeroom.

## ■ ESSENTIALS OF GOOD STOREKEEPING

Storekeeping is both an art and a science. It is an art as it involves the day-to-day receipt, storage and issue of materials; it is science, as it involves recording the store's transactions as per the prescribed principle and rules. Good storekeeping results from experienced and enthusiastic storekeeper and his assistants.

The essentials of good storekeeping are outlined below:

1. Allot a proper place for every item of store
2. Keep every item of store in the allotted place
3. Maintain proper records of stores and keep them up to date
4. Issue materials promptly to various departments
5. Storing the materials in an orderly fashion
6. Protecting materials against damage and pilferage
7. Issue oldest materials first
8. Classify and codify the materials for easy identification
9. Provide adequate space in between racks and almirah for easy movement of stores assistants
10. Undertake continuous verification of materials.

## ■ LOCATION AND LAYOUT OF STORES DEPARTMENT

The selection of appropriate site for establishing a storeroom is known as location of stores. The ideal location of storeroom must be such that the movement of the materials from the receiving department to the storeroom and from the storeroom to the production departments is minimum. Further, the ideal location of store is that where the most efficient transportation and material handling equipment could be utilised. The following factors for storage location should be taken into account in order to arrive at the best locality.

### 1. Material classification

Materials of same classification may be stored at a place irrespective of differences in size, weight and place of consumption. For example, one area may be designated for raw materials, sundry supplies and component parts, another area may be designated for semi-finished products, and another for finished stock.

### 2. Similarity of materials

Items of similar size, shape and weight may be stored together although they may be classified differently or required at different production departments. For example, all small items may be kept in one place and bulk items in another place.

### 3. Material handling considerations

Materials requiring similar handling equipment may be grouped together. For example, those materials which are to be moved by trucks alone, may be stored separately. Similarly, liquids which are to be specially measured and moved by trolleys may be placed together.

### 4. Character of materials to be stored

The character of materials to be stored affects the location of storage areas. Materials that are not damaged by weather can be stored in a shed. Material subject to corrosion must be stored in dry place. Materials whose character is changed by high temperature must be stored in cooled storeroom. Finished goods, which are damaged by dust, must be stored in dust proof bins.

### 5. Quantity, weight and bulk of materials

The quantity of each of the materials to be stored must be carefully considered in determining the location of storeroom. When the quantities of materials are known, the weight and bulk of materials can be determined and required space can be allotted.

#### *Layout*

Stores layout refers to physical arrangement of storage space and facilities so as to provide for most efficient receipt, storage, and issue of materials. The arrangement of storeroom includes arrangement of space for storing material records, files, and materials handling equipments. The basic principles of good store layout are:

1. The layout of any store must reduce distance to be moved by the store items, storage equipments, storage space and handling cost.
2. The store layout must be flexible enough to allow for changed condition and future expansion.
3. Free flow of materials into and outside the storeroom has to be ensured keeping the principle of minimum distance for moving the materials.
4. Provision for different storage facility for different types of materials.
5. Facilitating better supervision of stores.

A well planned layout offers the following advantages:

1. Full utilisation of storage space.
2. Easy accessibility to all the materials.
3. More security of all materials and stores records.
4. Lesser time to receive, issue and store materials.
5. Minimum spoilage, damage and other kinds of losses.

A specimen of stores layout of a small factory is given below:

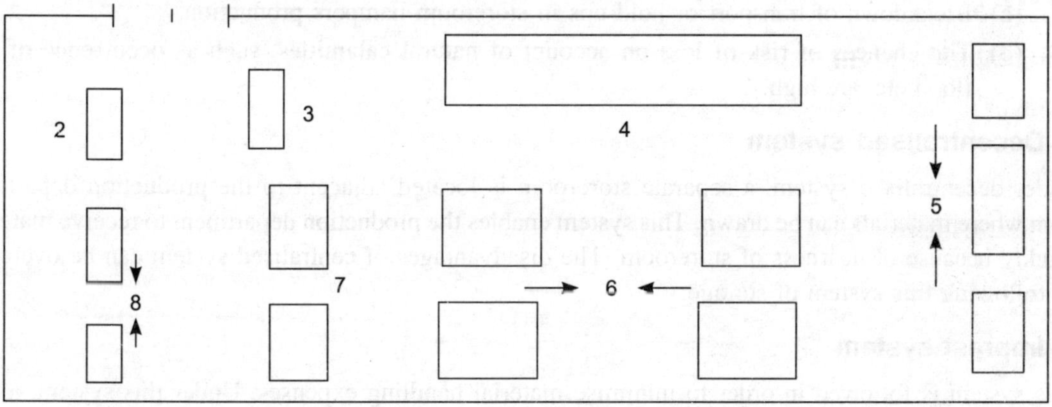


1. Entrance
2. Head Storekeeper
3. Issue Clerk
4. Filing Cabinet
5. Cabinet for storing
6. Bin-racks
7. Almirahs
8. Spare racks.

**Fig. 16.1** Layout of a small storehouse

## ■ ORGANISATION OF STOREKEEPING DEPARTMENT

The organisation of storekeeping department depends upon (a) design and layout of the factory, (b) the degree of centralisation required, (c) need for departmental storeroom, and (d) the relationship of manufacturing department with storekeeping. Generally speaking, storekeeping department can be organised under: (1) centralised system, (2) decentralised system, and (3) imprest system.

### 1. Centralised system

In centralised system all the materials are received and issued from one stores department. The advantages of centralised storing are:

(a) Few persons are required in the storeroom.

(b) As the entire staff of the storeroom are familiar with the materials stored, the system is not disrupted even if someone leaves or is absent.

(c) Better control is exercised over materials.

(d) Economy in records and stationery involving less clerical work and cost.

(e) Materials stored are less because of lack of duplication.

(f) Total space occupied is less.

(g) Stock taking of materials becomes easy.

(h) Because of concentration of experts in one stores room, it is possible to forecast the requirements of materials.

The disadvantages of centralised storing are:

(a) The centralised storeroom may be far away from some departments. So, transportation cost will be high to carry materials from the centralised storeroom to distant departments.

(b) The supply of materials to distant production department may cause delay, and inconvenience.

(c) Breakdown of transport or hold-ups in storeroom hampers production.

(d) The chances of risk of loss on account of natural calamities, such as occurrence of fire, flood etc. are high.

### 2. Decentralised system

Under decentralised system, a separate storeroom is located adjacent to the production department from where materials can be drawn. This system enables the production department to receive materials quickly because of nearness of storeroom. The disadvantages of centralised system can be overcome by following this system of storage.

### 3. Imprest system

This system is followed in order to minimise material handling expenses. Under this system, a sub-store is located near production department. The exact requirements of stores for each production department is decided in advance and sufficient materials are kept on hand in the beginning. At the end of the month, the sub-storekeeper obtains the quantity of materials required so as to replenish the exhausted stock.

## ■ DUTIES AND RESPONSIBILITIES OF STOREKEEPER

The stores department is headed by a competent authority, known as storekeeper. A storekeeper is an individual who takes care of the stores and keeps a watchful eye on the movement of both men and materials with a view to keeping in whole organisation moving. The type of storekeeper required to operate storekeeping function differs from store to store depending upon the nature, size and composition of the stores department. However, a good storekeeper must possess the following requisites:

(a) He must be hard working

(b) He must be honest

(c) He must have knowledge of accounts

(d) He must possess leadership abilities so as to command his subordinates to carry out store-keeping functions efficiently

(e) He must possess an academic qualification which depends upon the type of industry. For example, the storekeeper of an engineering storeroom should be a science graduate

### Duties of a storekeeper

1. To prepare and issue purchase requisition note for such types of materials which have reached re-order level
2. To receive the purchased materials from receiving department

3. To enter particulars of materials in the bin card
4. To keep materials in their appropriate place for easy identification
5. To issue materials to production department on the basis of material requisition note
6. To take back the surplus materials returned by production department
7. To undertake stock verification of materials frequently
8. To report on scrap, waste, surplus, obsolete materials to management for prompt action
9. To prevent unauthorised person from entering into stores, and
10. To equip the storeroom with materials handling equipment for economical handling.

### Responsibilities of a storekeeper

1. The storekeeper is responsible for materials which he receives. Therefore, at the time of receiving the materials into the storeroom he must verify the quantity, quality and the specification of materials.
2. He is responsible for the timely issue of materials. So, the storekeeper has to classify, and codify the materials, store them in the appropriate place.
3. He is responsible for every shortage of materials on account of theft, damage and spoilage.
4. It is the responsibility of the storekeeper to work in close coordination with purchase department, production department and accounts department, and for the smooth functioning of the factory.
5. He is responsible for the negligence of his own as well as of his subordinates.

## ■ STORE RECORDS

The following documents are used in stores department:

1. Materials receipt book,
2. Bin card,
3. Stores ledger card, and
4. Stock verification sheet.

1. **Materials receipt book:** This book records the receipt of materials by the storekeeper in a chronological order. This book forms the basis of stores accounting. Before the materials are stored in bins, they are verified in respect of quantity and quality. If there is any shortage or damage of materials, the storekeeper has to prepare a report of shortage or damage.

2. **Bin card:** A bin card is made out of a thick paper and is meant for recording the receipt, issue and balance of materials in stores. The bin card is attached to the bin or rack in which materials are stocked. It enables us to know the quantity of materials/on hand whenever materials are issued or when received from supplies or return from departments as surplus stock. A bin card helps the storekeeper to prepare purchase requisition to replenish the exhausted materials. It also helps in locating the discrepancy when physical stock verification is undertaken and compared balances with bin card. It contains particulars, such as Bin number, description of materials, code number of materials, maximum, minimum, re-order and danger level and columns for the quantity of materials received, issued and in balance.

The specimen of a Bin card is given below:

| | |
|---|---|
| Bin Card Number.............. | Maximum level............. |
| Name of Material.............. | Minimum level............. |
| Code No. of Material.............. | Reorder level................ |
| Location Code No. .............. | Danger level................ |

| Date | Refer ledger | Receipts | Issues | Balance | Initial of store-keeper | Remarks |
|---|---|---|---|---|---|---|
| | | | | | | |

**Fig. 16.2** Bin card

3. **Stores ledger card:** A stores ledger card is a record of materials showing receipts, issues and balance of materials both in quantities and values. It is maintained in stores accounting section and is outside the control of storekeeper.

Stores ledger card differs from Bin card in the following respects:

| Bin Card | Stores Ledger Card |
|---|---|
| 1. It records only quantities. | 1. It records quantities as well as values. |
| 2. It is maintained by the storekeeper. | 2. It is maintained by stores accountant. |
| 3. It is kept inside the storeroom. | 3. It is kept in cost accounting department. |
| 4. Transactions are individually posted | 4. Transactions are posted collectively. |
| 5. Entries are recorded before the transactions take place. | 5. Entries are recorded after the transactions take place. |

A specimen form of stores ledger card is given below:

| | |
|---|---|
| Code Number.............. | Maximum level............. |
| Name of the material.............. | Minimum level............. |
| | Reorder level................ |
| | Danger level................ |

| Date | Receipts | | | Issues | | | Balance | | |
|---|---|---|---|---|---|---|---|---|---|
| | Qty. | Rate | Amount | Qty. | Rate | Amount | Qty. | Rate | Amount |
| | | | | | | | | | |

**Fig. 16.3** Store ledger card

4. **Stock verification sheet:** This record is prepared at the time of stock taking in the storeroom. After physical verification is over they may be valued to incorporate the value of material to record in the Balance Sheet.

## ■ ISSUE OF MATERIALS

The storekeeper is expected to issue materials only when material requisition note is presented to him. Material Requisition Note is a document drawn on storekeeper by the departmental head. It consists of the following particulars:

1. The number of material requisition note and the data of requisitioning it.
2. The name of the department requisitioning it.
3. Full description and code number of materials required.
4. The quantity of mateials required.
5. The rate at which the issue is to be priced.
6. Total cost of materials.
7. Signature of person preparing the material requisition note to avoid misuse and excess withdrawal of material.

A specimen of Material Requisition Note is given below:

Requisition No.............. Date of Issue..............
Requisition for.............. department Job Order No..............

| Sl. No. | Quantity | Description | Code No. | Cost per unit | Amount | Remarks |
|---|---|---|---|---|---|---|
| | | | | | | |

**Fig. 16.4** Material requisition note

To avoid placing frequent purchase requisition notes sometimes an alternate document is made use of. This is known as Bill of Materials. By placing a Bill of Materials all types of materials required to complete a job can be drawn at a time. This saves considerable amount of time and reduces the clerical work.

Often, the materials issued by the storekeeper to various production department may have been found to be in excess quantity. Such surplus materials are also returned back to storeroom. Similarly, scrap, waste, and spoilt materials are also returned back to storeroom. Such returns of materials are always accompanied by a note known as Materials Returned Note. It is the duty of the storekeeper to properly account for such materials. A speciment of materials received note is given on the next page.

Bin Card Number .............. Sl. No. ..............
Name of the department returning the materials.............. Date..............

Please receive the undernoted materials

| Description of Materials | Reason for returning | Quantity | | | Rate | Value |
|---|---|---|---|---|---|---|
| | | Number | Quantity | Weight | | |
| | | | | | | |

Sd/-

**Fig. 16.5** Materials returned note

Frequently, materials which are not required by one department or found to be excess in one department may be required by another department. Although direct transfer of materials from one department to another department is to be discouraged, yet it is practised in certain circumstances where production process is hampered in the transferee department for want of materials and when materials to be transferred is heavy involving high transportation cost. Under such circumstances, a note is prepared to indicate the transfer of material as Material Transfer Note. This note is passed on to the stores department for making necessary entries and for forwarding to costing department. A specimen of Material Transfer Note is given below:

Issued from .............. Department Date..............
Issued to ..............Department From Job No. ..............
Sd/- ..............
Foreman

| Code No. | Description of materials | Quantity | Dimension | Rate | Amount |
|---|---|---|---|---|---|
| | | | | | |

Authorised by ..................
Received by ....................

**Fig. 16.6** Material transfer note

## ■ SIMPLIFICATION AND STANDARDISATION

### Simplification

Edvin. W. Ely has defined simplification as "the policy of management which seeks to avoid waste by eliminating unnecessary variety and non-essential differences in articles and commodities in everyday use". Simplification means avoidance of superfluous varieties, size, dimension, and grades of materials and component parts." In simple words, it means reduction of a variety of materials or parts. It is also known as variety reduction, as it is essentially a reduction process, a cutting down of varieties and types of materials. The basic principle of simplification is that a single item serves as many different applications as possible.

**Advantages of simplification**

1. It involves less amount of investment of raw materials and components,
2. It occupies less storage space,
3. It involves less material handling equipments,
4. It facilitates effective control over materials,
5. It involves less staff and less clerical work, and
6. Chances of obsolescence are less.

**Disadvantages of simplification**

1. Simplification may make the line of products too narrow and reduce the factory's ability to cater to the needs of the market.
2. The benefits of simplification may not always be realised in the short run unless the factory spends additional funds for required specialised facilities.

**The process of simplification includes the following steps**

1. Specify fixed types of items.
2. Limit the number of sizes, weights, or types of materials.
3. Issue instructions to staff regarding its use.

### Standardisation

Standardisation in a production sense means the reduction of a line of product to fixed types, sizes, and characteristics. E.C. Peck has defined it thus: Standardisation primarily means setting up standards or 'measuring sticks' by which extent, quantity, value, performance, or service may be gaged or determined, and is the crystalised best thought and practice of industry into definite forms for general use.

Standardisation differs from simplification in two respects, namely: (1) Simplification process is commercial and selective, whereas standardisation process is technical and creative, and (2) The purpose of simplification is to determine which sizes, items or varieties of product are most important and to concentrate production to the extent possible on them. Whereas the purpose of standardisation is to establish in use and practice the best design, size, quality, method or process for performing a desired production.

### *Scope of standardisation*

The American Standards Association outlines the scope of the standardisation process to include eight types of standards. They are:

1. Standardisation of favourable varieties of products.
2. Standardisation of nomenclature.
3. Standardisation of dimensions and proportions.
4. Standardisation of purchase specification.
5. Standardisation of methods of test.
6. Standardisation of ratings of machinery.
7. Standardisation of provisions for safety.
8. Standardisation of rules for operation.

1. **Standardisation of favourable varieties of products:** Standardisation to select the most favourable varieties closely resembles the process of simplification. In other words, this standard denote elimination of unnecessary types, sizes and grades, instead it concentrates on most favourable types, sizes, and grades of manufactured products.

2. **Standardisation of nomenclature:** In a factory, many difficulties arise due to the use of special or local names, ambiguous and misleading terms and unusual or little known symbols and abbreviations. To avoid this, it is necessary to establish standard nomenclatures. Some examples of standard nomenclatures relate to mathematical symbols, telephone and telegraphic symbols, topographical symbols. Abbreviations relate to plant illumination, noise control, electrical quantities, etc.

3. **Standardisation of dimensions and proportions:** Standardisation of dimensions and proportions are of prime importance from engineering point of view. The objective of proportional standardisation is to secure interchangeability of parts. This type of standard is indispensable for mass production. The savings arising out of this type of standardisation is substantial.

4. **Standardisation of purchase specifications:** The purpose of this standard is to buy materials on a carefully prepared statement of physical, chemical and other properties so as to ensure the right supply of materials by the suppliers.

5. **Standardisation of methods of test:** This standard ensures that the materials supplied by the supplier satisfy the specification written on purchase order. Various methods of tests have been standardised in order to check the quality and standard of the materials before they are actually used for production purpose.

6. **Standardisation of ratings of machinery:** This type of standardisation sets up methods for rating machinery according to efficiency of operation, useful life, safety, upkeep, etc.

7. **Standardisation of provisions for safety:** Standardisation of provisions for safety is useful to protect the worker's life, limb and health and also bring substantial savings to employer by way of direct and indirect costs.

8. **Standardisation of rules for operation:** These standards are concerned with the technical features of the operations of machinery, equipment and apparatus. They have been set-up in the forms of codes, rules, and schedules of instructions.

***Standardisation in a factory***

Standardisation in factories results in the utilisation of most economical and useful materials, machinery, equipment, processes, methods and practices in production and distribution. It also maintains suitable quality of product consistent with the economics of production and utility. The standardisation process in a factory can be organised under two methods, namely: (i) the standards divisions, and (ii) the standards committee.

Under standard division method, a separate standardisation department in charge of an officer is established. This department is responsible for standardisation work of the factory. The department develops new equipment and improvement in methods of production. It also looks after quality of the finished products.

Under standards committee method, instead of creating a separate department, a committee is set-up whose members change from time to time. Under this method, a committee is constituted for a particular project and after the work is done it is wound up. Such a committee holds frequent meetings, obtains the required information, conducts tests and experiments and after thorough deliberations offers recommendations.

**Advantages of standardisation**

The advantages of standardisation are derived by manufacturers, distributors and consumers.

**1. Advantages to manufacturers**

(a) Standardisation helps in less capital investment on raw materials, component parts, finished stock, special machinery and repair parts.

(b) It enables more economical production through
   (i) Longer runs, by less frequent changes in machine set-up.
   (ii) Proper estimation of production.
   (iii) Less idle equipment.
   (iv) Reduced waste in production.
   (v) Efficient utilisation of labour by means of specialisation.

(c) It facilitates simplified process of selling with a few varieties thereby increasing the rate of turnover.

**2. Advantages to distributors**

(a) Increased rate of turnover due to
   (i) Simplified selling,
   (ii) Elimination of slow moving stock, and
   (iii) Greater concentration of sales on fewer items.

(b) Decreased capital investment in
   (i) Stock in hand, and
   (ii) Storage space.

(c) Less deterioration in quality and obsolescence.

(d) Decreased

(i) Handling charges,

(ii) Clerical and accounting work, and

(iii) Selling expense.

**3. Advantages to consumers**

(a) Better quality of product through the manufacturere's ability to concentrate on better design and reduce manufacturing cost.

(b) Prompt delivery of goods.

**Disadvantages of standardisation**

1. When standardisation is excess, the resulting specialisation makes factory operations rigid and costly.
2. The lack of flexibility in the use of men, materials, and machines, sales and other activities, leads to dislocation when external factors, such as market shift, fluctuation in demand, and technology make changes necessary.
3. Excessive standardised operations and procedure make work irritating for employees and lessen individual initiative.
4. Unless standards are determined in a comprehensive manner by a central agency, the standards determined independently by various departments conflict with each other and thus defeats the very purpose of standardisation.

## SUMMARY

Storekeeping is one of the important aspect of materials management. Purchase of materials is of no relevance unless they are properly protected and preserved against hazardous conditions, bad weather, theft and deterioration. The place where materials are stocked is known as storeroom. The location of storeroom depends upon classification of materials, homogeneity, material handling considerations, physical property of material, quantity and weight of material. For efficient utilisation of storeroom there must be proper layout of stores. The organisation of stores and material management department depends upon the design of the factory, degree of centralisation required, the relationship between storeroom with other departments, such as production and accounts department. Stores and materials management department can be organised under:

(a) Centralised system,

(b) Decentralised system, and

(c) Imprest system.

The stores department is headed by a competent person known as storekeeper. He is responsible for the overall maintenance of the storeroom. His duties range from placing of purchase requisition to issue of materials. The important documents used in connection with storage and issue of materials are:

1. Materials received book

2. Bin card
3. Stores ledger card
4. Stock verification sheet
5. Materials requisition note
6. Materials returned note
7. Materials transfer note.

Simplification reduces excess and undesirable variety in products in order to eliminate waste and to attain economy. Standardisation means the reduction of a line of product to fixed types, sizes and characteristics.

## QUESTIONS

### A. Objective type

**I. Write *True* or *False* for the following sentences:**

(a) Storeroom does not store finished products manufactured in the factory.

(b) "Providing a place for everything and everything in its place" is the key to a successful stores in an organisation.

(c) Without efficient storekeeping no factory can maintain a favourable position.

(d) A storekeeper supervises the work of receiving, storing and issuing of items maintained in the storeroom.

(e) Centralised store system is more suitable for a large sized factory.

(f) A good layout need not give a good appearance.

(g) Volume of stores is an important factor in its location.

(h) Layout of a store should reduce to minimum the total handling cost.

(i) A storekeeper can reject a 'Material Requisition' if it does not bear the signature of competent authority.

(j) A storekeeper need not get signature of the person receiving the materials.

(k) A Bin Card is not filled by the storekeeper.

(l) A stores ledger card contains the quantity, and value of materials received, issued and in balance.

(m) Excess materials lying in a production department need not be returned to the storeroom.

(n) The returned material is received by the stores accountant.

(o) Materials from one department to another should be transferred through materials received note.

(p) Under a 'decentralised storekeeping' system several employees working out of one store room are responsible for the issue and control of all items.

(q) Interchangeability of parts among product models not only reduces investment in plant but also makes for continuous use of machinery.

(r) Parts and standard supply items used in small quantities are usually cheaper to buy than to fabricate.

(s) Whereas product simplification eliminates uneconomical variety, diversification adds new products, styles and sizes.

**II. Match the following:**

| | Column A | | Column B |
|---|---|---|---|
| 1. | Purchase requisition note | (a) | Person nominated by management |
| 2. | Purchase order | (b) | Stores attendant |
| 3. | Materials received note | (c) | Head of the department |
| 4. | Bill of materials | (d) | Laboratory technician |
| 5. | Material requisition note | (e) | Cost clerk |
| 6. | Stores ledger card | (f) | Foreman |
| 7. | Material verfication note | (g) | Purchase manager |
| 8. | Material transfer note | (h) | Production control department |
| 9. | Material inspection note | (i) | Storekeeper |
| 10. | Bin card | (j) | Material inspection clerk |

## B. Very short answer type

1. Mention the factors to be considered while locating storeroom.
2. What do you mean by centralised system of storage?
3. What do you mean by location of storeroom? How does it differ from stores layout?
4. What do you mean by decentralised system of storage?
5. What do you mean by impress system of storage?
6. State the requisites of a storekeeper?
7. Mention the important records used for recording stores.
8. What do you mean by bin card? Give its specimen.
9. What is stores ledger card? Give its specimen.
10. State four points of differences between a bin card and stores ledger card.
11. What do you mean by material rquisition note? Give its specimen.
12. What do you mean by material transfer note? Give its specimen.
13. Define simplification.
14. Define standardisation.
15. Distinguish between simplification and standardisation.
16. State the advantages of simplification.
17. State the disadvantages of simplification.
18. Mention the advantages of standardisation to the manufacturer.
19. Mention the advantages of standardisation to the distributor.
20. Mention the disadvantages of standardisation.

## C. Short answer type

1. Explain the objects and importance of storekeeping.
2. Outline the essentials of storekeeping.
3. State the principles and advantages of store layout. Draw up an imaginary layout of stores for a small sized factory.

4. Compare and contrast the merits and demerits of centralised and decentralised stores system.
5. What do you mean by centralised stores? State its merits and demerits.
6. Outline the duties and responsibilities of a storekeeper.
7. Briefly explain the various records used for recording stores items.
8. What do you mean by standardisation? Discuss its scope.
9. Explain how standardisation process can be organised in factories.
10. Explain the advantages and disadvantages of standardisation.

## ANSWERS TO OBJECTIVE TYPE QUESTIONS

I. (a) F, (b) T, (c) T, (d) T, (e) T,
(f) F, (g) T, (h) T, (i) T, (j) F,
(k) F, (l) T, (m) F, (n) F, (o) F,
(p) F, (q) T, (r) T, (s) T.

II. 1. (i), 2. (g), 3. (j), 4. (h), 5. (f),
6. (e), 7. (a), 8. (c), 9. (d), 10. (b).

# Chapter 17

# MATERIAL CONTROL

## ■ INTRODUCTION

In olden days, the function of controlling the materials in factories was thought of "minding the stores". This function was then performed by uninspired clerks with no training. There was no systematic way of controlling the materials and it was being performed haphazardly. When they came to know that materials were running out of storesroom, they simply used to arrange for more materials so that production would not be stopped. It was a misnomer to call such an approach as material control. One can label such a system as material miss-control. But, nowadays, because of growing knowledge of materials management, the material control manager has gained skill through training in this field. A strict control over material ensures exact quantity and quality of materials on hand at the time required with a minimum expenditure of investment.

## ■ DEFINITION OF MATERIAL CONTROL

The American Production and Inventory Control Society defines materials control as "the function of maintaining a constantly available supply of raw materials, purchased parts and supplies that are required for the manufacture of products. Functional responsibilities includes the requisitioning of materials for purchase in economic quantities at the proper time, and their receipts, storage and protection; the issuing of materials to production upon authorized request; and the maintenance and verification of inventory records".

Very often, the term "inventory control" is used to denote Material Control. But the term Material Control is used in the broadest sense and it includes inventory control as well. Inventory Control has been defined by the American Production and Inventory Control Society as "the technique of maintaining stock keeping items at desired levels, whether they be raw materials, work in process or finished products". The determination of desired levels and maintaining inventory at these levels is the core of the inventory control problem.

In brief, Material Control may be defined as the systematic control concerned with acquisition, storage, and usage of materials so as to minimise wastage and losses and, at the same time, avoiding excessive investment on materials.

When we analyse the above definitions we come to see that material control embraces the following:

1. Determining material requirements.
2. Preparing the purchase requisitions and placing orders with the suppliers.
3. Receiving purchased materials.

4. Inspecting purchased materials and delivering them to the storeroom for storage.
5. Entering receipts in stores records.
6. Issuing of materials to various departments.
7. Recording of issue in stores records.
8. Receiving, entering and issuing transactions from accounting records.

## SCOPE AND IMPORTANCE OF MATERIAL CONTROL

The scope of Material Control can be listed as follows:

1. Determining the policies to guide inventory control programmes.
2. Determining the technique of material control.
3. Determining the appropriate organizational structure for material control.
4. Determining the economic order quantities.
5. Determining the safety stock and recording quantities.
6. Determining the lead time.
7. Minimizing handling and storing procedures.
8. Determining effective layout of storeroom for effective utilisation of storage space and simplified receiving and issuing procedure.

The importance of Material Control can be outlined under the following points:

1. It ensures regular supply of material uninterrupted production.
2. It minimises investment of capital on purchase of materials. It also reduces danger of obsolescence.
3. It reduces inventory carrying cost.
4. It reduces cost of placing frequent orders.
5. It avoids duplication in ordering the materials.
6. It permits better utilisation of available materials by transferring them from one department to another, when required.
7. It avoids theft or loss of materials on account of carelessness.
8. It facilitates the location and disposal of obsolete and slow moving materials.
9. It simplifies the accounting of materials.
10. It makes use of modern techniques, such as standardisation, value analysis, import substitution which cut down the material cost.

## OBJECTIVES OF MATERIAL CONTROL

1. To maintain the required material in sufficient quantities. This is undertaken with the technique of level setting.
2. To ensure required quality of materials.
3. To minimise and eliminate loses due to wastages which may occur due to dust, rust, moisture, pilferage and bad and careless handling of materials.
4. To ensure that materials are purchased at minimum cost taking the advantages of trade discount and cash discount.

5. To ensure that materials received are in accordance with purchase order.
6. To avoid overstocking of materials which has adverse effects on capital cost, space cost, equipment cost and personal cost.
7. To report promptly and frequently to top level management for planning of production.
8. To facilitate prompt payment of suppliers so as to keep up prestige and goodwill of the factory.

## ■ PREREQUISITES FOR MATERIAL CONTROL

In order to ensure the above objectives, certain definite prerequisites must be fulfilled. They are as follows:

1. An adequate, well-arranged storeroom with (a) definite location of material, and (b) definite identification of material.
2. Centralisation of authority and responsibility under the supervision of a competent storekeeper.
3. A system for counting and inspection of materials on receipt.
4. Absolute control over issue of materials.
5. Adequate recording for receiving, storing and issuing the materials.
6. A system of continuous stock taking.
7. Provision for eliminating slow moving and obsolete materials.

## ■ ELEMENTS IN MATERIAL CONTROL

There are three elements in material control process. They are:

(a) Planning material needs,
(b) Fixing responsibility for performance, and
(c) Measuring the results.

### (a) Planning material needs

The basis for planning the material needs are sales forecasts, customer's orders, production authorisation, transfer from production departments. In addition to planning and procuring the exact quantity of materials they must be easily and readily made available without much internal transportation, i.e., material handling facility. Planning of materials is generally made a year in advance and altered to meet the changing conditions throughout the year.

### (b) Fixing responsibility for performance

The person who is responsible for purchasing the planned materials is the purchase manager. The responsibility fixed for the purchase manager relates to such questions as what to buy, when to buy and how to buy. The answers to these questions are to buy the right type of material, to buy at the right time and in right quantities.

### (c) Measuring the results

The purchased materials are compared with budgeted materials to know the efficiency in purchasing department. The buying reports help in this regard.

## TECHNIQUES OF MATERIAL CONTROL

Several techniques are available to control the materials. Most important among them are:

1. ABC analysis.
2. Level setting.
3. Economic order quantity.
4. Material verification.
5. Inventory turnover ratio.
6. Classification and codification.

### 1. ABC analysis

The ABC analysis underlines a very important principle: "VITAL FEW-TRIVIAL MANY". The ABC analysis as a technique of material control is a procedure in which materials are classified into high-value (class A), medium-value (class B), and low-value (class C). Generally speaking, the entire quantity and types of materials are not of equal importance in factories. Some materials are very costly while some are very cheap. Depending upon their relative economic value, the materials are designated as A, B, C and so on. In most of the factories, about 10% of the items constitute about 70% of the total value of the materials, the next 20% of the items accounts for about 20% of the total value of materials and the last 70% items constitute about 10% of the material value. But in terms of consumption of materials 'C' category of materials rank first and 'B' and 'A' rank second and third respectively. Therefore, 'C' class of materials should be stocked in bulk quantities so that production could be carried out continuously.

Under this technique, control is exercised in two ways. First, the investment of capital on materials are judiciously utilised in the sense that 'A' category of material constituting highest value of materials are not unnecessarily bought and stocked. Secondly, in terms of storage and preservation utmost control is exercised over 'A' category of material by an experienced person, a moderate control over 'B' category of materials and a loose control over 'C' category of materials. As control is exercised by selecting the items of materials, this technique is also known as selective control of materials. While exercising control over these categories of materials the following policies are adopted, general policy for class 'A' items:

1. This category of materials must be held at absolute minimum level. However there is a need to expedite their delivery.
2. They must be promptly recorded in all the stores documents.
3. A senior person must be in charge of such materials.
4. More than one supplier must be relied upon for such materials.
5. Frequent review of their consumption, purchase and follow-up should be made.

***General policy for 'B' class items***

1. These items should be ordered less frequently than 'A' class items, may be 4 to 6 times a year,
2. Stock and issue records must be necessarily maintained for this class of materials, and
3. Economic order quantities and re-order level should be carefully fixed for these items.

***General policy for 'C' class items***

1. Keep the stock of materials in relatively large quantities.

2. Simplified records can be maintained for such materials.
3. These materials need not be subject to tight material control and can be under the charge of even a junior person.

***Purpose of ABC analysis***

The object of carrying out ABC analysis is to develop policy guidelines for selective controls. Normally, once ABC analysis has been done, the following broad policy guidelines can be established in respect of each category.

| A Items (High consumption value) | B Items (Moderate value) | C Items (Low consumption value) |
|---|---|---|
| (1) Very strict control | Moderate control | Low control |
| (2) No safety stock | Low safety stock | High safety stock |
| (3) Frequent ordering | Once in a quarter | Bulk ordering once in 6 months |
| (4) Weekly control statements | Monthly control reports | Quarterly control reports |
| (5) Rigorous value analysis | Moderate value analysis | Minimum value analysis |
| (6) Accurate forecasting for material planning | Estimate based on past data | Rough estimate for planning |
| (7) Maximum efforts to reduce lead time | Moderate efforts | Minimum efforts. |

**Advantages of ABC analysis**

1. A strict control is exercised on materials representing high material cost.
2. Investment in inventory can be kept at minimum by budgeting the purchase of materials.
3. Storage cost is also minimised.

## 2. Level setting

Level setting as a technique of material control helps in avoiding the over and under investment of capital on materials and incidentally the overstocking and understocking of materials. The various stock levels are determined by the management and it is the duty of storekeeper to maintain the material in their respective levels. There are four different levels of maintaining the materials in storeroom. They are:

(a) Maximum level
(b) Minimum level
(c) Re-order level
(d) Danger level.

(a) **Maximum level:** It is a level beyond which no material is allowed for storage. This is because, if stock exceeds this level it will (i) involve more investment, (ii) require more space, (iii) more wastage due to damage, spoilage, theft, obsolescence, and (iv) more storage cost. This level is fixed after considering the following factors:

(a) Amount of capital available
(b) Rate of consumption of materials
(c) Time taken by the supplier to supply the materials
(d) Storage space available
(e) Market conditions and fluctuation in prices
(f) Seasonal availability of materials
(g) Possibility of loss due to deterioration, evaporation, etc.
(h) Government policy regarding import of materials
(i) Maintenance cost, such as insurance, salaries to staff etc., and
(j) Need of buffer stock i.e. safety stock in relation to actual stock.

(b) **Minimum level:** It is the level below which materials should not be allowed to fall. This level is fixed in order to avoid stoppage of production due to shortage of materials. This level is fixed after considering the following factors:

(a) Rate of consumption of materials.
(b) Time taken to supply the materials by the suppliers.
(c) Nature of item, as for example material specially purchased against customer's specific order when no minimum level is necessary.

(c) **Re-order level:** This level is fixed in between maximum level and minimum level. Whenever this level is reached, the storekeeper has to prepare a purchase requisition note for replenishing the stock of materials. This level is fixed after considering the following factors:

(a) Maximum usage of materials
(b) Time taken by the supplier to supply the material
(c) Economic order quantity
(d) Rate of consumption of materials
(e) Minimum level
(f) Possible unexpected delays in obtaining the fresh supplies, such as rains, war, labour trouble, transport inadequacy, etc.

(d) **Danger level:** This is a level which is fixed below the minimum level. This level indicates that materials have touched the lowest point and it is red signal given to storekeeper to arrange for emergency purchase of materials for replenishing the stock. On reaching this level, usually the storekeeper issues materials unless he receives instructions from production control department as to the department for which materials are to be issued.

## 3. Economic order quantity

One of the problems encountered by the purchase manager at the time of purchasing the materials is the quantity of material to be bought at a time. If large quantity is bought, the cost of carrying the materials, such as storage space, cost of insurance, interest on capital borrowed, obsolescence, etc. is high. However, when materials are bought in bulk the benefits according from quantity purchase, such as trade discount, free home delivery facility, after sales services, and credit facilities can be derived. On the other hand, if materials are purchased in small quantities, the cost of ordering the materials, such as cost of inviting quotation, cost of placing frequent orders, postage, and telephone and telegram expenses, and travelling expenses will be high. But the cost of carrying the materials will be less. Therefore, the quantity to be ordered at a time must be determined by considering these two factories, viz., (1) cost of acquisition, and (2) cost of carrying. Economic order quantity is taken at the point where the cost of carrying equals the cost of ordering the materials. Thus, economic order quantity gives us the most favourable quantity which is to be ordered at a time. The total investment in buying the economic order quantity is also less when compared to purchase of any other quantity.

## 4. Material verification system

It is a system under which the materials physically present in the storeroom are checked with the store records to know whether all the materials are intact. This process is also known as stock taking which helps accounting purpose. The physical verification of materials with the store records reveals discrepances and condition of materials. The discrepancy may be due to (1) clerical error, (2) wrong placement of materials in different racks, (3) incorrect counting, (4) incorrect weight, (5) omission in recording the issued material, (6) theft, (7) loss due to damage, leakage and evaporation, (8) excess issue of material. Material verification may be undertaken by the following methods.

(A) Annual stock verification, and

(B) Perpetual inventory system.

### *(A) Annual stock verification*

Under this system, all the materials kept in the storeroom are verified once in a year. The stock verification is undertaken at the end ot financial year. The stock verification under this system is undertaken by the storekeeper along with his assistants. During the period of annual stock taking, no material is issued or received. The following procedure is involved in annual stock verification.

1. An advance notice is served to all the heads of the department concerned regarding the stock verification.
2. The staff of storekeeping department is assigned duties for such verification.
3. Materials are arranged for easy verification.
4. Each item of material is checked by the concerned staff.
5. Reports are prepared for excesses, shortage and discrepancies.
6. Arrangements are made to dispose such material which are incapable of use.

The specimen used for stock verification is given below:

| Sl. No. | Code No. | Nomenclature | Unit | Actual Stock | Book Balance | Quantity | | |
|---|---|---|---|---|---|---|---|---|
| | | | | | | Excess | Shortage | Removal |
| | | | | | | | | |

Sd/ Storekeeper Sd – Verifier

**Fig. 17.1** Specimen of stock verification

**Disadvantages of annual stock verification**

1. The factory is to be closed during the period of stock verification as materials cannot be issued during this period.
2. Control cannot be exercised on shortage of materials, because it would have occurred long before the annual stock taking.
3. The system is expensive.

### *(B) Perpetual inventory system*

The disadvantages of annual stock taking can be obviated by the system of perpetual inventory control. Under this system of stock verification, materials are verified on a continuous basis. The verification is undertaken in such a way that all materials in the storeroom get checked up at least two or three times a year. The selected items of materials are counted at frequent intervals and compared with bin card and stores ledger card. Any difference between the book entries and items of materials denote discrepancies. Therefore, this difference should be investigated, reconciled and corrected at frequent intervals.

**Advantages**

1. As stock verification is undertaken on a continuous basis the need to close the factory does not arise as in the case of annual stock taking.
2. It enables preparation of interim profit and loss account and balance sheet because the data relating to closing stock is frequently available.
3. Control over materials can be constantly exercised as and when discrepanies are located.
4. This system avoids overstocking and understocking of materials.
5. This system reveals obsolete or slow moving materials which can be promptly dealt with.
6. It serves as a moral check on storekeeper and his staff because it is undertaken by people nominated by the management.

**Disadvantages**

1. Due to perpetual inventory system, the work of storekeeping becomes complicated as the stores are checked three or four times in a year. It also leads to confusion as regards the stocks available.
2. This system puts more mental pressure on the storekeeper as he is answerable for the stock position often and again when the discrepancy is noticed while checking materials.
3. The administrative work in the stores department increases due to frequent checking and naturally more staff will have to be appointed in the stores department.
4. It is very difficult to check the entire stock in the store three or four times in a year, particularly when the store is large with wide variety of stocks.
5. The staff of storeroom feels that it is an extra burden on their part to assist the stock verification authorities nominated by the management.
6. Perpetual inventory system is costly as it needs modern costly devices like computer or electronic data processing machine.
7. Supply of material from the stores to different departments may be delayed particularly when the periodical inspection work is in progress.

## 5. Inventory turnover ratio

Inventory turnover ratio as a technique of material control is used to know whether materials are fast moving or slow moving. Material turnover ratio is obtained when value of materials consumed is divided by average value of inventory. A high ratio indicates fast moving materials and hence necessary arrangements can be made to procure and stock such materials in required quantities. Whereas slow moving and obsolete materials need not be unnecessarily stocked in bulk quantities, thereby reducing excess investment on it. Inventory turnover rate can also be indicated by the number of days in which the average inventory is consumed. This is done by dividing 365 days by the inventory turnover ratio. If the length of the inventory turnover period, is short, material is said to be fast moving.

## 6. Classification and codification of materials

In a large factory where large quantities of a wide variety of materials are bought, there is a tendency to mix up all types of materials. So, unless they are properly classified and codified, and stored properly, it becomes very difficult to locate and issue them. Hence, production gets delayed to that extent. So, classification and codification of materials become essential. Classification means a standardised arrangement by groups of materials under a common designation according to similarities of kind, attributes or relations. Materials can be classified on the basis of general classification and according to the manufacturing process. On the basis of general classification, materials can be classified as (a) raw materials, (b) component parts, (c) work in process, (d) equipment and spare parts, (e) tools, (f) jigs and fixture used for holding materials, (g) packing materials, (h) scraps, and (i) sundry supplies. On the basis of manufacturing process, materials can be classified as pre-process stock, intermediate stock and finished goods.

Codification means assigning a code number or symbol to a store item. The following are different methods of coding the material:

1. **Alphabetical method:** Under this method, alphabetic letters are used for coding the materials.

2. **Mnemonic method:** When the letters are used to help memory, such a method is known as mnemonic letter. In fact, this is a modified form of alphabetic method. Under this method, usually the first letter or abbreviation of materials are used to codify the materials.

**Examples:**

| *Name of Material* | *Code* |
|---|---|
| Rubber | R |
| Screw | Sc |
| Ball bearing | BB |
| Building material | BM |

3. **Numerical method:** Under this method, numbers are used to codify materials. Where large variety of materials are used decimal system of codification can be used.

4. **Alpha-numerical method:** This is a combination of alphabetical and numerical methods wherein both alphabetic letters as well as numbers together are used to codify the materials.

**Examples:**

| *Name of Material* | *Code* |
|---|---|
| Plastic Sheet ¼ thick-II grade | Ps-142 |

**Advantages of classification and codification**

(a) It avoids use of long names,

(b) It helps in early identification of materials
(c) It helps in machine accounting
(d) It minimises clerical and paper work
(e) It ensures secrecy.

## ■ EVALUATION OF MATERIAL CONTROL

The following criteria can be used to evaluate the material control system:

1. The system must furnish timely, adequate and accurate information. This can be reviewed by determining the worth of economic order quantity as to purchase of right quantity of materials involving less capital investment or less storage space.
2. The system must be flexible to accommodate necessary changes: In today's dynamic production system, the accumulation and depletion of materials are natural. If data relating to additions and deletions of materials are not made available then the system of material control cannot be designated as effective one.
3. The system must be simple and understandable to operate: Where the material control is not simple, it becomes difficult to implement it and the system becomes waste.
4. The system should be economical to operate: The cost of operating the system should be less than material cost. Where a simple punched card system can be used, it becomes unnecessary to use a computer. Similarly, where material control can be exercised manually it is costly to use punched card system.
5. The system must permit "management by exception": The costly and valuable materials must be under the charge of senior and responsible person whereas usual items of materials can be taken care of even by a newcomer.

## SUMMARY

As materials cost constitute a significant portion of total cost of manufacturing a product utmost care must be exercised over materials. Material control embraces within it the control over purchase, storage and issue of material. Material control aims at reduction of unnecessary investment on purchase of materials and reduction in wastage and losses. The three elements in material control programme are:

1. Planning material needs
2. Fixing responsibilities for performance
3. Measuring the results.

The important techniques of material control are:

1. ABC Analysis
2. Level Setting
3. Economic order quantity
4. Material verification
5. Inventory turnover ratio
6. Classification and codification of materials.

## QUESTIONS

### A. Objective type

### I. Fill in the blanks:

1. Allotting symbols to the different items of stores is known as .................. .
2. Maintenance of inventory record on a continuous basis is known as .................. .
3. Under ABC analysis, 'A' stands for .................. value of materials.
4. Materials turnover is a ratio of .................. to .................. .
5. Two important opposing factors in fixing the economic order quantity are .................. and .................. .

### II. Write *True* or *False* for the following sentences:

1. Under the "Classification System", store items are arranged and placed in the stockroom in the order corresponding to the numeric or the mnemonic method of identification.
2. The "economic order point" indicates the minimum quantity to which stock may fall without any need for replenishment.
3. The taking of physical inventory is necessary under perpetual inventory system.
4. Building up of big inventories is always profitable because prices rise very fast.
5. More the number of purchase orders lesser will be the inventory carrying cost.
6. Material control strikes a balance between stockout situation and building up of large inventories.
7. Longer the lead time, larger will be the inventory.
8. The wages paid to the store staff is part of the inventory carrying cost.
9. EOQ strikes a balance between inventory carrying cost and ordering cost.
10. Classification C represents smaller number of store items having about 70% of the total value of stores material.
11. The numerical system of coding is the best and most popular codification system used for inventions.
12. Although the coding system eliminates the necessity of using long names, it uses a long chain of numbers which may be very confusing.
13. 'C' class items must be strictly controlled.
14. There can be considerable saving on inventory cost if only 'A' class items are strictly controlled.
15. Perpetual inventory system enables the management to ascertain stock at any time without the expense of physical stock taking.
16. In ABC analysis 'A' group of items consists of those materials the value of which is not high but which are used in large quantities.
17. The economic order quantity is the Reorder quantity.

### III. Choose the correct answer from the following alternatives:

1. Which of the following methods of material control aim at concentrating efforts on selected items of materials?

   (a) Perpetual inventory system (b) Material turnover

   (c) Level setting (d) ABC analysis

2. The classification of items in ABC analysis is made on the basis of
   (a) investment value of materials (b) consumption value of material
   (c) quantity of materials consumed (d) all of these
3. The storekeeper should initiate a purchase requisition when stock reaches
   (a) maximum level (b) minimum level
   (c) recorder level (d) danger level
4. Which one of the following techniques of material control helps in easy identification of materials in storeroom?
   (a) EOQ (b) Level setting
   (c) Material turnover ratio (d) Classification and codification
5. Which one of the following techniques of material control aims at minimising theft and losses of materials?
   (a) ABC Analysis (b) Material Turnover Ratio
   (c) Perpetual Inventory Control (d) Level Setting

## B. Very short answer type

1. Define material control.
2. What do you mean by ABC analysis?
3. Define classification of material.
4. Define codification.
5. Distinguish between Mnemonic and Decimal codification.
6. What do you mean by economic order quantity?
7. What do you mean by maximum level?
8. What do you mean by minimum level?
9. What do you mean by danger level?
10. What do you mean by re-order level?
11. What do you mean by carrying cost? Give examples.
12. Define Inventory Turnover Ratio.
13. What do you mean by ordering cost? Give examples.
14. What do you mean by perpetual inventory system?
15. Distinguish between annual stock taking and perpetual inventory system.

## C. Short answer type

1. Define material control. Outline its scope and importances.
2. Explain the objectives of material control.
3. What is ABC analysis of material control? What policies are to be followed in respect of each category of material?
4. Explain various levels of stocking materials.
5. Explain the significance of economic order quantity.

6. "The perpetual inventory system is an integral part of the material control". Explain the statement by bringing out its merits.
7. How are materials classified and codified? State the merits of classification and codification of materials.

### D. Long answer type

Explain the various techniques of material control.

## ANSWERS TO OBJECTIVE TYPE QUESTIONS

I. (1) Codification (2) Perpetual Inventory System (3) high
(4) material consumed; average stock (5) cost of ordering; cost of carrying

II. (1) T, (2) T, (3) F, (4) F, (5) T,
(6) T, (7) T, (8) T, (9) T, (10) F,
(11) T, (12) T, (13) F, (14) F, (15) T,
(16) F, (17) T

III. (1) (d), (2) (d), (3) (c), (4) (d), (5) (c).

# Chapter 18

# MATERIAL HANDLING

## ■ INTRODUCTION

"Material handling" refers to the study of the movement of materials from one place to another within the factory. Material handling constitutes the third phase of materials management, the other two being purchasing and storage of materials. The importance of materials handling cannot be underestimated in spite of the fact that mechanical equipments are largely being used. It has been estimated that one out of ten in the labour force is involved in handling materials and in a typical factory 50 tons of product must be handled to produce one ton of finished product.

In the words of Keith Lockyer, in many factories, at least one-quarter of the final cost is attributable to the handling of materials. The manager of a modern factory has realised that material handling is not merely a substitute for a man with a strong back and a weak mind, but instead is a vital element in the continuous flow of goods through a factory. Congestion of materials in the work areas and delays in the supplying of materials are removed through mechanical handling devices.

## ■ DEFINITION OF MATERIAL HANDLING

According to James Lundy, "Material handling includes any and all movements and packaging of materials, assemblies and products". Carson, Bolz and Young in their book, "Production Handbook" have given the following definitions of material handling:

1. "Movement and storage of material at the lowest possible cost through the use of proper methods and equipment."
2. "Lifting, shifting and placing of material which affects saving of money, time and place."
3. "Art and Science of conveying, elevating, positioning, transporting, packaging and storing of material."
4. The material handling division of the American Society of Mechanical Engineers has defined material handling as "the art and science involving the moving, packaging and storing of substances in any form."

## ■ OBJECTIVES OF MATERIAL HANDLING

The objectives of material handling can be explained as follows:

1. **Reduction in the cost of each part handled:** The main objective of material handling is to reduce the overall cost of material handling by reducing the number of handlings involved.

But the overall material handling costs can be reduced only if the unit cost, i.e., the cost of each part handled is reduced. This approach requires that cost of handling be allocated to its component parts which are involved.

2. **Reduction in the manufacturing cycle time:** Effective handling of materials from the stage of receipt to the stage of completion involves reduction in production time. By means of speeding up or by handling over short distance, it results in the reduction of inventory cost.
3. **Contributing towards a better control of the flow of goods:** In continuous manufacturing factories, where all the processes of production are predetermined, and where production of one process depends upon another process, material handling plan can effect considerable amount of savings in the flow of goods.
4. **Providing improved working conditions and greater safety:** The Factories Act requires adherence to safe handling practices. Safe handling of materials also reduces industrial accidents. This reduces the tangible saving in the form of reduced insurance rates and an intangible saving in the form of improved employee morale.
5. **Lesser rejection of goods:** Handling of materials carefully, to a large extent, reduces breakages of and damages to the finished products. This is more so in the case of fragile goods, such as glass and ceramics. Excessive damages and breakages add to the increased cost of production and so a careful material handling plan is necessary.
6. **Increase in storage capacity:** A well-designed material handling plan saves to an extent storage space in factories.
7. **Increased productivity at lower manufacturing cost:** A material handling system improves productivity by moving materials in the fastest, most efficient and economical way possible.

## ■ SCOPE OF MATERIAL HANDLING

The scope of material handling activity depends upon the type of factory, the type of product manufactured, the value of the product, the relative importance of material handling to the factory, the number of employees involved and the organisational structure of the factory.

The scope of material handling can be discussed under the following order:

1. **Traditional point of view:** Under the traditional point of view, the emphasis of material-handling is primarily on the movement of material from one location to another within the factory. The aim of material-handling engineer was to find out the best way to move things from one point to another point. He is mostly concerned with solving individual or isolated material handling problem situations. He had to move from crisis to crisis to meet the immediate needs of those who called for his services and most of his attention was given to those who shouted the loudest. He used to pay little attention to the possible inter-relationships between the various individual handling situations. Material handling functions in this fashion were neither very efficient nor progressive.
2. **From the point of view of the entire factory:** The attention of the material handling engineering centres on the overall flow of material in the factory. The management is concerned with the inter-relationships between all handling problems and the possibility of establishing a

general overall material handling plan. Its effort is directed towards integrating material handling plan for the entire factory.

3. **Systems point of view:** Under this systems, the material-handling engineer visualises the material-handling problems, the physical distribution activities, and all closely related functions as one, all encompassing system. This view is broader in scope can be compared to the earlier mentioned two points of view. This view conceptualises the total solution to the overall material handling problem in terms of a theoretical system.

## GUIDING PRINCIPLES OF MATERIAL HANDLING

The principles of material handling helps the material handling engineer in solving problems relating to material handling. James Lundy has enunciated the following principles of material handling:

1. **Eliminate as much as possible:** According to this principle, elimination of unnecessary material handling reduces the cost of material handling.
2. **Make accurate analysis:** In order to make a rational decision on material handling, this principle emphasises that the present cost and future cost of material handling must be determined.
3. **Use charts, diagrams and summaries to analyse problems:** As it is difficult to understand numbers, the material handling analyst has to make use of charts and diagrams.
4. **Remove handling tasks from among the duties of direct labour personnel:** This principle lays down that a separate set of employees are to be recruited for performing material handling. If direct labourers are utilised for this purpose their skill is underutilised.
5. **Avoid using handling equipment below its capacity:** This principle emphasises that material handling equipment must be used to its full extent.
6. **Use of unit loads:** This principle connotes the movement and storage of items in groups rather than individually.
7. Using more materials at higher speeds as well as in larger groups.
8. **More materials at constant rates of speed:** This is to prevent frequent overload and idle periods in the production departments.
9. **Use the space fully for storing and moving:** Empty space above the operating machines is wasteful, overhead conveyors can be used or goods can be stored to utilise the space fully.
10. **Use gravity to full advantage:** Gravity flow of materials and semi-finished goods does not involve power cost.
11. **Arrangement of equipment for the minimisation of transport distance:** Handling cost increases with increase in distance; so, equipments must be arranged for minimising transport cost.
12. **Avoiding backtracking:** This ensures smooth flow of materials.
13. **Avoiding rehandling of goods:** This is to ensure elimination of unnecessary putting-down and picking-up operations.
14. **Keep operations from being congested:** In a congested area, one may have to move some materials back and forth in order to gain access to an item being sought.

15. **Selecting the most flexible equipment:** The greater the flexibility of equipment, the more readily a change can be made when a system becomes obsolete. It is also possible to minimise capital expenditure by selecting equipment capable of performing a variety of functions.
16. **Using mechanical handling devices to eliminate normal activity:** This is helpful, especially when hot or heavy material or continuous handling is involved.
17. **Combining the movement and storage of materials:** Instead of storing items in one place and then carrying them to their destination, one can store materials on an inclined rack which feeds them forward, as needed.
18. Provide a means for having material handling equipment at the right place and at the right time.
19. Train operators in good handling techniques.
20. **Efficient handling is safe handling:** When safe conditions prevail, employees can devote their attention to output rather than self-preservation.
21. **Keeping passage ways lighted and unobstructed:** By this principle, damage and injuries can be reduced.
22. **Labeling of parts or containers clearly with handling instructions:** When the containers are not marked properly, wrong deliveries are frequent which are confusing and costly.
23. Treat the handling of scrap materials commensurate with other materials.
24. Have a well planned preventive maintenance programme for material handling equipment.
25. Assign the responsibility of promoting good material handling to one individual.

## Factors affecting the selection of material handling equipment

The following factors are to be considered when choosing material handling equipment:

1. **Type of material to be handled:** This includes size, weight and strength of the materials.
2. **Type of production:** For the sake of material handling purpose, the types of production can be considered as continuous production or batch production. If continuous type of production is envisaged, conveyor belts and overhead conveyors might be suitable. In the case of batch production, powered trucks and portable conveyors are useful.
3. **Factory building:** The determining factors are the number of floors, provision of lifts, heights of ceiling, floor level, etc.
4. **Handling costs:** It is difficult to assess material handling costs. However, a full study of cost should be made not only of labour but also of handling equipment and containers.
5. **Adaptability:** The carrying capacity of the equipment should match with the material handling problem. Wherever possible, the equipment should have flexibility to handle more than one material.
6. **Speed:** Rapidity of movement of materials within the limits of the production process should be considered.
7. **Space requirement:** The space required to install or operate materials handling equipment is an important factor in selecting the material handling equipment.
8. **Supervision required:** This refers to the degree of automaticity designed into the equipment.
9. **Ease of maintenance:** Equipment selected should be easily maintained at reasonable cost.
10. **Environment:** Equipment selected must conform to any environmental regulation.

**Types of material handling equipments:** Material handling is undertaken through the medium of (1) manpower, (2) gravity flow, and (3) mechanical means.

1. **Handling by manpower:** Traditionally, most of the materials and semi-finished products were handled by employees, but this resulted in loss of production time as the employees had to concentrate on handling material instead of producing goods. However, this is still used in small-scale industries, as it is very flexible, where it is essential to use employees for handling materials. The following points must be remembered:
   (a) Do not use skilled workers for moving materials, instead use unskilled workers.
   (b) Do not move in small quantities. Instead, use sacks or baskets to move in bulk quantities. This saves time in material handling.
   (c) The load to be carried should not be kept above the height of the shoulder or kept on the floor. Instead, keep the loads at the working height.
2. **Use of gravity:** Gravity always provides a cheap and reliable source of movement of materials. But, this is not always possible except in the case of multi-storey building.
3. **Mechanical equipments:** While gravity conveyor works only on a downward machine, mechanical equipments are used to handle materials on the same working level or above the working level. Some of the mechanical equipments used to handle materials are:
   (a) **Conveyors:** The term "conveyor" includes all equipments for conveying materials between two fixed points with continuous forward movement. Conveyors may be of the following types:
      (i) **Belt conveyors:** It consists of power-driven endless belt with terminal pulleys. They transport materials horizontally. It is mostly preferred because of its smooth noiseless operation and easy reversibility. It carries loaded materials in the forward direction and empty containers are carried in the reverse direction.
      (ii) **Suspension conveyor:** This runs above normal head height and carries containers for the movement of goods. This is mostly used in the finishing department where finished products are to be moved from the finishing department to the warehouse.
      (iii) **Pneumatic conveyor:** It is a system of tubes through which bulk materials are conveyed under pressure or vacuum system.
   (b) **Cranes:** Cranes are versatile lifting and transporting mechanisms that are made adaptable to a wide variety of jobs by the attachment of an almost indefinite number of specially designed grabs. Cranes are of three types, namely (1) fixed cranes, having a limited handling area, (2) travelling cranes which travel along a fixed track, and (3) portable cranes having considerable mobility.
   (c) **Lifts:** Lifts are vertical conveyors, usually working between various floor levels.
   (d) **Hoist:** It has a large steel bucket fitted with a flanged wheel running on guides of steel channels. It is a device which is complete in itself for receiving, elevating and discharging batches of materials.
   (e) **Chutes:** A chute is a wooden or metal trough inclined in such a way that the articles slide down when placed upon it. It is used for transporting stores from upper to lower floors, and can best carry loose materials and light packages.

(f) **Pallets:** A large elevated platform with a fork is called a pallet. A pallet is so designed that forks of the truck roll just pass into it. One pallet may be used to accommodate one package of roughly the same base area.

(g) **Industrial vehicles:** These include trucks, rail, cars, trailers, tractors, trollies, which are used to carry semi-finished products from one department to another department and finally to the warehouse.

**Advantages of mechanical handling**

1. The manufacturing cycle time can be reduced by the elimination of non-productive time in the manufacturing process. Research has indicated that at least 30% of the total time required in manufacturing is consumed by material handling.
2. Human fatigue in lifting and handling normally can be reduced and, in some cases, entirely eliminated.
3. Idle time can be brought to a minimum. Most of the waiting for work that occurs where intermittent and non-mechanical delivery of materials is involved can be eliminated by equipment that ensures a steady constant flow of materials.
4. The productivity of employees working on the product is increased by a reduction of time they would otherwise spend on handling materials.
5. Increased safety of handling results where materials are not "man-handled".
6. Storage space is conserved, particularly where mechanical equipment is used to stock materials vertically.
7. Non-productive, indirect labour can be released for more productive direct labour activities.
8. Certain types of mechanised handling equipment tied in with automatic machine controls and open up vast possibilities in the field of automation.

## Material handling cost

The cost of material handling arises from two sources. The cost of acquiring and maintaining equipment and the cost of operating the system. The material handling cost can be classified on the basis of variability and character of cost.

This is shown in the following Fig. 18.1.

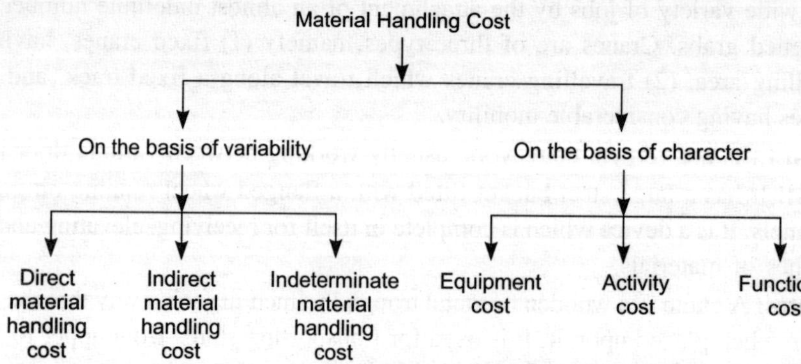


Fig. 18.1

On the basis of variability, material handling costs can bc classified into:

1. **Direct material handling cost:** Direct costs are commonly associated with the operation of material handling equipment. Both the equipments and man power costs are included in this category. Some of the examples of direct material handling costs are depreciation, interest on investment, wages of operating personnel, fuel and power, etc.
2. **Indirect material handling cost:** Indirect material handling costs are those associated with investment. Sometimes, these also include operation cost of an equipment but not in direct proportion. Examples of indirect material handling costs are the space occupied, repair parts, etc.
3. **Indeterminate material handling cost:** Indeterminate material handling costs are those which cannot be precisely determined or which are not known in advance or which do not lend themselves to the determination of a definite cost figure. This category might include some of the following costs: safety, paper work, plans for expansion.

On the basis of the character of costs, material handling costs can be classified into

1. **Equipment cost:** Equipment cost is related to the actual capital investment.
2. **Activity cost:** Activity cost is the expenditure required by a specified handling activity.
3. **Functional cost:** Functional cost is concerned with such organizational unit as receiving warehousing and the like.

In order to reduce the material handling cost to the minimum, the following suggestions are made:

1. Keep all handling to the minimum.
2. Handle as many pieces in one unit as is practical.
3. Provide large, heavy or bulky objects with handling aids, such as hooks.
4. Co-ordinate production planning, scheduling and dispatching.
5. Always consider handling problems in analyzing and designing the overall production system.
6. Modify existing building facilities to permit full use of available capacity.
7. Whenever possible, manufacturing processing should take place while the product is being moved.
8. Move the greatest weight or bulk material to the least possible distance.

***Plant layout and material handling system***

The plant layout engineer can facilitate material-handling by considering the following:

1. Avoid crowdest conditions.
2. Eliminate obstacles from materials flow.
3. Plan material movement in a direct path, i.e., avoid back tracking zig-zag flow, crooked paths.
4. Arrange for alternate paths in case of difficulty.
5. Beware of cross-traffic and take necessary precautions, avoiding particularly the traffic jams.
6. Keep related work areas close together.
7. Use product-type layout when possible.
8. Plan proper location of sub-assembly.

9. Combine operations to eliminate intermediate handling.
10. Minimize moves between floors and buildings.
11. Process heavy and bulky materials close to receiving.

### Production control and material handling system

Some of the specific ways in which material handling can be coordinated with production control are:

1. Provide direct, mechanical paths for material movement.
2. Move materials in lots, batches or containers of a predetermined quantity.
3. Store material in containers holding a specific number of pieces.
4. Use containers that facilitate identification of their contents.
5. Make optimum use of mechanical handling in picking, accumulation and loading.
6. Move material on a schedule and in lots to match production and to avoid such delivery, practical loads or duplicate moves.
7. Avoid verbal orders; instead, use written tags.
8. Coordinate handling schedule with purchasing and manufacturing.

### Safety and material handling system

It has been estimated that two-thirds of industrial accidents are caused by defective material handling systems. So, the material handling engineer must work closely with the safety engineer to ensure safety to both material handling methods and equipments. In order to provide safety, the following must be considered:

1. Install adequate guards and safety devices on handling equipment.
2. Use mechanical handling equipment for difficult hazardous handling activities.
3. Do not permit handling equipment or devices to be overloaded or operated beyond the rated capacity.
4. Use mirrors at busy aisle intersections to permit seeing around the corners.
5. Install adequate lighting.
6. Maintain floors in good conditions.
7. Avoid crowded conditions.
8. Make sure that operators are properly instructed in the method and use of equipments.
9. Use remote emergency switches and controls.
10. Isolate inherently dangerous equipment and operations.

### Material handling at the workplace

Material handling at the workplace is defined as that handling which must be done after material has been delivered and which is meant for use at the workplace and before it is picked up and moved to the next operation. It can normally be considered to cover not more than 3 or 4 feet in any direction from the centre of the machine, bench or workplace. Still, it constitutes an important area of cost reduction.

The following are the characteristics of material handling at the workplace:

1. Individual handling distances are relatively short.
2. The number of moves is usually high.

3. The greatest portion of the operational cycle time at an individual workplace is taken up by material handling.
4. Most of the workplace handling is classified as direct labour.

In planning an efficient workplace, the material handling engineer should give due consideration to the principles of workplace layout. These principles are outlined below:

1. Tools and equipments should be located close to and in front of the operator to minimise movements and efforts.
2. Provide a definite place for tools, equipments and materials.
3. Use gravity when possible to feed and remove materials.
4. Deliver material directly to the point of use.
5. Plan prompt and efficient removal of material from workplace.
6. Plan proper height relationship between material supply, point-of-use, and disposal.
7. Coordinate each workplace relative to preceding and following operations.
8. Leave sufficient space at the workplace for efficient delivery and removal of material.
9. Plan for storing incoming material and finished work awaiting removal at the workplace.
10. Make sure that handling equipment at workplace is properly integrated into the handling system.

## QUESTIONS

### A. Objective type

**I. Write *True* or *False* for the following sentences:**

(a) A belt conveyor is used to handle material, such as sand, stone, etc.
(b) Gravity type roller conveyors are used to carry materials from a lower elevation to a higher elevation.
(c) Overhead cranes are used in plants of very small size.
(d) Hand trucks are used in plants of very small size.
(e) Material handling equipments reduce accidents.
(f) It is always better to rely on equipment for labour saving.
(g) "Less wastage, spoilage and damage" is the golden principle of any material handling device.
(h) Every lifting machine is marked with an identification number and a safe working load.

**Ans.** *Try Yourself.*

### B. Very short answer type

1. Define material handling.
2. What are conveyors?
3. What is a crane?
4. What is a lift?
5. What are chutes?
6. What are pallets?

**C. Short answer type**

1. Explain the objectives of material handling.
2. Outline the principles of material handling.
3. State the factors which affect the selection of material handling equipment.
4. Explain the important material handling equipments.
5. Explain the various materials handling costs. Suggest ways to reduce material handling costs.
6. Outline the material handling programme to be designed to ensure safety in factories.
7. Outline the steps to be taken in planning material handling at the workplace.

Chapter 19

# PRODUCTION PLANNING

## INTRODUCTION

Planning is defined as deciding in advance what is to be done, how and when it is to be done. It is the first and foremost function of management on which all other functions are based upon. It involves projecting the future course of action of the entire organisation as well as every department of an industry. It bridges the gap between the present and the future. Production planning is a part of overall planning that decides future action and plans for production. Production planning defines what, how, where, when and why to produce and who will produce considering various factors which affect it.

## DEFINITION AND CHARACTERISTICS

Samuel Eilan defines production planning as the "direction and coordination of the firm's material and physical facilities towards the attainment of pre-specified production goals in the most efficient available way."

In the words of John L. Barbidge, "Production planning is the function concerned with planning, directing and controlling the methods to be used to make products and the way in which the production facilities, buildings, machines, equipments etc. should be laid out in the space available for the production." The features of production planning are as follows:

1. It is a part of the overall planning process. In its widest sense, production planning is related to planning, directing and controlling of production methods for the manufacturing of products,
2. Production planning is an universal function related to production,
3. It is pre-requisite to production control, and
4. It involves taking decision about the sequence of production while planning physical facilities, such as building, machines, equipments, etc.

## STEPS INVOLVED IN PRODUCTION PLANNING

Production planning involves the following steps:

1. **Determination of targets:** It involves fixation of production target for the planning period. Fixation of target is based on production capacity, production facilities, demand for the product, and past experience of production manager.

2. **Collection and interpretation of information:** The second step involved is collection of data, such as availability of new materials, labourers, machines and equipments, capital market potential, etc. The data may be collected from past benefits the factory should have accomplished, published reports of the Chamber of Commerce, government and other institutions. The data thus collected is to be analysed and interpreted. Based on the interpretation of data production planning.
3. **Developing plans:** Production planning involves developing of plans, such as policies, programmes, budgets, etc. These plans constitute the various elements of production planning. In order to develop these plans, many techniques, such as graphical technique, operation research techniques, etc. are used. Wherever necessary, these plans are modified. The plans are then sent to various executives for approval before they are implemented.
4. **Follow-up action**: Under this step, the results obtained after implementation of production planning techniques are compared with the past records. If there is any deviation, the reason for such deviation is identified and necessary steps are taken to avoid adverse variance. In case the result is favourable, efforts are made to retain it.

## ■ OBJECTIVES OF PRODUCTION PLANNING

The objectives of production planning are as follows:

1. To coordinate the production activities in a systematic manner. Whenever more than one product is manufactured, it requires balancing of activities both in terms of quantity and time.
2. To utilise the available resources to the maximum extent. Production process is affected by some hindrances, such as scarcity of material supply, idle time of workers, idle capacity of machines, defective production schedule and so on. By planning, these obstacles are overcome to make optimum utilisation of resources.
3. To maximise profits of the organisations by producing right quantity in right quality and at the right time for customers.
4. To dominate the market and capture the desired market share. This is yet another object of production planning. By forecasting the demand and by conducting market research it is possible to introduce new product according to the demand of the customers.
5. To reduce cost of production by exercising control over production.
6. To fulfil promised delivery dates given to customers.

### Importance of planning in production management

Planning plays a very important role in an enterprise. The success of an enterprise depends upon planning. Without planning, production becomes random in nature and results are meaningless. In present situation of uncertainty, rapid changes in production methods and techniques and cut-throat competition, production planning function has become an important function. The importance of production planning can be highlighted under the following points:

1. **Production planning sets objectives:** Production planning sets objectives of an enterprise. In order to achieve the objectives, it chooses out best alternative. After selecting the best alternative, it becomes imperative to prepare a plan to achieve the goal.

2. **Facilitates to meet unforeseen conditions:** By planning the production function it is possible to overcome abnormal conditions which may be of threat to production process. Production planning helps to meet the risk of uncertainty. This is because production manager can take precautionary measures to avoid abnormal situations.
3. **Proper utilization of resources:** Proper utilization of resources is possible because production planning helps in coordinating the efforts of various people. By the coordination of efforts of people, it ensures the best use of resources, such as men, materials, and machinery to the fullest extent.
4. **Basis for control:** Production planning provides the basis for production control which is another function of production manager. As a matter of fact, production planning and control go together because without planning there cannot be any control. While production planning sets targets and fixes standard time for completing the job, production control ensures production according to predetermined course of action by minimizing deviation from standard. The causes for deviation are identified and then removed in the next planning process.

## Data required by production planning department

The following information is required by production planning department for its successful functioning:

1. Data relating to design product, the type of process or operation involved, assembly or sub-assembly method
2. Sequence involved in production process
3. Specification of materials and the quantity of materials involved. This is to take advantage of large scale production
4. Economic order quantity and economic batch quantity which economises cost of production
5. Rate of production per hour, per day, per weak or per month
6. Elements of cost, viz. materials cost, labour cost, and overhead cost per unit
7. Number of orders on hand and their delivery schedules
8. Information about machineries, equipment and tools either required or available in the factory
9. Available production capacity
10. Availability of stock of materials and employees
11. Data relating to job specification, job analysis, job evaluation and merit rating techniques
12. Information about internal and external transportation
13. Power supply and power generation system
14. Losses and expected and allowed percentage of wastage
15. Extent of mechanisation and automation.

## Organisation of production planning department

A production planning department usually consists of three sections. They are as follows:

1. **Records section:** This section compiles and records information relating to:
   (a) The value of various materials and components on hand.
   (b) The number of customer's orders on hand.
   (c) Available plant, machinery, equipments and tools.

(d) Maximum, actual and normal capacity of production.

(e) The various operations involved, their sequence and time involved in each operation.

Thus, this department is concerned with collecting various information about stock, plant and machinery, tools and equipments. Labour force, production process, depreciation, quality and quantity of goods, time involved, delay and improvement, etc. The top management is involved in this section as valuable information is maintained in this section.

2. **Review section:** This section reviews the various consideration relating to alternate, schemes, production methods, operations, processes, tools and equipments, auxiliary services, etc. The various schemes that are approved are put in writing and various charts are drawn for implementation.
3. **Control section:** This section is concerned with translating plans into action and controlling the results. It is concerned with the collection of information relating to actual performance and comparing it with standard performance. If there is any variation it is identified and the appropriate measures are taken to set right adverse variance.

The production planning department must adopt systematic methods of observation, inspection and reporting at regular intervals. It must see that necessary corrective measures and modifications for the future should be made to obtain better results.

## ■ CAPACITY PLANNING

Capacity means a quantity of output in a given time and it is the highest quantity of output one can get during that time. The "capacity" of a factory is, however, an ambiguous concept. The simple statement that capacity is a quantity of output in a given time does not explain it fully.

In a single-product factory it is easy to talk about the quantity of output in a given time. But single product factories are very rare to find. Thus, the 'capacity', when expressed in terms of the final output units, varies depending upon the product mix in the case of multi-product organisation.

Time poses another problem. It was stated earlier that "capacity is a quantity of output in a given time, but how much time? In the case of continuous operation, such a steel mill, the term 'capacity' may mean the total amount that the plant can turn out per day or per week.

On the other hand, in the case of non-continuous type of processes, capacity would probably mean the expected output in a 48-hour work week, if the plant operates on a single shift basis.

## ■ INDIVIDUAL MACHINE CAPACITY

So far the term capacity was used in a broad sense, but in the final analysis, capacity comes down to individual machines. One needs to calculate how many time each type of machine requires while planning. The following steps are involved in calculating the number of machines required (the machine capacity required) for a given quantity of product output.

(a) First of all, the cycle time for the operation is determined.

(b) Next, the weekly work load is calculated by multiplying the cycle time per unit and the quantity of output required per week.

(c) Considering the machine utilisation factor, the total machine work load is divided by the number of hours it is likely to operate in a week to obtain the number of machines required.

## ■ CAPACITY BALANCE

For multi-product companies, the product mix changes from time to time, causing the load on different machines and departments to fluctuate. Machines also do not operate at evenly balanced speed and efficiency. Consequently, there will always be an imbalance between the work load of different machines.

Obsolescence and introduction of new products may cause part of the problem. This is because, yesterday's products require machines and equipments that are not needed much today. In such situations, more machines are added where today's demand consistently requires costly overtime work and where this demand is likely to continue. By making such changes it is possible to maintain a reasonable balance of capacity.

Another way to balance the capacity is to manipulate the demand. The sales department may be requested to try and generate demand for such product that will use up the idle machine and equipment. One can also try to outsource the job.

When capacity of machine is out of tune with its needs, there is always a few bottleneck spots. They set the limits to the plant capacity. The capacity of the plant is the capacity of the bottleneck operations.

Hence, if one wants to increase one's capacity one can do so by improving or by adding machines for successive bottleneck operation.

## ■ PLANNING FOR QUANTITY

Planning the quantity of product is based on demand forecasting. The demand forecast is the link between the evaluation of external factors in the economy which influence the business and the management of company's internal affairs. Fundamentally, there are two ways of obtaining forecasts of demand for the use of material. They are as follows:

### 1. Statistical exploration method

This method recognises the past material usage through statistical tools. It works reasonably well, where the general character of end items being sold is not changing.

### 2. Product explosion method

Yet, another method of demand forecasting is to start with parts and sub-assemblies which go into a single unit of the item. The unit material and time requirements are multiplied by the forecast quantity of the item to get gross demand implied by the forecast.

## ■ SPECIFICATION OF PRODUCTION REQUIREMENT

A forecast of the expected pattern of demand is not in itself an adequate basis for production planning. The demand forecast must be converted into a specification of production requirement.

Demand forecasts are usually given as a schedule of anticipated demand, for each month or year. This must be adjusted to make it be consistent with available production days.

The next type of adjustment required is an allowance for necessary operating inventories in the manufacturing and distribution system.

Finally, adjustment must also be made for forecasting errors. The adjustment to be made is one of increasing or cutting the quantities shown in the demand forecast until the risks and cost of carrying inventory and cost of ordering are unbalanced.

Once the adjusted demand forecast has been obtained, the task is to plan the production rate corresponding to requirements of production.

## QUESTIONS

### A. Very short answer type

1. Define production planning.
2. State the features of production planning.
3. Mention the three sections of production planning department.
4. What do you mean by capacity planning?
5. What do you mean by quantity planning?

### B. Short answer type

1. Explain the steps involved in production planning.
2. State the objects of production planning.
3. Explain the importance of planning in production management.
4. List out the various information based on which production planning is undertaken.
5. Explain the organisation of production planning department.
6. Write a note on capacity planning.
7. Write a note on quantity planning.

Chapter 20

# PRODUCTION CONTROL

## ■ INTRODUCTION

Production control refers to the regulation of the orderly flow of materials in the manufacturing process from the raw state to the finished product. Production control is a facilitating and coordinating activity concerned with the kind, amount, location, movement and timing of the various commodities under production. It is an organised activity of converting raw materials into useful products and production control is the control of these organised activities. The task of the production control department is to organise the most affective use of manpower, materials and machines.

## ■ DEFINITIONS OF PRODUCTION CONTROL

According to Spiegel and Lansburg, "Production Control is the process of planning production in advance of operations; establishing the exact route of each individual item or part; settling, starting and finishing dates for each important item; and finished product; and releasing the necessary orders as well as initiating the required follow-up to effect the smooth functioning of the enterprise."

Charles A. Koopke has defined production planning and control as "the coordination of a series of functions according to a plan which will economically utilise the plant facilities and regulate the orderly movement of goods through their entire manufacturing cycle from the procurement of all materials to the shipping of finished goods at a predetermined rate."

## ■ OBJECTIVES OF PRODUCTION CONTROL

The aim of production control is to produce the right product, in the right quantity, of the right quality, at the right time, and by the best and least costly methods. Good production control means less work in progress, decreased stock inventories, and more rapid turnover which, in turn, results in less capital tied up in idle material and greater earnings on the money invested. In the words of James Lundy, "A successful production control programme minimises the idleness of men and machines, optimises the number of set-ups required, keeps in-process investories at a satisfactory level, reduces materials handling and storage costs and consequently permits quantity and quality production at low unit cost. The objectives of production control can be enumerated as under:

1. To determine capacity of all manufacturing departments and to plan systematically coordinated and related production activities with the scope of the factory to meet sales requirements.
2. To translate orders received from sales department into orders on the production department and to ensure steady plans of production activities.

3. To coordinate the activities of different departments so as to maintain a good balance of activities.
4. To minimise the employment of production facilities with the general purpose of minimising operating costs and meeting delivery schedules.
5. To utilise the full capacity of production departments so as to undertake all the jobs without any refusal.
6. To maintain progress records to show actual against planned production and take necessary action to correct deviations as far as possible and advise the sales department when it is known that delivery promises cannot be maintained.
7. To maintain accurate record of all material and component stocks and movements in and out of stores in such a way as to anticipate future requirements and always to have material available for production to consumer's requirements.
8. To train staff in the effective performance of their duties.
9. Adhere to factory's production policy and ensure that production is achieved before the fixed target date.
10. To keep abreast with developments in modern techniques of production.

## ■ PRODUCTION CONTROL FUNCTIONS

Franklin and Moore, in his book, *Production Control*, has pointed out that the function of production control in a factory is comparable to that of the nervous system in the human body. It serves to coordinate the activities of a plant just as the nervous system regulates muscular movements. According to Carson and Young, (*Production Handbook*) production control serves as the 'eyes and ears' of manufacturing. Its role is to relieve the manufacturing supervisor from non-operating and recording duties so that he can concentrate on production, supervision and quality of goods. More specifically, the functions of production control are:

1. Initiate orders and provide authorisation to produce required quantity and quality of goods. To carry out this function, the production control department must:
   (a) Analyse in order to determine resource requirements and match these requirements with available capacity. Then the production control department is to inform the sales department which production order and delivery dates are feasible for customers.
   (b) Provide information to production department about the sequence of manufacturing, setting up of machines, employees to be utilised and materials to be used.
   (c) To issue production order which authorise the head of the production department to carry out production of goods.
2. Assist in the efficient utilisation of material resources, people and facilities. To achieve this, production control department would seek to:
   (a) Provide the requisite scheduling information to the production department on raw material, tooling, labour, and machine requirements by synthesising information obtained from industrial engineering departments.
   (b) Initiate purchase requisitions for raw materials and other component parts and send them to purchase department.
   (c) Assist in making cost and time estimates for order scheduling.
   (d) Provide detailed instructions for fabricating products.

3. Provide coordination and control for manufacturing activities. This function includes monitoring production activities, analysing production problems and communicating any need for corrective action to production personnel on time. These require production control department to:
   (a) Initiate reports to provide feedback information on the status of orders.
   (b) Compare actual work with scheduled requirements to identify orders falling behind schedules.
   (c) Inform the production personnel, as to what steps they should take and in what sequence, and schedule to accomplish the work.

## ■ PROCEDURE OF PRODUCTION CONTROL

Production control is concerned with recording the present events and comparing with planned production programme. Deviations between the actual performance from the planned programme is reported to management for taking corrective action. The following factors are involved in the practice of production control:

1. **Control of activities:** This involves the release of manufacturing orders and setting plans in motion at assigned times by means of despatching.

2. **Control of material movement:** This refers to the system of acquiring materials from suppliers and issuing them to production departments in accordance with production plan.

3. **Control of availability:** This refers to the observation of availability of tools specified by the production planning department.

4. **Control of due dates:** This refers to observation of delays or machine breakdown which results in delayed production.

5. **Control of quantity produced:** This refers to observation of work in process in order to determine whether right quantity of acceptable work has been processed.

6. **Control of labour efficiency:** This refers to observation and recording of the time taken on each unit of work and comparison with the time allowed on such job.

7. **Control of progress of orders:** This refers to the observation of the progress of orders by ticking off completed work on the production schedule.

## ■ ELEMENTS OF PRODUCTION CONTROL OR MECHANISM OF PRODUCTION CONTROL

There are six elements of production control. They are:

(1) Planning, (2) Routing, (3) Scheduling, (4) Dispatching, (5) Follow-up or expediting, (6) Inspection.

### 1. Planning

Production planning takes a given product or product lines and organises in advance the manpower, materials, machines and money required for a predetermined output in a given period of time. More specifically, the objectives of production planning are:

(a) To earn a prescribed level of profit
(b) To capture a desired share of market

(c) To operate the plant at a predetermined level of the efficiency
(d) To utilise effectively the available plant facilities
(e) To create specific number of jobs.

***Functions of production planning***

The functions of production planning include:

1. Sales forecasting.
2. Determination of production requirements to accomplish the sales forecasts.
3. Determination of the requirements raw materials.
4. Inventory management—both raw materials and finished stock.
5. Determination of labour requirements based on planned operating level.
6. Planning the design of the product to be manufactured.
7. Planning the quality of raw materials and fabrications materials and parts to be used.
8. Planning the sequence of operations.

Production planning is a series of related and coordinated activities performed not by one but a number of different departmental groups, each activity being designed to systematise in advance the manufacturing efforts in its area.

Production planning is based upon the following information:

(a) **Production material:** The information is derived from an analysis of the product into its separate components to determine the kind, grade, quality and quantity of each type of material required.
(b) **Availability of materials:** The balance of material on hand is known from the bin card.
(c) **Standard of quality for each unit:** This information is derived from engineering drawings and specifications.
(d) **Equipment capacity:** This information is derived from an analysis of machine capacity and consists of unit of work per hour capable of being handled by each machine.
(e) **Operation method:** This information is derived from technical experience.
(f) **Sequence of operations:** This information is derived from technical experiences assisted by an accurate knowledge of machine layout. It consists of a determination of the order in which operations shall be performed on each production item.
(g) **Operation time allowance for each operation on each unit:** This information is derived from time study and from technical experience.

## 2. Routing

Routing has been defined by Kimball and Kimball in, *Principles of Industrial Organisation,* p. 213, as "the selection of paths or routes over which each piece is to travel in being transformed from raw materials into finished product." Alford and Beatly in their book, *Principles of Industrial Management,* p. 403, have defined it as "the specification of the flow or sequence of operations and processes to be followed in producing a particular manufacturing lot." Routing establishes the operations, their path and sequence, and the proper class of machines and personnel required for these operations. It is closely related to plant and industrial engineering in setting up the most efficient operating methods and in establishing a material flow through the plant for a minimum handling and back tracking.

### *Routing procedure*

The routing procedure for a new product may consist of seven separate activities:

(a) **Analysis of the article to determine what to make and what to purchase:** This consists of analysis of the product and its components parts, to break them down into materials and decide which items to buy and which items to make. This decision is primarily based on the relative cost involved and, secondly on such factors as technical considerations, purchasing policies, and availability of equipment and personnel.

(b) **An analysis of the article to determine what materials are needed and of what kind and quantity:** Drawings, specifications, standards of quality and identification symbols are usually considered by the routing section into a parts list. A part list shows each part name, identification number, quality required and also indicates the kind and amount of materials required for each part. From this list, the inventory control section can determine the adequacy of the materials in stock or on order and then initiate the purchase of additional material needed.

(c) **Determination of the manufacturing operations and their sequence:** Based on estimates supplied by the industrial engineering department and together with technical considerations of machine capacities and product characteristics the sequence of operations in their sequence is listed on the route sheet. This form generally shows the part number and description and the material required and then may indicate for each operation its standard or estimated process time, the type of machine used, and tools required.

(d) **Determination of sizes of lot:** This means the quantity to be manufactured in any one lot or order. The size of the lot will depend upon type of industry and manufacture which may be (a) continuous industry, (b) assembly industries, (c) job order industry, and (d) batch order industry. While determining size of the lot, allowance for rejection must be made.

(e) **Determination of scrap factors:** For any number of units of input in the first operation, the output of good units expected is less than the input. The anticipated difference between the input and output is called scrap factor or shrinkage. Scrap factors are important in the planning of production quantities as a part of the routing functions as well as the scheduling or loading of various machines.

(f) **An analysis of the cost of the article:** While the function of cost estimating is primarily the responsibility of the costing department, it also requires contributory efforts of the routing section of the production control department and plant and industrial engineering departments. The estimate is based largely on the routing information obtained in steps 1 through 5 above.

(g) **The organisation of production control forms:** The type of manufacture exercises considerable influence upon the forms required by the plant departments. In producing a product, usually a production order is required. In addition to this form, material requisition, job cards, labour cards, inspection cards, move tickets, and tool tickets are also prepared to authorise and report on the work being done.

### *Factors affecting the routing procedures*

Routing is affected primarily by (i) the type of layout and manufacturing process, such as continuous, intermittent, job order or batch production processes, (ii) individual characteristics of the physical equipment, such as age, condition, degree of precision, capacity, range, speed, etc.,

(iii) availability of physical plant equipment, viz. machine load condition, breakdowns, absentee operations etc., (iv) human factors for example, operators vary in experience, capability, manual dexterity, physical limitations, intelligence and emotional stability, etc.

## 3. Scheduling

James Lundy in his book, *Effective Industrial Management,* p. 379, defines scheduling to "consist of the assignment of starting and completion times for the various operations to be performed." According to Alford and Beatty, scheduling is "fitting specific jobs into a general time table, so that orders may be manufactured in accordance with contracted liability, so that each component may arrive at and enter into assembly in the order and at the time required." Scheduling determines the programme for the operations, order of sequence of each operation and their starting and finishing time is decided so that the required materials, machines, and other factors may be kept ready as per the schedule. A schedule is a representation of the time taken to carry out a task. It is not merely a list of functions necessary, but it also takes into the account the time relationships between the various functions.

Scheduling and dispatching are closely related, and, in many small factories, both the functions are performed by the same individual or group. The preparation of a factory schedule requires attention to be paid to:

(a) The various job schedule
(b) The capacity, various sections or departments
(c) The efficiency of the various sections or departments
(d) The maintenance schedule
(e) Holidays
(f) Anticipated sickness or absenteeism
(g) existing commitments
(h) Availability of raw materials.

### *Machine loading*

To aid in production scheduling, planners prepare machine load charts to show the amount of work in terms of hours, days or week assigned and scheduled to each maching group of identical machines, or production departments. Load is the work assigned to a machine or an operation, and capacity is the volume of output capable of being produced in any convenient period of time. When the load is equal to the capacity, then the department, machine or operation is said to be fully loaded. If the load is greater than the capacity, then the plant is overloaded. If the load is less than capacity of the plant it is then underloaded. Ideally, every machine operator should know the task which has to be undertaken for atleast one week in advance. By doing so it will be possible:

1. To maximum utilisation of plant and personnel.
2. To establish and meet the target dates.
3. To improve morale of the operator.
4. To determine the need for new plant. It is possible to express load in hours of work, but it is– frequently convenient to express it in other physical terms such as:
   *Money*: a machine has an output of Rs. X an hour

*Weight*: a machine has an output of X tons an hour

*Length*: a machine has an output of X feet an hour

*Quantity*: a machine has an output of X parts an hour

Load can be derived from the schedule, and the schedule, in turn, can be drawn up considering the load. Since delivery dates determine the schedule, the need for considering the load, when setting a delivery date, is very essential. It is folly to set a delivery date without due regard for the load.

### *Scheduling procedure*

Scheduling usually starts with the master schedule. A master schedule is a weekly or monthly breakdown of the production requirements of the job or product to be manufactured in the concern. In addition to the master schedule, a manufacturing schedule is also prepared.Which contains the detailed outline of individual production function and their time sequence.

In preparing a schedule, the following rules should be taken into consideration:

1. Schedule first those jobs with shortest first operation, or
2. Schedule first those jobs with shortest last operation, or
3. Schedule jobs according to their total work content, or
4. Schedule jobs according to their date of receipt, or
5. Assign priorities to jobs according to the customer.

## 4. Dispatching

Dispatching may be defined as setting production activities in motion through the release of orders and instructions in accordance with personally planned time schedules and process routings. Dispatching is concerned with issuing work orders according to priority rules and the assigning of work to specific work places. Dispatching determines by whom work shall be done.

### *Functions of dispatch department*

1. The assignment of work to the machines or work places.
2. The authority to prepare, assemble, and issue to their point of use, the necessary materials tools, fixtures and gauges.
3. The issuance of the orders and production forms necessary for the performance of work and for the reporting of production, pay-roll, and cost data.
4. The responsibility for controlling the progress of material at each operation; for making the necessary adjustments to schedules and work assignments as conditions change or as unpredictable emergencies occur.
5. The authority to move work from one operation to the next.
6. The liaison function linking the plans of the routing and scheduling office with the performance of the manufacturing divisions.

Complexity of the activities of the dispatcher varies with the types of manufacture. The dispatching of repetitive orders, particularly where continuous production lines are involved, is very much simpler than the dispatching of work, materials tools and other items for a job order project that is seldom repeated.

### *Dispatching procedure*

There are two types of systems that may be used for dispatch work. These are:

1. **Decentralised dispatching:** It consists of issuing manufacturing schedules or work orders in a blanket fashion to the foreman or dispatch clerk within each department. The foreman or clerk then arranges the sequence in which the work orders will be processed within the department. He arranges the dispatch of material to work benches and machines. The chief advantage of this systems are: 1. Duplication of postings and elaborate reporting are minimised to a great extent, 2. It reduces complete authority of control of the dispatcher.

2. **Centralised dispatching:** It involves distribution of work orders from the central dispatching section to the individual machines or work benches directly. The capacity work load, backlog etc. are known to the central dispatching station in advance from where centralised control is exercised. The advantages of this system are:

   1. Centralised dispatching normally achieves a greater degree of control.
   2. It is more flexible when work load is high and the factory is running nearly at full capacity.

The different methods of dispatch communication are:

(a) Messenger service
(b) Pneumatic tubes
(c) Telantograph
(d) Teletypewriter
(e) Telephone
(f) Intercom system.

## 5. Follow-up or expediting

Follow-up is that branch of production control procedure which regulates the progress of materials and parts through the production process. Follow-up is closely interrelated with dispatching. It serves as a catalytic agent to fuse the various separate and unrelated production activities into the united whole.

### *Types of follow-up*

There are basically three types of follow-up:

(a) **Follow-up of materials:** This is the responsibility of purchasing department. When the materials are not received from the supplier as per the agreed date, the purchase manager can send a telegram quoting the reference number of purchase order. A duplicate purchase order copy can also be sent so that in case the original is lost the duplicate purchase order serves the basis upon which the supplier can supply the materials.

(b) **Follow-up of work in progress:** This is the responsibility of the foreman who is expected to note down the extent of work done for each day. This can be compared to planned production to know whether the required extent of work is performed. Otherwise, necessary action may have to be taken to expedite the production process.

(c) **Follow-up of assembly and erection:** This is the responsibility of Production Manager. Under this type of follow-up, the component parts which are to be manufactured to assemble them into finished product must be ensured as per the scheduled programme. Such component parts are manufactured in batches and it is the duty of the Production Manager to make sure that all component parts are manufactured in the required batches so that they all can be assembled to get a given number of finished products.

### *Preventing production delays*

The follow-up man or expediter is concerned with the delays that creep into factory production. He knows the delays through analysis of the production reports and from personal observation. He must not only take corrective measure after delay has occurred but also anticipate and prevent it before it actually occurs. As the saying goes an announcing prevention is far more valuable than a pound of cure where delays in production occur in factories. The common causes of delays are:

(a) **Errors in planning:** Production Manager is often responsible for this type of error. The error may relate to scheduling the equipment with work beyond its capacity to produce, underestimating manpower, scheduling uneconomically small lots, etc.

(b) **Lack of materials, tools or equipment:** This error creeps in owing to delivery failure which could have been prevented by closer follow-up by the purchase department.

(c) **Equipment breakdowns:** Maintenance engineer is responsible for this error. Preventive maintenance of machines could have avoided this error if followed in factories.

(d) **Excessive rejections:** Excessive damages caused to the products results in the production of good units. Care must be taken by production engineer to design the product by carefully allowing the experienced workers to work in such circumstances where excessive scraps are anticipated.

## 6. Inspection

The terms inspection and quality control are sometimes used interchangeably. Inspection implies the checking of goods in order to differentiate the good from the bad. It is the manufacturing function which judges production against established standard. It serves as a common instrument for quality measurement as well as quality control. Inspection has been defined by Alford and Beatly as "the art of applying tests, preferably by the aid of measuring appliances, to observe whether a given item of production is within the specified limits of variability.

### *Need for inspection*

Need for inspection arises as a result of faults in manufactured products because of (a) wrong tolerance allowances, (b) faulty design, (c) badly set or working machine tools, (d) falling off in concentration and vigilance of machine operators, (e) faulty materials being machined, and (f) complaints from customers.

### *Objects of inspection*

The object of inspection is to ensure that the entire work leaving the factory is of the required standard. The aims of inspection are not only to discover faulty products, but also to prevent their becoming faulty, and thus avoid scrap. More specifically the objectives of inspection are:

1. To detect errors in manufacturing poor quality products and report them to responsible official in production department for taking suitable action.
2. To protect the consumer from receiving a product that is below the quality level by sorting good units from those which are below standard.

3. To complete or compile information in conformity with the specification of the product for the use of engineering, production, purchasing and quality control departments.

### *Functions of inspection*

The functions of inspection department may be outlined as follows:

1. Inspection of raw materials to determine whether they are physically and chemically in accordance with specifications.
2. Inspection of process to determine whether the part is correctly formed and dimensioned in accordance with specifications.
3. Metallurgical inspection to determine whether the metallic structures, hardwares and other properties are as specified after the various processing operations have been performed.
4. Inspection of component parts to determine whether they conform to purchase specification.
5. Inspection of finished goods to make sure that sub-standard quality products are not delivered to customers.
6. Inspection of tools to determine whether the pattern and tool are capable of producing the parts in accordance with specifications.
7. Inspection of gauge and other measuring instrument to make certain that the equipment is capable of giving the desired results, whenever used.
8. Inspection of assembly department to determine and report error in design that result in poor performance.
9. Inspection of salvaging operations in which defects are reworked so that they bring the best price when sold.
10. Inspection of complaint department which receives reports on defective workmanship, investigate them and make recommendations to the manufacturing department to prevent future such occurrences.

### *Importance of inspection*

Inspection is an important part of the whole sequence of production because:

(a) It can affect the reputation of the factory as too many faulty products means an increase in customer complaints.

(b) It can prevent unnecessary work being performed on faulty parts.

(c) It ensures that incentive payments are made only for good quality work.

(d) It locates fault in machines, materials, tools, tool setting or bad workmanship.

(e) It ensures that increased productivity is not obtained at the expense of quality.

## ■ REQUIREMENT OF PRODUCTION CONTROL

The following are the requirements of a good production control system:

1. Complete detailed drawings and other engineering information.
2. Complete information regarding special tools, such as jigs and fixtures whether available or to be provided.
3. Complete information on times and costs of previous performances.
4. Accurate up-to-date information regarding the stores and finished stock that are to be used.

5. Exact knowledge of the progress of the work in process.
6. Complete tabulated data on power, speeds, and feeds of all machines.
7. Records of the best performances on similar work with best combination of tools, feeds and speeds.
8. Careful instruction of the workman by the speed boss or some similar person.
9. Careful following up and correction of the department schedule.
10. Careful inspection of all tools and appliances to make sure that they are up to standard conditions.
11. A financial incentive that will enlist the interest of the workman.

***Recent trends in production control***

The following trends towards measures to increase production control are becoming evident:

1. Manufacturing performance is improved by integrating controls at all levels of manufacturing endeavour from raw materials inputs to finished product output.
2. A more responsible, accurate and flexible control is found in the use of mechanical office equipment. Examination of practices to shorten the clerical and communication routines are also being initiated.
3. Computers are frequently being used to solve the more complex manufacturing processes. Data generating and quick analysis abilities of the computers are being applied to achieve efficient production control.

**Advantages of production control**

The advantages of production control can be viewed from (a) Factory's point of view, (b) Worker's point of view, (c) Shareholders point of view (d) Consumer's point of view, and (e) Societies point of view.

(A) **From factory's point of view:** Advantages of production control from factory's point of view can be classified under the following captions:

1. *Production control*
   (a) It increases the pace of production, and
   (b) It reduces production cost.
2. *Quality control*
   (a) It minimises the wastes, scraps and rework,
   (b) It minimises the rectification hours, and
   (c) It reduces the cost of inspection.
3. *Manufacturing cost*
   (a) It decreases maintenance cost,
   (b) It reduces raw material wastage,
   (c) It reduces material handling cost, and
   (d) It exercises better control over manufacturing cost.
4. *Advantages to management*
   (a) It helps in better planning of production.

(b) Through feed back an affective control system can be installed in different spheres of activities.

(c) It reduces conflicts with trade union and management and thus eliminate the possibility of strikes and lockouts.

(d) The management can efficiently and effectively install new techniques of production and automation, if necessary.

(e) It helps in easing the burden of the supervisor.

5. Advantages of Capital Investment:

(a) It helps in management of working capital, earnings and dividends, and

(b) It helps in reduced investment in machines and equipment by

(i) increased production per machine.

(ii) utilising idle hours of machines.

6. Advantages to Marketing Management:

(a) It increases goodwill and reputation of the factory by

(i) maintaining excellent quality of product.

(ii) satisfying customers by prompt delivery of goods.

(b) It helps in introducing new product in the market,

(c) It realises cost of advertising, and

(d) It reduces Market Research Cost.

(B) **From worker's point of view**

(a) It reduces the efforts of the workers.

(b) It reduces workers' fatigue.

(c) It leads to specialisation.

(d) It leads to efficient operations of workers.

(e) It leads to team spirit.

(f) It reduces number of accidents.

(g) It leads to higher earnings.

(h) It offers better working conditions.

(i) It ensures job security.

(C) **From shareholders point of view**

(a) It offers better security of investment.

(b) It leads to adequacy of returns.

(c) Value of their holding increases.

(D) **From consumer's point of view**

(a) It reduces cost per place, and

(b) It ensures better quality of products.

(E) **From society's point of view**

(a) Quicker and faster capital formation which leads to higher national income and per capita income which decides the standard of living of country's people.

(b) Better and efficient application of production control technique enables government to earn more revenue in the form of tax on account of higher earnings.

(c) National reputation and self-dependence is boosted up.

(d) The nation progresses towards prosperity and progress.

(e) Security of the nation is achieved.

## ■ PRODUCTION CONTROL TECHNIQUES

There are two techniques used under production control. They are as follows:

### 1. Programme evaluation and review technique (PERT)

PERT has become a very popular management technique for planning and controlling projects. Under PERT, the completion time is assumed to be uncertain and unknown. Therefore, the probability of activity completion time is estimated. Three time estimates are made for each activity-optimistic time, pessimistic time and normal time. Optimistic time is the best time that could be expected if everything went exceptionally well. Pessimistic time is the worst time that could be expected if everything went wrong.

The steps involved in PERT are as follows:

#### *(i) Preparation of the network*

First of all, a list of activities involved in a project is prepared. The predecessor and successor activities are determined. A network diagram is prepared on the basis of dependence between different activities and events. This is project planning phase of PERT. Events are numbered in ascending order from left to right.

#### *(ii) Network analysis*

Estimates of the time required to perform each activity are made. These estimates are based upon manpower and equipment availability. At this stage, the probability of completing the project or its special time can be computed.

#### *(iii) Scheduling*

Expected time for each activity is computed from the three time estimates. Earliest and latest starting time and finishing time for each activity are determined. Then the critical path through the network is determined. The slack time associated with the non-critical activities is also computed.

#### *(iv) Timo cost trade-offs*

If management wants to reduce the project completion time, crashing or compressing of the project is done. The cost of reducing the project completion time is computed. Time cost trade-off for the critical path is considered.

#### *(v) Resource allocation*

The feasibility of each schedule is checked with respect to manpower and equipment requirements. Replanning and rescheduling may be necessary if the resources are limited.

### *(vi) Project control*

Once the network plan and schedule are developed to a satisfactory level, they are finalised. The project is controlled by checking progress against the schedule, assigning and scheduling manpower and equipment and analysing the effects of delay. Whenever major changes are made in the schedule, the network is revised accordingly and a new schedule is prepared. Thus, monitoring of progress may require periodic updating of the project and rescheduling to ensure completion of the project in time.

**Utility of PERT**

(a) In construction industry, PERT is used in building large structures like factories, fly-overs, dams, etc.
(b) In installing plants, computers, officers and in reorganising new systems.
(c) In overhaul, maintenance and major repairs like refitting ships, steel furnaces, scheduling aircraft, etc.
(d) In general administration, for long-range planning, streamlining, corporate planning, manpower planning, etc.
(e) In marketing, PERT is used for advertising, development and launching of new products, distribution network.

**Advantages of PERT**

(a) It enables managers to plan carefully and study how the various parts fit into the whole project. It forces planning all down the line because each subordinate manager plans the event. It enables management to predict time and cost of a project in advance.
(b) It focusses attention on critical or bottleneck elements of the project so that a manager may either allocate more resources to them or keep a careful watch on them as the project progresses. It permits control by exception and better management of resources.
(c) PERT is a unique control technique as it assists management in controlling a project. Once the project begins PERT calls attention to review delay in the project completion date. It allows a manager to calculate the expected total time for the completion of the project at the time of formulation and planning. Therefore, PERT provides a forward looking type of control or a feed forward control. It serves as a readymade standard against which performance can be measured.
(d) PERT incorporates the statistical analysis in determining time estimates and enables determination of the probabilities concerning the time by which each activity as well as the entire project would be completed.
(e) It provides up-to-date information on the progress of the project so that the necessary steps may be taken (e.g., rescheduling, reallocation of resources, etc.), to minimise delays and interruptions.
(f) PERT focuses attention of the management on problems ahead, indicating relationship and coordination required thereby providing a sound means of control.

**Limitations of PERT**

(a) PERT is based on time estimates rather than known time for each activity. There may be errors in time estimates due to business bias.

(b) It emphasises only time and not cost.

(c) It is not practicable for routine planning of recurring activities. It is useful in complex projects consisting of numerous activities which are independent of each other and whose completion times are uncertain.

(d) For active control of a project, PERT requires frequent updating or revision of the calculations. It becomes an expensive and time consuming exercise. It requires highly trained personnel.

## 2. Critical path method (CPM)

CPM is used for optimising resource allocation and minimising overall cost for a given project. CPM was developed to help scheduling of routine plant, over-hand and maintenance building of a pilot model plant, etc. CPM uses two time and cost estimate for each activity (one for the normal situation and other for the crash situation). It is based on the assumption that the time which each activity in the project takes as precise and known. The relation between the amount of resources employed and the time needed to complete the projects is also assumed to be known.

The following steps are involved in the process of determining the critical path:

(a) Breakdown the project into various activities systematically. Arrange all activities in logical sequence and label them. Construct the arrow diagram.

(b) Number all the events and activities. Find the time for each activity considering it to be deterministic. Indicate the activity times on the arrow diagram.

(c) Calculate the earliest start time, earlier finish time latest start time and latest finish time. Construct a table showing earliest time, latest time, and normal time.

(d) Determine the total float for each activity on the basis of difference between the earliest time and latest time.

(e) Identify the critical activities and connect them with double line arrow. This gives the critical path.

(f) Calculate the total duration of the project.

(g) If it is intended to reduce the total duration, crash the critical activities.

(h) Optimise the cost by shifting resources.

(i) Update the network and smooth the network resources.

**Advantages of CPM**

1. CPM highlights the critical activities on which management should focus attention to reduce project completion time.
2. It helps management in diverting resources.
3. It provides a technique of planning and scheduling a project. Scheduling helps to determine completion date and to evaluate progress towards the completion of the project.
4. It gives complete information about the significance, size, duration and performance of an activity.
5. It helps to in identifying the sequence of jobs that determine the earliest completion date for the project.

**Limitations of CPM**

(a) It operates on the assumption that there is a precise known time that each activity in the project will take. But this may not be time in real life situation.

(b) It does not incorporate statistical analysis in determining time estimates.

(c) Each time, changes are introduced into the network and the entire evaluation of the project has to be repeated and a new critical path has to be determined.

(d) It is not suitable for a situation which does not have a definite start and definite finish.

## QUESTIONS

### A. Objective type

**I. Choose the correct answer from the following alternatives:**

1. The main factors which determine the place of production control in an organisation are
   (a) The type of production, size of plant, type of industry.
   (b) The type of computers used, the accounting techniques followed, the day-to-day control of operation.
   (c) Need of service to be given to customers, measurement of system employed, decision-making system.
   (d) Incoming orders, optimum control system.
2. The need of production control is much more felt in
   (a) advanced technology and developing economy
   (b) moderate technology and developing economy
   (c) obsolete technology and underdeveloped economy
   (d) advanced technology and underdeveloped economy
3. Production Control is said to be
   (a) factory's nervous system
   (b) factory's barometer to measure profit
   (c) factory's muscular movement
   (d) none of the above.
4. Advantages of production control occur in
   (a) manufacture only.
   (b) factory, shareholders, customers, workers.
   (c) workers, society.
   (d) consumer, workers, factory.
5. The routine of setting productive activities in motion through release of orders and instructions as known as
   (a) routing
   (b) dispatching
   (c) scheduling
   (d) expediting

6. In repeated order, Production Control is
   (a) simple
   (b) difficult
   (c) extremely difficult
   (d) complicated
7. The technique, which establishes operations and sequence and proper class of machines and personnel required for these operations is known as
   (a) routing
   (b) scheduling
   (c) dispatching
   (d) follow-up
8. The simple dispatching rules are
   (a) earlier due date, first come first served; shortest processing time
   (b) earliest due date, last come first served; longest processing time
   (c) longest due date, first come first served; longest processing time
   (d) longest due date, last come first served; shortest processing time
9. In the short run, the performance criterion that is most likely to be emphasised for production control is
   (a) to meet customer's requirement
   (b) achieve low production cost
   (c) optimise investment in inventories
   (d) improved plant utilisation and attain stability in production operations
10. In the long run, the major objectives of production control are to
    (a) adopt successfully to changes in customers' demand and to introduce new products.
    (b) reduce turnover.
    (c) avoid any unnecessary costs in the operation of the production control system itself.
    (d) to achieve maximum production at minimum cost and customer's satisfaction.
11. The goal of production control is
    (a) to match as efficiently as possible the production capacity of factory with the demands made by its market
    (b) to reduce inventories
    (c) to reduce manufacturing cycle time
    (d) to reduce gap between demand and supply of orders.
12. The major purpose of inspection is to
    (a) remove all defects to prevent delivery of substandard products
    (b) identify poor operations
    (c) develop information to facilitate corrective action
    (d) keep cost down by finding defects early in the cycle
13. The function of inspection is to
    (a) improve quality standards
    (b) check work against specifications
    (c) salvage poor work
    (d) raise employee workmanship

14. The responsibility of the production control department is to
    (a) keep work in process at a minimum
    (b) formulate production policy
    (c) schedule output to fulfill sales needs
    (d) avoid inventory losses

## II. Write *True* or *False* for the following sentences:

1. The inspection function should always be set-up as an independent department under the manufacturing division.
2. High precision inspection can be successfully carried out only through the centralised plan.
3. The chief inspector should have primary jurisdiction over the setting of quality standards.
4. A single ideal production planning and control system can be designed to apply to all types of manufactures.
5. Routing is primarily concerned with the reactive time at which production is to occur.
6. The term quality refers to the determination of standards and the measurement and control necessary to see that these standards are maintained.
7. The cost of manufacture increases rapidly with increased quality of product, but the compounding rate of increase in the value of quality decreases sharply.
8. Quality may be defined as the degree to which it meets the requirement of the customers.
9. Inspection involves more than setting up a way measuring quality characteristics and comparing them to quality standards.

## III. Match the following:

| Column A | Column B |
|---|---|
| 1. Routing | (a) Production order follow through |
| 2. Scheduling | (b) Sequence of machine operations |
| 3. Dispatching | (c) Rush orders and shortage |
| 4. Control board | (d) Issuing the instructions |
| 5. Expediting | (e) Progress of production |

## B. Very short answer type

1. Define production control.
2. State the elements of production control.
3. Mention the functions of production planning.
4. Define routing.
5. Define scheduling.
6. What do you mean by machine loading?
7. Define dispatching.
8. State the functions of dispatching section.
9. Distinguish between centralised and decentralised dispatching.
10. What do you mean by follow-up?
11. Mention the common causes of delays which are responsible for follow-up action?
12. Define inspection.

**C. Short answer type**

1. Outline the objectives of production control.
2. State the functions of production control.
3. State the functions of inspection department.
4. Outline the requirement of good production control system.
5. State the advantages of production control.

**D. Long answer type**

Explain the various elements of production control.

## ANSWERS TO OBJECTIVE TYPE QUESTIONS

| | | | | | |
|---|---|---|---|---|---|
| I. | (1) (a), | (2) (b), | (3) (a), | (4) (b), | (5) (b), |
| | (6) (a), | (7) (a), | (8) (a), | (9) (a), | (10) (d), |
| | (11) (a), | (12) (d), | (13) (b), | (14) (d). | |
| II. | (1) F, | (2) F, | (3) F, | (4) F, | (5) F, |
| | (6) T, | (7) T, | (8) T, | (9) F. | |
| III. | 1. (b), | 2. (a), | 3. (d), | 4. (e), | 5. (c). |

*Chapter* **21**

# QUALITY CONTROL

## ■ INTRODUCTION

The term "quality" is used to indicate a standard. From the manufacturer's point of view, quality may be defined as the sum total of a number of characteristics describable in a specification. In other words, the term "quality" does not carry with it the popular meaning of "best" in any absolute sense. A manufacturer views quality as "best for certain customer condition". The two customer's conditions are: (a) the actual end use, and (b) the selling price of the product. The term quality is attributed to the specification of dimensions, physical or chemical property, hardness, temperature, pressure or any other requirement of a product. Quality control starts with the customer's specification which is undertaken through various aspects, such as designing, research, scientific purchasing of raw materials, production planning, mechanical inspection, electrical testing, proper packing, and ultimate delivery to customers. Quality control, in a broad sense, refers to the systematic control of the variables encountered in manufacturing process which affect the excellence of the end product. The control of such variables is essential as reputation for uniformity and good quality output is a valuable asset to an industry.

### Definition and objectives of quality control

Alford and Beatty have defined quality control as "the mechanism by which products are made to measure up to specifications determined from customer's demand and transformed into sales engineering and manufacturing requirements."

In the words of Pharmaceutical Manufacturers Association of the USA, "Quality Control is the organized effort employed by the company to provide and maintain in the final product the desired features of properties, characteristics of identity, purity, uniformity, potency and stability within established levels so that all merchandise shall meet professional requirement, legal standards as the management of a firm may adopt."

Quality control is a statistical technique needed for systematic observation of size, form, quality and workmanship and control of variables encountered in a manufacturing process that affect goodness of end product.

The objectives of quality control are as follows:

1. To establish standards of quality which are acceptable to the customer and economical to maintain such standards.
2. To enable the setting and resetting of processes and machinery. It enables us to know the performance of similar machines and operations.

3. To keep up the quality of product during manufacture by taking remedial steps.
4. To locate and identify the process faults and defects of products and thus to control the scrap and waste.
5. To take different measures to improve the standard quality of product.
6. To see that products of lower quality do not reach customers.
7. To enable reduction in operating cost by not producing defective goods.
8. To develop quality reputation which is of prime importance in selling consumer goods.

### Importance of quality control

Quality control plays a very important role in the process of manufacturing. The problem of production adaptation to customer requirement has now become increasingly serious. Management uses a wide range of tools in manufacturing goods that involve good workmanship, design, materials and other characteristics. These quality products encourage customers even to pay premium prices. This also leads to customer satisfaction. If poor quality of goods are supplied to customers, they refuse to accept and instead go in for substitute products. This results in reduced sales. Hence, the need for quality control.

The importance of quality control can be highlighted under the following points:

(a) It increases the profit earning capacity of the business.
(b) It enables the industry to compete successfully.
(c) It reduces cost of production.
(d) It reduces operating losses by keeping scraps and wastes to a minimum.
(e) It improves the product design.
(f) It reduces bottleneck product line.
(g) It improves morale of the employees.
(h) It enhances satisfaction of customers.
(i) It increases reputation of the industry.

### Principles or essentials of quality control

There are three essentials of a good quality control:

1. **Fixation of responsibility for manufacturing the quality product:** The responsibility for quality control must be entrusted to someone or a group or persons best suited for the job. Otherwise, it leads to duplication and sometimes it amounts to the old saying "everybody's business becomes nobody's business" and thus quality is severely damaged.
2. **Setting up clear-cut standards:** Setting up standards becomes useful as it helps in increasing the variation of end products by comparing with predetermined standards. This adds to the excellence of the end product.
3. **Uniform application of standard of measurement:** A systematic routine must be followed to see that the promise is backed by performance, i.e. the predetermined excellence of the product is unaffected. According to W.C. Deming, "Not how much product, but how much acceptable product is what counts."

## Functions of quality control department

The functions of quality control department include the following:

1. Advises an inspection and quality control policy formulated.
2. Sets inspection standards in the light of design-engineering tolerances.
3. Prepares department budget requests and controls operating expenses.
4. Selects inspection points, including receiving room, department clearance and final inspections.
5. Selects inspection gauges and instruments and sees that maintenance keeps each in good working order at all times.
6. Collaborates with statisticians on choice of type of statistical quality control charts to be used.
7. Collaborations with statistician on designing efficient sampling plans and methods.
8. Issue of damage reports.
9. Training inspectors on duties, and in use of inspection standards.

## Mechanism of quality control

The mechanism of quality control comes from four basic tools. These are as follows:

### *1. Standards and specifications*

Standards and specifications contribute to a great extent to the programme of quality control. In other words, standards and specifications must be determined to achieve successfully the objectives of quality control. A specification portrays precisely the characteristics possessed by the product.

Establishment of standard is the task of the quality engineers. However, quality standards and specifications should be determined in close cooperation with purchasing, sales, manufacturing and inspection departments because these departments have something to contribute and are closely inter-related with each other, and the action of the one will affect the other. Quality standards are necessary for comparison. Such standards should be carefully preserved. In the absence of such preservation, the company will find the quality level of its product shifting as there is deterioration in physical standards or change through usage.

Standards must be definite and self-explanatory backed by appropriate drawings, specification sheets, blueprints, accurate formulae, etc. to avoid any confusion of what actually is required.

***Tolerance:*** Tolerance means possible variation from a desired, nominal measurement embracing a specified variable in quality. Tolerance permits the most economical production cost. Hence, it is important. Its permissible variation must be taken into account while standards and specifications are being established. These variations are the permissible variations from the basic standard or the ideal criterion. The "zone of acceptability" has two limits: (a) upper and (b) lower, and may be expressed as under:

$4 \pm 0.005$. Here 0.005 indicates that variations or limits (permissible) may be either plus 0.005 or minus 0.005, as the case may be, from the basic criterion, i.e., 4.

### *2. Inspection*

Inspection is the most common method of attaining standardisation, uniformity and quality of workmanship. Inspection acts as a diligent and intelligent guardian with stick of specified standards in its hand so that it may determine whether a given item falls within, this zone of acceptability. If the said item does not fall within this zone, it will be rejected and corrective measures are applied to see that the items, in future, conform to the specified standard. Thus, inspection is the art of applying tests, to observe, whether a given item of product is within the specified limits of variability.

Inspection helps to control quality, reduces manufacturing costs eliminates scrap, losses and assignable causes of defective work, aids distribution, and thus contributes to profit. In the absence of the technique of inspection, defective goods cannot be segregated and thus customers are deprived of getting goods of proper quality. Thus, the inspection process embraces, for each quality characteristic,

(a) Interpretation of the specified standard,

(b) Measurement of the product in the light of specification,

(c) A judgement whether a given item of product falls within the specified limits of variability, and

(d) Approval or rejection of the given item of product under inspection.

### 3. Statistical quality control

Statistical quality control makes use of statistical methods and principles with the aim of assessing not only the magnitude of "chance cause variation" but also to detect assignable cause variation. Because of the detection of "assignable cause variations" by these statistical method, it is possible to control various stages of production of a product.

Statistical quality control includes the following two major tools:

(a) **Quality control charts:** Control charts are pictorial means of presenting a mass of actual data so that their significance can be understood. A control chart may be defined as "a chronological (hour-by-hour, day-by-day) graphical comparison of actual product-quality characteristics with limits reflecting the ability to produce, as shown by past experience on the product characteristics."

Control charts for the purpose of statistical quality may be applied for attributes required simply by noting and recording the presence or absence of some quality characteristics by inspectors. A control chart simply determines whether a piece of product is satisfactory or defective. Quality control for variables requires measurement of product for each quality characteristics keeping a record of each measurement clearly showing whether it falls within the zone of acceptability or tolerance. It is the analysis of this sort which is the backbone of control charts.

(b) **Acceptance of sampling:** A sample means a small part taken from a quantity to give an idea of the quality of the whole. Samples and sampling methods are vital aspects of statistics as used in quality control. "Sampling inspection" involves examination of less than 100% of the production.

Acceptance of sampling is a device of sampling that determines whether the lot in question is to be accepted or rejected. Thus, acceptance of sampling throws light over in the uninspected residue of a lot.

### 4. Inspection devices

Most of the instruments used for inspection are known as gauges. These gauges investigate the dimensional fitness of a mechanical element in relation to its predetermined dimensional standards. The more commonly used gauges are: fixed sized gauges, micrometer gauges, air gauges, combination gauges, chrome-plated gauges.

Electronic inspection devices are becoming more popular in recent times. Such devices are used in testing and sorting of fruits, in checking internal characteristics of products such as testing of smoke, heat, humidity, acidity, etc. Electronic inspection devices readily reject faulty and defective articles.

### Factors affecting quality

(a) **Market:** Customer's demand has needs and his purchasing power are the main determinants of quality level.

(b) **Men:** For designing quality and for production of quality goods right type of men with required knowledge are essential.

(c) **Money:** Increased competition, more mechanization and lower profit margin make scrap and rework losses very serious. Cost of maintenance and improvement of quality increase to a great extent.

(d) **Management:** Without management's interest and active cooperation there can be no adequate quality.

(e) **Materials:** Owing to production cost and quality requirement, it is necessary to work with wide variety of materials having tight specification.

(f) **Machine and method:** Manufacturing equipments have become more complex to meet high volume of production and high level of quality goods. There machines and technology are highly sensitive.

## ■ INSPECTION

Inspection is the manufacturing function which judges production against established standards. It is both the instrument for quality measurement and a part of the activity of quality control, which however is often organised as an independent function. Inspection may be defined as the art of applying tests, preferably by the aid of measuring appliances to observe whether a given item of product is within the specified limits of variability.

The objectives of inspection are:

1. To detect errors in manufacturing and trends towards poor quality, and report them to responsible officials in the production department so that action may be taken to prevent making units of product that is not acceptable or a level of quality of product that is below the specified quality.
2. To protect the consumer from receiving a product that is below the quality level and limits specified, by sorting good units or lots from those which are below standard, permitting only what is good.
3. To compile information regarding the suitability of the product with specification for the use of engineering, production, purchase, quality control and other divisions responsible for the quality performance.

### Functions of inspection department

The functions of inspection department may be outlined as follows:

1. Raw material: To determine if the incoming goods are physically and chemically in accordance with specification.
2. Process inspection: To determine if the part is correctly formed and dimensioned in accordance

with specifications and is free from defects in material, improper processing or accidental injury and is completely processed and finished.

3. Metallurgical and Metallographic: To determine if the metallic structure, hardness and other properties are as specified after the various processing operations have been performed.
4. Purchase parts: To determine if purchased items conform to purchase specifications.
5. Finished goods: To assure management that an excessive amount of goods below the predetermined quality specification will not be delivered to customers.
6. Tool inspection: To determine if the patterns and tools which are purchased or made are capable of producing the parts in accordance with specifications.
7. Periodic gauge and other measuring instrument inspection: To make certain that the equipment is capable of giving the desired results, whenever used.
8. Assembly department: To determine and report errors in design or manufacture that should result in excess assembly time or poor performance.
9. Salvaging operations in which poor work is reworked to eliminate the defects, converted to other uses or converted to scrap material that will bring the best price when sold.
10. Complaints division: It receives reports on defective workmanship or material from the sales and service departments, investigates them and makes recommendations to the engineering or manufacturing departments to prevent future occurrences.

## Kinds of inspection

The various kinds of inspections are as follows:

1. **Tool inspection:** Tool inspection, as the term implies, is the application of inspection methods to tools, fixtures, jigs and gauges in advance of the work of production. If tools are incorrect, the work varies from the standards of quality established. Therefore, periodic inspection of all tools should be provided for particular attention to those points where wear and tear takes place.
2. **First piece inspection:** First piece inspection is based upon the importance of beginning a job rightly. If the first three or four pieces produced in a new lot are subject to inspection, there are chances that the tools may be properly set and that ensuring pieces will be up to standard.
3. **Working inspection:** Working inspection implies that the inspector shall check pieces at definite intervals to make sure that they are being produced to specification. In this way, a continuous inspection of production is maintained so that a minimum of defective parts will be manufactured.
4. **Operation inspection:** It is the completion of an operation before the work in process passes along to a succeeding process or machine. Next to final inspection, it is the most commonly applied of the several kinds.
5. **Inspection by sampling:** Inspection by sampling is less than 100% inspection, in which a certain proportion or percentage of pieces is taken from each lot, submitted to inspection and the lot judged according to this sample.
6. **Final inspection:** Final inspection is concerned with inspection after an article has been completely finished and is ready to be sent to the storeroom or shipped to a customer. It is

the step whereby the manufacturer has assurance that his product is meeting the established standards in all respects and will be satisfying to his customers when they receive it.

7. **Floor or patrolling inspection:** Floor or patrolling inspection takes place at or near the machines. It ranges from patrolling the shop and keeping an eye on the work in the machines to close inspection and careful measurement of the product where it is being produced. In continuous process industries, floor inspection is often conducted from an enclosed area in the line of work, the product flowing through this area as though it is one in the chain of machines.
8. **Centralised inspection:** When inspection is centralised, the parts are transported to special areas where precision measuring devices may be located and where the inspectors may make accurate measurements without much disturbance and interference that may occur in the production floor. The basic idea is the separation of inspection from manufacturing inspection or crisis may be located parallel to the flow of work through the shop and centrally with respect to the machine.

**Advantages of inspection**

1. It ensures whether quality of actual output conforms with the specified standard quality.
2. It facilitates rectification of defective output.
3. Inspection process ensures that the customer receives the product of desired quality and not the sub-standard goods.
4. It serves as a moral check on employees who undertake to ensure quality of goods.
5. Inspection facilitates good housekeeping.

**Disadvantages**

1. It involves increased cost of production owing to salary payable to inspectors.
2. It results in delay of the delivery of goods.

## STATISTICAL QUALITY CONTROL (SQC)

The SQC involves the statistical analysis of the inspection data which is based on sampling and the principles involved in normal curve. In the field of quality control the problems susceptible are statistical analysis and those of standardization, specification and inspection. Thus, it includes problems both of quality design and quality of performance. The principal applications of the statistical method for quality control are the following:

(a) Problems of quality of design

1. To assist in determining the essential characteristics of vital raw materials and finished product.
2. To determine to what extent variations in essential characteristics affect the value of a finished product.

(b) Problems of quality of conformance

1. To compare different methods of measuring the essential characteristics of finished product.

2. To determine whether significant variations in essential characteristics of finished products are due to variations in raw materials or in manufacturing processes, or can be assigned to pure chance within statistically determined limits of probability.

## ■ ACCEPTANCE SAMPLING

A widely used statistical quality control technique used for inspection by the method of attributes is acceptance sampling. In the place of 100% screening or sorting inspection, samples of a lot or process are selected carefully. Generally, inspection for defective pieces and the number of defectives forms the basis for the acceptance or rejection of the entire lot. When rejected, the balance of the lot is sorted to separate the defective pieces from the acceptable ones.

The operation of a sampling inspection plan involves taking the following steps in sequence:

(a) Segregation of the product into inspection lots.
(b) Selection of sample or samples from each lot.
(c) Inspection of each item in the sample or samples to determine their quality.
(d) Acceptance or rejection of each inspection lot on the basis of the inspection of the sample or samples.

**Uses of Sampling Inspection**

(a) Ascertaining acceptability and quality of incoming raw material, component parts and finished product.
(b) Ascertaining the acceptability and quality of outgoing product.
(c) Determining the acceptability of work-in-process for further processing in the plant.
(d) Improvement and control of the quality of the product.

### Acceptance sampling plans

Three types of acceptance sampling plan are in general use: single, double and sequential. The best known and most generally applicable are the Dodge and Roming Single and Double Sampling inspection tables. Both of them have been developed for each of the two kinds of consumer protection: (i) Lot for quality protection and (ii) average outgoing quality protection (AOQL).

The four types of tables developed by Dodge and Roming are:

(a) Single sampling lot tolerance tables
(b) Double sampling lot tolerance tables
(c) Single sampling AOQL tables
(d) Double sampling AOQL tables.

Dodge and Roming have outlined the single sampling inspection procedures as follows:

(a) Inspect a sample of *'n'* pieces.
(b) If the number of defects found in the sample does not exceed (c), accept the lot.
(c) If the number of defects found in the sample exceeds (c), inspect all the pieces in the remainder lot.
(d) Correct or replace all defective pieces which have been found.

### Double sampling

In double sampling, lots are not rejected always when acceptance criterion for the first sample exceeds, but the decision is sometimes postponed until a second sample is taken and the acceptance criterion for the combined samples exceeds. The procedure outlined by Dodge and Roming is as follows:

1. Inspect a first sample of $n_1$ pieces.
2. If the number of defects found in the first sample does not exceed $C_1$ accept the lot.
3. If the number of defects found in the first sample exceeds $C_2$ inspect all the pieces in the remaining lots.
4. If the number of defects found in the first sample exceeds $C_1$ but does not exceed $C_2$ inspect a second sample $n_2$ pieces.
5. If the total number of defects found in the first and second samples combined do not exceed $C_2$ accept the lot.
6. If the total number of defects found in the first and second samples combined exceeds $C_2$, inspect the pieces in the remaining lots.
7. Correct or replace all defective pieces found.

### Sequential sampling

In addition to single and double sampling, there is also a type known as sequential sampling. Where single sampling is used, the decision to accept or reject a lot must be made after inspecting a single sample from the lot and where double sampling is used, it may be necessary to take two samples. In sequential sampling, one, two, three or more samples may be required before it is possible to reach a decision to accept or reject the lot.

## ■ CONTROL CHARTS

A control chart is a statistical device used for the study and control of repetitive processes. A control chart is essentially graphic device for presenting data so as to directly reveal the frequency and extent of variations from established standards or goals. A control chart consists of three horizontal lines:

(a) A control line to indicate the designed standard or level of the process.
(b) Upper control limit (UCL).
(c) Lower control limit (LCL).

### Types of control charts

Control charts can be divided under two heads:

(a) Control charts of variables.
(b) Control charts of attributes.

### (a) Control charts of variables

Variables are those quality characteristics of a product which are measurable and can be expressed in specific units of measurement, such as diameter of TV valves which can be measured and expressed in centimeters, etc.

Attributes are those product characteristics which are not amenable to measurement. Such characteristics can only be identified by their presence or absence from the product.

Control chart relating to variables are of two types. They are as follows:

1. **Control chart for averages:** To prepare a control chart for averages small samples of the product (usually 4, 5 or 6 items) are taken from the production line at regular intervals in the order of production. These are carefully measured for the quality characteristics to be controlled and the actual measurement recorded. The average value of the characteristic for each of these samples is calculated and plotted on graph paper. After sufficient samples have been taken, usually 30 or more, an average sample is determined and this is plotted on the center line. An upper and lower control limit is then determined from the formula.

$$\text{Control limits} = \bar{x} \pm A_2\bar{R}$$

where $\bar{x}$ = The average sample averages

$A_2$ = A factor, the value of which varies with the size of the sample.

$\bar{R}$ = The average of the sample ranges.

For sample of 4, the value of $A_2$ is 0.729 and for sample of 5, the value is 0.577. The range is the difference between the highest and the lowest value in each sample and the average range $\bar{R}$ is the sum of the sample ranges divided by the number of samples.

The danger limits are determined from the formula.

$$\text{Danger limits} = \bar{x} \pm \sqrt{n}\, A_2\bar{R}$$

where $n$ = Sample size

When the sample size is 4, the danger limit is twice as far from the center line as is the control limit. When the sample size is 5, the danger limit is 2.336 times as far from the center line as the control limit.

Control charts for averages show variations in samples taken from a process in relation to the quality level being produced. This level may or may not be the desired level. Where it is not, steps must be taken to alter the process so that the average quality result is satisfactory. The upper and lower control limits are the guide to whether or not the process is under control. When a point falls outside these limits, action is indicated to determine the cause and to eliminate it.

2. **Control chart for range or 'R' chart:** The 'R' chart is used to show the variability or dispersion of the quality produced by a given process. 'R' chart (or σ chart) is the comparison chart to the $\bar{x}$ chart, and both are usually required for adequate analysis of the production process under study. The R chart is generally presented along with the $\bar{x}$ chart.

### (b) Control charts for attributes

The various control charts used for attributes are as follows:

(a) **C-chart:** The C-chart is designed to control the number of defects per unit. C-chart is used in situations wherein the opportunity for defects is large while the actual occurrences tend to be small. This happens, for example, if we count the number of imperfections in a piece of cloth, the number of air bubbles in a piece of glass, etc. Let 'C' stand for the number of defects counted in one unit of cloth (paper, roll of wire) and $\bar{C}$ for the mean of the defects counted in several (usually 25 or more) such units of cloth. The central line of control chart for C is $\bar{C}$ and the 3-sigma control limits are:

$$UCL = \bar{C} + 3\sqrt{\bar{C}}$$

$$LCL = \bar{C} - 3\sqrt{\bar{C}}$$

This formula is based on a normal curve approximation to the Poisson's distribution. The use of the C-chart is appropriate if the opportunities for a defect in each production unit are infinite but the probability of a defect at any point is very small and is constant.

***Uses of C-chart***

The important applications of C-chart are given below:

(i) The number of defects in a galvanised sheet or painted plate or enamelled surface of given area.

(ii) The number of defects of all types in air crafts, sub-assemblies or final assembly.

(iii) Number of defects observed in a roll of paper or sale of cloth etc.

(b) **P-chart:** The P-chart is designed to control the percentage or proportion of defect in each sample. Since the number of defects can be connected into a percentage expressed as a decimal fraction merely by dividing C by the sample size. The P-chart may be used in place of the C-chart. The P-chart has two advantages over the C-chart.

(a) Expressing the defectives as a percentage of production is more meaningful and more generally understood than would be the statement of the number of defects.

(b) Where the size of the sample varies from sample to sample the P-chart permits a more straight forward and less cultural presentation.

## ■ QUALITY CIRCLES

Quality circle means a team established to improve the quality of manufactured products. The concept is based on the premise that those working closest to the process are likely to have greatest insight into the improvement of way it is produced. This will be further enhanced if people work together as a team rather than as individuals. The nature and composition of the team depends on the particular circumstances.

### Conditions necessary for the success of quality circles

The success of quality circles depend the following conditions:

(a) Active support and commitment on the part of top level management,

(b) Proper coordination in the team,

(c) Commitment and ability of facilitators and leaders, and

(d) Proper education about the quality circle philosophy and sufficient training for facilitators, leaders and members.

The technique of quality circles involves individual workers to work together in problem-solving processes. The aim is to involve employees to actively participate in improvement process. As no work environment can be expected to be perfect, the people who face the problems are expected to identify, investigate and find solutions to the problems. As such, this concept envisages the involvement of rank and file employees – no employee should feel unwelcome to get involved in a circle. Employee participation may however depend upon the attitude of the employees and the time at his disposal.

Employees from the same work area are grouped in a circle. Although no limit is laid down to the number, an effective working of the circle requires around 10 members. The members meet regularly for about one hour every week, a superior who initially volunteers to start the circle may lead the same. A circle starts functioning after developing a programme, which is a detailed procedure, also called as quality circle cycle. The programme lists the different topics of discussion and the action taken. The activities and the results of the circle then are put forth for a management review.

Quality circle increases the involvement of employees by means of participation. It provides an environment of creativity and achievement. To employees, it provides an opportunity to train and develop. By mutual exchange of ideas, they reach full potential, work becomes more enjoyable and purposeful. When workers and different levels of management are brought together, communication is improved.

From the organisational point of view the advantages are mainly two folds: firstly, quality circles mark a commitment of companies to change the organisational culture. Secondly, it enhances of effectiveness business. It provides an answer to the question, how to manage human resources for business improvement.

### Process involved in quality circles

The process of quality circles involve the following steps:

1. **Identification of problem:** The members may be able to identify several problems in their area. Quality, productivity, cost reduction, housekeeping and safety are some of the general categories of problems which may be identified by quality circle. Techniques, such as brain-storming, may be used to help problem identification.
2. **Problem selection:** Problem selection is a prerogative of the circle. When several problems are identified, a selection of the problem for further process of the quality circle may become necessary.
3. **Problem analysis:** The circle members analyse the selected problems. If needed, the circle may take the assistance of experts and consultants.
4. **Recommendation to the top-management:** Finally, the circle makes its recommendations to its departmental heads in the first instance, normally once in 7–8 weeks selected cases of all circles are presented to the top management, normally once in 2–3 months, known as management presentation. In a management presentation, the leader and members describe to their manager what project they have been working on and what recommendations they wish to make regarding this.

It is the top management which decides whether the recommendations should be accepted and implemented.

## Constituents of quality circles

The various constituents of quality circles are as follows:

1. **Top management:** Top management consists of the executive at the higher level. Without an enthusiastic support from the management, a quality circle cannot be expected to succeed. For continuous growth of programmes, management must support circles by
   (a) providing assistance in training,
   (b) providing accommodation for circle meeting,

(c) Publishing circle activities,

(d) Giving assistance in implementation of approved solutions, and

(e) Giving explanation where circle solution is rejected.

2. **Steering committee:** A steering committee is at the highest level of the division or unit. This committee is headed by a top executive of that division or unit. He is designated as the chairman of the committee. Some of the functions of this committee include

(a) The promotion of quality circle movement,

(b) The formulation of rules and regulations governing quality circles. The same must be reviewed periodically,

(c) To look after the progress and activities of quality circles. In case of expansion of quality circles they must be controlled by splitting into two circles. The committee must lay down the rules for these,

(d) Expenses for the functioning of the quality circles like training, expenses towards provisions of meeting facilities, pointing of documents, etc., have to be sanctioned by the committee

(e) An annual quality circle convention must be organised. All circle presentations must be assembled. Selection of the best presentation is done by the committee, and

(f) Evaluation of the progress of the quality circle must be periodically undertaken on the basis of quality improvement, cost reduction, product innovation, work satisfaction, communication, team spirit, attitude.

3. **The facilitator:** The facilitator plays an important role in the structure of quality circle. He is responsible for conducting all circle activities. His functions include.

(a) Liaisoning with the coordinator in all quality circle activities,

(b) Execution of all quality circle policies, procedures and code of conduct,

(c) Forwarding of monthly reports of quality circles assigned to him and to the coordinator, and

(d) Arranging for assistants from other departments for quality circles assigned to him.

4. **Circle leader:** The circle leader is to be chosen by the members of the quality circle. Due to lack of training on the part of workers, a foreman or supervisor may be initially chosen as a circle leader. Subsequently, members may decide to have leaders by rotation. His functions include:

(a) To lead the circle,

(b) To encourage members to participate,

(c) To provide agenda of the meeting,

(d) To make regular progress report,

(e) To present work solutions made by the circle to the steering committee through the facilitator, and

(f) To ensure that the code of conduct is followed.

5. **Non-members:** Workers, who are reluctant or unwilling to join a circle, are non-members. Nevertheless, they must be encouraged to give suggestions to circle members.

6. **Coordinator:** The coordinator regulates the circle activities throughout the organisation. An executive from the quality assurance department is usually given this task. His duties include

(a) Implementation of all policies, rules and regulations laid down by the steering committee,
(b) Coordination of quality circle activities of all the facilitators,
(c) Making arrangements for training of members, leaders and facilitators,
(d) Maintaining all records of activities and monthly reports of quality circles, and
(e) Communication with all the employees on matters relating to the programme.

## Total quality management

Total Quality Management (TQM) is a collection of concepts and techniques aimed at improving business performance by ensuring quality to meet a customer's expectation. The essential elements of TQM are as follows:

1. **Commitment:** A management to continually improve the quality of products and services sounds an obvious necessity. Management participation and demonstration by example are the best ways of convincing the work force that the managers are serious about quality and that the same should be expected of everybody. Commitment should be demonstrated by actions from the very beginning. Perhaps, with the publication of sound quality policies and the formation of quality steering committee and quality councils involving top managers and directors.

   Proper working conditions, adequate education and training, good communication and cooperation, modern leadership, appropriate quality tools and job satisfaction are some of the ingredients of a system that can motivate. Such a system needs a change in attitude and culture, something that is impossible unless there is real commitment. TQM requires a commitment to education, training on well-established and up to-date, innovative quality improvement techniques.
2. **Scientific knowledge:** Scientific knowledge helps in the creation of proper conditions so that all employees can take responsibility for the quality of their own tasks and accept ownership of certain quality problems as they arise. Employee's flexibility and adaptability then become a way of life. Quality output is seen as an expected reward rather than a forced obligation. One of the main advantages of scientific knowledge is that it provides a common language which can facilitate communication between the different departments and individuals.
3. **Involvement:** Involving everybody in the common pursuit of quality ensures that all interdependent processes can function to their maximum capacity. Maximum efficiency can only be achieved by the utilisation of the valuable experience of the people nearest to the process. This experience shared through open, honest and adequate communication, when helped by modern quality improvement techniques, can achieve results far superior to the ones obtained through isolated efforts or through a compaign of unsupported slogans and exhortations.

## International organisation for standardisation (ISO)

The abbreviation ISO stands for international organisation for standardisation. It is a world wide quality certification organisation. It awards certificates based on reviewing the applications made by firms. Firms use these certificates to demonstrate to customers and suppliers that they have met the minimum necessary standards.

## ISO 9000 series

ISO 9000 is a group of generic standards which specify what should be in a company's quality system, whatever the product or service. Set up by the International Organisation for Standardisation (ISO) in

Geneva, ISO 9000 standard was started in 1989 to provide a universal framework for quality assurance among its 12 member nations.

ISO 9000 standards do not refer to the technical specification of products but to the systems producing them, assuring that products consistently have the quality that buyers expect. The standard consist of five parts.

### ISO 9000

It is a quality standard that sets out the methods by which a management system incorporating all the activities associated with quality can be implemented in an organisation to ensure that all the special performance requirements and the needs of the customer are finally met. The system applies to the quality management systems a company uses not its products.

### ISO 9001

It provides the model for an organisation which is involved in the management or design as well as in producing the product or service. Thus, in service organisations or organisations provide professional services where the service is offered or designed to meet the specific needs of the customer.

### ISO 9002

It is an appropriate model for many manufacturing industries producing standard items or service organisations, such as retailing outlets providing a standard service.

### ISO 9003

It is only used for those organisations whose product is already manufactured and is simply inspected before being supplied.

### ISO 9004

It requires that a company's service be defined with specific characteristics documented, such as dependability, capacity safety, security, courtesy and accuracy. The standard also addresses the importance of employee involvement and motivation in providing quality service and vesting a service quality loop, which enables internal and external measurement of customer service.

A broad scope of quality systems is covered by the ISO 9000 services, such as management responsibility. Contract review, document control, purchasing, process control, inspection and testing, design control, handling, storage, packaging and delivery, quality records, quality audit, training and servicing.

## Certification process by ISO 9000

The certification process usually involves the following steps. The firm audits and reviews its operations to measure the existing quality standards against ISO 9000 standards and identifies areas for corrective action.

It then decides whether to use consultants to help with the certification or build up its own network of information sources to answer questions and keep the teams going in the right direction.

A quality manger is designated to organise and manage all activities. A quality manual detailing what is done in each specific area to conform to the requirement of the standard is then drafted by the team involved with quality systems and implemented. Inter-quality audits are conducted to highlight areas of non-conformance in each department.

If the firm feels that it is ready for assessment, it submits its quality manual for the assessors to review and see if the documentation meets the requirements of the standard. Then the facility is audited to ensure that the firm's practices comply with the requirements. Training of personnel is verified through records and on-site interviews.

When a supplier's quality system is verified to conform to the requirements of the selected standard (ISO 9001, 9002 or 9003) the registrar issues certificate to the supplier asserting to that conformance. The certificate is then listed in a register which is available to the public and the supplier is allowed to display the registrer's mark on advertising and stationery, as evidence of registration.

The benefits obtained after certification include improvements in documentation, communication, morale and responsiveness, increase in customer satisfaction and sales and decrease in rework, wastage and annual audit.

## QUESTIONS

### A. Very short answer type

1. What do you mean by quality?
2. Define quality control.
3. Mention three essentials of quality control.
4. What do you mean by statistical quality control?
5. List out four tools of quality control.
6. What do you mean by acceptance sampling?
7. State the uses of sampling inspection.
8. What do you mean by double sampling?
9. What do you mean by sequential planning?
10. What is C-chart?
11. What is P-chart?

### B. Short answer type

1. Outline the objectives of quality control.
2. Explain the importance of quality control.
3. Outline the functions of quality control department.
4. Explain the factors which affect the quality of the product.
5. Outline the functions of inspection department.
6. Explain the various kinds of inspection.
7. Write notes on
   (a) Control chart for averages
   (b) Control chart for range
   (c) C-chart
   (d) P-chart.

# Chapter 22

# WASTE MANAGEMENT

## ■ INTRODUCTION

Waste management is that aspect of production management which is concerned with minimising or eliminating all kinds of waste in a factory. Waste not only means unwanted portion of produced goods but also unutilised resources or improper utilisation of resources. One way of eliminating waste is judicious use of resources. Resource management and waste management are thus complimentary to each other. Waste can also be minimised by adopting efficient method of production. Proper supervision also contributes to the reduction of wastage in factories.

## ■ MEANING OF WASTE

Waste in industry may be defined as the ineffective use of time, materials, skill, money, equipment, machinery, space, etc.

## ■ CLASSIFICATION OF WASTE

1. On the basis of the state in which waste is obtained, it is classified into three types, viz. (a) solid waste, (b) liquid waste, and (c) gaseous waste.

The components of solid waste are paper, garbage, metal, glass, plastic and such other materials.

Liquid waste is defined to mean such contamination of water or such alteration of the physical, chemical or biological properties of water or such discharge of any sewerage or trade effluent or any other liquid or solid substance into water that is likely to change its physical appearance, odour or render such water harmful and injurious to public health.

The components of gaseous waste are dust, fumes, poisonous gases and so on.

2. From the accounting point of view, wastes are classified as:

(a) Waste,
(b) Scrap,
(c) Spoilage, and
(d) Defectives.

These are explained below:

### Waste

The residue which is left behind by a production process is known as a waste. Wastage is inevitable and is inherent in the technological process. It has comparatively insignificant value. It cannot be reused nor reworked so as to convert it into good units. Waste comprises of (a) invisible loss as for example, shrinkage in a tanning industry, evaporation in an oil refinery, loss in energy transmission, etc. (b) visible loss that cannot be collected, as for example, sound in construction industry and (c) unsoluble portion of collected loss, as for example saw dust in furniture making industry, charnings in a machining operation, cuttings in a garment industry, ash in coke industry and so on. In certain cases, waste involves further costs of disposing it, e.g. the cost incurred for the disposal of effluent, obnoxious gases, etc.

Whenever a waste occurs, it is necessary to prepare a report to facilitate accounting and controlling such wastes. A specimen form of waste report is given below:

**Report on Waste**

Dept.________ Period________

| Production Order no. | Units of Product | Waste Qty. | Percentage of Waste to Production |
|---|---|---|---|
| | | | |
| Total | | | |

## Scrap

A scrap refers to the incidental residue derived from certain type of manufacture recoverable without further processing. The main feature of scrap is that it has some disposable value and it arises from normal production process. Scrap arises from faulty operation, inproper supervision, wrong tool setting, defective process and use of defective raw material.

### *Types of scrap*

(a) Normal scrap: This is considered to be inevitable in the manufacturing process and hence it is predetermined or anticipated much in advance of production.

(b) Administrative scrap: This arises owing to the decision taken by management, such as use of a different method of production or a different design of product.

(c) Defective scrap: This arises mainly due to the use of sub-standard quality of materials or bad workmanship.

### *Differences between a waste and a scrap*

1. The degree of involvement of waste is more when compared to the inherence or the element of inevitability in scrap.

2. The chance of re-use scrap in the same production process is high when compared to waste.
3. Scrap has a higher saleable value when compared to waste.

Examples of scraps in engineering industry takes the form of turnings, borings, filings, etc. from the metal. In leather industry, it takes the form of pieces of leather. In timber industry, it takes the form of saw-dust.

To facilitate accounting of scrap, a daily and weekly scrap report is to be prepared. This reveals the unexpected items and abnormal variations in scraps. A specimen form of such a report is given below:

**Scrap Report**

Name of the Production Dept.....
Scrap report for the week ending.......

| No. | Description | Units Issued | Units Scrapped | Percentage of Scrap | Cost | Remark |
|---|---|---|---|---|---|---|
| | | | | | | |
| Total for the week | | | | | | |

## Spoilage

Spoilage is man-made scrap. It results when materials are so damaged in manufacturing operations that they are taken out of process and disposed of in some manner without further processing. They cannot be repaired or reconditioned into a product of acceptable quality. It is either sold as second hand product or reused for further manufacturing as a basic raw material. Spoilage occurs due to faults in operation, bad workmanship, use of defective machines and faulty setting of tools.

Spoilage differs from scrap in the following two respects:

(a) Spoilage occurs more towards the finishing stage with higher loss of added value whereas scrap occurs in the beginning and intermediary stage of production with less added value.

(b) Spoilage arises because of some defects in production process or materials which may or may not be inherent in the production process, whereas scrap arises as a result of inherent production process. Thus, it can be said that scrap is inevitable whereas spoilage is not so in all cases.

To facilitate accounting and control of spoilage a spoilage report is prepared. A specimen form of spoilage report is given as follows:

**Spoilage Report**

Dept. No.......... Date.............

Production order no.........

| Units Produced | Units Spoilt | Normal Spoilage | Abnormal Spoilage | Reason | Action Taken |
|---|---|---|---|---|---|
| | | | | | |

## Defectives

Defectives refer to imperfect products which are transformed into the standard specifications by the application of additional material, labours or both. Defective differs from spoilage in one important respect, viz., defectives can be reworked and restored to original condition but spoilages cannot be rectified. Defectives occur on account of the following reasons:

(a) Sub-standard raw materials
(b) Bad maintenance of machines
(c) Wrong setting-up of tools
(d) Bad workmanship
(e) Machines used for unscheduled operations
(f) Lack of control, such as temperature, humidity, etc.
(g) Unsuitable design of the product
(h) Improper working conditions.

Defective goods should be separated from spoilages to facilitate reconditioning of work. However, reconditioning work is justifiable only when the revenue earned by the sale of rectified defective goods is more than the cost incurred in rectification of defectives. The rework to be done on defectives should be authorised by a senior official. For this, a defective work report is to be prepared and attached to production order representing the defective work. A specimen form of defective work report is given as follows:

**Defective Work Report**

Production order no…….. No…………..
No. of units……………… Date…………
Dept. responsible………..
Nature of defective……..

| Job No. | Description of Additional Work Required | Rework Cost | | | |
|---|---|---|---|---|---|
| | | Material Cost | Labour Cost | Overhead | Total Cost |
| | | | | | |

1. From the point of view of causes leading to wastage, it is classified as (a) material waste, (b) time waste, (c) energy waste, (d) equipment waste, (e) money waste, and (f) space waste.
2. From the point of origin, waste can be classified as (a) industrial waste, (b) commercial waste, and (c) office waste.
3. From the point of view of causing health problem, waste is classified into (a) hazardous waste, and (b) non-hazardous waste.

### Causes of industrial waste

1. **Waste of time:** This arises when a worker does not do his job in the factory. This is also known as idle time. The reasons for not working may be classified into two types.
   (a) The worker does not want to exert himself. This may be because of several factors. The work may be monotonus, extremely fatiguing or psychologically demotivated, and so on.
   (b) The worker may have to wait for work. Such situations are waiting for spares, waiting for tools, waiting due to machine breakdown, waiting due to lack of power, etc.
   Another aspect of wastage of time is to take more time for the completion of the work than what it should normally require. Here again the causes may be manifold. Lack of training, inefficient machines, substandard raw material, improper design causing excessive scrap, inefficient materials handling, etc. are some such causes.

2. **Waste of materials:** Material wastage can occur in many ways and may be examined under the following heads:
   (a) Design
   (b) Manufacturing operations
   (c) Distribution
   (d) Storing

   At the design stage, improper specification for materials, unrealistic tolerance, choice of inappropriate materials, use of costly materials, where cheaper ones may serve the purpose, etc. contribute to waste of material.

   During manufacturing operations, waste of materials occur due to excessive rejections, excessive consumption of costly materials, and poor handling methods.

   At the distribution stage, wastage may occur due to damage of products. This again may be because of several factors, such as choice of wrong type of transportation, wrong packaging, or inefficient handling equipment.

   Wastage can occur in storing due to unproductive stock piling, pilferage, deterioration, obsolescence, etc.

3. **Wastage of equipment and machinery:** Another important source of wastage is in the area of machinery and equipment. It is obviously desirable to keep the equipment and machinery busy for as long as possible to derive maximum benefit. If the machineries remain idle, it is wastage. Again, the causes may be many. There may be delay in getting the job, due to faulty planning and scheduling procedures. There may be frequent breakdown, due to poor maintenance or there may not be sufficient work-load to keep the machine busy for most of the time. Frequent change over from one product to another leads to considerable idle machine time.

4. **Wastage of space:** A common cause for wastage of space is because of the fact that most organisations reserve some "space for future expansion". However, it must always be remembered that there is optimum size beyond which it would be uneconomical to expand an existing organisation. In other words, there is always a limit to expansion.

5. **Wastage of manpower:** Wastage of manpower can occur owing to delays caused by waiting for materials and tools, waiting for instructions or idling due to non-availability of job. Human efforts can also be wasted due to unnecessary or fatiguing work. Improper selection, training and placement are also causes of wastage of manpower.

### Methods of dealing with the waste

1. **Recycling of waste:** Recycling of waste means use of waste as input in the same process. For example, cotton yarn of inferior quality can be used in manufacturing coarse cloth in the same industry.

2. **Reuse of waste:** Reuse of waste takes place when waste material is used for manufacture in some other processes. For example, bagassee obtained in sugar industry can be used in paper making in paper mills.

3. **Disposal for profit:** Some by-product which are not required by the industry can be sold for profit. For example, in oil refinery, kerosene can be sold at its market price to fetch income besides recovering its cost.
4. **Disposal as scrap:** Iron filing, leather cuttings, wood pieces etc., which are part pieces obtained in manufacturing process, can be sold at least to recover its cost.
5. **Obsolete stock disposal:** Obsolete stock and unused materials are owing to discontinuation of a particular product which are another form of waste and can be sold as second-hand materials to other industries for whom they may be useful.
6. **Damaged materials:** They can be returned back to the supplier and replacement obtained. Otherwise, credit note may be obtained.
7. **Sales as junk material:** These are outrightly treated as waste. It is disposed at throw-away prices only to utilize the space efficiently and avoid accumulation of garbage in the factory.
8. **Sale to dealers:** Some form of waste can be sold to dealers or agents who deal with such waste, may be directly or by conducting an auction.
9. **Sale to employees:** If employees are interested in buying such waste products or materials, it can be sold at a concessional rate.
10. **Donations:** Laboratory equipments, journals and magazines, research reports, etc. can be donated to schools and colleges.

### Wastivity *vs* Productivity

Wastivity and productivity are interrelated concepts. If wastivity is reduced, productivity can be increased. In other words, productivity is the elimination of waste of all forms.

### Measurement of waste

Waste can be measured by adopting any of the following methods. A standard is established in respect of waste based on past performance. If the actual waste exceeds the standard waste it indicates the inefficiency in the organisation

$$\text{Wastivity} = \frac{\text{Waste}}{\text{Input}}$$

$$\text{Gross wastivity} = \frac{\text{Total waste}}{\text{Total input}}$$

$$\text{Net waste} = \text{Total waste} - \text{Waste recycled within the system}$$

$$\text{Net wastivity} = \frac{\text{Net waste}}{\text{Total input}}$$

### Measures to reduce excessive wastage in industries

The measures that are to be taken to avoid excess wastage can be enumerated under the following headings:

1. **Measures related to production method**

   (a) Replacing defective machines,

(b) Redesigning the improper designs,
(c) Avoiding overloading of machines,
(d) Avoiding excess utilisation of resources,
(e) Solving problems associated with new and old products, and
(f) Avoiding shrinkage, leakage and eraporation process.

2. **Measures related to materials**
   (a) Avoid use of sub-standard quality of materials,
   (b) Avoid obsolete materials, and
   (c) Reduce the variety of materials.
3. **Measures related to labour**
   (a) Ensure adequate training to employees,
   (b) Ensure adequate supervision,
   (c) Avoid excess overtime work, and
   (d) Avoid idle time of employees.
4. **Measures related to handling and storage of materials**
   (a) Proper storage of materials as soon as they are received,
   (b) The corks of containers should be tightly closed,
   (c) Material handling equipments must be used to handle heavy and bulk quantity of materials, and
   (d) Proper case must be taken to avoid theft and misappropriation of material.
5. **Measures related to disposal**
   (a) Make available scrapped, spoilt or defective materials ready for sale,
   (b) Select the best buyer. Quotations can be obtained and the revenue receivable should be compared with market price, and
   (c) Control the quantity of losses. Physical control is to be exercised over such materials before they leave the factory and there must be frequent review of quantities produced, repaired and sold.

Special productivity techniques are employed to investigate, locate and finally eliminate the areas of wastes. Some of these techniques demand sophisticated know-how and considerable time and money, while some are relatively inexpensive and do not demand anything more than commonsense and logical reasoning. The most commonly used techniques are as follows:

1. Work study
2. Value analysis
3. PERT/CPM
4. Market research
5. Operations research
6. Statistical quality control
7. Inventory control
8. Ergonomics.

# QUESTIONS

## A. Very short answer type

1. What do you mean by waste?
2. Give four examples of solid waste.
3. What do you mean by liquid waste?
4. What do you mean by scrap?
5. Distinguish between a waste and a scrap.
6. Give four examples of scrap.
7. What are spoilages?
8. Distinguish between spoilage and scrap.
9. What are objectives?
10. State four factors which give rise to defectives.
11. Distinguish between wastivity and productivity.

## B. Short answer type

1. Explain the various types of waste.
2. Explain the causes of industrial waste.
3. Explain the various methods of dealing with waste.
4. Suggest measures to reduce excessive wastage in industries.

Chapter 23

# TIME STUDY

## INTRODUCTION

Time study is the analysis and determination of time necessary to perform a given task. It replaces the old practice of using past performance, judgment or trial as a method of establishing the time allowed for the performance of a task.

The concept of time study was first coined by F.W. Taylor. He evolved and laid down a definition and explanation of time study.

Frank Gilbreth and his wife, Lillan Gilbreth, well known as pioneers in motion study, made a major contribution in the field of time study. They became interested in the problem of fatigue and the methods by which it could be reduced and the concept of relaxation allowances developed from their pioneering work.

From 1911 onwards, an American Industrial Consultant, Charles E. Bedaux, further developed Taylor's time study and devised a common unit in terms of which the quantity of work in any job could be recorded. It was intended to provide a standard upon which bonus assessment could be based and by which the amount of work in different jobs could be compared. His principal contribution was the introduction of the rating factor.

The object of time study is to determine by direct observation the quantity of human work in a specified task, and hence to assess the proper time for the task.

## TIME STUDY EQUIPMENT

In order to make time study, certain equipment is essential. Basic time study equipment consists of:

1. **The stopwatch:** Two types of watches are in general use for time study, namely the fly back and the non-fly back types. A third type—the split hand stopwatch—is used sometimes.
2. **The study board:** The study board is simply a flat board, on which to place the forms for recording time studies. It may have a fitting to hold the watch so that the hands of the work study man are left relatively free and the watch is in a position to be read easily. A strong spring clip fitted to the board holds the forms on which the study is recorded.
3. **Time study forms:** Studies can be made on plain paper, but it is convenient to have printed forms of a standard manner and that no essential data are omitted.

## TIME STUDY PROCEDURE

The major steps included in a formal study are as follows:

### 1. The objective

The objective of the study is to be clearly defined. This includes a definition of the use of the results, the precision required and the desired confidence in the estimation of the time parameters. The purpose of the study and the necessary preparations are reviewed with the supervisor of the operating department.

### 2. Selection of the job for the study

Job selection for the sake of conducting time study is undertaken for the following reasons:

(a) Whether the job is a new one not previously carried out.

(b) Whether there has been a change in material or method of working and a new time standard and is required.

(c) Whether a particular operation appears to be a "bottleneck" holding up subsequent operations.

(d) Whether standard time is required prior to the introduction of an incentive scheme.

(e) Whether to investigate the utilisation of a part of the plant where the output is considered low.

(f) When the cost of a particular job appears to be high.

### 3. Selecting a worker

The next step is to select a worker whom the work study man will observe during his study period. It is a good policy to ask the foreman and workers' representatives to suggest the suitable worker to be studied first, emphasizing that he should be a competent steady person. His rate of working should be average or slightly better than average. It is important, especially where the job is likely to be done on a large scale by a large number of workers, to take studies on a number of qualified workers. A qualified worker is defined as: "one who is accepted as having the necessary physical attributes possessing the required intelligence and education and has acquired the necessary skill and who knowledge to carry out the work in hand to satisfactory standards of safety, quantity and quality"

### 4. Breaking the job into elements

It is found, in practice, that a worker's rate of working may vary not only from cycle to cycle of a job, but frequently within each cycle itself. This obviously would make it difficult to make an overall rating for the period of the study or even a separate rating for each cycle. Hence, it is customary before starting a time study to breakdown the job into what is called "elements" except those having a very short cycle time. The definition of an element is as follows:

An element is a distinct part of a specified job selected for convenience of observation, measurement and analysis.

The "work cycle" is defined as "the sequence of elements which are required to perform a job or yield a unit of production. The sequence may sometimes include occasional elements". A work cycle starts at the beginning of the first element of the operation or activity and continues to the same point repeating of the operation or activity, and continues to the same point albeit in repetition of the operation or activity.

### Reasons for breakdown of elements

A detailed breakdown into elements is necessary:

(a) To ensure that production work (or effective time) is separated from unproductive activity (or ineffective time).

(b) To permit the rate of working to be assessed more accurately.

(c) To enable the different types of elements to be identified and distinguished so that each may be treated appropriately.

(d) To enable elements involving high fatigue to be isolated and to make the allocation of fatigue allowance more accurate.

(e) To facilitate checking the method.

(f) To enable a detailed work specification to be produced.

### Types of elements

There are eight types of elements. The standard definition of each along with example is listed below:

(a) **Repetitive element:** Repetitive element is an element which occurs in every work cycle of the job. Examples are: picking up a part prior to an assembly operation, putting aside a finished component, etc.

(b) **Occasional element:** It is an element which does not occur in every work cycle of the job, but which may occur at regular intervals. Examples are: clearing machine table, and adjusting machine setting.

(c) **Constant element:** It is an element for which the basic time remains constant whenever it is performed. Examples are: switch on a machine or measure a dimension.

(d) **Variable element:** It is an element for which the basic time varies in relation to some characteristics of the product, equipment or process. The example is cleaning the rusted surface where time varies depending on the amount of rust.

(e) **Manual element:** It is an element performed manually by a worker.

(f) **Machine element:** It is an element automatically performed by a power-driven machine. The examples are: glass bottles, press car body shell to shape.

(g) **Governing element:** It is an element occupying a longer time than that of any other element which is being performed conveniently. An example is 'boil kettle of water' while 'setting out teapot and cups.'

(h) **Foreign element:** It is an element observed during a study which, after analysis, is not found to be a necessary part of the job. Examples are: unexpected tool breakage, and call from foreman for discussion.

### Use of stopwatch

There are two principal methods of timing with the stopwatch.

(a) **Flyback timing:** In flyback timing the hands of the stopwatch are returned to zero at the end of each element by pressing a KNOB and are allowed to start immediately for recording the next element, the time for each element being obtained directly.

(b) **Cumulative timing:** In this method, the position of the stopwatch hand is recorded at the commencement of the study and at the end of each element without ever returning it to zero.

For individual element, times are determined by substraction of successive readings. The purpose of this procedure is to ensure that the whole time during which the job is observed is recorded in the study.

### 5. Rating of time study

Time study is based on a record of the observed times for the purpose of doing a job. Along with an assessment of the effectiveness of working of the observed worker in relation to a concept "combining one or more factors necessary to carrying out of the job, such as speed of movement, effort, dexterity, consistency." Assuming that the worker also takes suitable rest, which is allotted to the job, this optimum. effectiveness applied to the 'effort' portion of the job "will enable him to produce, without becoming more than healthy tired, what is defined as standard performance over the working period."

Thus, "standard performance results when the work in a job is done at ideal degree of effectiveness and the appropriate relaxation allowance is taken in full." It has been found that in the long run this performance can be maintained throughout without over-exertion and deterioration of health.

A scale has therefore been fixed which gives this effectiveness a value of 100 and this is designated as the standard rate of working. Observers are trained in various ways who should be able to recognize the standard rate of working and assess the degree to which a worker's observed speed and effectiveness varies from the '100' concept. The procedure in which this assessment is noted simultaneously with the observed time is known as 'Rating'.

The definition of 'Rating' issued by the British Standard Institute is as follows:

*"Rating is the assessment of the worker's rate of working relative to the observer's concept of the rate corresponding to standard pace."*

The definition of 'Standard performance', as issued by the British Standard Institute, is as follows:

"Standard performance is the rate of output which qualified workers will naturally achieve without over-exertion as an average over the working day or shift provided, they know and adhere to the specified method provided they are motivated to apply themselves to their work." Thus, performance is denoted as 100 on the standard rating and performance scale.

The rate of working is most generally accepted as corresponding to the standard rating and is equivalent to the "speed of motion of the limbs of a man of average physique walking without a load in a straight line on level ground at a speed of 4 miles an hour." Thus, it is a brisk, business like rate of walking.

### 6. Determination of basic time

After having recorded a number of observed time and corresponding ratings for each of the elements of a job, the next step is to determine the basic time for each actual time noted. Thus, process is termed 'extension' and consists of determining what time would have been taken to perform each element had the worker been working at the standard rate of performance, i.e., 100. Each observed time for each element is multiplied by the corresponding rating and the result is divided by the standard rating (100).

Thus,

$$\text{Basic time} = \frac{\text{Observed time} \times \text{Observed Rating}}{\text{Standard Rating}}$$

Basic time is defined as the time for carrying out an element of work at standard rating.

## 7. Completing the study summary sheet

The time study man enters the basic time for each of the constant elements listed on a study summary sheet and the number of occasions on which the element is observed, i.e., its frequency. He note the relationship between basic time and the controlling variable against the elements or records a reference to the graph sheet on which the basic time derived has been analysed.

To complete the summary, the time study man must enter a record of any occasional elements observed and also any foreign elements which may have appeared during the study. Usually, the contingency basic minutes are expressed as percentage of the total basic minutes of repetitive work observed during whole of the study.

### *Relaxation allowance*

After establishing the basic time per cycle required by the qualified worker to perform each element at standard rate of working, it is necessary to find out what percentage of time should be added to each element to allow for fatigue, personal needs and other contingencies.

Relaxation allowance is added to the basic time with an intention to provide the worker an opportunity to recover from the physiological and psychological effects of carrying out specified work under specified conditions. It also considers time for personal needs. The extent of the allowance depends on the nature of the job.

Following are the principal factors for which the relaxation allowance per cent is computed:

(a) Motions
(b) Personal needs, including basic fatigue
(c) Thermal conditions
(d) Atmospheric conditions
(e) Visual fatigue
(f) Other influences of environment.

Personal needs, including basic fatigue, are common to all work and hence are termed as constant allowances. The basic fatigue allowance is that assumed to be adequate for a seated worker engaged on light work in good working conditions using hands, legs and senses normally.

### *Contingency allowance*

A worker's job sometimes may include a number of minor activities which may be infrequent that otherwise economic work measurement cannot be undertaken. To account for this, a contingency allowance expressed as a percentage of the basic times may be included in the work content for the job. The contingency allowance covering the activities must be clearly specified and carefully computed for the particular conditions relating to each job. The activities must also be listed. Examples of such activities are:

(a) Sharpening of tools
(b) Obtaining special materials
(c) Obtaining a special purpose equipment from a central tool room
(d) Consultation with the supervisor
(e) Consulting a manual or work order for specifications.

***Calculation of standard time***

The standard time for the job is the sum of the standard time for all the elements of which it is made up plus the contingency allowance.

***Motion study***

Motion study has been defined by F.B. Gilbreth as "the science of eliminating wastefulness resulting from the use of unnecessary, ill-directed and inefficient motions." Motion study consists of dividing work into the most fundamental elements possibly studying these elements separately and in relation to one another, and from these studied elements when timed, building methods of least waste.

***Elements of motion***

The concept of 'motion' is essential in the discussion of motion study. Manual work is generally performed with the motions of hands which are also known as 'Therbligs' F.B. Gilbreth has listed these motions as:

1. Search or find
2. Select
3. Grasp
4. Position
5. Assemble
6. Plan
7. Transport empty
8. Transport loaded
9. Avoidable delay
10. Unavoidable delay
11. Rest for overcoming fatigue
12. Hold
13. Dissemble
14. Inspect
15. Release load and
16. Preposition.

**Rules of human motion**

The rules of human motion, as enunciated by Parker, are reproduced below:

(A) Rules pertaining to the use of the human body:

1. There should be balanced distribution of the work between the two hands so that they begin as well as end their work at the same time.
2. Both hands should not be idle during the same period, except during the rest period.
3. The work of the two hands should follow opposite and symmetrical motion pattern.
4. The lowest practical and usable ciassification of body motions should be employed.
5. Maximum use should be made of the momentum developed by body motions. If the momentum cannot be effectively used but must be overcome by muscular action, every effort should be made to eliminate or reduce the momentum.
6. Smooth flow of motions produce less fatigue and are preferable to short motions involving stops and changes in direction. In other words, continuous curved motions are preferable to straight line motions involving sudden and sharp changes in direction.
7. Ballistic movements are easier, faster and more accurate than controlled movements.
8. Sequence of motions should be arranged to build rhythm and automation into the operation.
9. Hands should be relieved of all work that can be done by the feet or other parts of the body.

(B) Rules pertaining to the arrangement of the work place:

10. Tools and accessories should have a definite location and should be conveniently located for easy accessibility.
11. Tools, materials and other devices should be easily accessible and close to the working areas.
12. Gravity feed bins should be used to deliver the material close to the point of use and at a height which will eliminate lifting or change in direction in carrying the material from the bin to the point of use.
13. Use of "drop delivery" or ejectors whereby the operator may deliver the finished article by releasing it in the position in which it was completed, without moving his hands to dispose it of.
14. Adequate illumination should be provided for workers to look at things properly.
15. The height of the work place and chain should be such that the operator should either be able to sit or stand in performing his work.
16. Chair is to be provided to the operators to make good posture possible.
17. The hands should not perform any work that can be done more effectively by a jig, fixture or foot-operated device.
18. Where possible, the colour of the work place should be selected so as to aid visual perception and reduce eye strain.
19. Proper ventilation by air, which is conditioned for temperature and humidity, should be provided for comfort and health.

## MICRO-MOTION STUDY

Micro-motion study is the subdivision of an operation into motions and their analysis for the improvement of the work cycle. Detailed bodily movements, especially highly skilled motions, are recorded and the time is measured by taking motion pictures at a constant speed with a micrometer from the background.

### Advantages of motion study

1. The worker is able to produce more units per hour and earn more wages by simplifying the movements and reducing the sequence. The employer is also benefitted by the increased production.
2. It helps the production controlling department in routing the work through the department.
3. It helps in carefully planning material handling equipments which not only increases speed of production but also reduces material handling cost.
4. It helps the foreman to know causes for where the progress is slow and enables him to teach the workers the best method of performing the task.
5. It helps the personnel department to induct the right type of workers.
6. It leads to increased safety measures.
7. It provides good working conditions to the employees.

### Difference between time study and motion study

| Time Study | Motion Study |
|---|---|
| 1. Time study is a technique of work measurement. | 1. It is a technique of method study. |
| 2. Time study is a quantitative analysis leading to the establishment of a standard time irrespective of the ultimate use of the results. | 2. Motion study is a qualitative analysis of work situation which leads to the improvement of an operation. |
| 3. Time study is used to measure the operation time, the unit being 0.01 minute with the help of a stopwatch. | 3. Motion study is used to measure the time of motion elements, the time being recorded to 0.0005 minute by means of a micrometer. |
| 4. By conducting time study, a standard time is fixed for determining wages and maintaining efficiency in production. | 4. By conducting motion study the best method of performing an operation is established. |

## QUESTIONS

### A. Object type

**I. Choose the correct answer from the following alternatives:**

1. The father of time study is
   (a) Mr F.B. Gilbreth
   (b) Mrs. F.B. Gilbreth
   (c) F.W. Taylor
   (d) H.L. Gantt
2. The real founder of motion study was
   (a) F.W. Taylor
   (b) F.B. Gilbreth
   (c) H.L. Gantt
   (d) H. Emerson

**II. Write *True* or *False* for the following sentences:**

1. 'Motion study' of a work cycle should be made only after improvement based on operation analysis has been achieved.
2. Motion study raises employees' productivity and reduces fatigue by selecting the fewest basic motion.

3. Micro-motion study achieves its biggest improvements in repetitive manufacture where many operators do identical jobs.
4. Time study is useful only for wage incentive purposes.
5. Time study is more applicable to repetitive than to job-order manufacture.
6. In setting the standard time for a task the analyst should include allowance for fatigue and unavoidable delay.
7. Production methods can be improved only while taking time standard.

## B. Very short answer type

1. What do you mean by 'time study'?
2. State the utilities of time study.
3. What do you mean by 'motion study'?
4. Distinguish between time study and motion study.
5. What do you mean by 'micro-motion' study?
6. Mention the advantages of motion study.
7. What is Therblig?

## C. Short answer type

1. Explain the procedure involved in time study.
2. Write notes on (a) Relaxation allowance (b) Contingency allowance.
3. Enumerate rules involved in motion study.

## ANSWERS TO OBJECTIVE TYPE QUESTIONS

I. 1. (c), 2. (b).

II. 1. T, 2. T, 3. T, 4. F, 5. T,
6. T, 7. F.

# Chapter 24

# WORK STUDY

## ■ DEFINITION OF WORK STUDY

Keith Lockyer, in his book, *Production Management*, has defined work study as "a management service based on those techniques, particularly method study and work measurement, which are used in the examination of human work in all its contexts and which lead to systematic investigation of all the resources and factors which affect the efficiency and economy of the situation being reviewed in order to effect improvement". Work study is one of the important tools of management which indicates the areas requiring investigation so as to set right the defects in manufacturing. Work study is especially concerned with productivity. Mostly, it is used to increase the amount produced from a given quantity of resources without further capital investment except sometimes, on a very small scale. In a nutshell, the objective of work study are as follows:

(a) The most effective use of plant and equipment,

(b) The most effective use of human effort, and

(c) The evaluation of human work.

## ■ VALUE OF WORK STUDY

There is nothing new about the investigation and improvement of operations in the workshop or elsewhere. Managers have been doing this ever since human effort was first organized on a large scale. The prime value of work study lies in the fact that its systematic procedure enables quite ordinary men to achieve results as goods as those of a less systematic genius.

Work study succeeds basically because it is systematic, both in investigation of the problem being considered and in the development of its solution. Obviously, systematic investigation is time consuming. The factory manager or shop foreman in his day-to-day work is usually not free from interruptions for long. But again, it is absolutely essential to obtain all the facts on what is happening in the course of an activity. This is because, unless all the facts are known, it is impossible to be sure that any alterations in procedures which are made are based on accurate information and will be fully effective. The implication is that work study must always be a full time responsibility of someone who is a staff and not a line position.

## ■ BASIC PROCEDURE OF WORK STUDY

There are eight steps in performing a complete work study. They are:

1. SELECT the job or process to be studied.

2. RECORD from direct observation everything that happens using suitable recording techniques.
3. EXAMINE the recorded facts critially.
4. DEVELOP the most economical method.
5. MEASURE the quantity of work involved in the selected method and determine a standard time for doing it.
6. DEFINE the new method and the related time.
7. INSTALL the new method with the standard time as agreed standard practice.
8. MAINTAIN the standard practice with the help of proper control procedure.

## ■ TECHNIQUES OF WORK STUDY

Work study includes two closely related techniques, viz. (1) method study, and (2) work measurement.

### 1. Method study

Method study is the systematic recording and critical examination of the existing and proposed ways of doing work as means of developing and applying easier and more effective methods and reducing costs.

Method study is primarily concerned with finding better ways of doing things and it imporves efficiency by elimination of unnecessary work, avoidable delays and other forms of waste. The following are some of the reasons for undertaking method study.

(a) Bottlenecks generating high work in progress, long delivery times or unbalanced work-flow,
(b) Idle plants giving rise to underutilization of resources,
(c) Poor morale on account of trivial complaints, high absenteeism. These may arise from tedious work,
(d) Inconsistent earnings, and
(e) Poor quality, which may arise from poor working methods or conditions.

#### *Steps involved in method study*

The following steps are involved in a method study:

1. **Selection of the task to be studied:** The selection of the task to be studied is a managerial responsibility. To conduct method study, it involves incurring of expenditure. So, an estimate of the likely costs should be made before starting the study. If the study is not justified by the cost incurred, then it should be avoided and not conducted at all. Three basic factors must be considered while selecting a job for method study. They are: (a) economic factor, (b) technical factor, and (c) human factor.

2. **Recording the facts:** The second step in the method study is recording the facts by direct visual observation. The facts must be recorded preferably at the time and place of occurrence. The following are some of the important methods used for recording:

(a) **Process charts:** These are charts which show the sequence of events diagrammatically by means of a set of a "process chart symbols". Their purpose is to provide an unambiguous record of the processes so as to analyse and improve each process of operation.
(b) **The multiple activity chart:** It is a chart which is used to show the time relationship between two or more men, machines or materials. Time is recorded on the left hand side and

a brief description of the activities on the right hand side. From the chart, the ratio of working to non-working time can be determined so as to balance the work within the available time.

(c) **SIMO chart (simultaneous movement chart):** In this chart, the movement of two or more parts of a worker's body is recorded.

3. **Analyse the facts and develop new method:** The facts are analysed by asking the following questions:

(i) *Purpose*
- What is being done?
- Why is it being done?
- What else could be done?
- What should be done?

(ii) *Place*
- Where is it being done?
- Why there?
- Where else could it be done?

(iii) *Sequence*
- When is it done?
- Why then?
- When else could it be done?

(iv) *Person*
- Who does it?
- Why that person?
- Who else could do it?

(v) *Means*
- How is it done?
- Why that way?
- How else can it be done?

These questions are asked in the above order. If the purpose is discarded, all other questions are meaningless. If this is changed, then the sequence, person, and means may be altered. Thus, a new method is developed.

4. **Define and install:** This step implies presentation to the management, preparation and installation of method study.

5. **Maintain:** This step implies checking and overhauling of the method study.

## 2. Work measurement

The procedure involved in measuring or forecasting the rate of output of an existing or newly designed operation as well as in determining how much time is consumed for various productivity and non-productivity activities of a process, operation or job is known as 'work measurement'. The term 'work measurement' is generally used to denote all the techniques of time measurement of work system.

### *Utility of work measurement*

The management of a factory makes use of work measurement as a technique for:

(a) **Evaluation of work methods:** A stopwatch time study is used to measure the various elements of the production process that is used to indicate the source of delay and areas where time may be reduced.

(b) **Determination of standard time:** Standard time is the time required by a normal operator, working under normal conditions and with normal skill and speed to complete one unit of work of satisfactory quality. Standard time serves as the basis for:

(i) Fixing incentive system of wage payment.

(ii) Evaluating the actual performance of an individual.

(iii) Determining the number of operators for a specific volume of output.

(iv) Estimating the cost of jobs performed at the operation.

### *Objectives of work measurement*

(a) To compare the efficiency of alternative methods. Other conditions being same, the method requiring minimum time forms the best method.

(b) To balance the work of members of teams, so that forms as far as possible, each member has a task which takes equal time to perform.

(c) To determine the number of machines an operator can run.

(d) To enable schedules of work to be prepared by reasonably relating accurate assessments of human work to plant capacity.

(e) To serve as the basis of realistic and fair incentive schemes.

(f) To provide information on the basis of which estimates for tenders, selling prices and delivery schedules may be prepared.

(g) To serve as a basis for labour budgeting and budgeting control systems.

(h) To enable estimates to be prepared for future labour requirements and costs.

### *Procedure in work measurement*

Work measurement is carried out in three stages. These stages are:

(a) **Analysis:** The work to be studied is broken down into its constituent parts or elements.

(b) **Measurement:** The time for an operator to carry out each element is determined.

(c) **Synthesis:** The elements are combined together to form a logical pattern of work and a total standard time established.

### *Work measurement techniques*

The various work measurement techniques are as follows:

1. **Synthesis:** Synthesis is a technique for building up the time for a job at a defined level of performance by totalling element time obtained previously from time studies on other jobs containing the elements concerned, or from 'synthetic data'.

Synthetic data is the name given to tables and formulae derived from the analysis of accumulated work measurement data arranged in a form suitable for building up standard time, machine process time, etc. by synthesis.

Synthetic times are used as substitute for individual time studies in the case of jobs made up of elements which have recurred a sufficient number of times in jobs previously studied to make it possible to compile accurate representative time for them.

**Advantages of synthesis**

(a) They are more reliable as they are based on the data derived from a large number of studies.

(b) They are economical. It has been claimed that savings of up to 90% of the cost of time study may be effected.

(c) They often eliminate the need for prolonged individual studies.

(d) They are valuable in estimating time standards for production planning and estimating for quotation purposes.

2. **Analytical estimating:** "Analytical estimating is a technique whereby the time required to carry out elements of a job at a defined level of performance is estimated from knowledge and practical experience of the elements concerned."

It is used for measuring non-repetitive work when it has not been possible to compile sufficient data to enable the synthesis of basic time for all the elements involved. The same principle of breaking the job down into elements is observed as in other work measurement techniques, except that those elements for which time to be estimated are of longer duration than elements for timing and rating. The technique serves all the basic purposes of work measurement, through it is slightly less precise owing to the greater reliance on judgment. Its successful use includes the areas of engineering maintenance as well as engineering construction its use is likely to be extended to many aspects of process work and other fields.

The success of this technique lies very much on the character and ability of the estimator and working knowledge of the qualified person. His judgments are also more likely to be accepted by workers.

The essential features of analytical estimating are:

(a) The employment of craftsman skilled and experienced in the work concerned as estimators.

(b) Giving these craftsmen a thorough training both in method and time study.

(c) The making of an initial method of the job in as much details as economically possible.

(d) Breaking the job down into elements and determining a time for each element based on standard performance. Where possible, element times are derived from time study data or synthetic time, where no such data exists, and times are estimated on the basis of the estimator's experience.

(e) When all the element times at 100 ratings have been determined they are added together and the total basis time for the operation is worked out. Relaxation allowances are added as a percentage of the total time along with any additional allowance.

There are many practical problems in the application of analytical estimation which make it unsafe for use by inexperienced work study men. The guidance of an expert should be sought.

3. **Predetermined motion time systems (PMTS):** In addition to synthetic data arrived at by time study of job elements, there are several ways of obtaining standard data based on the elementary

human motions on which all human work is based. The first of the well-known system is called "work factor", which originated in 1934 in a large manufacturing corporation in Philadelphia. The object was to eliminate the element of human judgment in conventional stopwatch time study. Special measuring devices were employed to calculate the basic time values and the means of modifying the values for different classes of motions through thousands of observations. In 1941, the Methods Engineering Council in Pitsburg made some refinements in the systems hitherto made public and a parallel work was done by the Methods Time Measurement (MTM) Association.

Work factor recognise certain basic motions which are modified by elements of difficulty, which tend to make movements slower, weight or resistance, directional control, the need for care, change of direction and stopping a motion by manual control. Each such factor is called a "work factor" and modifies the basic time value.

In MTM, the basic motions are analysed in greater details and the predetermined times, therefore, need no modification. Several British companies have adopted these systems under the general headings of PMTS (Predetermined Motion Time System) – the "British Standard Term".

The theory behind the systems is that manual work in industrial conditions can be regarded as consisting of different combinations of a relatively small number of basic motions. Since it has been demonstrated that within practical limits the time required for skilled workers to perform any one of these basic motions is constant, by synthesis it is possible to construct patterns of basic motions for such work and to build up time values from them.

All such systems require a fairly lengthy period of intensive training under expert guidance, and trainees are unlikely to be able to apply the methods satisfactorily unless, they are already skilled and experienced in the methods analysis before assimilating special instructions.

**Advantages of PMTS**

(a) Once personnel are trained to use them the tabulated values are ready for immediate use and do not have to be built up within any individual organization.

(b) They are universal in character and not confined to a limited number of elements. Time standards for most of the physical activities can be built up from the basic times.

(c) Attention is focussed on the method before the time can be set and offer made is more precise means of recording than any other existing system.

(d) Because of detailed breakdown, any change in a method can immediately be identified.

**Disadvantages of PMTS**

(a) Some research workmen have pointed out that after time for a particular motion is influenced by the motions preceding and succeeding it. It may not therefore be valid to add times for individual small motions in the way required by the systems.

(b) The systems are generally restricted in their application to repetitive jobs and are generally uneconomic for non-repetitive jobs.

(c) The systems have limitations when applied to restricted work and are not universally applicable.

# QUESTIONS

## A. Objective type

**Choose the correct answer from the following alternatives:**

1. Work study comprises of two main techniques, viz.
   (a) Time study and job evaluation.
   (b) Method study and work measurement.
   (c) Value analysis and work measurement.
   (d) Time study and motion study.
2. Work study is most useful where
   (a) production activities are involved.
   (b) Industrial relationships are to be improved.
   (c) Worker is to be proved wrong.
   (d) The image of manager is to be improved.

**Ans.** 1. (b), 2. (a)

## B. Very short answer type

1. What do you mean by work study?
2. State the objectives of work study.
3. Mention the two techniques of work study.
4. What do you mean by method study?
5. State any four reasons for which method study is conducted.
6. What is work measurement?
7. State the utility of work measurement.
8. State the objects of work measurement.
9. List out the steps involved in work measurement.

## C. Short answer type

1. List out the steps involved in work study.
2. Explain the steps involved in method study.
3. Explain the techniques of work study.

Chapter 25

# PRODUCTIVITY

## ■ MEANING OF PRODUCTIVITY

According to the *Oxford Illustrated Dictionary* of productivity means efficiency in industrial production to be measured by some relationship of outputs to inputs.

## ■ DEFINITION OF PRODUCTIVITY

It is defined as the quotient obtained by dividing output by one of the factors of production. In this way, it is possible to speak of productivity of capital, investment or raw materials according to whether output is being considered in relation to capital, investment or raw materials.

In economics, productivity is the ratio of what is produced to what is required to produce it. Usually, this ratio is in the form of an average expressing the total output of some category of goods divided by the total input, say, raw materials or labour.

Very often, productivity is linked closely with labour input. In this sense, the International Labour Organisation has defined it as "the ratio between the volume of output as measured by production indices and corresponding volume of labour input as measured by employment indices".

## ■ PRODUCTION *vs* PRODUCTIVITY

The term 'productivity' is often confused with the term 'production'. Many people, think that the greater the production, higher is the productivity. This is not necessarily true. Production is concerned with the activity of producing goods or services, whereas productivity is concerned with the efficient utilization of resources (input) in producing goods or services (output). If viewed in quantitative terms, production is the quantity of output produced, while productivity is the ratio of the output produced to input used.

Suppose that a company manufacturing electronic calculators produced 10,000 calculators by employing 50 people at 8 hours per day for 25 days. Then, in this case

$$\text{Production} = 10{,}000 \text{ calculators}$$

$$\text{Productivity (of labour)} = \frac{10{,}000}{50 \times 8 \times 25 \text{ man-hours}}$$

$$= 1 \text{ calculator per man-hour}$$

Suppose this company increased its production to 12,000 calculators by hiring 10 additional workers at 8 hours per day for 25 days. Then, the

Production = 12,000 calculators

Productivity (of labour) $= \dfrac{12{,}000 \text{ calculators}}{60 \times 8 \times 25 \text{ man-hours}}$

$= 1$ calculator

Clearly, the production of calculators has gone up by 20% (from 10000 to 12000) but the labour productivity has not gone up at all. Thus, it implies that an increased production does not necessarily mean increased productivity.

## ■ OBJECTIVES OF PRODUCTIVITY

1. To eliminate waste in all forms.
2. To reduce cost and make items cheaper.
3. To provide better standard of living to maximum number of people.
4. To improve working conditions and reduce fatigue.
5. To earn more revenue for the government.
6. To help the worker in earning higher wages.
7. To enable the shareholders to get higher dividend.
8. To enable the management to get more capital.

## ■ BENEFITS OF PRODUCTIVITY

The improvement of total production of a product or service results in the reduction of the total cost per unit. Therefore, improving the total productivity results in two favourable management strategies.

1. Reduction of the selling price of a product or service without sacrificing the present profit margin.
2. Increase in the profit margin without reducing the selling price.

If strategy (1) is adopted as result of improvement in total productivity;

(a) 'Consumers' will benefit through savings by purchasing the product or service at lower prices for the same quality or even better quality in some cases,

(b) The 'organisation' will most likely benefit through a gain in market share and thus might, in turn, create greater revenue-generating opportunities and take advantage of the economies of scale,

(c) The 'employees' of the organisation will benefit through increases in real wages or salaries, when the organization sincerely shares the productivity gain with its employees.

If strategy (2) is followed as a result of total productivity improvement;

(d) The shareholders or owners of the organization will benefit through larger dividend on their shares. The organisation will also have a better chance of reinvesting the profits in new products, services, processes and ventures.

## FACTORS AFFECTING THE INDUSTRIAL PRODUCTIVITY

The following factors affect the industrial productivity:

### 1. Human factors

Human factors, which affect productivity, are as follows:

(a) Human nature.

(b) Human behaviour.

(c) Ability to do work which is determined by education, training, experience, aptitude of employees.

(d) Willingness to do work. This, in turn, is affected by motivation, morale, wages and incentives, for workers participation in management, promotion policy and other physical facilities, such as good lighting, ventilation and other working conditions.

### 2. Technological factors

The various technological factors, which influence productivity, are as follows:

(a) Size of the factory.

(b) Product design, standardization, simplification, specialization.

(c) Regular material and power supply.

(d) Automation and degree of mechanization.

(e) Regional and maintenance facilities.

(f) Location and layout of factory.

(g) Material handling system.

(h) Production planning and control system.

(i) Research and development facilities.

(j) Quality control system as well as inspection method.

(k) Inventory control techniques.

### 3. Managerial factors

Some of the managerial factors which affect productivity, are as follows:

(a) Structure of good organization.

(b) Good relation between superior and subordinates.

(c) Extent of delegation of authority.

(d) Extent of centralisation of authority.

(e) Various levels of management.

### 4. Financial factors

Availability of huge finance facilitates the organization to spend on research and development, recruitment of professional managers, adoption of latest technology, ability to stock materials, etc. definitely affect productivity.

### 5. Sociological factors

This include attitude of people towards work, management, training development, education, etc.

### 6. Government policy

This include:

(a) Taxation policy,
(b) Industrial licensing,
(c) Enactment of labour laws, and
(d) Monetary policy.

## ■ TECHNIQUES FOR PRODUCTIVITY IMPROVEMENT

Some of the techniques which improve productivity are as follows:

1. **Work study:** Scientific analysis and improvement of work in all its aspects is a very useful technique of increasing productivity. Work study results in improvement in plant layout, material handling system, process design, working conditions, etc. These, in turns, help to minimise defective work and waste.

2. **Research and development:** Constant research and development leads to the discovery of better techniques of production and improvement in existing machinery, equipment, etc. The rate of technological progress is a direct determinant of productivity.

3. **Incentive schemes:** Wage incentive schemes seek to motivate employees by paying extra renumeration. Profit sharing or bonus, labour welfare measures and good working conditions also help in this regard. All these schemes foster a sense of belonging and closer human relationship. As a result, there is reduction in idle time caused by absenteeism, labour turnover, accidents and disputes.

4. **Production planning and control:** Scientific task planning ensures timely supply of inputs, proper maintenance of plant, efficient work, scheduling and regulation of day-to-day activities in the plant. It facilitates full utilisation of plant capacity and achievement of production targets.

5. **Worker's participation in management:** Worker's participation in management is considered an effective tool for improving productivity. It helps in developing mutual understanding and cooperation between management and labour. Joint consultation, suggestion scheme, two way communication, grievance procedure are the main forms of workers participation in management.

6. **Automation:** Mechanisation, automation and rationalization constitute the major breakthrough for increase in productivity. These schemes are effective, provided the productivity gains are equitably shared with workers. Such measures increase the speed and accuracy of work.

7. **Management by objectives (MBO):** MBO is a process whereby the superior and subordinates jointly identify the specific measurable goals, definite results expected of each individual and jointly assess the contribution of every individual. It is an approach for integrating the individuals with the organisation. A link is created between the organisational goals and individual's targets so that an employee can see how his work contributes to the goals of the organization. Subordinate's participation in setting goals and action plans and in reviewing performance provides a good measure of self-control. As a result, there is improvement in the understanding, motivation, and morale of the individual.

8. **Job enrichment:** Job enrichment is the process of redesigning a job in order to enlarge its scope and to give the worker more to do. Its purpose is to improve job satisfaction, motivation and morale of workers. When the job is engineered to workers the de-humanisation element is reduced so as to improve productivity and to reduce cost. It provides an opportunity for the satisfaction of higher level needs.

The following methods can be adopted for job enrichment:

(a) Give workers new and more varied tasks to perform,

(b) Provide greater freedom and self-control in performing jobs,

(c) Give opportunity to do the whole task rather than its element,

(d) Give workers greater responsibility for their own work, and

(e) Supply production report (feedback) directly to workers.

9. **Flexitime:** Flexitime is a relatively new work pattern which is a major departure from tradition. It allows the workers to set their own work hours subject to a minimum number of hours per week. During a particular period, all workers are required to be present. Such a period is called "core hour". Subject to these limitations, workers are given the freedom to decide when they will work.

Flexitime helps to reduce worker alienation and to raise productivity. It reduces the tyranny of supervisors and provides job opportunity to working mothers, aged persons and students. It has greater motivational value than four days of work in a week. By permitting workers the right of self-determination, flexitime reduces tardines, overtime and short term absenteeism.

10. **Quality of work life (QWL):** QWL is a new technique for improving productivity and quality of work. A QWL programme consists of the following elements:

(a) **Labour-management:** A major change is required in the philosophy and attitude of management and labour. The attitude of antagonism and opposition must be replaced by a feeling of togetherness. Supervisors and workers must learn to work together and to mutually solve problems. Management must take the initiative unilaterally to develop mutual cooperation and constructive relationship on the production floor. Management must provide the conditions to motivate workers to increase productivity. These conditions include good pay, proper working conditions, and job security etc.

(b) **Collective bargaining:** The collective bargaining agreement must be based on the mutuality of interests on the shop floor.

(c) **Participative management:** Management must adopt a more open and democratic style in place of the classical style of use of authority. Employees must be permitted to participate in the decision-making process.

## ■ PRODUCTIVITY INDEX

If we measure output and input and find out their ratio, we get productivity index.

There are many factors that affect productivity. These factors are so interlinked that sometimes it becomes difficult to say, for example, whether increased productivity is the result of better machineries, better skill or better management. However, we have seen that, in general, elimination of wastage improves productivity. Therefore, productivity is inversely proportionate to wastage. Lower the wastage, higher the productivity and vice versa. Hence, if we wish to measure productivity, we must develop relationship between the output and the wastage of input factors. In other words, we can say that for a given output, lower the input greater is the productivity. Here "input" may mean any single factor, such as capital, manpower, machinery, time, fuel, etc., or it may mean a combination of several of them.

1. **Labour productivity:** This is defined as "the ratio of output to input of man hours." Expressed in the form of formula, it is

$$\frac{\text{Total production in length, weight, volume}}{\text{Man hours worked}}$$

2. **Machine productivity:** This is given by the following formula:

$$\frac{\text{Total production in length, weight, volume}}{\text{Machine hours worked}}$$

3. **Material productivity:** This is given by the following formula:

$$\frac{\text{Total production in length, weight, volume}}{\text{Material consumed in length, weight, volume}}$$

## ■ TOTAL *vs* PARTIAL PRODUCTIVITY

Comparison of output with all the input factors taken together is called total productivity. Comparison, of output with any one of the input factors, keeping all other factors constant is called partial productivity.

## ■ MEASURES TO BE TAKEN FOR INCREASING LABOUR PRODUCTIVITY

Labour productivity can be improved by the joint efforts of the government, employers and employees. Following steps may be taken to increase labour productivity:

(a) Recruitment and selection of right type and required number of employees.
(b) Training of the employees.
(c) Provision of good working conditions for employees.
(d) Adopting production planning and control techniques.
(e) Standardization and simplification of work.
(f) Fixation of reasonable rate of wages and incentives.
(g) Conducting time, motion and work studies.
(h) Adopting job evalution and merit rating techniques.

## QUESTIONS

### A. Very short answer type

1. What do you mean by productivity?
2. Distinguish between production and productivity.
3. State any four objectives of productivity.
4. What do you mean by productivity index?
5. What do you mean by labour productivity?

6. How is machine productivity obtained?
7. What do you mean by total productivity?
8. What do you mean by partial productivity?
9. State any four measures to be taken to improve labour productivity.

## B. Short answer type

1. State the benefits of productivity.
2. Explain the factors which affect industrial productivity.
3. Explain the various techniques used for improving productivity.

# Chapter 26

# AUTOMATION

## ■ DEFINITION OF AUTOMATION

Automation is a term which is applied to denote the recent developments in the design and application of machine tools in the production process. Although automation has been a part of industry's vocabulary from the earliest times, its utility and contribution has become more common in recent times. Automation involves the application of automatic control mechanisms with an element of self-regulation. It implies the process of moving the materials in and out of machines and the operating of machines automatically, all without human control. Automation requires machines, tooling, and mechanical handling devices so integrated as to become, in effect, one continuous machine.

Bethel, Smith and Atwater define automation, as "the addition of handling and control equipment to automatic machines for continuous automatic production through a series of operations without human guidance and control."

According to John Diebold, "Automation deals both with automatic operation and the process of making things automatic. In the latter sense, it includes several areas of industrial activity, such as product and process redesign, the theory of communication and control and the design of machinery."

## ■ BASIC CONCEPTS OF AUTOMATION

Peter, F. Drucker has enunciated three concepts of automation. They are as follows:

### First concept

There is a basic pattern of stability and predictability behind the seeming flux of phenomena.

This concept refers to research undertaken in order to know the new technology to do things in a better way. As in other sciences, even technology of automation has a basic pattern of stability when it is referred to research. When we consider other branches of science, all the steps involved in research, such as observation, analysis and interpretation, are stable. This basic pattern is also equally applicable to the technology of automation having the feature of forseeing the innovation in the areas of designing, production, distribution and customer service.

### Second concept

It focuses on the process which it sees as an integrated and harmonious whole.

This principle emphasises the totality of manufacturing process but not on the individual factor of production. The focus is on one integrated and harmonised process through the automation of overall process. In such a system, there are provisions for processing, transferring, packaging, inspecting and controlling the materials throughout its flow. Thus, the integrated process is the best process that will produce maximum output, with less human efforts and at the lowest cost of production.

### Third concept

The new technology has a concept of control to maintain equilibrium between ends and means, output and effort.

To improve efficiency it is always essential to introduce a system of control. The control device may be sometimes installed in the machine itself so that any defect in production can, in turn, be reconverted into finished product. Thus, control implies rejection of certain things which are unnecessary for the process or adjustment of the process to make the product satisfactory.

## ■ FORMS OF AUTOMATION

When automation is introduced in factories it takes three forms, viz.

### 1. Integrated mechanisation

This form of automation is installed in factories where continuous production takes place without stoppage. The entire process of production is undertaken by automatic machines. The role of employees is restricted to start, stop, inspect, maintain and repair the automatic machines. In the words of James Lundy an integrated automation permits an operator to set up a system that without further manual control, transfers parts from one station to another, processes the parts at each station, inspects them and rewards them, if necessary. The examples of industries where this form of automation is employed are chemical industries, pharmaceutical industries, glass manufacturing industries, and such industries where production is integrated and continuous.

### 2. Feedback control

This refers to a system of control exercised by automation. In order to maintain efficiency, the process of operation is predetermined and the actual process is compared with the predetermined one. In case if the actual course of action differs, necessary corrective action is taken. Feedback control ensures necessary adjustments in its operation to move along the predetermined course of action. The aim of this form of automation is to check the deviation in order to conform to the standard by correcting or adjusting such variations.

### 3. Computer technology

Whereas the above two forms are used in the production departments, computer technology is applied in the office and administration division of the factory. The chief device that constitute this form of automation is electronic computer. The component of modern electronic computer is a punch card input system, an arithmetic unit and a memory device having stored punch cards. Computers are used for accounting and decision-making process. In addition to computers, data processing equipments are also used. This consists of electric tape punching, reading typewriters and tabulating card machines. This is largely used in production planning and control process.

## ■ GUIDING PRINCIPLES OF AUTOMATION

There are four guiding principles of automation. They are as follows:

### 1. Automaticity

This principle implies that the entire production process is undertaken by automatic machines with least interference of employees. Automatic machines can be installed both in continuous manufacturing or intermittent industries. In the former type, automation embraces a complete process, fabrication or assembly. In the latter case, only a segment or section of a factory alone is covered by automatic machines, the rest being undertaken by employees.

### 2. Reduction of human labour

Automation is based on the principle of reducing the manual and mental labour. In the course of manufacturing, very often it involves carrying materials and semi-finished goods from one place to another place. Under such circumstances, automatic material handling equipments, such as elevators, conveyos, etc. are used. Similarly, to reduce mental labour, computers are used to calculate, tabulate, process and to present the required information.

### 3. Control

Any system of automation without a system of control is incomplete. As it was pointed out earlier, a control device forms an integral part of automatic machines. The automatic control system with the 'Feedback' arrangement enables management to detect variations and to rectify them.

### 4. Focus on process

This principle emphasises the process of work rather than human skill. The continuous process of work helps in increasing both quantity and quality of goods. This holds good particularly in mass production which helps management to set up the machinery with a view to have harmonised process. This ensures the output of one machine to constitute as the input of another machine until production is complete.

## ■ ADVANTAGES OF AUTOMATION

1. Automation results in the reduction of the cost of production, as automatic machines reduce the number of employees to minimum. Thus, the increase in wages payable to them gets saved by installing automatic machines.
2. Automation increases the quantity of production as it can be worked continuously without stoppage.
3. Goods produced through automatic machines will be of uniform quality.
4. It helps in expediting the production process and in delivering the goods on the promised date. This adds to the reputation of the factory.
5. It is more safe to perform the work through automatic machines than mannually operated machines.
6. It helps in automatic planning, scheduling and dispatching of work without bothering much the production control staff.

7. Automation leads to decreased scraps, defectives, and wastages in the production process.
8. As automation ensures continuous production, it reduces the piling up of inventories which cause hindrance for the movement of men and other type of materials.
9. It increases the standard of living owing to provision of better quality of goods at cheaper prices.

## ■ DISADVANTAGES OF AUTOMATION

1. The initial investment on automatic machines is very high. Small scale industries cannot afford to invest such huge amount of capital on automatic machines.
2. It lacks flexibility, as whenever the design of the product is to be changed, it may not permit so easily.
3. Whenever the volume of production is to be reduced, especially during the period of depression, automated factory goes waste as it cannot be put to any other use. But the depreciation is to be still provided without getting any output.
4. In an integrated automated system, failure of one part leads to failure of the entire system.
5. It leads to unemployment and therefore trade union is opposed to automation.

## ■ IMPACT OF AUTOMATION

1. Automation eliminates routine and monotonous job in factories. Instead, it is turning every job into a more challenging one. Some such jobs are those which require set-up ability, knowledge of maintenance, highly skilled employees involving payment of high wages.
2. Automation definitely improves the quality, reduces prices, expands the market, offers new line of product and creates more civilised communities.
3. Automation definitely leads to unemployment. As a measure of caution, it is better to install automatic machines gradually, i.e., step by step but not all of a sudden.
4. It leads to more competition by the entry of competitors in the field of production.
5. Automatic equipments are immensely used not only in the field of production but also in other institutions, such as banking, insurance, and government organisations.

## ■ CYBERNETICS

Cybernetics is defined as that field of knowledge which deals with the science of communication for the purpose of control. Whenever automations is introduced, the control is exercised either mechanically or electrically. This involves the following phases:

(a) The receipt of signal indicates a significant deviation from the standards of correct performance.
(b) The evaluation of the signal and the determination of the corrective action should be taken.
(c) The "Feedback" of information regarding the corrective action to a device which controls the performance of the operation.
(d) The corrective adjustment of the process by the device to restore the satisfactory performance.

# QUESTIONS

## A. Very short answer type

1. Define automation.
2. Mention the basic concepts of automation.
3. Mention the guiding principles of automation.
4. Define Cybernetics.

## B. Short answer type

1. Explain the guiding principles of automation.
2. Explain the basic concepts of automation.
3. State the advantages and disadvantages of automation.
4. Discuss the impact of automation in the recent times.
5. "Automation is inevitable we have to live with it." Explain.

# Chapter 27

# VALUE ANALYSIS AND VALUE ENGINEERING ERGONOMICS

## ■ VALUE ANALYSIS

Value analysis was developed as a cost reduction technique in U.S.A. in 1947. The credit for it goes to Lorry, D. Miles who was working at general electricals and who subsequently became the president of SAVE (Society of American Value Engineers). Value engineering was developed because of the inherent desire in mankind to make and sell cheaper poducts, keeping the utility of the products the course same.

### Value

The term "value" has different meaning. Most often, value is evaluated in terms of cost of a product. Performance is another basic factor chosen for the evaluation of value. Thus, a product or service is generally considered to have good value if it has appropriate performance and cost. Hence, it may be concluded that:

(a) Value may be increased by decreasing costs while maintaining performance, and

(b) Value may be increased by increasing performance of the employees.

#### *Types of values*

(a) **Cost value:** It is the cost of manufacturing a product or service.

(b) **Use value:** It is also called as functional value. It considers the work done, functions performed or services rendered.

(c) **Esteem value:** It involves qualities and appearance of a product (e.g., a T.V., car) which attract persons and create in them a desire to possess.

(d) **Exchange value:** A product is said to possess exchange value if the same can be exchanged for something else.

#### *Value approach*

It is an organized system dedicated to every effective means of identifying and thus eliminating the unnecessary costs. An unnecessary cost is one which neither adds to quality nor to life or appearance.

### Source of unnecessary cost

As the product makes progress through its life cycle, a number of factors contribute to continued inclusion of unnecessary costs in the product. These are briefly discussed as follows:

(a) Lack of information: Lack of information or its proper use by the decision makers quite often increases the costs.

(b) Lack of utilisation of the creative mind: Normally, the first workable solution is accepted instead of developing and analysing ideas, not only from the performance point of view but also from economic standpoint.

(c) Temporary circumstances: Sometimes, due to emergency circumstances, certain make shift arrangements are made, and these decisions tend to become permanent. They save in the cost of the product, year after year.

(d) Honest wrong beliefs: A good idea can be destroyed by honest wrong beliefs. These beliefs are the chief stumbling blocks to creativity. For example, we may honestly believe that something cannot be done or we may believe that there is a good reason why we should not do something, or we may believe that certain material is not at all good to work with, and so on.

(e) Habits and attitudes: Some jobs are done the way things are done just by force or habit, while an unbiased observer may be able to point out the way in which it can be done better.

(f) Human factors: Ineffective communication, misunderstandings and personality clashes become increasingly responsible for unnecessary costs in the more complicated system.

(g) Impact of technological advancement: It is possible to reduce the cost of an old product by the use of new processes, new products, and new materials. Cost, which is felt necessary at the time of design and development of the product, can possibly be eliminated by the use of advanced technological know-how.

Value approach has two elements, namely: (i) value analysis, and (ii) value engineering.

Value analysis is a special type of cost reduction technique which, unlike other methods, does not blindly accept the product design. Rather, it critically investigates and analyses the different aspects of materials, design and production of each and every component of the product. A component to be a part of the product must perform some function and serve some purpose. Value analysis examines the design, function and cost of each and every component in order to produce it economically without decreasing its utility, function or reliability. Value analysis is normally applied to existing rather than to new products.

## Objects of value analysis

The objects of value analysis is to generate promising ideas to

(a) simplify the product
(b) use cheaper and better materials
(c) modify and improve product design
(d) use efficient processes
(e) reduce the product cost
(f) increase the utility of the product by economical means
(g) save money or increase the profit.

**Advantages**

1. Value analysis is a much faster cost reduction technique.

2. It requires less expenditure because the value analysis team can be formulated out of the staff available in different sections like purchase, production, finance, etc.
3. Value analysis reduces production costs and adds to sales income of the product.

### Value analysis procedure

Following steps are involved under value analysis:

1. **Identifying the product:** The first step is to identify the product for which value analysis is to be carried out. The product should be one which, if redesigned, can add to the sales income and would not become obsolete in near future. Value analysis may be applied to the product as a whole or to only some of its component parts.
2. **Collecting relevant information:** The information relevant to the product may be as follows:
   (a) Technical specification with drawings,
   (b) Manufacturing processes, machine layout and instruction sheets,
   (c) Time study details and manufacturing capacity,
   (d) Completing cost data and marketing details, and
   (e) Latest developments in related products.
3. **Defining different functions:** Function specifies the purpose of the product or what the product does, what is its utility, etc. There can be three functions of a product, viz. (a) primary function, (b) secondary function and (c) tertiary function. Having identified the functions, specify value content of each function and identify the high cost areas.
4. **Creation of different alternatives:** Know functions of each component part and its manufacturing details, generate ideas and create different alternatives so as to increase the value of the product. The value analysis team can hold brainstorming sessions. All suggestions feasible or non-feasible are recorded without any criticism. The persons are encouraged to express their views freely.
5. **Critically evaluate the alternatives:** The different ideas recorded under step-4 are compared, evaluated and critically assessed for their virtues, validity and feasibility as regards their financial and technical requirements. Ideas which are technically sound and involve lower costs are further developed.
6. **Development of the best alternative:** Detailed development plans are made for those ideas which, during step-5, appear most suitable and promising. Development plans comprise of drawing sketches, building of models and conducting discussion with the purchase section, finance, and marketing divisions, etc.
7. **Implementing the alternative:** The best found idea under step-6 is converted into a prototype manufacture which ultimately goes into operation and its results are recorded. The product cost and functional analysis is carried out to assess the net saving as the result of value analysis.

## ■ VALUE ENGINEERING

Value engineering is the application of the concepts of value analysis at the design or pre-manufacture stage of the component parts with a view to cut down the unnecessary costs, without impairing the function or utility of the product.

## ■ ERGONOMICS

The study of man-machine relationship in order to improve the efficiency and job satisfaction of workers is known as ergonomics. It is also known as human engineering. The main objective of ergonomics is to assist in design and operation of man-machine environment system which will ensure physical and mental ease to the human beings. The details of equipments, most often, are determined by the engineering requirements rather than keeping the workers convenience in view. It is here that need of the study of ergonomics arises. The attempt should always be made to design the machines and equipments in such a manner that not only the user but also those in the vicinity should be protected against dangers of accidents. Guards for the moving parts, barriers for dangerous spots are some examples of safety measures that need to be installed in all factories.

Ergonomics is the study of the people at work and of work methods. It includes the study of equipment's design, hours of work and environmental conditions of work. Its purpose is to improve productivity and job satisfaction.

Ergonomics should be able to increase the usefulness of many machines and tools. There seems to be enough room for improvement in control indicators and work space management. To have the insight of the concept of Ergonomics, we have to understand the concept of "Work Study". Work study is comprised of Motion Study and Time Study.

The elements of motion can be used to break down any job to show the details of hand work. Various principles of effective motion can be stated as follows:

1. Successive movements should be so related that one movement passes easily into that which follows.
2. The order movements should be so arranged that the mind can attend to the final aim.
3. The sequence of movements is to be so framed that an easy rhythm can be established.
4. The continuous movements are preferable to angular movements involving sudden changes in the direction of movements.
5. The number of movements should be reduced as far as possible.
6. Simultaneous use of both hands should be encouraged.
7. Fixed positions should be provided for tools, materials, etc.

### Motion study techniques

The tools and techniques of motion study may be divided into three classes:

(a) **Process analysis:** It is the process of making a component or performing an activity before undertaking a thorough investigation of special operations in the process chart. The chart graphically represents, the separate events that occur during the performance of a task. The chart begins with the raw material entering the factory and follows it through every step, such as transportation to storage inspection, machining, operations and assembly till it becomes a finished unit.

(b) **Equipment utilization:** In order to have a complete breakdown of the process, the series of operations are plotted against time scale. This diagram is called an activity chart. In order to eliminate unnecessary waiting time for the operator and for machine it is important to perform the following three steps : (i) get ready, (ii) do, and (iii) put away.

(c) **Operation analysis:** The overall study of the process should result in a reduction in the amount of travel of the operator, materials and tools and should bring about orderly and systematic procedure.

## Psychological aspects

There are three main types of psychological contributions to Ergonomics:

1. Principles and practice of human relations to obtain cooperation in changes.
2. Research on methods to ensure that adequate experimental and statistical controls is there to make findings accurate.
3. Recognition of psychological characteristics of workers, such as perception, speed and tendency to boredom under certain conditions.

**Job methods:** In fact, the decisions should be jointly made by engineers and psychologists to have deep insight of the problem.

**Equipment design:** Ergonomics equipment design involves knowledge of not only the motion and time study analysis but many other areas to fit man over machine.

Motion and time studies attempt to adopt the man to the machine, whereas ergonomics places more stress on changing the machine, if necessary.

## Tools and techniques used in ergonomics

1. Experimental design
2. Mathematical modelling
3. Game theory
4. Linear programming
5. Field testing
6. Statistical sampling.

# QUESTIONS

## A. Very short answer type

1. What do you mean by value?
2. Mention different types of values.
3. What do you mean by value analysis?
4. List out some source of unnecessary cost.
5. List out the objects of value analysis.
6. State the advantages of value analysis.
7. What do you mean by value engineering?
8. What do you mean by Ergonomics?
9. How is psychology related to Ergonomics?
10. List out four tools of Ergonomics.

## B. Short answer type

Explain the procedure involved in value analysis.

# Chapter 28

# PERSONNEL FUNCTIONS

## ■ EVOLUTION OF PERSONNEL MANAGEMENT

In the olden days when factories were of small size, the number of employees were few in number. The problems of employees were less in number and the employers used to attend all the problems of employees in person. Gradually, when factories became large in size the employer could not attend to the problems of employees directly and there was a gap between employer and employee and to bridge this gap, personnel management has been developed. The development of personnel Management can be traced back to the period of Industrial Revolution. As and when the industries were expanded they were managed by professional managers instead of the owners. As a result of separation of owners and employees, the working and living conditions of the employees deteriorated. This led to the formation of trade unions with a view redress their grievances. In England, a few pioneering industrialists, such as Robort Owen and Boutton, paved the way for the development of modern personnel management. In U.S.A., the scientific management movement led by F.W. Taylor gave opportunity to the development of personnel management. The Hawthorne experiments conducted by Elton Mayo and his associates, known as human relation movement, gave further impetus to the growth and development of personnel management.

The development of personnel management in India dates back to 1929–31. During this period, the report of the Royal Commission on Labour in India recommended the appointment of labour officers to check corruption while recruiting the employees. Until the period of independence, to look after the welfare of employees, welfare officers were appointed. Subsequently, with the enactment of Industrial Dispute Act in 1947, welfare officers soon became industrial relations officer, who used to participate in collective bargaining, conciliation and adjudication. With the rapid growth of industries, the Indian industries demanded many skilled and semiskilled workers. This led the Government to cover recruitment aspect of personnel management by law. The Apprentices Act 1961, and the Employment Exchange (Compulsory Notification of Vacancies) Act, 1959 have regulated recruitment in respect of workers. Today, all matters pertaining to personnel management are governed by statutes in our country.

## ■ DEFINITION OF PERSONNEL MANAGEMENT

1. According to British Institute of Personnel Management, London, "personnel management is concerned with the people at work and with their relationship within the enterprise."
2. According to Indian Institute of Personnel Management, "Personnel Management function is primarily concerned with the human relationships within an organisation. Its objective is the

maintenance of those relationships on a basis which, by consideration of the well-being of the individual, enables all those engaged in the undertaking to make their maximum personnel contribution to the effective working of that undertaking."

3. According to William Springal, "Personnel Management is concerned with the attaining of maximum individual development, desirable working relationships between employers and employees and an effective moulding of human resources as contrasted with physical resources".
4. Edwin B. Flippo in his book, *Principles of Personnel Management,* p. 4, defines Personnel Management as the personnel function which is concerned with the procurement, development, compensation, integration and maintenance of the personnel of an organisation for the purpose of contributing towards the accomplishment of that organisation's major goals of objectives.
5. Michael Jucious, in his book, *The Management of Labour Relations,* p. 36, defines personnel management as the field of management which has to do with planning, organising, directing and controlling the functions of procuring, developing, maintaining and utilising a labour force, such that (a) the objectives for which the company is established are attained economically and effectively, (b) objectives of all levels of personnel are served in the highest possible degree, and (c) objectives of society are duly considered and served.
6. In the words of Dale Yoder, "Personnel Management is that phase of management which deals with the effective control and use of manpower as distinguished from other sources of power."

## ■ IMPORTANCE OF PERSONNEL MANAGEMENT

In order to study the importance of Personnel Management, it is worthwhile to consider at this stage the various aspects dealt with by Personnel Management. It includes three closely related aspects, viz. (i) personnel aspect, (ii) welfare aspect, and (iii) industrial relations aspect. The personnel aspect includes recruitment, selection and placement of personnel, training and development, promotions and transfers, wage administration, etc. The welfare aspect is concerned with the provisions of amenities to the workers and living conditions, health and safety, etc. The industrial relations aspect is concerned with factory's or organisation's relations with employees, such as union, management relations, collective bargaining process, disciplinary action, grievance handling and settlement, etc.

As regards the importance of personnel management, experts on management subject treat management as synonymous with personnel management. In the words of Reusis Likert, "All the activities of any enterprise are initiated and determined by the persons who make-up that institution of all the tasks of management, managing the human component is the central and most important task, because all else depends on how well it is done."

The importance of personnel management is increasingly realised because of complexity in the manager's job. This is because of the difficulty involved in selecting, retaining, and motivating the employees with required competence. The workers must be treated as our asset rather than a source of problem. This is because the success of a factory, to a large extent, depends upon the management of men.

Among all the factors of production, human factor is the most complex factor in a factory. They possess a number of characteristics, perceptions, needs, and behavioural patterns that complicate factory administration. It is just not enough to recruit workers in a factory but also to see how they react to a given situation. Personnel management deals with these human aspects in a factory.

## ■ PRINCIPLES OF PERSONNEL MANAGEMENT

The following are some of the important principles of personnel management:

1. Care and skill should be exercised in the selection of employees.
2. Introduction to the job should be friendly, skillful, and adequate.
3. Each employee should be made to feel that the efforts are really appreciated.
4. Careful and thoughtful consideration should be given to the probable effect of each rule, notice and practice on employees.
5. Employees should take part in planning those things which affect their working conditions.
6. There should be a sense of security and reasonable freedom from worry.
7. There should be a constant and intelligent effort on the part of management to be absolutely fair in every policy and every practice.
8. Each employee should have a feeling of pride in the worthfulness of his work and his factory.
9. The organisational set-up should be such that there is no confusion in any one's mind as to his duties or responsibilities.
10. Conditions should be such that working proves to be a satisfying social experience as well as a means of making livelihood.

### Objectives of Personnel Management

The term 'objective' refers to some pre-determined goals which are sought to be fulfilled individually or collectively in any factory. There are three broad objectives of personnel management, viz. (1) To maintain good relationship within the factory, (2) To enable each person to make his personal contribution to the organisation, and (3) To achieve these things through respect for human personality and the well being of the individual. In the words of Michael J. Jucions, personnel functions are expected to help in the attainment of the following goals:

(a) Producing and distributing an acceptable production service.
(b) Continuous yielding of satisfactory profits in investors and satisfactory wages, salaries and other personnel values to employees at all levels.
(c) Meeting community and social obligations.
(d) Attaining the forgoing objective economically and effectively.

## ■ FUNCTIONS OF PERSONNEL MANAGEMENT

The functions of personnel management can be classified under two headings, viz. (1) Operative functions and (2) Managerial functions.

### 1. Operative functions

Operative functions of personnel management are as follows:

#### *(A) Employment*

This function involves

(a) tapping the sources of labour supply,

(b) selection of employees,
(c) introduction of the worker to the factory's policies and to his departmental head, and
(d) maintaining records of all hired, discharged and laid off employees.

***(B) Promotion, transfers, discharges, demotions and separations***

This function involves

(a) Establishment of lines of promotion,
(b) Establishment of lines of policies regarding transfers,
(c) Formulating policies regarding discharge and demotions, and
(d) To deal with separation initiated by the employees.

***(C) Formulation and direction of training programmes in keeping with factory objective***

***(D) Job analysis and evaluations***

This function involves,

(a) Analysis of all jobs of office, supervisory and manual workers, and
(b) Evaluation of each job according to some scheme that will show the relative worth of each.

***(E) Fixeration of wages and incentives***

This involves

(a) Formulation of wage plan,
(b) Study of the cost of living and community wages with recommendations to management in relation to the factory's practices,
(c) Formulation of policies for rewarding employees's suggestions, and
(d) Supervising bonuses of profit sharing programmes.

***(F) Health and sanitation***

This includes provision of

(a) First aid to the injured,
(b) Hospitalisation programme,
(c) Sanitation,
(d) Health education, and
(e) Conduct studies to eliminate fatigue, monotony, mental strain, occupational diseases.

***(G) Industrial safety***

This includes

(a) Imparting safety education,
(b) Study of the causes of accidents,
(c) Safety inspection and providing guidance to Employees Safety Committees,
(d) Formulation of safety-practice code,
(e) Fire protection, and
(f) Watch and ward service.

***(H) Financial aids to employees***

This function includes

(a) Employees Mutual Benefit Societies
(b) Profit sharing unions
(c) Mutual Savings Programme
(d) Pension Plans
(e) Workmen's Compensation Insurance
(f) Special discount on factory's products.

***(I) Employee service activities***

It includes provision of

(a) Recreational activities
(b) Housing facilities
(c) Canteens
(d) Transport facilities
(e) Educational facitities.

***(J) Research, record keeping, reports and follow-up***

It includes:

(a) Maintaining all files and records of employees,
(b) Periodic check of all records for promotions, wages increase, transfers, etc.,
(c) Special reports to executives and supervisors,
(d) Study and analysis of personnel trends and programmes of others, and
(e) The personnel audit.

***(K) Employee-employer cooperation***

It includes:

(a) Various forms of employee-employer relations,
(b) Procedure for promoting company welfare in terms of improved product and competitive position, and
(c) Procedure for lay-offs, discharge and promotion.

## 2. Managerial functions

The managerial functions of personnel management pertains to the activities concerned with planning, organising, directing and controlling.

***(A) Planning***

Planning determines in advance a personnel programme. It involves ability to think, analyse and to take decisions about personnel problems.

***(B) Organising***

After the plan is formed, the people available have to be grouped and their relationship established in a which should enable the employees to achieve organisational objectives. Organisation function involves grouping of the activities required to attain the planned objectives, defining responsibilities of the people in the organisation, delegating appropriate authority to them to enable them to discharge their respective responsibilities and establishing structural relationship to generate coordination of the individual efforts towards accomplishment of the factory's objectives.

### *(C) Directing*

This function is concerned with getting the work done through subordinate by the seniors. It consists of issuing orders and instructions by the seniors to the subordinate the execute the functions of a factory by implementing the plans. This also involves senior's expectation from his subordinates to take initiative in the given task. However, much depends upon the motivating factor behind the directing function.

### *(D) Controlling*

It is concerned with periodical performance appraisal, employment counselling, personnel research, etc. with a view to ensure that it conforms to the laid down standards. This function leads to innovations and new ideas relating to planning, motivation, etc.

## ■ QUALITIES OF PERSONNEL MANAGER

The important qualities required for a successful manager are:

### 1. Sense of vocations

As the Personnel Manager has to deal with persons, it is very necessary for him to possess a feeling of humanity and concern for his fellow workers. It is the lack of this feeling which is responsible for disappointment and discouragement in a personnel job. He must create a better social and industrial order among employees.

### 2. Sense of social responsibility

Factory is a part of society whose success depends upon the effective cooperation of the people working in the factory. The Personnel Manager must create facilities for deriving better cooperation of the workers. He must appreciate employees of the factory as social units and deal with them in the social background of the factory.

### 3. Capacity to leadership

The Personnel Manager occupies the position of leadership in the Personnel Department. He should speak frankly with labour union and other groups of workers. He should be in a position to convince others about his view points and this is possible only when he has all leadership equalities.

### 4. Personnel integrity

Personnel Manager must be a man of integrity and trustworthy so that all employees of the factory can share their problems and grievances without reservation.

### 5. Ability for persuation

The Personnel Manager must persuade the management of the factory to implement the proposals or suggestions made by him so as to solve the problems of employees. On the other hand, he must also persuade the employees to reconcile with the objects and philosophy of the factory.

### 6. Dynamic personality

Dynamic personality of the Personnel Manager is as a result of number of abilities, such as knowledge and intelligence in handling personal problems, ability to mix with employees, cheerful disposition, courtesy, social awareness, personal dignity and experience.

### 7. Other qualities

(a) Loyalty to the factory
(b) Sense of responsibility
(c) Respect for the opinion of others
(d) Decisiveness
(e) Interest in subordinates
(f) Willingness to support both to his superiors and subordinates.

### Responsibilities of personnel manager

The responsibilities of a Personnel Manager can be summarised under the following points:

1. He is responsible for the top management for all personnel matters and help the chief executive in formulating the personnel policies.
2. He is responsible for departmental managers involving the personnel problems arising in their respective department.
3. He is responsible for selecting the right type of employees for the factory.
4. He is responsible for fixation and administration of wages and salaries.
5. He is responsible for proper maintenances of records pertaining to the employees in the factory.
6. He is responsible for maintenance of industrial peace.

## ■ ORGANISATION OF PERSONNEL DEPARTMENT

The organisation of personnel department depends upon the following factors:

1. Size and nature of the factory
2. Number of employees, working in the factory
3. Relative importance of personnel department in the factory
4. Attitude and managerial philosophy of the factory.

Herzberg has suggested three bases for organising personnel department. They are

### 1. Functional organisation

This basis of organising personnel department is suitable in large sized factories. The personnel department is headed by a competent person known as Personnel Manager. Under this type of organisation, the personnel department is subdivided into small sections, such as Employment Section, Training and Development Section, Wage Administration Section, and so on. These sections are headed by Assistant Personnel Manager under the supervision of Chief Personnel Manager. The Chief Personnel Manager reports to the Managing Director. The following chart shows functional organisation of personnel department.

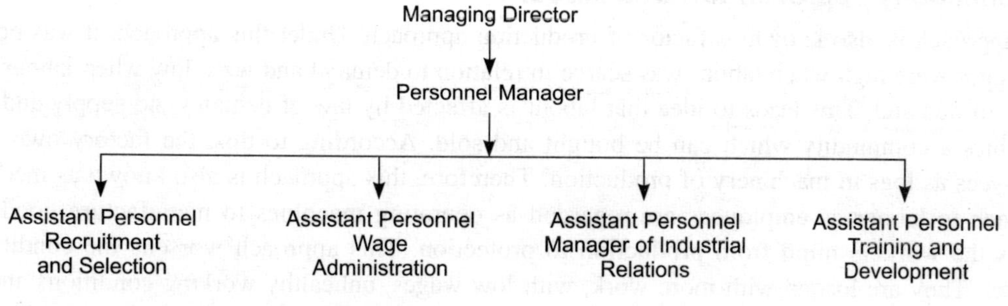


**Fig. 28.1** Chart showing functional organisation of personnel department

## 2. Service Basis of Organisation

In most of the factories, the Personnel Department is considered as service rendering department. On this basis Personnel Department can be divided into line functions and staff functions. The following chart shows this type of organisation.

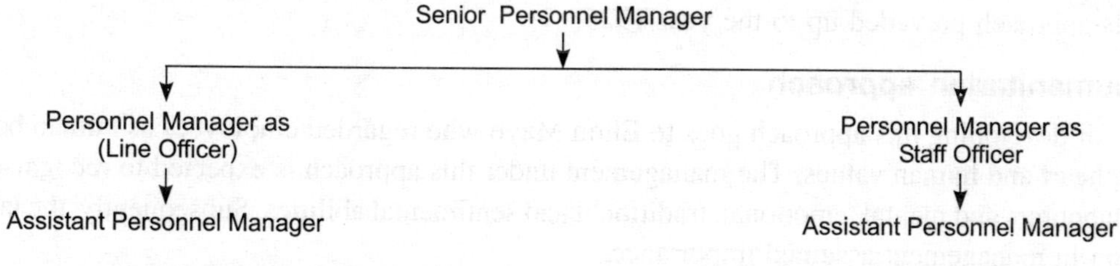


**Fig. 28.2** Chart showing organisation of personnel department on the basis of service

## 3. The clienele Basis of Organisation

Under this basis, the Personnel Department is organised on the basis of work force, such as male workers, female workers, and child workers. This type of organisation can be shown under the following chart.

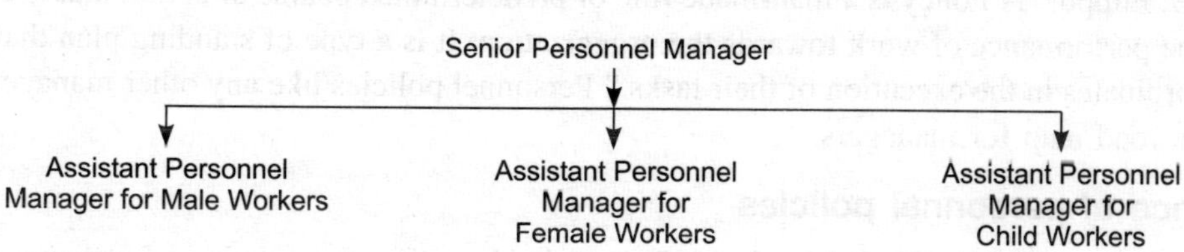


**Fig. 28.3** Chart showing organisation of personnel department on the basis of clients

### Philosophy of personnel management

The attitude and behaviour of management towards its labour force is known as philosophy of Personnel Management. The philosophy of personnel management is always affected by the outlook of management and their level of thinking. The management adopts a number of approaches while dealing with employees although none of them have been accepted by employees in full. These approaches have been dealt with hereunder in order to evaluate and know the impact on the workers and personnel management policies.

### 1. Commodity approach towards labour

This approach is also known as factor of production approach. Under this approach, it was observed that wages were high when labour was scarce in relation to demand and were low when labour was in excess of demand. This leads to idea that labour is affected by law of demand and supply and labour resembles a commodity which can be bought and sold. According to this, the factory owners take employees as logs in machinery of production. Therefore, this approach is also known as mechanical approach to labour as employees are regarded as operating machines to manufacture goods. This diverts the workers mind from production to protection. This approach worsens the conditions of workers. They are loaded with more work, with low wages, unhealthy working conditions and other types of exploitation. This leads to the struggle of employees and eventually to trade unionism. The commodity approach of labour prevailed up to the end of 19th century and was later substituted by the protective approach.

### 2. The protective approach

This approach is also known as paternalistic approach. The employers have now recognised the fact that welfare of employees has a direct effect upon their productivity. Hence, a set of labour welfare measures have been introduced in factories. This view was proposed by the British industrialist Robert Owen. This approach prevailed up to the year 1925.

### 3. The humanitarian approach

The credit for developing this approach goes to Elton Mayo who regarded employees as human beings with mind, heart and human values. The management under this approach is expected to recognise the dignity of labourers and mental, emotional, traditional and sentimental abilities. Subsequently, the labour participation in management assumed importance.

## ■ PERSONNEL POLICIES

In order to discharge the duties and responsibilities of the Personnel Department, it is necessary to formulate personnel policies in advance. In the words of Michael Jucious, policies are basic rules established to govern functions so that they are performed in line with the desired objectives. According to Edwin B. Flippo, "A Policy is a man-made rule or predetermined course of action that is established to guide the performance of work towards the organization. It is a type of standing plan that serves to guide subordinates in the execution of their tasks." Personnel policies like any other managerial policy serves as a road map for managers.

### Importance of personnel policies

1. **Help in achieving the objectives of organisation:** The formulation of policies makes the efforts of each worker as well as the management goal oriented.

2. **Uniformity in decisions:** Well drafted personnel policies bring continuity, uniformity, and consistency in various decisions relating to the employees. They eliminate ad-hoc decisions, partiality for some and subdual of others.

3. **Encouragement to decentralisation:** Decentralisation means distribution of work among different persons and departments. Personnel policies accomplishes every type of work because of the existence of good relationship between superior-subordinates.

4. **Helps in controlling:** The personnel policies enables to compare the actual performance with the predetermined performance and in case of any difference it helps us to take necessary steps to make actuals to conform to the predetermined ones.

5. **It increases the morale of workers:** The personnel policies, which are nothing but the goals and the means to realise it, enables the workers to know the philosophy and objectives of the factory. They take policies as guide to accomplish the objectives. This increases the morale of workers.

6. **It guarantees security:** The personnel policies are common for both members and non-members of the trade union. Therefore, workers need not necessarily fall prey to the whims of the supervisors and managers.

7. **Guide to management:** Personnel policies guide the management as to who has to do the work, when and how. It also helps the management in solving personnel problems.

## ■ OBJECTIVES OF PERSONNEL POLICIES

As mentioned earlier, policies serve as guidelines to the achievement of objectives and of the factory. Its success or failure is measured on the basis of the objectives for which these were initially formulated. They are formulated to achieve the following objectives:

### 1. Maximum use of human resource

The best use of manpower can be ensured only when employees are scientifically selected and placed on a suitable job. The process of matching the job with individuals is an important aspect in factories. Profits cannot be maximised until the factory does not utilise the manpower to the best of its capabilities. Personnel policies define jobs and their responsibilities and thus helps in their proper manning.

### 2. Maximum individual development

Personnel Policies must encourage healthy and constructive competition among the workers so that they may be motivated for their maximum development.

### 3. Sound industrial relations

The efficiency of a factory, to a large extent, depends upon industrial peace. A harmonious relationship must prevail between employer and employees. Bringing about good industrial relations is also the central idea of mental revolution coined by F.W. Taylor. Personnel policies aims at maintaining sound industrial relations.

### 4. Other objectives

These include: (a) proper recognition of work force and protection of their prestige, and (b) safeguarding the interests of labour and management.

### Contents of a personnel policy

Personnel policies should consist of:

1. History of the factory's growth.
2. Employment practices and conditions of employment.
3. Grievance handling procedure.
4. Safety rules and regulations.
5. General practice, such as procedure of getting pay, leave policy etc.

6. Relation between employer and employee.
7. Financial aid to employees.
8. Medical facilities to employees.
9. Educational opportunities to employees.
10. Leave pay, holiday with pay.
11. Sickness benefits or allowances.
12. Freedom to discuss any item of interest with management.
13. Social security and other compensations.
14. Collective bargaining.
15. Procedure for disseminating information regarding factory policies.
16. Discipline.

## Characteristics of good personnel policies

Good personnel policies should contain the following characteristics:

1. They should be specific as to principles but in general avoid minute details.
2. They should be permanent in nature but should not be inflexible.
3. They should possess organic unity of purpose in keeping with the other policies of the organisation.
4. They should recognise the fact that some workers prefer to deal with management on an individual basis rather than through an organised group.
5. They should recognise the desire of many workers for recognition as groups in many of their relationships.
6. They should recognise individual difference.
7. They should be formulated with due regard for the interest of all parties concerned—the employees, the public, the consumers, and the owners.
8. They should conform to government regulations.
9. They should provide for adequate means for becoming generally known to all the facts available.
10. They should be the result of careful analysis of all the facts available.

## Factors affecting personnel policies

### *1. Laws of the country*

The various laws and labour legislation govern the various aspects of personnel matters. Policies should be in confirmity with laws of the country.

### *2. Social values and customs*

These are the codes of behaviour of any community which should be taken into account in framing the policies.

### *3. Management philosophy and values*

Management does not work together for any length of time without clear breed philosophy and set of values which influence their actions concerning the work force.

### 4. Stage of development

All changes, such as size of operations, scale of technology, innovations, fluctuations in the composition of work force, decentralisation of authority and change in financial structure, influence the adoption of personnel policies.

### 5. Financial position of the factory

The personnel policies cost money which will be reflected in the prices of the product. Because of this, prices set the absolute limit to organisation's such policies.

### 6. Union objectives and practices

How all the employees are organised? What is their bargaining capacity? What are their pressure techniques? All these factors are responsible for personnel policy.

### 7. Type of work force

The assessment characteristics of work force and what is acceptable to them is the responsibility of an effective personnel staff. A policy which is not appropriate is hardly worth implementation.

## RECENT TRENDS IN PERSONNEL MANAGEMENT

The following are some of the recent trends in the area of personnel management:

1. **The selection and utilisation of minority groups:** From the stand point of recruitment and selection of new employees, emphasis in modern days is to select neglected and weaker sections of the society. The policy formulated by the government regulation has added more importance to this changing trend.

2. **Better methods of training and placing disadvantaged individuals:** Recognising the social responsibility of business, factories in modern days hire, educate and train those employees such as physically handicapped, Ex-service men, etc. who are not otherwise eligible for such employment.

3. **Automation of personnel records:** With the introduction of data processing equipment most of the factories are making use of automatic machines for maintaining personnel records. Instead of making use of paper files, nowadays magnetic tapes are made use of for storing applicant's data, performance ratings, job history, test results, promotions, payroll data and the like.

4. **Merit rating and appraisal:** Merit rating is conducted by recognising the management potential through experimentation with sample of the individual's behaviour rather than through total reliance on tests and interviews.

5. **Determining opinions of the employee and attitudes:** The management is heavily relying upon the opinions of employees instead of depending upon outside consultants. Management of factories has now fully understood that incorporation of employee's feelings and opinions in formulating plans will motivate the employees and thus increase their efficiency.

6. **Morale of employee:** The importance of the morale employees' recognised in most of the factories today. Research is undertaken to study the effect of good working conditions on employees, better employer and employee relationship, better motivation so that morale of employee is improved leading to better performance.

7. **Basic and applied research by personnel management:** Increasing emphasis is made on research covering a wide range of topics in the area of personnel management. Some of these topics relate to technical and managerial obsolescence, organisational and environmental aspects, and so on.

## QUESTIONS

### A. Objective type

**Write *True* or *False* for the following sentences:**

1. Personnel Management is an extension of general management.
2. To be more effective, personnel management should be attended to only now and then.
3. Personnel Management consists of both managerial and operative function.
4. Planning, organising, direction, and control are examples of operative functions.
5. The growing mechanisation of industry is decreasing the importance of personnel management.
6. Because of the confidential nature, personnel policy statements should not be distributed to employees.

### B. Very short answer type

1. Define personnel management.
2. Mention the objectives of personnel management.
3. What do you mean by the philosophy of personnel management?
4. Define "personnel policy".
5. Mention the objectives of personnel policies.

### C. Short answer type

1. Outline the principles of personnel management.
2. Mention the qualities of personnel manager.
3. Explain the organisation of Personnel Department in a factory.
4. Explain the various approaches to the personnel management.
5. Discuss the importance of personnel policies.
6. Define personnel policy. State its contents.
7. Outline the characteristics of good personnel policy.
8. Explain the factors which affect the formulation of personnel policies.

### D. Long answer type

Explain the functions and responsibilities of personnel manager in a modern factory.

## ANSWERS TO OBJECTIVE TYPE QUESTIONS

(1) T, (2) F, (3) T, (4) F, (5) F, (6) F.

Chapter 29

# RECRUITMENT AND SELECTION OF EMPLOYEES

## ■ MANPOWER PLANNING

Manpower is considered as the most valuable and important asset of a factory. Leon, C. Magginson in his book, *Personnel and Human Resource Administration,* views manpower as the total knowledge, skill, creative abilities, talents and aptitudes of an organisation's work force as well as the values, attitudes and benefits of an individual involved. In thc words of Bruce, P. Coleman, manpower planning is the process of determining manpower requirements and the means for meeting these requirements to carry out the integrated plan of the organisation. Many factors have contributed to the great interest of manpower planning in modern days. These factors are:

(a) Job requirements are changing fast with the change in technology.
(b) Increased need for skilled workers.
(c) National concern about labour and employment.
(d) Increased reliance on the efficiency of human resources.
(e) Changing patterns of modern management process.
(f) Mechanisation and automation introduced in factories.
(g) Expansion in the size of factories.

## ■ OBJECTIVES OF MANPOWER PLANNING

The important objectives of manpower planning are:

1. **Making correct estimate of manpower requirements:** This is the first and foremost objective of manpower planning. The forecasting of manpower helps in recruiting the right type of man on the right job. The additional workers in a factory are created by discharge, retirement, lay-offs, retrenchment and separations. Employees under such circumstances are not available all of a sudden. Manpower planning helps in the correct estimate of manpower requirements.

2. **Managing manpower according to the need of factories:** Manpower planning avoids overstaffing and understaffing in factories. To a large extent the employees available within the factory can be utilised without relying on external sources. It encourages the existing employees and, in turn, creates favourable psychological climate for motivation.

3. **Help in recruitment and selection:** Sound manpower planning helps in recruitment and selection. It helps in pursuing sound procedures of recruitment so that best workers may be available at the time of requirement. It also reduces the cost of recruitment.

4. **Maintaining production level:** Manpower planning undertakes to estimate the separation of workers on various grounds in advance. By making proper arrangement it undertakes to make alternative arrangement for substituting the workers who might leave and go from the factories. This is possible by two types of analysis, known as workload analysis and workforce analysis.

5. **Other objectives:** Other objectives of manpower planning include making development programmes of employees effective—establishing industrial peace, reduction in labour cost, and effective utilisation of labour force.

## TYPES OF MANPOWER PLANNING

### 1. Short-term manpower planning

It involves the matching of present employees with the jobs. They are offered so that they may perform their function efficiently. However, it may not always be possible to have a perfect match between jobs and individuals. So, necessary adjustments have to be made in the jobs so as to make employees fit to the job. The problems under such circumstances can be studied under the following:

(a) When an employee is less qualified than the requirements, the following steps can be taken:
   1. Providing training
   2. Change in the job
   3. Transfer.

(b) When the employees is more qualified than the requirement of job the potentials of employees are not exploited to the fullest extent and hence, the following adjustment can be made:
   1. Job enlargement
   2. Additional charge
   3. Promotion to higher position.

### 2. Long-term planning

In the long run, the management plans the manpower requirements for a long-term usually between 10 to 15 years. Long run planning considers such factors as organisational structure, technology, method of production, possible expansion of factory, and so on.

***Manpower planning can also be classified as***

1. **Replacement planing:** Replacement planning is connected with recruitment or promotion to fill expected losses. It considers ages, health problems and identifies sources of replacement.

2. **Adaptive planning:** Under this planning, the future events are known in advance and alternatives are considered and best course of action is taken.

3. **Contingent planning:** Under this planning, potential hazards are identified and advance strategies are developed.

## STEPS IN MANPOWER PLANNING

The steps involved in manpower planning has been beautifully summarised by Geisher in his article, "Manpower Planning: An Emerging Staff Function." The process of manpower planning includes forecasting, developing and controlling by which a firm ensures that it has the right number of people and the right kind of people at the right place at the right time doing work for which they are economically most useful.

Manpower planning consist of the following steps:

1. Forecasting future manpower requirements.
2. Making an inventory of present manpower resources and assessing the extent to which these resources are employed optimally.
3. Anticipating manpower problems by projecting present resources into the future and comparing them with the forecast of requirement to determine their adequacy, both quantitatively and qualitatively.
4. Planning the necessary programmes relating to selection, training, development, transfer, motivation and compensation to ensure that future manpower requirements are properly met.

## PROCEDURE OF APPOINTING AN EMPLOYEE IN A FACTORY

The procedure involved in appointing a person in a factory can be studied under the following heads:

1. Receiving of labour placement requisitions.
2. Recruitment of workers.
3. Inviting application forms.
4. Checking references.
5. Screening out unqualified and incomplete applicants.
6. Conducting employment tests.
7. Conducting oral interviews.
8. Conducting medical examination.
9. Final approval.
10. Placement and induction.

### 1. Receiving of labour placement requisitions

The function of appointing the required number of employees in a factory starts with receiving the labour placement requisitions. A labour placement requisition is a request made in written form from various production and service departmental heads. It contains particulars such as (a) job specifications, (b) educational qualifications, (c) experience, (d) skill, (e) age requirements, and (f) the number of persons required for such department. The actual number of persons required in production department depends upon sales forecasts and schedule of production for various product. The determination of employee's skills is known from engineering department. The labour placement requisitions, which are received from time to time by the Personnel Manager is consolidated so that all the required number of persons for all the departments may be appointed at the same time. This also reduces the cost involved in procuring the labour force.

### 2. Recruitment of workers

The term 'recruitment' applies to the process of attracting potential employees to the factory. It is a systematic means of finding and motivating available candidates to apply to the factory for employment. Since it is the process of searching for prospective employees, it is concerned with the range of sources of supply of labour and the recruitment practices and techniques. As the ultimate success or failure of the factory depends upon the right type of employee appointed, it is essential that the Personnel Manager taps the right source of supply for the labour force in his factory. There are two sources of recruiting. The employees, viz., 1. Internal source and 2. external source. This is presented in the following chart:

Sources of Recruitment

**Internal Sources**

1. Promotion
2. Transfer
3. Recalling retired employees
4. Trainees
5. Deputation

**External Sources**

1. Friends and Relatives of the present employees
2. Technical Institutes and Colleges
3. Advertising
4. Employment Exchange
5. Direct recruitment at gates
6. Waiting lists
7. Recruitment through Trade Unions
8. Use of Special Consultants for Recruiting

***Internal sources***

The internal source of supply of manpower refers to recruitment within the factory so as to conserve the existing manpower and avoid the complicated and expensive procedure of recruiting persons from external source. Internal source of recruitment offers the following advantages:

1. It enhances the general morale of the employees of the factory.
2. It builds loyalty among the employees by creating a sense of security.
3. It reduces labour turnover in the factory.
4. It creats a sense of sincerity among the employees.

However, internal recruitment suffers from the following disadvantages:

1. It severely narrows down the area of selection.
2. It leads to stagnation and conservation in the service.
3. Fresh candidates with talents are denied a chance of entry into the factory.
4. It does not compel the existing employees to keep abreast of new development in their fields.

The following are the important sources of internal recruitment:

1. **Promotion:** Under this source, vacancies are filled up through promotion, from the lower cadres. This gives encouragement to the employees in general besides creating vacancies at the lower levels which gives employment opportunities to the unemployed.

2. **Transfers:** Very often existing employees, who are found competent to take up a newly created vacancy, may be taken over to the department where he is more suited. Thus, transfer involves the change of place of work by an employee without any change either in status or remuneration.

3. **Recalling retired employees:** When no qualified and competent employers are available to fill up the vacancy caused by the retired employee, such a position can be filled in by recalling the retired person. But care must be taken to see that he has necessary ability and interest to continue in the factory.

4. **Trainees:** In modern days, a large number of prospective employees are offered training even before they are appointed as full time permanent employees. On such successful training, if the candidates are found suitable, they may be absorbed without resorting to external source.

5. **Deputation:** This source of recruitment is available only in big factories with branches in different localities. Instead of recruiting a stranger, who may not have adequate experience, it may be desirable to depute some of the experienced staff and other skilled employees until the new branch is firmly established. Subsequently, it can be left to the choice of the deputed staff either to continue with the branch or to come back and resume the work in the main factory.

### *External resources*

External source refers to recruitment of employees from outside the factory. External source of recuitment offers the following advantage:

1. A wider field of selection is available.
2. Fresh viewpoints and a broad outlook may be attracted.
3. Experienced and trained employees may be procured.

External source of recuitment suffers from the following disadvantages:

1. Prolonged training has to be given to new recruits involving huge expensis on training.
2. It reduces incentive to work hard among the existing workers because they feel that however excellently they may work, they have no chance of getting promotions in their factory.

The following are the important sources of external recruitment.

1. **Friends and relatives of the present employees:** The management may consider the recommendations of friends and relatives of the existing employees. It is presumed that the present employees, who are loyal to the organisation, will be in a position to introduce good, honest, and efficient workers.

2. **Technical institutes and colleges:** Under this source the factory keeps contact with educational institutions, notifies vacancies and contacts them to recommend meritorious and outstanding candidates for appointment. However, candidates who complete the course alone are considered for recruitment. But it is useful for the recruitment of technical personnel at higher level. In India, recruitment through universities and technical institutes is not common. This is due to the absence of close contact between such educational institutions and factories. Some factories like Hindustan Lever make recruitment through this course.

3. **Advertising:** In this case, advertisement with necessary details, is wanted in the newspaper, trade journals, radios and TV. Press advertisement gives full particulars about the job requirements, educational qualifications, experience, salary expected or offered and other service conditions. Suitable condidates are appointed through tests and interviews.

4. **Employment exchange:** In India, the government has set up employment exchanges in all towns. These exchanges are useful for providing jobs to unemployed persons. Those persons interested in employment have to register their names. An employer or factory informs the employment exchange about vacancies available from time to time and the exchange sends a list of suitable candidates for consideration and selection. Recruitment through employment exchanges are very common in India.

5. **Direct recruitment at gates:** Under this source, the employer displays a notice of recruitment at the factory gate and interested persons are asked to come for recruitment on a particular day, date and time. Selection is made out of the persons present at the gate. This source is convenient and

economical and it saves the expense and botheration of searching for the sources of manpower. This method is useful for temporary recruitment of unskilled persons.

6. **Waiting lists:** Some of the applicants, who had applied previously but were not selected, may be given an opportunity to come and take up the vacant job.

7. **Recruitment through trade unions:** Trade union leaders often recommend the required number of persons to the factory. But there is a danger in this source of recruitment, in the sense that the person recruited through the recommendation of union leader would always support the union and may work contrary to the ideas and ideologies of the factory.

8. **Use of special consultants for recruiting:** These are special consultants who keep the record of the persons called for interview. Consultancy service of recruitment and selection are popular in foreign countries. These agencies are mostly business firms whose incomes are derived from fees charged from clients. Many such agencies are well staffed with competent specialists and maintain high standards of ethical practice. In India, we have Tata consultancy service, ABC consultants, Farguson and Company, etc. "Unlike public agencies, private agencies are seldom used for obtaining blue collar workers. Rather, they provide technical, semi-professional or highly specialised personnel. Some private agencies operating in India have specialised in supplying blue collar workers to foreign countries particularly to Middle East and Gulf countries."

### 3. Inviting application forms

After resorting to any of the above mentioned source of recruitment, the next step in the selection process is receipt of filled in application forms from the prospective employees. The factory may sometime prepares standard blank application form in advance and it may be issued to the requisitionists after collecting a normal fee. Sometimes, the candidates themselves are asked to write applications on their own to know their abilities and hand writing. The application forms must bear three important categories of information. They are (a) biographic data, such name, age, sex and status, (b) education and past experience, and (c) references. Application forms should be as simple as possible and must incorporate questions having a bearing on the fitness of the job applied. Different colours of application forms can be made use of for different categories of employees.

### 4. Checking references

One of the information which the employer expects from the prospective employees is reference of reputed persons from whom the employer can know the honesty, efficiency and sincerity of employees. On receipt of the filled-in application form the employer writes to the persons referred to by the prospective employees requesting him to express the frank opinion of the incumbent under reference. But this information cannot always be relied as the prospective applicant would give the names of reference of the person to whom he knows well and speak good about him. It is always desirable, in case of appointment of a person who had in service in some other factory to check from the former employee. This gives an idea to on what ground the employee left the factory. To know the opinion, use of telephone mail service or even personal visit can be resorted to. To avoid delay, some factories use the printed form of checking reference and only a few columns are left blank which are to be filled in by the referee with either recommending or not recommending the candidate.

### 5. Screening out unqualified and incomplete applications

In these days of unemployment, it is common to observe that thousands of applicants apply for the job although they may not be really competent and fit for the job. With increased, application forms it becomes difficult even to select the right candidate. So, unless incompetent applications are screened out, it involves too much of time and more confusion in selecting the right candidate. For screening out the undesirable applicants a criterion may be fixed. First of all, incomplete application forms may be outrightly rejected. Then, on the basis of experience, merit, age, skill, and such other criterion the incompetent candidates may be screened out. Now, it becomes easy to deal with a limited applicants and this facilitates the selection of right candidates.

### 6. Conducting employment tests

According to Lee, J. Cronhach in *Essential of Psychological Testing,* p. 21, "A test is a systematic procedure for comparing the behaviour of two or more persons." In the words of Milton L. Blum, "A test provides a sample of an individual's behaviour, performance or aptitude. Employment tests can be classified under the following categories:

(a) **Performance test:** Performance test is designed to measure what the applicants know about a particular job or their degree of proficiency in performing certain job. This type of test is used for selecting employees at lower levels, such as a welder or a typist.

(b) **Aptitude test:** This test is used to know the nature and efficiency of the candidate for routing work. This test shows whether the candidate has the interest and ability to do the work.

(c) **Intelligence test:** The intelligence test was the first type of test to be used in personnel work and probably it is still the most popular. Under this test, the candidate's mental ability, debating power and reasoning abilities are known for new and difficult situations.

(d) **Dexterity test:** This type of test is used to discover a person's cleverness or strength of his hands. Many jobs require the skilful use of one's hands and body, and standardized dexterity test can simplify the selection of persons to fill the vacancies.

(e) **Interest test:** This type of test is designed to measure the applicant's preferences for certain activities compared to other activities.

(f) **Personality test:** This type of test is undoubtedly the least useful of all those mentioned above because of their lack of validity. Many personality tests have been devised for the purpose of measuring such characteristics as emotional adjustment, self-confidence, originality and other traits. But until more is known about personality, it is doubtful whether these tests can be of much value in the selection process.

All the above tests must be properly administered as they serve the purpose of (1) scientific selection, (2) training, (3) vocational guidance, (4) forecasting the success of employees, and (5) placing the employee on the job most suited to him. The test to be administered must possess the following features:

1. reliability, i.e., even if different persons conduct the same test, it must reveal the same result,
2. validity, i.e. it tests the areas for which it is designed,
3. objectivity, i.e. there must be one and only one answer to each and every question,
4. comprehensiveness, i.e. all possible types of questions relating to the areas to be included, and
5. utility, i.e. it should be simple, easy to conduct it, and it should not involve much expense.

### 7. Conducting oral interviews

Spriegel defines interview as the purposeful exchange of ideas, answering of questions and communication between two or more persons. An interview is an art of conversation through which fitness of a person for the particular job is measured. While conducting interviews, the interviewer, looks for symptoms that indicates the fitness or inability of a person to do a job. The purpose for which an interview is conducted is:

(a) to obtain additional information through direct contact,
(b) to know the personality of the candidate,
(c) to verify the information given by the applicant in the application, and
(d) to test the power of expression, presence of mind or other capabilities of a person which cannot be ascentained from the application form only.

The success of interview depends to a large extent, on the conditions surrounding it and the abilities of the interviewer. The following are some of the principles of good interviewing:

(a) Conduct the interview in private.
(b) Make the applicant feel at ease.
(c) Give the applicant the full attention.
(d) Eliminate all personal prejudicies of interviewer.
(e) Keep control over the interview to make sure that it is not be too lengthy.
(f) Arrive at some conclusion, *i.e.* what action to be taken.

Usually, an interview committee consisting of personnel, "manager as the chairman and representatives from the particular department for which selection is to be made is constituted. Interviews can be effectively conducted through a well developed procedure which is generally as follows:

1. The preparation of a list containing the criteria required for the particular job should be carefully observed during the interview.
2. The creation of a proper atmosphere for the interviewee so as to encourage the candidates to answer questions smoothly.
3. Preparation of a scheme giving guidelines for conducting the interviews. This helps in judging the qualities and abilities of the candidates from prepared questions.
4. Development of a rating scale for assessment of the different qualities and abilities of the candidates.

## 8. Conducting medical examination

The physical examination or medical examination as a tool of selection is used to ascertain the physical fitness of an employee to a job. A proper matching of job requirements with physical ability results in greater utilisation of manpower. In addition, a thorough check-up before confirmation of employee services prevents infection which may spread to other employees within no time. This is more dangerous as the employer is responsible for paying heavy compensation to accidents and disease caused by pro existing ailments.

Physical examination may include:

(a) Family medical history.
(b) Personal history of previous illness.
(c) Height, chest and weight measurement.
(d) Physical examination of skin.
(e) Examination of eyes, nose, ears and teeth.

(f) Chest X-ray.

(g) Check-up of heart and blood pressure.

(h) Blood test.

## 9. Final approval

The selection of an employee in small factories is made by the Personnel Manager himself. But in medium and large sized factories, the final selection lies with the line management. This is on the ground that if a manager is to be held responsible for results, he must also be vested with the authority to select his subordinates. The personnel department, therefore, operates with delegated authority in order to fulfil its responsibility to assist the line officers in the acquisition of personnel. It merely sorts out the applicants according to their qualifications and after the initial screening, sends only a few to each line manager for final selection. Therefore, it is the line management, not the personnel department, that has the final decision in the procurement of manpower.

## 10. Placement and induction

The acquisition of manpower is not completed until the appointed employee is put on the job, and introduced to his co-workers and his supervisor. In majority of the factories, this step is totally forgotten and there is a gap between the selection of an employee and his successful employment. The process of bridging this gap is known as induction. It involves the orientation of new employees to the work situation. Soon after the selection, an employee must be thoroughly introduced to the factory and his job. This introduction may cover the history of the factory, the products manufactured, and how it is made, benefits of employees from the organisation, structure of the factory, and how the employee fits into it, factory rules and regulations and the specific duties and responsibilities involved in the job. Job introductions serve as excellent starting point for factories to sell themselves and infuse confidence in new employees.

# QUESTIONS

## A. Objective type

**Write *True* or *False* for the following sentences:**

1. Assessing the current personnel situation involves an enquiry into what each worker is doing, how, why, and what qualifications and experience are needed for his job.
2. Assessment of future demand and supply of personnel necessitates an examination of the objectives of the enterprise and the internal and external sources of personnel.
3. Personnel planning is nothing but striking a balance between the existing and future demand and supply of right number and kinds of personnel.
4. Recruitment is a positive function in that it seeks to induce as many candidates as possible to apply for jobs in a factory.
5. Only factories that offer fat salaries to their staff attract good condidates.
6. Image of a factory has nothing to do with a candidate's choice of job in it.
7. Government regulation have nothing to do with recruitment by factories.

8. Internal transfers, promotions and demotion are examples of internal source of recruitment.
9. Recuitment from internal source cause resentment among employees of the factory.
10. Employees of a factory do not favour recruitment from external source.
11. Time lag between receipt of applications and placement of candidates is an important consideration in the choice of a source of recruitment.
12. Costs involved in the choice of a source of recruitment do not matter at all.
13. Employment exchanges mainly provide highly qualified and experienced candidate.
14. Recruitment is negative function whereas selection is a positive function.
15. Screening of applications is necessary to pick out candidates who fit the job requirements.
16. The object of interview is to ascertain whether a candidate is really suitable for the job applied for by him.
17. Blank application forms are filled after the main interview is over.
18. Proficiency tests judge a candidate's merit better than aptitude best.
19. An interview is a device to see if the candidate knows all that he claims to know.
20. Checking reference may be a worthwhile exercise.
21. Final selection of a candidate is done by the Personnel Manager.

## B. Very short answer type

1. What do you mean by manpower planning?
2. State any four objects of manpower planning.
3. Distinguish between short-term and long-term manpower planning.
4. Distinguish between recruitment and selection.
5. State the merits of internal source of recruitment.
6. State the demerits of internal source of recuitment.
7. What do you mean by performance test?
8. State any two merits and demerits of external sources of recuitment.
9. What do you mean by aptitudes test?
10. What do you mean by inteliigence test?
11. What do you mean by dexterity test?
12. What do you mean by interest test?
13. What do you mean by personality test?

## C. Long answer type

Explain the procedure involved in selecting an employee in a factory.

## ANSWERS TO OBJECTIVE TYPE QUESTIONS

| | | | | |
|---|---|---|---|---|
| 1. T, | 2. T, | 3. T, | 4. T, | 5. F, |
| 6. F, | 7. F | 8. T, | 9. F, | 10. T, |
| 11. T, | 12. F, | 13. T, | 14. T, | 15. T, |
| 16. T, | 17. F, | 18. T, | 19. T, | 20. T, |
| 21. F. | | | | |

Chapter 30

# TRAINING AND DEVELOPMENT

## ■ INTRODUCTION

Training refers to the process of increasing knowledge and skill of an employee for doing a particular job. Soon after a worker is selected and inducted into a job, we may not expect full contribution from 'raw' human resources in attaining the objective of the factory. For ensuring satisfactory job performance, training is essential for all levels of management. Training eliminates personnel obsolescence and improves their competence and capability in discharging duties efficiently. Training serves not only the purpose of motivation but also as means of developing various methods of work. The terms training and development are often used synonymously. But there exists a difference between the two. While the term training in viewed as a process by means of which the aptitudes, skills, and capabilities of individual employees to perform specific jobs are increased, the term development implies the nature and direction of change induced among employees through the process of education and training. Several factors have contributed to the increased adoption of training and development opportunities in factories. They are:

1. In recent times, the need for skilled labour is increasingly felt in developing countries like ours. Skill of labourers can be increased by means of training and development.
2. The growth and development of new technology has made training facilities very essential in factories.
3. Persistent obsolescence of manpower has demanded adequate training facilities in modern days.
4. The policy of government relating to the employment of socially and economically backward class of persons have further underlined the need for training for employees.
5. Employers have also recognised the fact that only trained employees alone can improve the productivity of the factory.

## ■ IMPORTANCE OF TRAINING

The importance of training employees results in the following advantages:

1. It makes sure the availability of skilled workers at all levels of management.
2. It increases potential abilities of workers and thus to improve the performance to their maximum attainable level through training process.
3. It enables to perform the work more accurately and precisely so as to maintain the quality of products.
4. It minimises the excessive scraps, defectives and wastages in the production process.

5. It minimises the number of accidents, as the unskilled and semiskilled workers are more prone to industrial accidents.
6. Training facilities reduce fatigue.
7. Training enables the workers to work speedily and thus increase the earnings of employees.
8. When the speed of production increases, overtime work can be avoided and therefore the payment of overtime premium also does not arise.
9. A trained worker does not feel like joining other factories and thus it reduces the labour turnover.
10. Training improves relationship between the employees and the management.
11. New techniques can be easily implemented through trained employees.
12. The practice of standardisation can be adopted in a factory where trained employees are available.
13. Team spirit and team work can be promoted when employees are fully trained.
14. Training enables the employees to occupy higher positions of authorities among promotions.
15. As trained worker's work do not require any consultation and because of less spoilage resulted from their performance, the supervision cost can be minimised.

In order to attain the above advantages, the training programme must be based on the following principles:

1. The training programme must suit the size of organisation, requirements of personnel to be trained and financial availability of the factory.
2. It must be flexible.
3. Training programme must recognise individual differences, such as interest, learning speed, etc.
4. Training should be based upon job analysis which indicates need for training and the nature of the training to be provided.
5. A training programme must always accompany payment of incentives.
6. Trainers and instructor's must be carefully selected.
7. The training programme must include executive development as well.

## ■ ORGANISATION OF TRAINING PROGRAMME

Following steps are involved in a training programme:

1. **Assessing training needs in the factory:** The assessment of needs of training can be made from the facts such as identifying production problems, analysing jobs, preparation of check-lists and its use to know the extent of training. Such an assessment will help in determining as to how many persons are to be trained and what kind of training is to be offered to them.

2. **Contents of training:** The contents of training depends upon the types of employees who are to be trained. In this respect, there are four distinct groups of employees for whom training is required. They are: (a) rank and file, (b) supervisory staff, (c) middle management, and (d) top management. The duties and responsibilities of each group of employees differ. Hence, on the basis of these category of employees training programme is to be outlined. Techniques, such as organisation analysis, operation analysis, employee analysis, help in determining the contents of training.

3. **Selection of training method:** A number of methods of training are available in practice. The Personnel Manager has to select the best method suited to his factory.

4. **Preparation of training:** This includes preparation of trainer to impart training and the trainee to receive the training.

5. **Conducting the training:** It includes the following steps:

(a) Fixation of time table for training.

(b) All jobs must be taken into account and training for performing each and every job must be offered.

(c) For offering training, stipend is to be paid for workers who are to learn.

6. **Examination of the trainee's job:** After imparting the required training, the performance of trained employees must be checked up. Whenever he makes any mistakes, he must be guided and he must do the same work till he gets competence.

The principles of training may be enumerated as under:

1. Training should be given in proper atmosphere and that too systematically through duly qualified and trained instructors.
2. Training should be of reasonably long duration so as to enable workers to understand theory and develop skills for managing job accurately.
3. Training should be given at all levels. This means that training programme of a factory should include induction training job training, training for promotion and refresher training.
4. The level of training should be high. It must be comprehensive and latest trends should be brought to the notice of the participants.
5. Training should not be of theory alone. It should be supplemented by practical training and it should be made interesting to all participants.

## ■ METHODS OF TRAINING

Training may be imparted through the following the important methods:

1. **Individual instruction:** Under this method, a single, individual is selected for training. This mode of training is undertaken where a complicated skill is to be imparted to an individual.

2. **Group instruction:** This mode of training is offered to a group of individuals who have to perform similar type of work. Where general instructions are applicable to this method is commonly adopted.

3. **Lecture method:** Here the instructor orally communicates the practice to be followed by the learners. Under this method, whenever there is any doubt, they may be classified.

4. **Demonstration method:** Where the performance of work is to be shown visually by the instructor for better understanding, this method can be followed. This is more concerned with practical than theoretical aspect.

5. **Written instructional method:** The medium of training is followed where future reference is to be made by the learners. This method is mostly followed where standardised production system is followed.

6. **Conference:** Conferences is organised frequently where experts in the field share their ideas and bring to the notice of learners the new areas and techniques that can be used to increase production.

7. **Meeting:** Meetings as mode of training involve a group of people who discuss the various problem confronting them. It involves exchange of ideas and views and later on, coming to a firm conclusion based on various proposals and alternatives.

## ■ METHODS OF TRAINING OF OPERATING EMPLOYEES

The methods of training employees in a factory may be classified into two types:

(A) Internal training methods.

(B) External training methods.

### A. Internal training methods

Under this method, training is imparted within the factory itself.

The following methods fall under this category:

1. Induction and orientation.
2. On the job training.
3. Apprentice training.
4. Vestibule training.
5. Training by skilled, experienced and old workers.
6. Helper system
7. Retraining.

A brief explanation of the above methods are given below:

### 1. Induction and orientation

This type of training is offered to the newly-recuited employee. For him everything will be new and strange in a factory. Therefore, before asking him to perform the work he will be familiarised with all departments and also on the nature of job. Once he gains confidence he undertakes to work on his own without the assistance of others.

### 2. On the job training

Under this method, the employee who is still new to the job is trained by placing him on the job by the foreman or the supervisor. No additional training equipment is needed under this method. This method is simple and inexpensive. It is flexible in the sense that it can be started and stopped and adjusted depending upon the requirements of the employees. There is considerable scope to evaluate the performance under this method of training and mistakes can be immediately corrected.

### 3. Apprentice training

This method of training is offered to learners who cannot be trained effectively through "on the job" training programmes because of the extended period of time required to learn the job. The apprentice training lasts for several years varying from 2 years to 7 years. During this period, the learner is paid a fixed amount in the form of remuneration which is called as stipend. Usually, an agreement is reached between the employer and employee where the employee guarantees to work for a minimum period after acquiring apprentice training. Once the prospective employee successfully completes the training, he can be directly absorbed into the factory. In India, the Indian Apprentice Act was passed in 1961 and was amended in 1977. Under this scheme, 131, 127 apprentices were provided training as on June 1985.

## 4. Vestibule training

A vestibule training is one under which a classroom is set up along with regular production area in which an attempt is made to simulate an actual production situation. This method of training is adopted when a large number of workers are to be trained in similar skills, uniformly and more quickly. As the employees learn the process of doing the work in vestibule classroom, the possibility of committing mistakes and slowness in producing goods is quite less. However, this method of training is costly as it involves setting up a situation where the actual process of doing and learning takes place. Moreover, it also involves payment of salaries to the skilled instructors which becomes a burden to the factory.

**Advantages of vestibule training**

1. The time and skill of the instructor can be more efficiently used as the learners are under close supervision of the instructor.
2. Regular production is not hampered by the learners as they concentrate on learning before they take up production.
3. Intensive training can be offered to learners at each and every stage which is not possible in 'on the job training'.
4. More time can be devoted in training learners when compared to other methods.

**Disadvantages of vestibule training**

1. This method is costly when compared to other methods.
2. The time involved is more for training when compared to other methods.
3. This method is well suited only to employees who are to be promoted.

## 5. Training by skilled, experienced and old workers

Under this method, a new employee is attached to an old and experienced employee who is expected to watch the process of doing work and to do the same type of work by himself. This type of training is very common in small scale industries which cannot afford to appoint experts in the field of training.

## 6. Helper system

This system of training is also known as "understudy" system of training. This method presumes that a worker will learns by helping another worker to do his job. Under this method, a worker is placed on a given task with the purpose of serving as an understudy to the man doing the work. The understudy is taught by the man actually working on the job, to whom he is understudy. But care must be taken to see that the instructor does not take the assistance of the learner only to reduce his burden. Instead, he must take equal interest in making the person under his control to learn.

## 7. Retraining

Retraining is mostly imparted to the existing employees for the following reasons:

(i) To keep the alround skills of employees as a reserve in case of need.

(ii) When the retrenched workers are called back after lay off period owing to several reasons.

(iii) When the new technology demands new method of production.

(iv) When a worker is not in a position to do his normal allotted work due to illness, accidents or incapacity due to age, but who can take up other jobs which are within his reach.

### B. External training methods

External method of training is resorted in such circumstances where the facility of internal sources are not available. Special training institutes have come into existence which are either owned privately or by government. In such training institutes, employees of the factory may be deputed for a specific duration to learn the required skills and abilities. The following are some such institutes which often special training courses: (a) National Productivity Council set up at various regions of our country, (b) Industrial Training Institutes, (c) Small Scale Service Institutes in different states, (d) Small Scale Industries Associations in different states, and (e) Government tool room and training centres.

## ■ METHODS OF TRAINING SUPERVISORS AND FOREMAN

Supervisors and foremen occupy the position of lower level management in managerial hierarchy of a factory. The supervisor and foremen come into direct contact with the employees and, as such, they must necessarily possess the required leadership abilities, technical competence, managerial talents, organising abilities and communication skills. Technical competence is necessary as the supervisor and foremen have to teach the newly recruited employees as to how to do the work. Whenever workers deviate from the normal work routine, they must be properly guided by foremen and supervisor. Occupying position of lower level management, supervisors and foremen must exhibit managerial talents. They must plan the production process, organise the production system, direct employees to carry out the production and control the process of operation. They must serve as the leaders of their immediate subordinates and must command respect from them. In order to achieve these traits they must be trained. In the words of Scott, Clothier and Spriegel, the primary objectives of executive training include the following: (1) to provide adequate leaders, (2) to increase the efficiency of performance of current executives, (3) to serve as a means of control in operation, (4) to develop a unity of purpose and improve morale.

Before the actual training programme is devised for supervisors and foremen, it is necessary to know their duties and responsibilities in a factory. This enables the management to provide the training so as to suit the requirements of these lower level managers. The supervisor is responsible for maintaining the (1) quality of goods, (2) speed of production, (3) bring in discipline among workers, (4) machineries and equipments, (5) good relation with other departments, and (6) handling labour problems.

## ■ METHODS OF TRAINING FOREMEN AND SUPERVISORS

### 1. Induction

As in the case of operative employees even the lower level managers, such as supervisors and foremen, must also be properly inducted in their jobs. They must be told about the ideals and main objectives of the factory, the expectations of management from supervisors and foremen, their duties and responsibilities and so on. The familiarisation with all aspects of factory itself enables the supervisors and foremen to know more about their positions and what they should contribute to the overall objectives of the factory.

### 2. Lecture or classroom method

Lecture constitutes the medium of instruction under this method. As foremen and supervisors do not require much of demonstration, this method is more suited for them. Experts in the field can be engaged to train through lectures. But it addition to lectures, audiovisual aids, such as technical films, slides and overhead transparencies could also be used.

### 3. Conferences

Under this method, the trainees are brought together to learn while in group. They have an exchange information of discuss and opportunity to the subject matter of their interest and arrive at a definite conclusion. As the knowledge of experienced persons is pooled together, a conference can change attitudes and even develop analytical abilities. The leader of the conference should take lead to stimulate, interpret and extract the opinions of the group engaged in discussion.

### 4. Training within industry (TWI)

Under this method, training is offered within the industry. This may take the form of:

(a) **Job instruction:** The supervisor gains the ability as to how to impart clear instructions to his subordinates.

(b) **Job relations:** Under this programme, the supervisors develop the leadership qualities, the ability to handle labour problems and the ability to establish good relations with everybody.

(c) **Job methods:** Under this programme, the supervisor gains the skill to improve methods of doing work along with best utilisation of inputs.

(d) **Job safety:** Under this programme, he learns to prevent industrial accidents that commonly occur in factories.

### 5. Training outside industry

Wherever necessary facilities are not readily available within the factory, they may be trained outside the factory. A number of such training institutes have been established all over the country. Some such training institutes, which offer training facilities to foremen and supervisors, are: (1) Foremen's Training Institute, Bangalore, (2) National Productivity Council, (3) The Institute of Supervisory Development, Kerala, and (4) the Institute of Industrial Supervisory Management, Jamshedpur. The training offered in these institutes may be full time or part time.

## ■ METHODS OF TRAINING EXECUTIVES OR MANAGERIAL EXECUTIVE DEVELOPMENT

The success of a factory depends how well it is managed. The management of a factory, in turn, depends upon the type of managers. Well qualified and experienced managers are highly responsible for leading the factory towards attainment of its goal. Orientation of managers go a long way in improving the efficiency of a factory. Hence, the importance of training executives is felt by most of the factories.

## ■ DEFINITION OF MANAGEMENT OR EXECUTIVE DEVELOPMENT

According to Dale S. Beach, Management development is a systematic process of training and growth by which individuals gain and apply knowledge, skills, insights and attitudes to manage effectively.

In the words of Jucious, Executive development is the programme by which capacities of executives to achieve the desired objectives are increased. For the successful executive development, it is necessary to fulfill at least the following pre-requisities:

(a) Support of the organisation's basic philosophy of management.

(b) Adequate resources like—time, money and manpower.

(c) Personnel involvement of the Chief Executive.

(d) Collaboration and team work between line and staff management.

## ■ NEED FOR EXECUTIVE DEVELOPMENT

The need for executive development arises on account of the following factors:

### 1. Technological and social changes

The rapid growth of technological and social factors has made it imperative to train the managers. Some of the technological factors which demand executive development are invention of electronic computers, implementation of automation, research in marketing leading to competition among factories. Among the social factors, the most important are: enlarged voice and elevated role of labourers, excessive government regulations over factories, increased interest of public in industries. Therefore to cope up with these factors and to project a good image, it is universally accepted that executive training is necessary.

### 2. Professionally managed factories

In modern days, there has been a marked shift from owner-manager to one who is professionally employed. Management today is considered as a distinct profession and day after day it is gaining more importance as a body of knowledge. The professional managers are to be trained in order to make them acquire the necessary skills and abilities to manage, supervise and control the activities of the factory. Even today there exists a gap between the full fledged theoretical managers and the recognised standard of practising managers. To fill this gap, executive development is necessary.

### 3. Research orientation

Over the past few decades, there has been an increase in research conducted in the field of principles and techniques of general management and various functional managements such as personnel management, financial management, production management, and so on. This contribution is widely accepted in all factories. In order to communicate and execute them in factories it is necessary to orient managers.

### 4. Recognition of social responsibilities of business

The recognition of social responsibilities of factories has made it more obligatory to develop executive skills. This is on account of increased responsibility of management towards a large section of people, such as owners, employees, government, and public at large.

## ■ METHODS OF EXECUTIVE DEVELOPMENT

The methods of executive development can be classified under two headings. They are:

(A) On-the-job methods

1. Coaching and understudy
2. Job rotation
3. Special projects
4. Committee assignment.

(B) Off-the-job methods

1. Special course
2. Role playing
3. Case study
4. Conference training
5. Multiple management
6. Management games
7. Sensitivity training
8. Programmed instructions.

## (A) On-the-job method

This method is best suited person when the executive is fully committed to the need for developing his subordinates. He must not only be competent but also willing to train his subordinates. The following are some of the methods which fall under this category:

### *1. Coaching and understudy*

Under this method, the senior person teaches job knowledge and skills to a subordinate. He also checks his performance and advises him to improve his performance and avoid committing mistakes. The senior person not only coaches but also counsels the subordinates. Often, the senior delegates his powers to the subsordinates in order to enable him to learn from such situations. He can give an opportunity to his subordinate to participate in decision-making process affecting the department.

In 'understudy' method of training, the superior trains his subordinates so as to enable the latter to assume the position of former when promoted, transfered or retired. Usually, a senior employee of a department is selected for this type of training by the departmental manager. The trainee is asked to handle the routine problems which confronts the departmental manager. The trainee is also given chance to supervise other workers to develop leadership qualities. The main advantage of this method is, it offers practical training, i.e., it emphasises learning by doing. However, this method creates friction and jealously among other workers.

### *2. Job rotation*

Under this method, the executive from one department is transferred to another department on a coordinated and planned basis. The idea behind this method is to broaden the background of the executives in the factory. This method facilitates all round development in the personality of the executives. In today's complicated problems faced by executives to confine to one branch of knowledge is not sufficient. He must be exposed to a variety of problems which may crop up in all the departments of the factory. This method provides an opportunity to the executive to work in various departments and face various problems arising from different situations. This method establishes good cooperation among all the departments. It injects new ideas in different departments. But the chief drawback of this method is that the work in various departments may be disrupted by the limitations of individuals to adjust to the new jobs. This disadvantage can be overcome by lengthening the interval of rotation and rotating fewer personnel at a time.

### *3. Special projects*

Under this method, the trainee is assigned a project that is closely related to the work of his department. For example, a trainee may be assigned to develop a system of cost control while executing the order of a customer. The trainee will accumulate all the elements of cost, anslyse them, check the accuracy, and then make written recommendations about it. Thus on the one hand, he will learn the techniques of cost control and on the other, keep the cost of production at low level.

### *4. Committee assignments*

Under this method, an adhoc committee is constituted and a problem is assigned to it. A committee assignment provides the necessary background to the trainee as he can learn the implications involved in solving a problem. After a thorough discussions and deliberations the committee members recommend the decision taken by them to the authority who constituted the committee.

## (B) Off-the-job methods

### *1. Special course*

Formal training course can be developed to train executives in a number of ways. One such approach is the factory itself. It may develop such a course which can be imparted either through the available experts within the factory or by experts from other institutions. The topics dealing with the structure of the organisation, factory policies, etc., can be taught by a senior executive, while topics like production planning, operation research, business games, can be taught by university professors or from Indian Institutes of Management. The second approach to this method of training is to depute executives to attend to courses offered by universities or special management bodies. Some such courses are offered by the Institute of Cost and Works Accountants of India (ICWA), the Institute of Chartered Accountants of India, the Institute of Company Secretaries of India and such other institutes. Factories can sponsor trainees to these courses by meeting the fees of the course. The contents of course include the nature and purpose of organisation, management principles and techniques, human relations, technical knowledge and skills, and economic, social and political environment.

### *2. Role playing*

This technique is used for training in the field of human relations. Its purpose is to give trainees an opportunity to learn human relations skill through practice and to develop insight into one's own behaviour and its effect upon others. It can be used in sales training because it involves dealing with other people. Under this method, a particular situation or a problem is created and it is assigned to two or three trainees. The trainees after having understood the prevailing situation, have to play their role. An example could be a supervisor handling a grievance with employees.

### *3. Case study*

It is a learning technique in which a real situation or a series of actual events is presented to trainees for their analysis and consideration of possible solutions to problems identified. Their findings are normally compared with the way in which the real life situation is subsequently developed.

A case study is a serious examination of a situation involving a problem. It provides, in details, the background data to the problem concerning the company, markets, policies, plans, personalities and human relations, etc., as appropriate to the particular case. When a serious problem is unresolved, the case study involves an analysis of the problem such as where did the company go wrong? Which type of action taken is correct? This finally enables us to suggest a suitable solution to the problem.

### 4. Conference training

Under this method, a group meeting is conducted according to an organised plan in which the executives seek to develop knowledge and understanding by participation. The executives can learn from comparing his opinion with those of others. Conferences may be of three types, viz. (a) directed conference, (b) the consultative conference, and (c) problem solving conference. Under the directed conference method, the programme coordinator directs the trainees in various concepts and techniques by lectures as well as prepared materials. This is more of theoretical nature. Under the consultative conference, the executive under training learns by consulting the fellow executives and leader of the conference. Under problem-solving conference, a problem is assigned to an executive who has to view it under the prevailing conditions and take an appropriate steps to solve it. For example, labour problem relating to strike may have to be solved by a labour officer by analysing its causes.

### 5. Multiple management

Under this method, more than one level of management is constituted to advise the top management for making decision. For example, two boards of directors may be constituted one consisting of juniors and another of seniors representing shareholders for the purpose of training. Members of junior board become a prerequisite to the membership of the senior board. The junior board of directors are at free will to exercise their discretion in developing ideas for solving managerial problems. Under this method, the executives gain benefit from experience. This method helps in identifying those executives who are good at management. A compared to other methods, it is also less expensive.

### 6. Management games

A management game is a dynamic training exercise which simulates model of a business situation. Using a set of mathematical relationships which is built into the model, the decisions are processed so as to produce a series of performance reports. These decisions and reports pertain to a specific time period, such as a day, month or year depending on the model. Decisions are then made for the next period by means of processing and preparing reports. Management games are previously used to learn from experience without involving any wrong decisions in an actual or real situation. Management games are exciting and powerful educational tools with numerous applications in research, problem solving, executive testing and selection. In managerial decision-making a brief discussion of a typical game play is presented under the following paragraphs.

The game session begins with a brief discussion. In this discussion, the instructor describes for the participants the type of company they are about to manage: the economic environment, the general nature of the products and the competitive force they will face. The scope of their authority, the functions to be performed, the decisions to be made and the information they will receive are all discussed. In addition to the mechanics of the play, the purpose of the exercise and manner in which it relates to the entire educational programme are covered. After the discussions the participants meet other members of their management team. The management teams determine their organisation, set objectives, decide on short and long range plans necessary to achieve these objectives and introduce necessary controls and procedures. In addition to the desire to maximise net profit, other objectives will be set concerning share in market, stabilised production, inventory control and personnel policies.

While the participants are engaged in operating in their companies, other people observe their performance. Some of them may be visitors, but others may have been specifically selected to follow the proceedings so as to provide feed back later on the human interactions evidenced. In some cases, elaborate facilities are available for observing and recording the actions of the participants.

At the end of the game play, a discussion session takes place. This session is held to focus attention on the lessons which had been taught. The participants have an opportunity of reviewing their performance, discussing management principles with other members of the group and receiving feed back from the game administrator and to observe. Later on, a report is prepared and presented to the Board of Directors which is guided along specific channels by a previously prepared check list.

### *7. Sensitivity training*

Sensitivity training is a general term which is used to describe a number of similar, highly participative learning methods whose purpose is to improve trainee's skills in working with other people by increasing the ability to (a) appreciate how others are reacting to one's own behaviour, (b) gauge the state of relationship between others, and (c) carry out skilfully the behaviour required by the situation. In a typical sensitivity training group, which is also known as 'T Group' session, a group of strangers, linked by their similar backgrounds is given a problem to discuss in a laboratory or workshop. No leader is appointed and the group is given no instructions as to procedure. Each member has to start from the very beginning to develop a role and a working relation with his colleagues. The senior manager may attempt to take a lead. After some time, they are aware of their true impact upon people and of the characteristics and personalities of their colleagues. The specific areas of learning under this method are.

(a) Increased sensitivity to emotional reactions and expressions in oneself and in others.

(b) Greater ability to perceive and to learn from the consequences of one's action through attention to feelings, one's own and those of others.

(c) Clarification and development of personal values and goal consonant with a democratic and a scientific approach to problems of social and personal decision and action.

(d) Development of behavioural skills to support better integration of intentions and actions, and

(e) Ability to transfer laboratory learnings to back home situations.

### *8. Programmed instructions*

Programmed instruction is defined as the application of the science of learning to the task of training and education, programmed instruction, teaching by films, programmed illustration, and so on. While on the one hand, it provides instruction to the learners, on the other it provides necessary feedback for each response. The success of this method depends upon proper programming of instructions.

### Recent trends in training

1. Informal on-the-job employee training is in vogue.
2. There is a rise in the trend towards training employees engaged on automatic machines and office automation.
3. Formal employee training is concentrated in highly paid professional and technical workers. Business management, engineering and technical training is increasing.

4. At present, training is given generally in marketing, finance and management. But it is more specific to each factory. It is related to real problems of the factory and an action-oriented approach in learning has gained importance.
5. More emphasis is placed on training in attitudes and behaviour of all levels of employees as it is almost non-existent in employee training. This is necessary to bring a change in the Indian permissive work culture where the commitments, awareness and work patterns lack precise definition. The thrust of training inputs is on effective organisation which requires to be mission directed, value oriented and oriented towards common purposes as a term to achieve targets and tasks. In this context, training in leadership, organisational behaviour and change of attitudes will gain momentum.
6. The employee-management participation will be increasingly evident in the field of production and productivity. The training activity for education of workers and management personnel in participative skills will need augmentation. The style of management plays an important role in the consultative and participative process.
7. Another change in emphasis in training activities is more towards development as district from pure training. Training implies preparation to carry out the specific skill requirements of a job, whilst development involves the much wider concept of enabling employees to develop and grow with the organisation of which they are a part, while training packages have a limited role to play, solutions have to be specific to the problems identified.
8. The adoption of a development rather than pure training approach brings with it the need to monitor the progress of employees throughout their career as compared to the present approach where it is mostly entry training.
9. As communication is at the root of any factory effectiveness, communication skills receive a good deal of attention in training.
10. Self-development becomes important and training centres in factories can assist in the self-development process by providing employees services such as interval libraries, video-cassettes, tapes, provision of reading lists covering topics of importance.

To conclude, a good deal of innovation in training techniques and development of professionalism of training staff is called for to carry out employee training at all levels. Top management support and commitment, preferably direct involvement in training activities, goes a long way in improving training methods.

## QUESTIONS

### A. Objective type

**Choose the correct answer from the following alternatives:**

1. The conference method is most suitable for training
   (a) plant technicians (b) clerical workers
   (c) machine operators (d) supervisors.

2. Which one of the following managerial development programme is easiest to teach?
   (a) Organisational skills (b) A proper attitude towards management
   (c) Technical knowledge (d) Administrative skills.
3. Which one of the following goals of training is typically a part of developing a proper attitude towards managerial responsibility?
   (a) Indoctrinating the manager with the factory's philosophy.
   (b) Improving the manager's understanding of his relationship with other employees.
   (c) Teaching the manager to think like an executive.
   (d) All of the above.

## B. Very short answer type

1. Distinguish between training and development.
2. Mention the steps involved in a training programme.
3. Mention the principles of good training programme.
4. What do you mean by on-the-job training?
5. What do you mean by apprentice training?
6. How is apprentice training different from regular on-the-job training?
7. What is vestibule training?
8. What is a helper system?
9. What is re-training?
10. What is role playing?
11. What is a case study?
12. What do you mean by conference training?
13. What is multiple management?
14. What do you mean by sensitivity in training?

## C. Short answer type

1. Outline the importance of training employees in a factory.
2. Briefly explain the various media through which employees in a factory are trained.
3. Explain the various methods of training operating employees in a factory.
4. Explain the various methods of training supervisors in a factory.

## D. Long answer type

What do you mean by executive development? Explain various methods of executive development.

## ANSWERS TO OBJECTIVE TYPE QUESTIONS

(1) d, (2) c, (3) d.

Chapter 31

# JOB EVALUATION AND MERIT RATING

## ■ INTRODUCTION

In olden days when the division of labour was less, payment of wages and salaries were not so difficult. Employers used to follow a simpler method of wage payment and employees adjusted themselves to the differences in wages and salaries. With modern complex conditions these simpler methods of wage payment methods are often quite unsatisfactory. Because of these complexities, managements have established wage policies that is fair to both employer and employee. In modern mass-production factories, the type of work differs to a great extent. It is difficult for a manager to compare these jobs to judge which is more or less important among all jobs. Under such circumstances, there is a tendency to pay more wages without considering the conditions warranting it and without any rational purpose. In such cases, instead of paying more wages to deserving employees, it might have been paid to an aggressive worker seeking larger wages. This results in inequalities in the payment of wages. To avoid such a defective system of wage payment, it is necessary to consider factors which affect the performance of work on a job by the employees. This calls for a systematic and scientific procedure and principle of wage payment. But the problem is how to measure the performance of work on various job? The performance of work on jobs are related to such factors as skill requirements, knowledge requirements, physical effort involved and responsibility for materials, money or safety to mention only a few. By analysis, each job in regard to these specific features, a rational job hierarchy is developed from the data so gathered and thus different rates pay is fixed for different types of jobs. The subject matter of establishing differential payment for the various jobs, the rewarding of individual effort and merit, and the forming of a logical basis for the promotion of employees, is known as Job Evaluation and Merit Rating.

The phrase "Job Evaluation" is used in a broad as well as in a narrow sense. Viewed in its broad sense, it means determination of appropriate base salary or wage rates for specific combinations of duties that are called "Jobs" in factories. In its narrow sense, job evaluation is a term applied to those approaches to job rate determination which attempts to systematise the process that are essential to achieve equality and employee satisfaction in respect of wage scales. In job evaluation one assesses selected job factors which are regarded as important for the effective performance of the job according to one of several alternative methods. The resulting numerical job gradings then form is the basis of an equitable wage structure.

## ■ DEFINITIONS

In connection with the study of Job Evaluation, one often comes across identical terms which are interchangeably used. It is worthwhile to note the definitions of such concepts. The concepts are defined as follows:

1. **Tasks:** A task simply refers to one of the simple activity, such as typing.

2. **Position:** A position entails two or more related tasks which collectively require the attention of one employee.

3. **Job:** A job involves a group of positions which are similar in function, skill requirements, knowledge requirements and responsibilities.

4. **Job analysis:** It refers to the process of examining a job in detail in order to identify its component tasks. Information on job content is useful to a factory for a large number of applications. For example, the personnel department needs data for recruiting, work study department requires data in order to plan work measurement. The information is also required for organisation manuals, salary gradation, job evaluation and so on. It is collected by one of the members of personnel known as job analyst by observation, interview, questionnaire and examination of existing records.

5. **Job description:** Job description refers to a broad statement of the purpose, scope, responsibilities and tasks which constitute a particular job. Job descriptions specify the nature of managerial responsibilities in outline. Job description serves as a basis for the study of job specification, job evaluation and merit rating.

6. **Job specification:** Job specification refers to a detailed statement of the knowledge and the physical and mental activities required to carry out the tasks which constitute the job.

7. **Job evaluation:** According to Kimball, "Job evaluation represents an effort to determine the relative value of every job in a plant or an organisation and to determine what the fair basic wage for such a job should be."

In the words of Alford and Beatty, "Job evaluation is the application of the job analysis technique to the qualitative measurement of relative job worth, for the purpose of establishing consistent wage rate differentials by objective means."

Amrine, Ritchey and Hulley, in their book "Manufacturing Organisation and Management" defines job evaluation as "a systematic procedure for determining the relative worth of job within an organisation and for establishing an adequate wage structure."

## ■ PRINCIPLES OF JOB EVALUATION

A. L. Kress, a leader in the development of job evaluation, has set forth eight principles of job evaluation. They are:

1. **Rate the job and not the man:** The requirements of the job are usually definite and fixed. The man on the job may have plus qualifications or may not quite measure up to the job requirement. A job rating plan should not be confused with any plan to grade employees. The man on the job may be paid more or less than the job itself is worth, in relation to other jobs. Each element should therefore be rated on the basis of what the job itself requires.
2. The elements selected for rating purposes should be easily explainable in terms that will avoid any overlapping which might lead to rating the same qualifications under several headings. The elements should be as few in number as will cover the necessary requisites for every job.

3. Success in job rating is absolutely dependent on a uniformity of understanding with regard to the definitions of the elements and on consistency in the selection of the degrees of those elements.
4. Any job rating plan must be sold to foremen and employees. Success in selling it depends on a clear-cut explanation and illustration of the plan.
5. Foremen should participate in the rating of jobs in their own departments.
6. The greatest degree of cooperation from employees, in job rating, will be achieved where they themselves have an opportunity to discuss the ratings.
7. In talking to foremen and employees, avoid discussion of money values. Talk point values and degree of each element.
8. Too many occupational wages or rate ranges for given labour grades should not be established.

## OBJECTIVES AND ADVANTAGES OF JOB EVALUATION

The usual objectives of job evaluation are as follows:

1. To eliminate wage inequalities.
2. To establish sound wage differentials among the jobs.
3. To provide a sound wage base for incentive and bonus plans.
4. To establish a sound wage structure.
5. To facilitate the maintenance of a consistent wage policy.

The following are the advantages of job evaluation programme:

1. Wage rates can be fixed accurately in an organisation by deciding the proper worth of different jobs.
2. Job evaluation technique is useful for proper selection, training, promotion, transfer of employees within the organisation. These activities can be performed objectively and impartially due to job evaluation.
3. It facilitates effective control on the entire organisation and eliminates nepotism and wastage.
4. Job evaluation eliminates or at least minimises the grievances of the workers about the absolute and relative wage rates. It avoids confusion in the minds of employees as regards the wage rates fixed by the management.
5. Job evaluation technique raises the morale of the employees and also efficiency of labour force in factories.

## PROCEDURE IN INSTALLING JOB EVALUATION

Lytle in his book, "Job Evaluation Methods", New York, The Roland Press Co., pp. 28-29 has outlined steps to be taken in installing a plan of job evaluation as follows:

1. Choose the most suitable method and the main techniques.
2. Choose the major job characteristics, then the minor ones and apportion limiting values.
3. Start selling the proposition to all concerned and seek suggestions.
4. Build definitions, measuring scales, or comparison techniques and assign relative values.
5. Design forms or questionnaires and collect preliminary descriptions.

6. Edit preliminary descriptions and establish grades or classes.
7. Identify and evaluate key jobs, first on major characteristics, then on minor characteristics.
8. Evaluate remaining jobs on all characteristics keeping proper relativity to key jobs and harmonise job titles.
9. At this stage, make sure to consider the union representatives concerned in weightings.
10. Make inter-company survey on key jobs only, but try to find at least one per class.
11. Translate abstract values into money values tentatively.
12. Plot the end jobs and the most sure key jobs on a scatter diagram.
13. Observe trend line and decide range limits.
14. Readjust all rates relative to line, standardise and put into working form; finally, fix all operating procedures.

## METHODS OF JOB EVALUATION

There are four methods of job evaluation. They are: (1) ranking method, (2) job classification method (3) point method, and (4) factors comparison method.

### 1. Ranking method

This method is also known as grading method, as it involves assigning grades to various jobs in order of their relative importance. Under this method of job evaluation, the following steps are involved: (a) making a thorough job analysis, (b) expressing the findings of this analysis in a job description, and (c) ranking each job by arranging them in ascending order, starting with the job of minimum and ending with the maximum requirements of various characteristic feature of jobs. Ranking can be based on the following factors: (a) difficulty of work, (b) volume of work, (c) responsibility involved, (d) supervision required, (e) supervision of others, (f) knowledge, training and experience necessary, and (g) conditions under which work is done.

After the ranking is complete, the jobs are generally grouped into ten to twelve groups, according to their position. The jobs are then evaluated by determining the wage rates prevailing in similar factories. Accordingly wage rates are increased either by a fixed percentage or by a fixed amount.

### 2. Job classification method

Under this method of job evaluation, standard grade descriptions are used in classifying the various jobs. As and when each job is reviewed, it is placed into the category having the most appropriate description. This is quite opposite to what happens in the job ranking system, since in that system, jobs are first ranked and then divided into grades.

### 3. Point method

Point method of job evaluation is by far the most widely used method in factories. It consists of a "yardstick" containing various factors, such as skill, education, responsibility and so on that are inherent in the jobs. The degree of importance of each factor is determined by arbitrary decision, and a suitable point value is specified for each factor. This is illustrated in the Fig. 31.1.

| Factors | Degree and Points | | | |
|---|---|---|---|---|
| | 1st Degree | 2nd Degree | 3rd Degree | 4th Degree |
| **Skill** | | | | |
| 1. Education | 14 | 28 | 42 | 56 |
| 2. Experience | 22 | 44 | 66 | 88 |
| 3. Initiative | 14 | 28 | 42 | 56 |
| **Effort** | | | | |
| 4. Physical demand | 10 | 20 | 30 | 40 |
| 5. Mental demand | 5 | 10 | 15 | 20 |
| **Responsibility** | | | | |
| 6. Equipment | 5 | 10 | 15 | 20 |
| 7. Material | 5 | 10 | 15 | 20 |
| 8. Safety of others | 5 | 10 | 15 | 20 |
| 9. Work of others | 5 | 10 | 15 | 20 |
| **Job conditions** | | | | |
| 10. Working conditions | 10 | 20 | 30 | 40 |
| 11. Hazards | 5 | 10 | 15 | 20 |

**Fig. 31.1** Degree and points assigned to job factors.

In the above figures, the various degrees connote the following definition:

**1st degree:** Requires the ability to read and write, add and substract whole numbers.

**2nd degree:** Requires the use of simple arithmetic, such as addition and subtraction of decimals and fractions, together with simple drawings and some measuring instruments, such as slide caliper, scale.

**3rd degree:** Requires the use of fairly complicated drawings, variety of precision measuring instruments, trade knowledge in a specialised field.

**4th degree:** Requires a basic technical knowledge sufficient to deal with complicated and involved mechanical, electrical, or other engineering problems.

In the evaluation of any particular job, its description is compared to the job factors on the evaluation form and the degrees, which are most appropriate, are assigned. The total points for all the factors then determine the relative position of that job as compared to others.

## 4. Factors comparison method

This method was introduced by Eugene Benze in the year 1928. The plan consists of analysing jobs on the basis of five factors; namely mental requirements, skill requirements, physical requirements, responsibility and working conditions. The jobs are ranked according to each of these factors, one factor being taken at a time and each job is compared with the other with respect to its worth on this factor alone. The relative weightage of this factor in each job is done by applying money value (i.e. rupees) to the ranking. There is no predetermined definition of the degree to which the factor affects job worth, and no range of limits is set on the worth of the factor. The following Fig. 31.2 illustrates this method of job evaluation:

| Job | Average Rank | | | | |
|---|---|---|---|---|---|
| | *Mental requirement* | *Skill requirement* | *Physical requirement* | *Respon-sibility* | *Working conditions* |
| Pattern maker | 1 | 12 | 1 | 1 | 16 |
| Riveter | 12 | 3 | 12 | 14 | 8 |
| Casting Inspector | 3 | 7 | 4 | 4 | 10 |
| Arc Welder | 8 | 9 | 7 | 9 | 3 |
| Crane Operator | 5 | 14 | 10 | 7 | 6 |
| Watchman | 15 | 5 | 15 | 11 | 2 |

**Fig. 31.2** Average ranks of 6 key jobs under factor comparision method of job evaluation

After all the jobs have been rated on each factor, a wage rate for each job is determined by obtaining the sum of money weightage determined for each of the five job factors. These wage rates become the basis for determining the wage scale.

## ■ MERIT RATING

Merit rating of an employee is the process of evaluating his performance on the job in terms of the requirements of the job, for the purposes of placement of workers on an appropriate job, selection for promotion, providing financial reward and so on. In the words of Alford and Beatty Merit, rating is the evaluation of appraisal of the relative worth of a man's services on his job.

## ■ DEFINITION OF MERIT RATING

Jame Lundy, in his book 'Industrial Management' defines merit rating as "the process of evaluating an employee's performance on the job." According to Amrine, Ritchey and Huliey, "Merit rating is concerned with employee appraisal. It is a systematic and impartial procedure for determining the excellence with which an individual is performing a job" (*Manufacturing Organisation and Management*, p. 429).

Kimball and Kimball define merit rating as "the evaluation of any given worker as to his fitness for a given job in terms of assigned factors by which he may be intelligently appraised (*Principles of Industrial Organisation*, p. 433).

Very often, it is difficult to measure the factors relating to the employee's performance when compared to standard. Under such circumstances, judgement serves as the only means of evaluation. But the judgment criterion as a source of appraising employee's performance is subject to personal prejudices and bias. For this reason, the trade union oppose merit rating programme and instead advocate paying all workers on the same job the same wage rate. But, for efficient workers, this is not acceptable. So, they demand a range of wage rates to be paid to each job on the basis of their performance, attitude and potential on the job.

In designing a merit rating system, the employee's traits are to be analysed. A rating form, known as rating scale, is used to reveal a variety of factors which are commonly used. However, it must be remembered that greatest weight should be placed on those factors that are measurable such as quantity of output, whereas the subjective factors which can be appraised by personal judgment should be given less weightage because of difficulties in justifying ratings. The factors used in a systematic rating of employees usually include: (1) quantity and quality of output, (2) attitude, as indicated by attendance records, safety records, cooperation with others and dependability, and (3) potential traits, as indicated by leadership ability, appearance, initiative, desire to learn and judgment.

## ■ OBJECTIVES OF MERIT RATING

Merit rating serves the following purposes

1. It furnishes a periodic record of the relative value of each employee, as judged by his seniors.
2. It determines and justifies wage differentials existing for the same job.
3. It provides more accurate information on which promotions, transfers, and lay offs may be based.
4. If provides a means of evaluating the selection and training techniques used.
5. It provides information for counselling employees, so that the means of overcoming weaknesses can be pointed out and programmes for self improvement developed.
6. It provides with a more effective tool for rating their personnel.
7. It establishes better employer-employee relations through mutual confidence, which comes as a result of frank discussions between leader and follower regarding ratings.
8. It ensures better supervision as the supervisors must observe the employees closely if they are to rate them accurately.

## ■ ADMINISTRATION OF MERIT RATING PROGRAMME

Merit rating system considerably influences the wages and salaries payable to workers. Therefore, utmost importance must be given for proper administration of merit rating programme, which otherwise leads to friction among employees. The management of a factory must give more attention to the design, installation and maintenance of the merit rating programme. By proper planning and installation of a merit rating programme, problems which encounter a merit rating programme can be prevented. The administration of a good merit rating programme is possible when the following factors are considered.

### 1. Frequency of rating

There is no standard pattern followed as regards the frequency with which merit rating is undertaken. However, new employees are rated just before their learning period ends in order to determine whether they should be retained or dismissed. In case of existing employees, rating may be carried out at an interval of six months, and wages can be revised accordingly.

### 2. Rating forms

A rating form consisting of various traits such as: (a) Interest, (b) knowledge, (c) quality of work, (d) judgment, (e) initiative, (f) industriousness, (g) reliability, (h) credibility, (i) health, and (j) appearance can be used to rate the employees. The rater reads the definition, considers the behaviour of the employee and enters in the appropriate column the degree of possession of trait. Necessary space for comments is provided on the back of the form.

### 3. Person to rate

As a matter of principle, rating should be done by the employee's immediate supervisor, who only knows the employee, and results produced by his efforts. This can, however, be checked by the Supervisor's senior as means of cross-check to know thoroughness of the job rather than to find fault with individual's rating. A final check can then be made in the personnel department using post rating as a guide to avoid any unusual changes that would have occurred while rating.

### 4. Setting-up a rating system

First of all, the various factors to be considered for merit rating must be established. These factors may relate to physical and mental ability, dexterity, interest, initiative, judgment and so on. Each factor should measure an exclusive trait. This requires careful definition of each of these factors so that the trait is easily recognised. Then the degree of possession of each trait should be carefully defined. Most scales provide for five major degrees of differentiation. The technique of rating to be used is then determined.

### 5. Training the rater

The raters must be trained in the technique of rating preferably under conference method. The technique of rating must be explained to them and necessary forms must be furnished to them. They may be asked to rate the performance of employees in small groups until they are well acquainted. The rating by the rater should not be based on general impression of the person who is being rated; rather it should be based on actual analysis of the performance of employee concerned.

## ■ METHODS OF MERIT RATING

The methods used for merit rating are as follows:

1. Rank order method.
2. The paired comparison method.
3. Man-to-man rating scale.
4. Graphic rating scales.
5. Forced choice.
6. Critical incident.
7. Field review.
8. Performance standard.
9. Appraisal by objectives.

### 1. Rank order method

Under this method, the rater is expected to keep a list of all the employees under his supervision. The various characteristics which are to be possessed by the employees are then determined. Ranks are assigned to these characteristics, depending upon the fulfillment of traits by the employees. This is illustrated in the Fig. 31.3.

This method is effective for differentiating the extremes of ability, personal characteristics of other kinds and performance. However, it is not analytic unless a number of rankings are made, one for each of a number of traits and performance characteristics. Again, the use of such a technique requires that the ratings of people in a group must all be done at the same time.

| *Grades* | *Exceptional* | *Very good* | *Good* | *Average* | *Poor* | *Total* |
|---|---|---|---|---|---|---|
| Characteristics | | | | | | |
| 1. Quantity of work | | | | | | |
| 2. Quality of work | | | | | | |
| 3. Initiative | | | | | | |
| 4. Fact | | | | | | |
| 5. Loyalty | | | | | | |
| 6. Judgement | | | | | | |
| 7. Cooperation | | | | | | |
| 8. Leadership | | | | | | |
| Total | | | | | | |

**Fig. 31.3** Figure showing rank order method of merit rating

## 2. The paired comparison method

Paired comparision method is defined as the ranking of a series of items by means of a series of comparisons between all possible pairs of items. This method is used when it becomes difficult to compare an individual's rating with the entire group of employees but easy to compare the two. The comparisions are carried out on a matrix, as shown below:

| | A | B | C | D | |
|---|---|---|---|---|---|
| A | | B | C | D | |
| B | | | C | D | |
| C | | | | D | |
| D | | | | | |

**Fig. 31.4** Paired comparison method.

## 3. Man-to-man rating scale

This method is used to rate foreman, or superintendent or salesman. Under this method, a five-step scale is constructed in which each step represents a known person. The highest step on the scale, as for example leadership, is represented by that person who, in the opinion of the rater, possesses leadership qualities to the highest degree among his colleagues in the type of activity engaged in by those to be rated. Other persons are selected to represent high level, middle level, low level possession of the trait. Persons to be rated are then slotted into the scale by comparing them in the trait in question with the individuals representing scale levels; hence, the name man-to-man rating.

### 4. Graphic rating scales

Graphic rating scale provides a series of traits and their definition. The rater placed a mark opposite to these traits on a line representing the full distance from 'highest' to 'lowest' rating. This approach is one of the most commonly used rating forms in industry today.

### 5. Forced choice

Under this method, the rater selects from a number of groupings of unrelated "personal characteristics" statements, one that is most similar and that is least similar to the rates. Numerical values are assigned on a statistical basis, and thus scores are obtained.

### 6. Critical incident

The rater keeps a running record of activity incidents which were 'critical' for successful and unsuccessful performance. When this method is used over a period of time, it identifies those types of activity which are characteristic of successful and unsuccessful employees in specific types of jobs. Thus, it furnishes the basis for continuing appraisals of subordinates and for day-to-day discussions with them for corrective and developmental purposes.

### 7. Field review

Under this method, a specialist in appraisal and development work meets supervisors and staff members and observes the persons to be appraised. After discussions with them, he writes out an analytic appraisal and reviews it with the supervisor for certification. This is an effective method, especially when applied to managerial personnel and when the specialist is properly qualified.

### 8. Performance standard

In this a standard is fixed to measure the achievement of employees. Many degrees are available to the rater to rate by using different signs. A tick mark (✓) in the standard box means that performance meets normal expectations (standard). A plus sign (+) in the standard box means that the performance is slightly better than standard but not sufficiently better to warrant a rating of above standard. Similarly, a minus sign (–) in the same box indicates some deficiency in performance, but not sufficient to warrant a below standard rating.

It is possible to compute a score in order to arrive at a total performance rating by taking the important elements into consideration. For example, if standard O is given a value of zero and each ✓ is given a minus value, such as –1, –2, –3, – 4 and each step above the scale is a plus value, such as +1, +2, +3, +4, these values multiplied by the importance degree (1, 2 or 3) are totalled and then divided by the number of items provide an index number to be considered for purposes of giving a total performance rating.

### 9. Appraisal by objectives

This approach is also known as "Management by Objectives". This method entails the preparation by subordinates appraisals of written statements covering his understanding of the objectives of (a) his senior's job (b) his own job, (c) the proper criteria of performance from his view point. (d) the situation, including problems to be overcome, and (e) his plan of action to accomplish the objectives. This report is discussed with the supervisors for purposes of communication, analysis, modification or approval and appraisal. The subordinate participates throughout and has largely appraised himself in the process.

## DIFFERENCES BETWEEN JOB EVALUATION AND MERIT RATING

| *Job evaluation* | *Merit rating* |
|---|---|
| 1. Job evaluation means determining the relative worth of jobs in our organisation. It is the critical study of the various jobs in order to assess their relative importance. | 1. Merit rating is the evaluation of the personality and performance of each employee by his senior. It is a critical study of qualities, knowledge, abilities, etc. of an employee. It is a type of performance evaluation. |
| 2. It is mainly useful for creating a fair and satisfactory wage system or structure. It acts as a base of compensation system. | 2. It is mainly useful for promotion of employees to the higher post. It acts as a base of promotion and transfer employees. |
| 3. Job evaluation is useful for explaining relative wage rates and for removing doubt among employees as regards wages, promotion, etc. | 3. Merit rating acts as a guide to employees for better performance and self development in future. |
| 4. It is concerned with the evaluation of job and not concerned with the employees. | 4. It is concerned only with the rating or evaluation of employees and not of jobs. |
| 5. It is useful for creating satisfied labour force. | 5. It is useful for manpower development and for raising efficiency of the labour force. |
| 6. Job evaluation is prior to merit rating as it rates the jobs themselves. | 6. Merit rating is next to job evaluation as it rates employees on these jobs. |
| 7. It determines the wage structure acceptable both to the employers and the employees. | 7. It provides a scientific base for determining fair wage for each individual worker according to his ability and performance. |

## QUESTIONS

### A. Objective type

**I. Choose the correct answer from the following alternatives:**

(a) The assessment of the requirements of a job is known as

1. job assessment
2. job grading
3. job analysis
4. job evaluation

(b) Job evaluation is
1. an assessment of the contribution a job makes to the profitability of a company.
2. a method of determining the relative worth of jobs.
3. a procedure to assess the skills required by a worker in a particular job.
4. a comparision of the relative earnings in a group of jobs to assess their relative value to the workers concerned.

(c) Merit rating is
1. an assessment of the different methods available to do a job in order to select the methods which provides the lowest cost permit of work produced.
2. the assessment and grading of ideas put forward in our organised suggestion scheme.
3. the assessment of the market appeal and sales attraction of a product in comparison with similar competitive products.
4. the systematic assessment of the behaviour and ability of workers in their work.

## II. Write *True* or *False* for the following sentences:

1. Job evaluation studies deal with the occupation as well as with the employee holding the position.
2. Separate job evaluation studies should be conducted for salaried employees and wage employees.
3. Job evaluation is the comparative appraisal of workers on different jobs.

## III. Match the following:

| Column A | Column B |
|---|---|
| 1. Job analysis | (a) Wage rate differentials |
| 2. Job specification | (b) Prevailing occupation pay levels |
| 3. Job evaluation | (c) Compensation on basis of output |
| 4. Merit rating | (d) Study of an occupation |
| 5. Wage survey | (e) Job composition |
| | (f) Pay increase and promotions. |

## B. Very short answer type

1. Define a task.
2. Define a position.
3. Define a job.
4. Define job analysis.
5. Define job description.
6. Define job specification.
7. Define job evaluation.
8. Define merit rating.

## C. Short answer type

1. Outline the various principles of job evaluation.
2. Explain the objectives and advantages of job evaluation.
3. State the procedure involved in installing a job evaluation programme.
4. State the objectives of Merit Rating.
5. Explain how a merit rating programme is administered.
6. Explain the various methods of merit rating.

### D. Long answer type

Define job evaluation. Explain the various methods of job evaluation.

## ANSWERS TO OBJECTIVE TYPE QUESTIONS

I. *Choose the correct answer:*

(a) 3 (b) 2 (c) 4.

II. *True or False:*

1. F 2. T 3. F.

III. *Match the following:*

1. (d) 2. (c) 3. (a) 4. (f) 5. (b).

# Chapter 32

# PROMOTION AND TRANSFER

## ■ INTRODUCTION

One of the important objectives of personnel department is to ensure adequate supply of manpower. Although training of employees and proper recruitment serves this purpose, this is not an end in itself from the point of view of getting necessary manpower. This must, in turn, be followed by an efficient administration of manpower. Maintenance of discipline among the workers, promotions, transfer, discharges constitutes an essential part of labour administration in factories. Disciplinary action need to be taken in respect of those employee who transgress the rules and regulations of the factory. In order to motivate the efficient and meritorious employees, promotions are necessary. In order to get maximum benefit from employees, transfers are necessary, besides giving an opportunity to the employees to get themselves acquainted and trained in the different departments of the factory. Often workers are to be punished by demoting them to a lower cadre when they lack the sense of responsibility. Employees are often discharged from services for several reasons.

## ■ DEFINITION OF PROMOTION

According to Scott, Clothier and Spriegel, "A promotion is the transfer of an employee to a job that pays more money or one that enjoys some preferred status." In simple words, promotion may be defined as a shift to a position or rank in which responsibilities correspondingly increase. Promotion need not necessarily imply an enhanced earnings, as for example, a charge from an hourly rate to a salary may be considered a promotion even though there is no actual raise in pay. However, promotion necessarily involves an increase in responsibilities of the employee who is promoted. The various classes of employees who can be promoted are manual workers, supervisors, technical workers, office staff and executives.

## ■ REASONS NECESSITATING PROMOTION

A well planned promotional policy improves the morale and increases the efficiency of workers. It also provides an opportunity for sincere workers to serve with loyalty. The following reasons are attributed for promotions in factories:

1. It leads to increased personal satisfaction of employees owing to increased salary and status.
2. When employees expect promotion they continue to serve the factory without searching employment elsewhere. Thus, promotion reduces labour turnover.
3. It creates a feeling of content with the present conditions and encourages ambition to succeed within the factory.

4. It increases interest in training and in self-development as a prerequisite to promotion.
5. It serves as reward for employees in recognition of their abilities, such as hard work, punctuality, sincerity, etc.

## ■ PROMOTIONAL POLICY

In formulating the promotional policy it is very essential to note that personal favouritism to a selected few must completely be avoided. This is because it leads to labour unrest due to frustration among the deserving candidates who are denied their legitimate promotions. The promotion must be based on traits such as merit, seniority, training acquired as they are more rational and accepted by employees. The following measures are to be taken in preparing a promotional policy:

1. The management should prepare an impartial, clear and long term promotional policy for all categories of workers. Such a policy should be framed after consulting trade unions and workers. The policy should clearly indicate the lines of promotion.
2. Wide publicity should be given about promotional policy through official manuals so as to give full and fair information about promotion rules, workers will know the experience, skill, knowledge etc. required for promotion.
3. The promotional policy should give preference to employees within the factory as against appointing employees to such positions from outside.
4. The basis of promotion must be made very clear so that there is no scope for misunderstanding by any employee.
5. Promotional policy should be supplemented by suitable training opportunity to eligible candidates. This enables the workers to get competence for promotion.
6. An opportunity must be given to every employee to justify himself as to why not he be promoted in preference to other candidate if he is a deserving candidate. With a view to make promotion a motivating factor, the promotional policy should be able to point out the promotional ladder within the factory which will indicate the positions that the junior-most employees are likely to reach. The promotional ladder is an arrangement of the several positions within a factory in the form of steps of a ladder starting from the lowest rank right up to topmost position. Besides giving a clear picture as to the future opportunities for the fresh recruits in each job classification it is bound to make him increasingly faithful in the discharge of his present duties, so that he can prepare himself to reach the next stage in the hierarchy.

This is shown in the following Fig. 32.1.

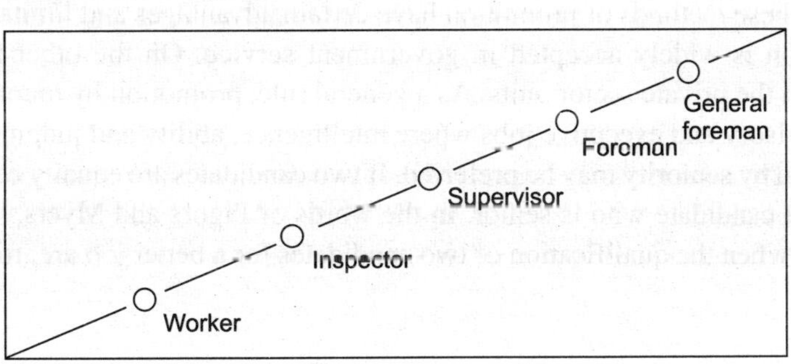


**Fig. 32.1** Positions to be filled in the promotional ladder in a factory

## ■ BASIS OF PROMOTION

There are two bases on which employees may be promoted, viz. (1) merit, and (2) seniority:

### 1. Promotion on merit

Merit as a basis of promotion is widely accepted by majority of the people. However, it is often discounted by a few on the ground of management's integrity to promote on merit. Moreover, it also becomes difficult for the supervisors to recognize merit. In spite of this, promoting on the basis of merit is considered as the soundest method.

### 2. Promotion on seniority

Seniority refers to the relative length of service of employees. Usually, length of service is computed on the basis of the current continuous employment. The seniority promotion plan is as old as civilization itself — seniority provides certainty and dependability. It reduces rivalry and jealousy. Although it was a popular basis in olden days, in modern business, seniority is quite inadequate as a universal promotional system. However, this method, when combined with the ability on the part of workers to do the job satisfactorily, can be readily accepted by workers.

## ■ SENIORITY *vs* MERIT IN PROMOTION

1. In promotion by seniority, the period of service of an employee is taken as a basis for giving promotion. In the case of promotion by merit, the ability, capacity, education and other merits are taken into consideration for promotion.
2. Management generally prefers promotion by merit while workers and trade unions prefer promotion by seniority.
3. Promotion by seniority is easy, simple and acceptable to all workers in general. It avoids disputes among workers. Promotion by merit is difficult to assess and disputes among workers are possible.
4. Promotion by seniority creates a sense of security among all workers. It also reduces the rate of labour turnover. On the other hand, promotion by merit is preferred by capable, ambitious and efficient workers.
5. There is no possibility of injustice to any worker when promotions are given strictly as per seniority. However, injustice to one or other worker by the management is quite possible when promotions are given on the basis of merit.

In brief, both these methods of promotion have certain advantages and limitations. Seniority, as a method of promotion is widely accepted in government service. On the other hand, promotion by merits is preferred in the private sector units. As a general rule, promotion by merit should be preferred in the case of supervisory and executive jobs where intelligence, ability and judgment are important. In other jobs, promotion by seniority may be preferred. If two candidates are equally competent, preference should be given to a candidate who is senior. In the words of Pigors and Myers, "Seniority should be considered but only when the qualification of two candidates for a better job are, for practical purposes, substantially equal.

## TYPES OF PROMOTION

Dale Yoder has classified promotions into two types, viz. (1) horizontal, and (2) vertical. Horizontal promotion refers to a promotion within a particular job classification, usually with increased salaries. For example, the promotion of a junior engineer to a senior engineer is a horizontal promotion, as it is within one job classification. On the other hand, if promotion takes place from one job classification to another, which is totally distinct, it is termed as 'vertical promotion'. For example, if a financial controller is promoted as general manager owing to his abilities and skills, it is a vertical promotion. Vertical promotion provides more opportunities, and greater scope for a person to utilize his experience, outstanding abilities and merits.

## DEMOTION

Demotion refers to a change in one's position and status from a higher cadre to a lower cadre with lesser responsibilities. Demotions are generally resorted to when there is a lapse on the part of the person who has been promoted. Generally, demotion takes punitive measure against an erring person. For example, the office manager may be demoted as office supervisor when there is slackness of work, dishonesty and disloyalty on his part. Demotion, in a way, amounts to degradition of position to a lower rank. A person can also be demoted in case of his gross inefficiency while discharging his duties. Sometimes, demotions are necessary to reverse a wrong promotion of a person who lacks the required abilities to discharge a responsible task. As far as possible, demotions should be avoided as it results in unpleasant consequences among the workers.

## TRANSFER

According to Scott, Clothier and Spriegel, "A transfer is the moving of an employee from one job to another." More precisely, a transfer is the shifting of an employee from one job to another within a department or from one department to another. A transfer need not necessarily involve a change in status, responsibilities, and salary. The main purpose of transfer is to ensure continuity in work in spite of labour shortage arising out of illness or resignation.

### Need for transfer

The need for transfer arises on account of the following:

1. When a worker is capable of handling a better job independently after having progressed in his present job.
2. When there is a vacancy which is to be filled up in another department, transfer can be resorted to.
3. When the interest of worker in the present job decreases, he can be transferred to another job where he can serve with more interest and enthusiasm. Monotony is one such reason where an employee looses his interest on a job.
4. When the relation between a senior and subordinate is not healthy, the subordinate can be transferred to another job.
5. When a worker is to be trained to acquire more experience, he can be transferred to such job where he can gain more experience.

6. Where the pressure of work is low in a department and there might not be enough work for some of the employees.
7. Where surplus staff exists in some department due to initial mistakes in posting employees to various departments.
8. When an employee requests on his own for his convenience, a transfer might be effected from one department to another department. Where transfers are made at the request of the employees, the management should lay down clearly the circumstances under which such a transfer will be effected. The reasons for requests for transfers should be convincing. In case of genuine reasons, transfers might have to be effected without any delay in the interest of employees concerned.

Whenever a transfer is effected, a form is made use of to effect such a transfer. Copies of such a form are sent to the personnel department, to the pay roll department and to the concerned departments. A specimen of transfer form is given below:

TRANSFER

| | |
|---|---|
| Name.............. | Date on which employee leaves...... |
| Pay roll effective date........... | Present job............ |
| Clock No............. | |
| Reason for transfer............ | |
| From: Department............. | Occupation.......... |
| Shift............. | Occupation............ |
| Transfer approval | Receiving approval |
| Foreman........... | ................. |
| Superintendent............ | ................. |
| Manager................. | ................. |
| | New clock no........... |

**Fig. 32.2** Transfer form

Whenever transfer involves any additional wage payment, adjustments are to be made for the payment of the same. Where no additional payment is stipulated the same old rate applies.

## Discharge

In general, discharge refers to termination of an employee from his services in a factory. The following are the circumstances under which the employees are discharged from the factory:

1. When the volume of work does not justify retaining the persons involved.
2. When a person fails to produce according to the requirements of the job due to his incapacity or deliberately restricting production and there is no suitable place to which he can be transferred.
3. When an employee violates the basic policy of the factory.
4. When any person endangers the safety of others in the factory.
5. When a person is involved in any moral misconduct.
6. When a person commits any theft of serious nature.

7. When a person is involved in any financial misappropriation.
8. When the factory is running under the conditions of depression under which production is to be curtailed owing to falling prices.
9. A person can be dischared on the grounds of inefficiency, dishonesty, drunkenness, carelessness, or indifference.
10. A person can be discharged on account of insubordination, uncleanliness, cause of discord, negligence, wastefulness and physical unfitness.

In order to avoid unnecessary grievances over discharges, it is desirable to establish rigid rules regarding discharge. A service agreement must be reached regarding discharge of employees under appropriate circumstances at the time of recruitment. Before an employee is discharged, it may be desirable to find out a way out to avoid it, as for instance he may be transferred to another department. A common procedure followed for discharging a worker is to suggest or recommend a discharge by the head of the department and it is executed by the personnel manager. Before an employee is discharged, the case may be reviewed so as to revoke the order of discharge. It is desirable to maintain a record in order to enter all the causes of discharge in order to demonstrate or prove that the discharge is justified and is not due to unfair discrimination or to the personal prejudice of the head of the department. In this connection, the following points may be considered:

(a) To keep a permanent record of all merit ratings made by the foreman may be kept. Such a record is especially valuable if there is rating of the traits that resulted in the discharge.
(b) Permanent record of ratings of the defendant's traits made by others than the foreman.
(c) A memorandum of the attempts made by the foreman to help the defendant to overcome this weakness.
(d) A copy of warning that had been sent to him.
(e) The letter of discharge, especially if the letter states the causes of the discharge.

Discharge may be of two types: (1) temporary, and (2) permanent. The former is also known as lay-off. Sufficient notice must be given in case of lay-offs so as to entable the employees to know the exact period for which they are to be laid off. However, the management should see that the discharged worker will not go with any unpleasant feeling against it. This implies that the discharged employee must be told the reason and sufficient notice must be served in advance, so that the employee can try to get an alternate job somewhere else. The amount of compensation payable to the discharged worker is a significant point to be noted. This depends upon experiences, skills, educational qualifications and other talents possessed by the employee.

## QUESTIONS

### A. Objective type

**I. Write *True* or *False* for the following sentences:**

(a) Promotions have better impact over worker's satisfaction than transfer.
(b) Promotion on the basis of merit is to be favoured as compared to seniority.
(c) In case of promotion of manual worker, promotion by merit is preferred to seniority.

(d) Discharge relates to permanent separation whereas lay-off relates to temporary separation.

(e) Whereas promotion encourages employees, demotion discourages them.

## B. Very short answer type

1. Define promotion.
2. Mention any four factors which necessitates promotion.
3. What do you mean by promotional policy?
4. What is a horizontal promotion?
5. What is a vertical promotion?
6. Distinguish between a horizontal and vertical promotion.
7. What do you mean by demotion?
8. Distinguish between promotion and demotion.
9. Define transfer.
10. What do you mean by discharge?
11. Distinguish between transfer and discharge.
12. Distinguish between discharge and lay-off.

## C. Short answer type

1. What do you mean by promotional policies? Outline its contents.
2. Mention the basis of promotion. Which do you prefer? Give reasons.
3. Define transfer. Outline the circumstances when transfers take place.
4. Define discharge. Mention the circumstances under which an employee may be discharged.

# ANSWERS TO OBJECTIVE TYPE QUESTIONS

(a) T (b) T (c) F (d) T (e) T

# Chapter 33

# SAFETY, HEALTH AND WELFARE OF EMPLOYEES

## ■ INTRODUCTION

The success of production in factories, to a large extent, depends upon the safety of employees. With the advent of factory system of production the number of industrial accidents have increased to an alarming extent. Safety in factories is essential both from the point of view of employees and employers. A safety programme increases the efficiency and morale of employees which ensures speedy production. On the other hand, an unsafe working environment may cause loss of arm, leg or sight which results in sufferings and hardship to the employees. Industrial accidents also diminish the working and earning abilities of workers. Apart from the fact that workers suffer from industrial accidents, their dependents are also forced to face hardship. From the point of employer, the production process suffers whenever industrial any accident occurs. The employer has to meet all the medical expenses of the victim in addition to the payment of compensation in accordance with the requirements of Workmen's Compensation Act. In addition to this, it involves loss of time in the process aiding the injured worker, investigating the accidents, preparing reports and discussing the events which led to occurrence of accidents. Further, the employer has to incur expenses in recruiting and training another employee in the place of injured worker. There is also the psychological effect in the minds of co-workers of the injured, and they may hesitate to perform similar type of job which led to accident. The quality and quantity of output may also decrease in such an event. An accident may also result in damage of machinery. When delivery dates are not maintained promptly owing to industrial accident there can also be the loss of orders from customers. The enactment of Factories Act of 1948 has made the manager of factories to give utmost importance to the element of industrial safety.

## ■ MEANING AND DEFINITION OF INDUSTRIAL SAFETY

Industrial safety refers to various measures taken by the management to prevent the occurrence of accidents in the factory. Accident is defined as an undesirable consequence when contact is made between an energy source and a person or object resulting in damage or injury.

R.P. Blake, in his book, *Industrial Safety* defines accident as "any occurrence that interrupts or interferes with the orderly progress of the activity in question".

The National Safety Council of U.S.A. describes an accident as "an event or rapidly occurring series of events, arising out of an unsafe act or an unsafe condition and culminating in an unpremediated injury. In any such series of events, it will be found that (a) some agency, such as a machine, tool, object, or material was involved, (b) the injured was performing some task or job at the time, and (c) contact was made in some manner between his body and the agency.

"Accident Prevention" is the term commonly applied to a programme of integrated and coordinated activities directed towards the prevention and control of accidents. In its broad sense, it includes a concern for safe equipment, safe work methods, design, promotion of safety awareness from an individual, education in safety at all levels in the organization and managerial support for the moral and ethical responsibilities that underlie any successful safety programme. Since accidents generally happen to people and not to equipment and processes the focus of accident prevention begins with the organisation as a whole. From there it is shifted to the specific responsibilities of management, supervision and employees for safety and accident prevention.

## ■ CAUSES AND CONSEQUENCES OF INDUSTRIAL ACCIDENTS

The causes of industrial accidents can be grouped under three headings, viz. (1) contributing causes, (2) immediate causes, and (3) accidents.

### 1. Contributing causes

Contributing causes of industrial accidents can be grouped under the following:

(A) **Supervisor's safety performance**

(a) Safety instruction inadequate
(b) Safety rules not enforced
(c) Safety not planned as part of the job
(d) Infrequent employee safety contacts
(e) Hazards not corrected
(f) Safety devices not provided.

(B) **Mental condition of the victim**

(a) Lack of safety awareness
(b) Lack of coordination
(c) Improper attitude
(d) Slow mental reaction
(e) Inattention
(f) Lack of emotional stability
(g) Nervousness
(h) Temperamental.

(C) **Physical condition of the victim**

(a) Extreme fatigue
(b) Deaf
(c) Poor eyesight
(d) Physically unqualified for job

(e) Heart condition

(f) Crippled.

## 2. Immediate causes

The immediate causes can be classified into two categories:

(i) **Unsafe working conditions**

The unsafe working conditions, which leads to accidents, may be listed as below:

(a) Inadequately guarded machines.

(b) Defective conditions, such as rough, sharp, slippery, decayed, corroded, where employees work.

(c) Unsafe design or construction.

(d) Hazardous arrangement or process, such as piling, storage, aisle space, exits, layout, over loading, etc.

(e) Unsafe ventilation which permits the accumulation of dusts and gases.

(f) Unsafe lighting.

(g) Poor housekeeping.

(ii) **Unsafe acts of persons**

The unsafe acts of persons include the following:

(a) Operating without authority.

(b) Operating at unsafe speed.

(c) Making safety devices inoperative.

(d) Using unsafe equipment, hands instead of equipment or with equipments unsafely.

(e) Unsafe loading, mixing or combining.

(f) Taking unsafe position or posture.

(g) Working on moving or dangerous equipment.

(h) Distracting, teasing, abusing.

(i) Failure to use safety clothing or personal protective device, such as helmets, goggles, hand-gloves, etc.

## 3. Accidents

(a) Fall

(b) Slip

(c) Slide

(d) Strike against

(e) Caught in between

(f) Erupt or explode

(g) Burn.

## ■ CONSEQUENCES OR EFFECTS OF INDUSTRIAL ACCIDENTS

The consequences or effects of industrial accidents can be summarised under the following:

1. Time lost by injured employee
2. Time lost by fellow employee who stops work:
   (a) Due to curiosity
   (b) Due to sympathy
   (c) To assist.
3. Time lost by supervisors in:
   (a) Assisting the injured
   (b) Investigating causes
   (c) Re-scheduling work
   (d) Re-training replacement
   (e) Preparing accident reports
   (f) Attending enquiries.
4. Time spent by first aid staff
5. Damage to equipment
6. Interference to production
7. Payment of compensation
8. Reduced output of the injured employee upon his return
9. Loss of profit due to idle equipment
10. Lower morale of work-force
11. Non-recovery of overheads by the injured person while he is a non-producer.

## ■ COST OF INDUSTRIAL ACCIDENTS

The cost incurred in connection with industrial accidents may be classified into: (a) Direct cost, and (b) Indirect cost.

### (a) Direct cost

The direct cost involved in industrial accidents is either: (1) medical expenses of injured employee (2) compensation payable to employees as per the requirements of Workmen's Compensation Act.

### (b) Indirect cost

These are the hidden cost which are at least three or four times greater than the direct costs. They take the following forms:

(a) Costs to be incurred when production is stopped during accidents.
(b) Costs of recruiting and training new employee so as to fill the position of injured worker.
(c) Loss or damage to property including machines.
(d) Loss of order owing to delay in deliveries.

(e) Fees paid to doctors and first aid staff.
(f) Loss in the earnings of profit due to accident.

## ■ ORGANISATION OF SAFETY DEPARTMENT

A safety organisation may be set up in several ways to suit the size and need of the factory. Safety department can be organized under any of the following:

1. **Line organisation:** This type of organisation is usually found in small factories where duties and responsibilities of Safety Director is delegated to a line officer as an additional duty. The merit of this type of organisation is that the total responsibility of industrial accident may be fixed on the line officer. But the demerit of this organisation is the line officer is overburdened with this additional duty.

2. **Establishment of separate safety department:** In a large size factory, a separate safety department may be set up with Safety Director appointed on a full time basis. The Safety Director reports to the Chief Executive for industrial accidents. There can be one or two assistants under the control of Safety Director. The functions performed by Safety Director are outlined below:

(a) Formulating and administering the safety programme.
(b) Advise on all safety matters for the guidance of management and all departments.
(c) Report to management periodically, i.e., daily, weekly or monthly on safety programme.
(d) Maintain accident records.
(e) Supervise or advise on safety training.
(f) Coordinate with medical department on proper placement of employees.
(g) Personal plant inspection.
(h) Keep informed on the latest safety information.
(i) Ensuring for compliance with laws and recommendations of insurance company.
(j) Consulting government agencies and insurance companies on safety problems.

3. **Safety committees:** A safety committee is often constituted to look into the causes and consequences of industrial accidents. When a safety committee is established it requires the initiative of executive, control and support in order to be effective. Generally, the number of members in a committee must be small in number for effective work, but at the same time, to include the breadth of knowledge and experience involved in the factories' operation. The formation of a committee must also involve preparation of a written statement including (1) scope of the committee's activity, (2) extent of committee's authority, and (3) procedure as to time and frequency of meetings, attendance requirements, agenda, records to be kept and reports to be submitted.

The responsibilities of a safety committee are:

(a) Reporting unsafe conditions.
(b) Investigating accidents and apprehension of accidents.
(c) Inspecting new equipment installations, observing employee work practices and looking for unsafe conditions.
(d) Influencing others to work safely.
(e) Setting an example of working safety for others to follow.
(f) Attending meetings and contributing to the knowledge and expertise of others at safety meetings.

## ■ SAFETY ORGANISATION CHART

A typical organisation chart of safety department that is used in a large sized factory is given below:

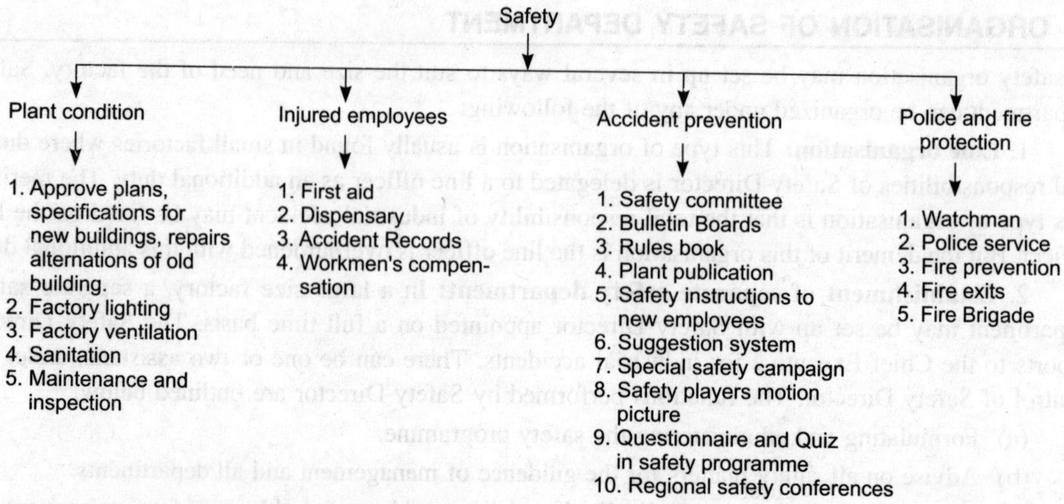


**Fig. 33.1** Chart showing activities of a typical safety department

## ■ FUNCTIONS OF SAFETY DEPARTMENT

The functions of safety department can be summarized by suggesting to provide or arrange for "MOST SAFE PLACES" for working in factories. Each of the alphabets in the above phrase denote the following:

1. *'M' for machinery:* It implies knowing the sources of mechanical power, transmission of power, material handling equipments.
2. *'O' for openings:* It implies closing of pits, shafts, ducts, drains and stairways.
3. *'S' for stacks:* It implies systematic storage of raw materials, semifinished products and finished products in addition to packing materials, such as sacks boxes and cartons.
4. *'T' for tools:* It implies maintenance of all types of tools, such as hammers, screwdrivers, spanners and saws.
5. *'S for structure:* It implies proper maintenance of floors, walls, ceilings, aisles, passage ways, platforms and roads.
6. *'A' for atmosphere:* This implies provision of good atmosphere by eliminating dust, gases and fumes.
7. *'F' for fire:* This implies provision of fire extinguishers, sprinklers, fire points and fire exits.
8. *'E' for electricity:* This implies provision of wires, cables, switches, electric motors and lighting. It would also include other services, gas, steam, compressed air, etc.
9. *'P' for pressure vessels:* It implies maintenance of boilers, compressors, etc.
10. *'L' for ladder:* It implies provision of steps, trestles, scaffolds and other means of access.
11. *'A' for attire:* This implies provision of personal protective clothing, hats, helmets, goggles, earmuffs and footwear.

12. *'C' for cranes:* It implies maintenance of hoists, escalators, conveyors, ropes, chains, hooks.
13. *'E' for explosives:* It implies safe keeping of flammable liquids, liquefied petroleum gases, and other dangerous substances.
14. *'S' for signals:* It implies provision of warning lights, telephones, signs, posters and bells.

## ■ STEPS IN A SAFETY PROGRAMME

The following steps are involved in any safety programme:

1. *Ensuring cooperation with plant manager:* The Manager's desire for safety achievement must be clearly visible through his action to achieve it.
2. *Ensuring cooperation with superintendent:* The superintendent must make safety an integral part of the operating organisation.
3. *Appointment safety director:* One person must be designated to develop and codify needed plant safety information, methods and procedures and advice on their implementation.
4. *Analysing accident records:* After his appointment, the safety director should analyse, the accident reports for the past year or two to learn, if possible, the how, who, where, when and why each accident has occurred.
5. *Arranging meeting of operating executives:* All foremen, superintendents and operating heads should then be summoned to a general meeting presided over by the Plant Manager.
6. *Inspection of operations:* Following this meeting, each foreman should make a complete inspection of his department.
7. *Mechanical safeguarding:* The safeguarding programme should then be developed and carried out, making sure that the most serious conditions are corrected first.
8. *Making general announcement:* Workers should be acquainted with the accident prevention plan.
9. *Organisation of educational work:* Formulate a programme to maintain interest and supply information on safety to management, foremen and workers.
10. *Engineering revision:* Consider methods for improving machinery, equipment and processes to eliminate hazards and increase production efficiency.

## ■ MEASURES TO ELIMINATE OR MINIMISE ACCIDENTS

The following measures can be taken to eliminate or minimise industrial accidents:

1. Plant housekeeping
2. Safety inspection
3. Safety education and training
4. Safety advertising
5. Safety committees
6. Machine safeguarding
7. Personal protective equipment
8. Safe design of machines
9. Enforcing safety rules

10. Job safety analysis
11. Maintenance
12. Accident investigation
13. Material handling.

### 1. Plant housekeeping

A good plant housekeeping for the purpose of presenting industrial accidents include building maintenance. The various places where accidents normally occur in a factory are: (a) stairways, (b) passageways, (c) floors. Therefore, stairways should be kept clear of all materials and should be properly illuminated. Passageways should be clear for the safety of pedistrian traffic and trucks. Floors should be free from holes, uneven surfaces and obstructions. Windows must be cleaned so as to allow good lighting into the factory. A regular and systematic programme of plant housekeeping can help in the removal of major accidents.

### 2. Safety inspection

Safety inspection is one of the principal means of locating accident causes. It assists in determining whether safeguarding is necessary to eliminate or remove hazards before accidents and personal injuries occur. It is best to plan surprise periodic inspections so that safety conditions are maintained at a high standard throughout the factory. All exits, fire escapes, fire alarm system, emergency lighting system and places seldom used should be thoroughly inspected to determine their adequacy and readiness to meet an emergency situation. Similarly, chains, cables, ropes and other equipments, which are subject to excess strain in handling heavy materials, should be inspected. Along with the scheduled inspections, a careful survey should be made as to the adequacy and safety of equipment in the plant. Recommendations should be made for replacement of defective and obsolete equipment as well as for the purchase of any additional equipment that may be necessary. Such recommendations should be followed up until the corrections are completed.

### 3. Safety education and training

Educating employees for ensuring safety has a direct and profound impact on the minds of employees. This is accomplished by employee safety meeting, labour-management safety committees, safety films, safety posters, safety contests, safety awards, factory publications, suggestion systems and numerous other educational devices. In addition to education designed to make them alert to hazardous conditions employees should also be trained in safe practices. The safety training must also include first-aid treatment for restoring consciousness, bandaging wounds, and stopping the flow of blood.

### 4. Safety advertising

Safety advertisements are to be designed to convey an appropriate message, through visuals how an employee is likely to involve in accidents. If they are changed frequently, they will attract the attention of most of the employees. Safety advertisement, containing warnings, instructions and effective slogans will have lasting impressions on the minds of employees. In addition to wall posters, pamphlets can also be used to illustrate safety do's and dont's.

### 5. Safety committees

This has already been discussed under the topic organisation of safety department.

### 6. Machine safeguarding

Moving parts of machine are extremely dangerous and they should be protected by guards to prevent injuries from occurring. Machine guards can be designed in such a way that they remain on a permanent basis.

### 7. Personal protective equipment

The use of personal safety devise does not eliminate the hazard. But it protects workers when used and makes them out of danger. In modern days, a number of safety equipments are available. They vary from safety hats to safety shoes. For head protection equipment such as helmets, and ear protectors can be used. For face and eye protection, goggles, face shields and welding helmets are available. For hand, foot and leg protection, gloves, safety shoes and foot guards can be made use of.

### 8. Safe design of machines

Although most of the accidents are attributed to the acts of employees, the importance of the worker's environment and physical surroundings should never be ignored in determining the cause of industrial accidents. In fact, good plant layout and design can go a long way in preventing accidents. The following requirements in safety design may be considered to prevent accidents:

(a) Provide ample space around individual machines or process units for normal operations, adjustments, usual repairs.

(b) Arrange machines in a logical sequence to give a direct flow of material.

(c) Provide efficient, safe and flexible facilities for moving material in process and removing finished products.

(d) Provide ample and convenient facilities for packing and storing finished goods.

(e) Select central locations for elevators, tool cribs, emergency rooms.

(f) Provide exists to evacuate the working force rapidly in case of fire.

(g) Provide means for the safe and quick cut off of mechanical power, electric current, steam, gas, not only at the individual machine but also from rooms and buildings.

(h) Provide heat, ventilation, air conditioning and facilities for the removal of dust, fumes, and vapours.

(i) Provide adequate natural and artificial lighting whenever employees work.

(j) Provide for the safe routing of outside traffic, both pedestrian and vehicular.

### 9. Enforcing safety rules

This measure imply the disciplinary action to be taken against those workers who violate safety rules. Sometimes, they may also be discharged from factory after warning. The first step towards safety rule observance is that all supervisors must become familiar with the rules and follow them continually. The good example set by supervisors have much influence on workers.

### 10. Job safety analysis

More accidents can be prevented through the analysis of each job in the factory. This analysis of job can be taken by safety analyst. Under this measure, the safety analyst breaks a job into its various elements to analyse individual motions to unearth possible hazards. On finishing his study, he is able to determine the right type of employee and proper placement of employee on the right job. Thus, accidents are considerably reduced.

### 11. Maintenance

Worn-out machinery often constitutes a serious hazard. The breakdown or inefficient operation can cause injury. In addition to machine, the machine guards are subjected to wear and tear and such defective equipment often gives employees a false sense of security and protection. Slippery floors around machines also may cause injuries. Defective machine tools are also a constant source of employee injury. Each of these safety hazards can be controlled through preventive maintenance involving inspections, repairs, records and reports.

### 12. Accident investigation

Accident investigation brings to light previously undetected hazards that may be corrected on the, job in which the accident had occurred. This measure is based on the maximum learning by experience. The purpose of the investigation is to bring forth facts which can be used to prevent of recurrence of accidents. Investigation of accidents serves the purpose of information to the workers so as to prevent by drawing attention of the workers to the possible cause of the accident and results. Accident investigation also helps in determining the liability or compensation payable to the accident victim.

### 13. Material handling

Handling of materials cause a large percentage of accidents in factory. Sometimes manual handling of materials is considered as more safe and efficient. To avoid back strains hand cart, trolleys, etc. are often made use of. To handle rough substances, hand gloves are preferred. Mechanical handling equipments, such as cranes, hoists, conveyors also cause injuries. Special attention may be paid in such circumstances to avoid accidents.

## ■ FIRE PROTECTION AND CONTROL

Fire starts when flammables and a source of ignition occur simultaneously. When the quantity of ignitables is large, the fire hazard increases. A combination of congested materials, a hot spark, or overheated electrical equipment may result in occurrence of fire. The other common causes of fire hazards in a factory are:

1. Smoking
2. Poor housekeeping
3. Defective heating equipment
4. Defective electric equipment and wiring
5. Open flames
6. Spontaneous ignition
7. Explosive atmosphere.

1. **Smoking:** Smoking of beeris, cigarettes, cigars is the major cause of fire. Therefore, it is necessary to prohibit use of match boxes, automatic lighters and smoking materials in factories. As smoking is a widespread habit its absolute prohibition requires constant reminders. The areas prone to fire accidents must be designated with NO SMOKING.

2. **Poor housekeeping:** Proper storage of materials and removal of waste materials are important in prevention of fire. Combustible materials must be stored in metal containers. Provisions should be made for the prompt removal of drippings of flammable oils, grease and fluids.

3. **Heating and electrical equipment:** Overheated surfaces and defective equipment may be the cause of a serious fire. All high temperature equipment should be insulated or isolated from combustible material.

4. **Open flames:** The use of open flames, welding torches and the like should be preceded by careful preparation of the area in which they are used.

5. **Spontaneous ignition:** When the ignition temperature of materials is high fire results from it. This process is accelerated by the presence of decomposing organic materials, chemical reaction and so on. Control of such an incident involves better housekeeping, storage of combustible materials in a well-ventilated, cool area.

6. **Explosive atmosphere:** A flammable dust, gas, or vapour present in the air causes an ignition to accelerate throughout the factory leading to an explosive atmosphere. Ignition prevention generally consists of appropriate ventilation, exhaust system, as well as the elimination of ignition source. On the other hand, the concentration of combustibles should be kept low.

## Fire prevention in factories

The following guidelines may be followed for preventing fire occurrence in factories:

1. Management must accept that a fire prevention policy must be set up and regularly reviewed.
2. An estimate should be made regarding the possible effects of a fire in building, plant and machinery, semifinished and finished goods workers, customers, and records.
3. Identify the fire risks, considering sources of ignition, combustible materials and means whereby fire could spread.
4. Estimate the magnitudes of the risk to establish priorities.
5. Establish clear lines of responsibilities for fire prevention.
6. Appoint a fire officer responsible to the Board.

## Precautions to be taken to prevent fire occurrence

1. Doors and other openings through which employees can escape at the time of occurrence of fire must not be locked and unobstructed.
2. Heating apparatus and main switches to be put off daily at the closing hours.
3. Furnaces and boilers to be checked up frequently.
4. Fire detection and alarm system tested at a specified time.
5. Smoking to be prevented during working hours.
6. Combustible materials must be kept away from heaters.
7. Flammable liquid containers should be tightly closed and kept away from the source of ignition.
8. Waste paper baskets should be emptied at regular intervals.
9. Workmen's clothes, shoes should be kept in separate rooms away from combustible materials and other sources of heat.
10. Electric motors must be kept clear of all accumulation of materials.

11. Fire extinguishers and other fire appliances should be kept in their appropriate places with fire buckets filled with water or sand.
12. Fire instructions, fire-exit and no-smoking notices clearly displayed.
13. Sprinkler and fire detector head must not be obstructed.
14. Raw materials and semifinished goods should not be dumped on floors. Instead, they must be properly arranged and stored in their appropriate places.
15. Weeds and grass cuttings should be removed from building especially from storeroom.
16. Water supply of sprinkler should be tested frequently.
17. Connections of electrical fittings should be checked regularly.
18. Leaks in roof should be repaired on time.
19. Gates and fence, which might admit strangers, must be secured.
20. Special fire extinguishing systems, such as dry powder and carbon dioxide, must be arranged.

## HEALTH OF EMPLOYEES

The health of employees has been one of the major concerns of employers since the beginning of the factory system. This is because it is only when workers are in good physical condition, can they work efficiently. The recognition of employees' health has assumed more importance ever since Factories Act of 1948 was passed in our country.

In the traditional sense, health implies "the mere absence of an ascertainable diseasse". But in its present connotation, health is the outcome of the interaction between the individual and his environment. Thus, industrial health refers to the maintenance of a healthy environment in the factory, conducive to healthy working conditions for the benefit of the employees. The basic objective of industrial health is prevention of disease and injury, rather than curing it. In accordance with this dynamic approach, industrial health may comprise measures for (1) protecting the workers against any health hazards arising out of their work or the conditions under which it is carried on, (2) fostering the adaptation of workers to the jobs and work environment and thus contributing towards the workers' physical as well as mental adjustments, and (3) promoting the establishment and maintenance of the highest possible degree of physical and mental well-being of the workers.

The maintenance of good healthy environment in factories is of particular interest to the Factory Manager. This is because (1) health of employees contribute continuous work in factories. An estimate, in U.S.A. place that the lost time arising from disabling, illness is as high as 2% and indicate that for every person incapacitated because of illness, at least two others were handicapped because of prevalent disease to the extent of 10 to 50% of their efficiency, (2) health of employees reduces the absenteeism in factories. It is estimated that absenteeism due to industrial disease is about 3% of the total absenteeism (3) it reduces excess labour turnover in factories, (4) it reduces the compensation payable to employees on account of disease developed because of industrial processes, (5) it minimises spoilage of goods produced in factories, (6) it improves morale of employees, increased productivity per employee and a lengthened span of working years for an employee. In fact, industrial health service is as much a productive and positive part of the organisation as any other in modern industry. Its accomplishment in maintaining the human resources of the organisation is to be accepted as an important activity just as in the maintenance of machinery in modern factory. Sections 11 to 20 of the Factories Act of 1948 deal with the provisions ensuring the health of the workers in the conditions under which work is carried on in the factories. These provisions are as follows:

1. Cleanliness: According to Section 11 of the Factories Act, every factory shall be kept clean and free from effluvia arising from any drain, privy, or other nuisance. Accumulation of dirt and refuse shall be removed daily by some effective method. The floor of every room shall be cleaned at least once in every week by washing using disinfectant where necessary.
2. Disposal of waste and effluents: Section 12 of the Act deals with this provision. This has already been explained earlier under the chapter Industrial Sanitation.
3. Ventilation and temperature: Section 13 of the Act deals with this provision. This has already been discussed earlier under the chapter "Industrial Ventilation".
4. Dust and Fumes: Section 14 of the Act deals with this provision. This has already been discussed earlier under the chapter "Industrial Air Conditioning and Ventilation".
5. Artificial humidification: Section 15 of the Act deals with this provision. This has already been discussed earlier under the chapter Industrial Air Conditioning.
6. Overcrowding: Section 16 of the Act deals with this provision. Section 16 (1) provides that there shall not be overcrowding in any room of the factory so as to be injurious to the health of the workers employed therein. Section 16 (2) lays down that there shall be at least 500 cubic feet of space for every worker.
7. Lighting: Section 17 of the Act deals with this provision. This has already been explained earlier, under the chapter, "Factory Lighting".
8. Drinking water: Section 18 of the Act deals with this provision. This has already been explained earlier under the chapter, "Industrial Sanitation".
9. Latrine and Urinals: Section 19 of the Act deals with this provision. This has already been discussed earlier under the chapter, "Industrial Sanitation".
10. Spittoons: Section 20 of the Act deals with this provision. This has already been discussed earlier under the chapter, "Industrial Sanitation".

## Measures to check ill-health of workers

The following measures check the ill-health of workers in factories:

1. Conducting a thorough physical fitness examination at the time of selection of workers.
2. Offering first aid treatment when the symptoms of disease is observed.
3. Medical check-up of employees in the dispensaries set up by the factories.
4. Supply of healthy food to employees from canteens started by factories.
5. Educating employees on health programmes through posters, films, health contests, publicity programmes and developing a healthy consciousness on the part of employees.
6. Elimination of workers with communicable disease.

## Welfare of employees

Welfare facilities are provided by the factories in order to fulfill some particular needs of employees. Welfare facilities are also termed as employee services and are offered as "conveniences" or "necessities" for employees. According to a report of the International Labour Organization, "workers welfare" should be understood the provision of mean such services, facilities and amenities which may be established in or in the vicinity of undertaking so that the persons employed there should be able to perform their work in a healthy, congenial surroundings. They should be provided with amenities conducive to good health and high morale. Such services instill a feeling of group solidarity and loyalty to the factory. The *Encyclopaedia of Social Sciences* (Vol. XV, 1935) defines labour welfare as "the voluntary efforts of employers to establish within the existing industrial system, working and sometimes living and cultural conditions of the employees beyond that which is required by law, the custom of the industry and general well being of the working population.

## Types of welfare facilities

Welfare facilities offered to employees in a factory can be classified into two types:

1. Statutory
2. Non-statutory.

Types of Welfare Facilities

**1. Statutory**

(a) Washing facilities
(b) Facilities for storing and drying clothes
(c) Facilities for sitting
(d) First aid appliances
(e) Canteens
(f) Shelter, rest and lunch rooms
(g) Creches

**2. Non-statutory**

(a) Housing
(b) Transport
(c) Recreational
(d) Educational
(e) Information
(f) Professional
(g) Financial

**Fig. 33.2** Chart showing types of welfare facilities offered in factories

### 1. *Statutory welfare facilities*

The provision of statutory as facilities are governed by the Factories Act of 1948. The various provisions in this regard are follows:

(a) **Washing facilities:** Section 42 of the Act deals with this provision. This has already been covered under the chapter "Industrial sanitation".

(b) **Facilities for storing and drying clothes:** Section 43 of the Act deals with this provision. This has already been covered under the chapter "Industrial Sanitation".

(c) **Facilities for sitting:** According to Section 44(1), in every factory, suitable arrangements for sitting shall be provided and maintained for all workers who are obliged to work in a standing position. This has been done in order that the workers may take advantage of any opportunities for rest which may occur in the course of their work.

(d) **First aid appliances:** According to Section 45 (1), there shall, in every factory, be provided and maintained first-aid boxes with the prescribed contents so as to be readily accessible during all working hours. There shall be at least one such box for every 150 workers.

(e) **Canteens:** According to Section 46 (1), where more than 250 workers are ordinarily employed, a canteen or canteens shall be provided and maintained by the occupier for the use of the workers.

(f) **Shelters, rest-rooms and lunch rooms:** According to Section 47 (1), in every factory, wherein more than 150 workers are ordinarily employed, there shall be a provision for shelters, rest-rooms and a suitable lunch rooms where workers can eat meals brought by them with provision for drinking water.

(g) **Creches:** According to Section 48 (1), in every factory wherein more than thirty women workers are ordinarily employed, there shall be provided and maintained for them a suitable room or rooms for use of their children under the age of six years.

**2. *Non-statutory facilities***

(a) **Housing facilities:** One of the serious problems faced by employees in modern factories is housing. This can be solved in large factories by constructing quarters which can be let out to employes at subsidized rent.

(b) **Transport facilities:** To help the workers to come and work on time, transport facilities may have to be provided. Large-sized factories can afford to provide this facility by owning their own vehicles.

(c) **Recreational facilities:** In order to eliminate monotony and strenuous work recreational facilities may be offered. This can take the form of indoor and outdoor games, cinemas, and picnics. The recreational facilities, besides ensuring health, also promotes good-will and a pleasant attitude of the workers, thereby leading to efficiency of employees.

(d) **Educational facilities:** Educational facilities are to be extended not only to the employees but also to their children. Education for employees take the form of training for improving their abilities, skill and efficiency, while the education for children of employees is to be provided by starting schools and colleges.

(e) **Information facilities:** The latest information about the factory can be brought to the notice of employees through the notice boards and factory magazine. The notice board is usually reserved for official notices. Factory magazine may contain both official and general information which may be of interest to employees.

(f) **Professional services:** Professional services, such as medical, legal, personel counseling, are highly useful to the employees in a factory.

(g) **Financial facilities:** The employees may be encouraged to form a credit cooperative societies to cater to their financial needs. Those who have surplus funds may be encouraged to deposit the money to earn more interest, while others who are in need of loans may be offered from the deposits received from employees. Sometimes, loans can also be given by factories to the employees and the amount can be recovered from the salary or wages payable for them.

## QUESTIONS

### A. Very short answer type

1. Define an accident.
2. State the objectives of industrial safety programme.
3. Outline the industrial safety functions.
4. Define safety organization.
5. Define safety committee.
6. What do you mean by industrial welfare?

### B. Short answer type

1. "Industrial accidents involve both direct costs and indirect costs". Discuss.
2. Outline the functions of safety department.
3. Explain the steps involved in a safety programme.
4. Explain the causes of fire hazard. State the guidelines which can prevent occurrence of fire in factories.
5. Explain the provisions of Factories Act relating to health of employees.

### C. Long answer type

1. Explain the causes and consequences of industrial accidents.
2. Explain the organizational structure of a safety department.
3. Explain the measures to be taken to prevent industrial accidents.
4. Define industrial welfare. Explain various types of welfare facilities offered in factories.

Chapter 34

# METHODS OF WAGE PAYMENT

## ■ INTRODUCTION

One of the major problems that confronts the management of every factory is the determination of a satisfactory wage structure. This problem has been further complicated because many direct remunerations have been devised which have social and psychological implications with a worker's wage. From the point of view of employer, the selection of a particular system of wage payment determines the future earning capacity of the factory. From the point of view of employees, choosing the appropriate plan plays a prominent role in determining employee satisfaction, productivity, morale and turnover. Therefore, management of every factory must determine how much of wages and salaries are to be paid to employees. The determination of wages payable to employees is based upon thorough analysis of all factors affecting such remunerations.

## ■ DEFINITION OF WAGES AND SALARIES

According to Alford and Beatty, "Wages are the aggregate earnings of an employee for a given period of time, such as a day or week, and are equal to the product of an hourly rate times the number of hours or the product of a piece rate times the number of pieces, plus any premiums or bonuses earned."

These earnings may be expressed in money, in which case they are called nominal wages or in goods and services purchasable with money, in which case they are called real wages.

### Definition of wage rate

The wage rate is the wage received by an employee for a unit of time, excluding special payments for overtime and night work and incentive earnings.

### Definition of standard wage rate

A standard wage rate is one established by job evaluation as the basic rate of wages to be received by employees for satisfactory performance of a given job.

### Definition of wage scale

A wage scale is an assembly of all properly evaluated standard wage rates set forth in sequence according to the evaluation of the job and the size of the rate.

### Definition of wage schedule

A wage schedule is an assembly of rates applicable to a given classification of work. Wage schedules are formal announcements of rates for the information of workers, supervisors and official instructions for payroll computations.

### Definition of salary

Salary is compensation paid to an employee for personal services rendered on a weekly, monthly or annual basis.

### Wages *vs.* salaries

When construed in a broad sense, wages cover all forms of compensation paid to the employees of a factory. Accordingly, wages include basic wages, bonuses, commissions or any other form of monetary payment. By its popular usage, the term wage is used to denote the remuneration given to those employees who are employed on production process. On the other hand, the term salary is used to denote payment of remuneration to those employees who manage, supervise and control the activities of employees. They mainly constitute managers, supervisors, accountants, inspectors, foremen and the like.

## ■ WAGE AND SALARY POLICIES

It is very difficult to prepare a comprehensive wage and salary policies in a factory. Usually, the following matters are considered while compiling a wage policy.

1. Basis of remuneration, i.e., number of hours worked or number of units produced, should be fixed for various groups of employees.
2. Establishment of wages and salary level that will enable the factory to maintain production costs that are competitive and thus assure stability in the earnings of profit.
3. Determination and use of fair wage differentials between jobs, based upon the skill, experience, responsibility and working conditions.
4. Measurement and recognition of individual merit through merit rating or through incentive system of payment of wages.
5. Establishment of fair standards of performance which can be reasonably and consistently attained.
6. Establishment of a plan of "promotion from within" the factory that will assure every employee an opportunity for advancement consistent with his ability and performance.
7. Establishment of a normal work week schedule indicating the hours of the day and the days of the week in which the work is to be performed.
8. Determination of extra remuneration for overtime and night shift work. Special work schedules should be anticipated and arranged, whenever possible to allow the worker time to adjust himself to the new situation.
9. Determination of wage and salary payments to be made for vacations, holidays and sick leave to the various groups of employees.
10. Provisions for giving prompt attention to complaints on wage and salary matters in order that adjustments that may be necessary, may be made before grievance develops.

## ■ ORGANISATION FOR WAGE AND SALARY ADMINISTRATION

The position of wage and salary administration in the organisation varies from factory to factory. In big factories, usually a staff department is set-up for advising and assisting the entire organisation on wage problems. This department is most commonly found in the personnel department. In small factories, the wage and salary functions may be assigned to controller or treasurer. In such a situation, it is to be ensured that the function of wage administration should not be subordinated to the other duties of controller or treasurer.

The functions performed by the wage and salary administrator are as follows:

1. Assist in formulation of wage and salary policies.
2. Analyse and classify the jobs according to their requirements.
3. Job specification and job evaluation.
4. Wage and salary surveys.
5. Merit rating of employees.
6. Approval of wage rate changes.
7. Study of the effects of wage incentives, profit sharing, "cost of living", bonuses and other special wage plans, affecting the morale and performance of employees.

## ■ CHARACTERISTICS OF A SOUND WAGE PLAN

The following are the essential characteristics of a sound system of wage payment:

1. The system must be agreed upon both by employer and employees.
2. The wage system must be such that it must minimise labour turnover.
3. It should reduce absenteeism and late attendance.
4. Wage system should include incentives for efficient and exceptional type of workers.
5. The cost of operating the system must be less.
6. The system of wage payment must take into account the working conditions of the employees.
7. It should guarantee a minimum amount of wages.
8. Wage system must be flexible and capable of being adjusted in case of need.
9. Wage system must be in commensurate with the earnings of the factory.
10. It should be consistent with government policy.

## ■ FACTORS INFLUENCING WAGES

Many factors influence the remuneration payable to employees in a factory. In addition to payment of basic wages (calculated either on the basis of time rate or piece rate) certain other forms of indirect remunerations are also paid. These take the form of leave with pay, holiday with pay, overtime premium and so on. They are referred to as fringe benefits. As a part of wage determination process, management must take all the factors which influence the wage payment. These factors are as follows:

1. Labour legislation
2. Collective bargaining
3. The labour market
4. Geographic location

5. Cost of living
6. Ability to pay.

1. **Labour legislation:** A number of laws have been enacted which have a marked influence on wage payment. They are: Payment of Wages Act, 1936, the Minimum Wages Act, 1948, the Workmen's Compensation Act, 1923, the Payment of Gratuity Act, 1972, the Employees Provident Fund (and Miscellaneous Provisions) Act, 1952, the Employees State Insurance Act, 1948, the Maternity Benefit Act, 1961 and Payment of Bonus Act, 1965.

2. **Collective bargaining:** Members of trade union often force the employer to pay as per the wage scale fixed by the trade union. This arises on account of collective bargaining of members of trade union. Usually, an agreement is entered into by the trade union and the employer in respect of fixation of certain wages. The wages remain in force until they are revised by the trade union. The trade union may also decide the incentive system that may be introduced in a factory. This factor can influence even other factories where there may not be a trade union with a view to pay uniform wages thereby satisfying the workers of their factories. Usually, the union of big factory will take the lead which will be followed, in turn, by small-sized factories.

3. **The labour market:** In a labour market, usually the supply and demand for a particular type of labour tends to seeks a balance. However, a perfect balance between demand and supply of labour is rarely observed. This difference between demand and supply of labour factor leads to the payment of different rates of salariès and wages for different categories of employees. The shortage of qualified workers for certain jobs may have considerable influence on the wages demanded by persons possessing specific skills.

4. **Geographic location:** Wage differentials prevail in different localities as in the case of our country, where the wage rates are different in south when compared to the north. The wage rates applicable in towns are different when compared to rural areas.

5. **Cost of living:** The cost of living index to a large extent, determines the fixation of wages in factories. An increase in the cost of living index always results in the fixation of higher wages and vice versa. The trade union take this factor as a strong reason for demanding higher wages. However, the management may not necessarily accept cost of living index as the basis for increase in wages, because sale income and profit may not coincide with cost of living index of employees.

6. **Ability to pay:** "Ability to pay" as a factor which influences the wages is often used by the employers to turn down. The workers demand for higher wages while the employees may claim more wages in commensurate with more profit earned by the factory, the employer may counter claim as to the factory's break-even-point in respect of costs and profit picture.

The ability to pay the wages, however, depends upon the wage policy of the factory. This is, because the factory cannot afford to pay wages at an exorbitant level at the expense of its customers or owners. But, at the same time, it must also pay wages at an acceptable level in order to maintain stability in labour force. Otherwise, it will lead to excess labour turnover.

## ■ METHODS OF WAGE PAYMENT

There are numerous systems of wage payment which are being used today. They are presented in the chart for clear understanding.

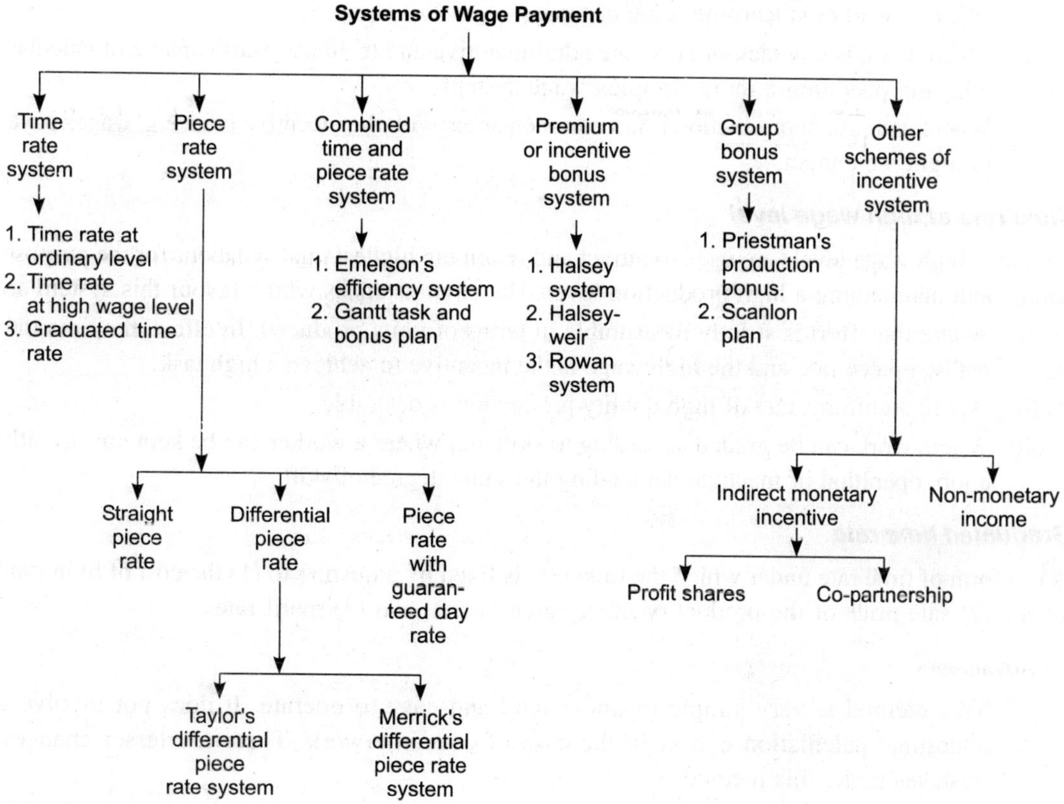


## I. Time rate system

The system under which the payment is made to the employees, according to the time for which they work, is known as time rate system. Time rate system can take any of the following forms:

### 1. *Time rate at ordinary level*

Under this system, time rate is fixed before hand and workers are remunerated at this rate for the hours of work done by them. The rate can be fixed either per hour, day, week or month. The formula for calculating wages under this method is.

*Earnings*: Time taken × Time rate. Suppose the time rate fixed in a factory is Re.1/- per hour, if an employee works for 8 hours in a day he will be paid Rs. 8/- i.e., 8 hrs × Re.1/- = Rs. 8.

Time rate at ordinary level is suitable under the following circumstances:

(i) Where services rendered by employees cannot be tangibly measured, e.g. watchman, office staff and other indirect workers.

(ii) Where quality of a product is the first consideration and where care and skill are more essential, e.g. tool-making, testing and inspection.

(iii) Where the speed of operation is governed entirely by process time and the operator has little or no control over the rate of production, as continuous process industries, such as chemical plants and oil refining.

(iv) Where a worker is learning a job or trade.

(v) Where there is any lack of adequate administrative and technical staff capable of calculating time and operating a more complex wage system.

(vi) Where increase in production is not commensurate with the incentive paid, e.g. wages payable to night watchman.

### 2. *Time rate at high wage level*

Time rate at high wage levels are used to attract and retain the highest quality labour for the purpose of obtaining and maintaining a high production level. The circumstances which favour this system are:

(i) Where the effort is strictly measurable in terms of units produced. In effect, the time rate is really a piece rate and the high wage is the incentive to achieve a high task.

(ii) Where a uniform rate of high quality production is desirable.

(iii) Where work can be graded according to skill and where a worker can be kept consistently at a job, operation or machine demanding the same degree of skill.

### 3. *Graduated time rate*

This is a form of time rate under which the time rate is fixed by adjusting to (1) the cost of living index numbers, (2) sale price of the product or other agreed basis, and (3) merit rates.

**Advantages**

1. This method is very simple to understand and easy to operate. It does not involve any additional calculation except in the case of overtime work. There are lesser chances of mistakes under this method.
2. This method does not give scope for jealousy and hatred amongst the workers as all of them earn the same wages. So, we don't come across rival groups being formed when this system is implemented.
3. Workers are not in a hurry to work and so there is little chance of breakage of tools and accessories.

**Disadvantages**

1. This method discourages efficient workers, as no distinction is made between efficient and inefficient workers. All are paid the same rate of wage payment.
2. The workers tend to work slowly as they are certain about their wages. So, in order to ensure that there is no waste of time, a supervisor is appointed and this increases the total cost of labour.

## II. Piece rate system

Under this system, wages are paid on the basis of number of articles produced by the workers. This method of wage payment offers a direct financial incentive to the workers who can earn more wages by producing more number of articles with their ability, energy and speed of work. Piece rate system of wage payment can be of the following types:

(A) Straight piece rate,

(B) Differential piece rate, and

(C) Piece rate with guaranteed day rate.

### (A) Straight piece rate

In this method, each unit of production is termed as a piece. For each piece a rate of payment is fixed which is known as a piece rate. The total wages are calculated by multiplying the number of pieces manufactured by the piece rate. Expressed in the form of formula.

Earnings = No. of pieces produced × Rate per piece.

This system of wage payment is suitable under the following circumstances:

(a) Where there is an urgent necessity to increase production.

(b) Where individual output can be easily and quickly determined and priced.

**Advantages**

1. This system offers an incentive to the employees in as much as they can earn more wages by producing more units.
2. As the workers tend to work on their own initiative the need for supervision can be obviated.
3. Labour cost can be conveniently charged to the units produced.

**Disadvantages**

1. Fixation of piece rate is not an easy job. A lower piece rate leads to discontentment among employees.
2. With a desire to produce more units in order to earn more wages, the workers may sacrifice quality for the sake of quantity. To ensure quality of the products, there is a need to appoint a quality control inspector, whose salary may again increase the total labour cost.
3. Excessive speeding up of work may lead to more spoilage and defective work. The cost of rectification may result in increased cost of production.
4. It is difficult to exercise discipline over the workers in the matter of their arrival and departure, because time is not the criterion for wage payment.

### (B) Differential piece rate system

Under differential piece rate system, the wages of workers vary at different stages within the range of output. This variation is sometimes more, sometimes less and sometimes in proportion to output. Sometimes workers feel that beyond a certain stage any further effort is not worthwhile. It is at this stage that an additional incentive is given to increase the output. Differential piece rate system is useful under the following circumstances.

1. Where production is undertaken on a continuous basis in order to maximise the output.
2. Where learners are to be encouraged.
3. Where time required to complete a job can be conveniently fixed.
4. Where output can be identified with the individual workers.
5. Where production process is standardised.

The two systems, which work under this principle are:

1. Taylor's differential piece rate system.
2. Merrick's differential piece rate system.

1. **Taylor's differential piece rate system:** This system was designed by F.W. Taylor in 1880. The features of this system of wage payment are as follows:

(a) Day wages are not guaranteed.

(b) A standard is established for each and every task by means of time and motion studies.

(c) Two differential piece rates are applicable for payment of wages to employees. The first rate is called a 'low piece rate' and second one is known as a 'high piece rate.' Low piece rate is used to remunerate those employees whose efficiency is below standard and high piece rate for those who are above standard.

(d) Taylor's original system of wage payment includes a low rate which is 83% of the piece wage rate. The high piece rate is 125% of the piece rate plus 50% incentive in the form of bonus (or 175%) of the given piece rate.

The main purposes of Taylor's differential piece rate system are:

(1) To discourage less than average workers by denying guaranteed wages and fixing a low piece rate for low level of production, and

(2) for rewarding the efficient workers by offering a high piece rate for higher level of production.

To illustrate with an example, let low piece rate be 0.60 per unit.

High piece rate be 0.90 per unit. Standard output be 0.40 units a week.

If the output of A, B and C is 32 units, 37 units and 42 units respectively, the earnings of A, B and C will be:

A = 32 units @ 0.60 per unit = 19.20

B = 37 units @ 0.60 per unit = 22.20

C = 42 units @ 0.90 per unit = 37.80.

**Advantages**

1. This system attracts only the efficient workers.
2. With the efficient labour force, the output increases considerably.
3. The incident of overhead with increase in production is less.

**Disadvantages**

1. This leads to discontentment among employees, particularly learners and sub-standard employees by setting a low piece rate.
2. This method is also not suitable for those employees whose efficiency is just below the border line, i.e. efficiency level is by small margin.
3. It does not guarantee even the minimum wages, which brings in frustration among the employees.
4. Workers develop hatred and jealously with each other because of differential wage rates.

2. **Merrick's differential piece rate system:** Under this system, three graded piece rates are used instead of two as in the case of Taylor's differential system. The features of this system are as follows:

1. Minimum day wages are not guaranteed and thus remuneration is solely on the basis of output.
2. The three rates of remuneration are as follows:
   (a) Up to 83% standard output, ordinary piece rate is paid.
   (b) Between 83% to 100% standard output, 110% of ordinary piece rate is paid.
   (c) Above 100% standard output, 120% of ordinary piece rate is paid.

To illustrate with an example, let normal piece rate be 0.60 per unit, let standard output be 40 units per week, let the output of workers A, B and C be 32 units, 37 units and 42 units respectively a week.

Their remuneration will be:

A = 32 units @ 0.60 per unit = 19.20

B = 37 units @ 0.66 per unit = 24.42

B = 42 units @ 0.72 per unit = 30.24.

**Advantages**

1. When compared to Taylor's system, this system offers better terms for earning the increased wages. Under Taylor's system, to earn a high piece rate wage an employee has to improve the efficiency to 100% whereas to earn an incentive under Merrick's system an employee has to reach only 83%. Thus, psychologically the employees feel that Merrick's system is a better system of wage payment to Taylor's system, as it is felt that it is within their reach to attain 83% efficiency.
2. Having thus reached the 83% level of efficiency employees strive to achieve even 100% efficiency.

**Disadvantage**

1. This system is mostly suitable at intermediate range of efficiency, i.e., it makes a good grading plan.

### *(C) Piece rate with guaranteed day rate*

This is a modified system of piece rate system, under which employees are remunerated on piece rate system provided that his total wage is greater when compared to time rate system. Suppose, if the worker's piece rate earnings fall below this level on account of low efficiency, he will be paid on the basis of time rate system. An alternative form of this method is the guaranteed time rate which is paid either per hour, day or week, plus a piece rate payment for output above a stated minimum.

This system of wage payment enjoys all the advantages of straight piece system. One more advantage of this system is, it avoids insecurity by providing a minimum guaranteed wages. Thus, a worker is not penalised when his piece rate earnings are low owing to circumstance beyond his control.

One disadvantage of this method is that the minimum guaranteed wages removes the incentives to improve the efficiency of workers.

## III. Combined time and piece rate system

This system of wage payment is based on the time rate and piece rate system of wages. The following methods of wage payments fall under this classification: (a) Emerson's efficiency system, and (b) Gantt task and bonus plan.

### *(a) Emerson's efficiency system*

This system was introduced by Emerson who was an associate of F.W. Taylor. This system is suitable to (a) encourage slow workers to improve their performance, and (b) facilitate an easy transfer from time wages to payment by results. The main features of this plan are:

1. Day wages are guaranteed.
2. A standard time is fixed for each job or operation or a volume of output is taken as standard.

3. Below $66\frac{2}{3}\%$ efficiency the workers are paid on hourly rate.
4. From $66\frac{2}{3}\%$ up to 100% efficiency, payments are made on the basis of step bonus rates.
5. Above 100% efficiency, and additional bonus of 1% of the hourly rate is paid for each 1% increase in efficiency.

The following formula is applicable:

$$\text{Earnings} = \text{Hours worked} \times \text{Rate per hour} + \text{Emerson's Bonus Percentage} \times \text{Hours worked} \times \text{Rate per hour}$$

### *(b) Gantt task and bonus plan*

This system was introduced by Henry, L. Gantt. It is a combination of Time Rate System with a step bonus and differential piece rate system of wage payment. The purpose of this method of wage payment is to reward those who reach high level of production. The method also guarantees the minimum day wages and, at the same time, encourages less skilled employees. Remuneration under this system is computed as follows:

Output below standard — Time rate wages
Output at standard — Step bonus of 20% on the time rate
Output above standard — High piece rate on workers' whole output.

**Advantages**

1. It provides security for less efficient workers.
2. It is beneficial to more efficient workers by offering a high incentive.
3. The increased output because of increased efficiency reduces the fixed cost per unit.

**Disadvantage**

1. The trade union may not agree to the piece rate fixed. Instead, it may seek a high guaranteed time rate.

## IV. Premium or incentive bonus system

The term "incentive" has been defined as "the stimulation of effort and effectiveness by offering monetary inducement or enhanced facilities." It is clear from this definition that an incentive could be a monetary incentive, i.e., cash bonus system or non-monetary like fringe benefits. Incentives can also be paid to individual worker or collectively to a group of workers. In the former case, the worker directly gets his share of premium for his increased efficiency, while in the latter case, the incentive is shared by all the workers in an agreed proportion for their collective effort.

The incentive system, in fact, is a compromise between time rate system and piece rate system. Under time rate system, the workers do not gain anything even if they complete production in less than the allowed time. On the other hand, under piece rate system, employers get nothing, if the time is saved. So, under incentive system, both the employer and employees benefit from the time saved.

The incentive systems have the following characteristics:

1. In all incentive systems of wage payment, minimum wages are guaranteed.
2. For every job, a standard time is fixed by conducting time and motion study.

3. If a worker completes the job within the time allowed, he will be paid incentive bonus on the time saved.

### Essentials of good incentive system of wage payment

David, W. Belcher in his book, *Wage and Salary Administration*, enumerates the following essential requirements of a good incentive system of wage payment:

1. An incentive wage plan should be explained and discussed with all employees and supervisors before it is installed. Employees' acceptance and cooperation is much more likely if they have a part in its inception.
2. The plan should allow for earnings to be in direct proportion to employees' output above the work standard.
3. An incentive plan should be easily understood and easy to calculate by the employees. A complicated plan leads to doubts and distrust in the workers' mind.
4. The incentive should be paid in the same month during which the efforts are put. It should not be postponed.
5. The spread between the guaranteed and the incentive pay rate should be large enough to encourage extra effort on the part of the employees.
6. All incentive systems should guarantee a minimum wages. This infuses an element of security among the employees.
7. The standard once set should not be changed unless (i) there is an error, or (ii) a change in work condition has been effected.
8. The standards should be scientifically set and it must be within the reach of employees to attain it.
9. The entire production process should be standardised, such as standard work methods, standard work places, standard materials, standard control processes, etc.
10. Equitable adjustments should be provided for an employee who fails to meet the standard for reasons beyond his control.
11. Standards of output must be based on established and recognised quality requirements. Employees should not be paid for substandard work. In fact, some provision may be necessary to control waste if it is excessive.
12. A good working condition is to be created to enable the workers to attain the standard.
13. An incentive system should be extended so as to include even indirect workers.
14. No upper limit be fixed for earnings of the workers.
15. The incentive system should be conducive to setting up standard cost and budgetary control.

The following are the most important types of incentive system of wage payment:

### *A. Halsey system*

The plan was introduced by F.A. Halsey, an American Engineer in 1891. The features of this incentive system are:

(i) A standard time is allowed for each job. A worker, who takes standard time or more than standard time, receives his time rate.

(ii) If the job is complete in less than standard time, the employee is paid an incentive of 50% of the time saved. The remaining 50% of the incentive is shared by the employees.

The following formula is used to compute wages under this method:

$$\text{Earnings} = \text{Time taken} \times \text{Time rate} + \frac{50}{100} \text{ of time saved} \times \text{Time rate}$$

This is illustrated by taking the following example:

Let time rate = Re. 1/- per hour

Let time allowed = 12 hours

Let time taken = 10 hours.

In the above example, the time saved is 2 hours, being the difference of time allowed (12) minus time taken (10)

$$10 \times 1 + \frac{50}{100} \times 2 \times 1$$

$$10 + 1 = 11$$

In other words, the worker receives 11 hours pay for 10 hours of work.

**Advantages**

1. Time wages are guaranteed and thus it offers a security to employees.
2. As the incentive is also shared by employer he is interested in improving the working conditions in factories.
3. This method of wage payment is comparatively easy to operate and understand.

**Disadvantages**

1. Workers are dissatisfied because employer's share half of the incentive earned by employees.
2. It is difficult to fix a standard time in actual practice.

### *B. Halsey-Weir system*

This system of wage payment was introduced by G. J. Weir in England. This is, in fact, a modified form of Halsey system. All the features of Halsey system also apply to this system, except the percentage of incentive payable to employees is $33\frac{1}{3}\%$ of time saved. The remaining $66\frac{2}{3}\%$ is shared by the employer.

### *C. Rowan system*

This incentive system was introduced by James Rowan of Scotland. Even under this system, the incentive is paid on the time saved as in the above mentioned two methods. But a different method is used to calculate the bonus. Under this system, bonus hours are calculated as the proportion of the time taken which the time saved bears to the time allowed, and they are paid on the basis of time rate system.

The following formula is applicable to compute wages under this system:

$$\text{Earnings} = \text{Time taken} \times \text{Time rate} + \frac{\text{Time saved}}{\text{Time allowed}} \times \text{Time taken} \times \text{Time rate}$$

Considering the example illustrated under Halsey system, the total earnings under the Rowan system are:

$$10 \times 1 + \frac{2}{12} \times 10 \times 1$$

$$10 + 1.66 = 11.66$$

**Advantages**

1. This system is more suitable to beginners and slow workers.
2. The employer benefits more from this system. ($66\frac{2}{3}\%$ of incentive); so he provides good working conditions in factories.

**Disadvantages**

1. This system of wage pay is not easily understood by employees.
2. This system is not beneficial to workers at high level efficiency.

***Comparison of Halsey and Rowan schemes***

In order to study the comparison between Halsey and Rowan system of wage payment, the following table may be considered:

| *Time rate per hr* | *Time allowed* | *Time taken* | *Time saved* | *Time wages* (1) × (3) | *Bonus* | | *Total* | |
|---|---|---|---|---|---|---|---|---|
| | | | | | *Halsey* | *Rowan* | *Halsey* | *Rowan* |
| (1) | (2) | (3) | (4) | (5) | (6) | (7) | (8) | (9) |
| 2 | 10 hrs | 10 hrs | – | 20 | – | – | 20 | 20.00 |
| 2 | 10 hrs | 8 hrs | 2 | 16 | 2 | 3.20 | 18 | 19.20 |
| 2 | 10 hrs | 6 hrs | 4 | 12 | 4 | 4.80 | 16 | 16.80 |
| 2 | 10 hrs | 5 hrs | 5 | 10 | 5 | 5.00 | 15 | 15.00 |
| 2 | 10 hrs | 4 hrs | 6 | 8 | 6 | 4.80 | 14 | 12.80 |

An observation of the above table reveals the following points:

1. Rowan system provides better bonus than the Halsey scheme until the work is completed in half the standard time, i.e., 5 hours.
2. When the work is completed in half the standard time, the bonus is the same under both the scheme.
3. When the work is complete in more than half the standard time, bonus under Halsey scheme is greater.

## V. Group bonus system

When bonus is paid collectively to a group of employees, it is known as group bonus system. In assembly type of work, such as radio, T.V., typewriter, refrigerators, automobiles, etc., production depends upon the collective efforts of a group of workers as a whole. In such cases, the output of individual worker cannot be measured and as group effort is inevitable. The work of each worker is dependent upon the work done by one or more co-workers. So, the workers constituting the group is considered for paying incentives. This system is applicable under the following circumstances:

1. Where individual output cannot be measured.
2. Where output depends upon combined efforts of a group.
3. Where management wants to encourage team spirit.
4. Where workers constituting a group are almost of equal skill.
5. Where indirect workers are also to be included under incentive system.

**Advantages**

1. This method of wage payment infuses cooperation and team spirit among the employees.
2. Absenteeism is reduced, as an absentee employee weakens the team which he does not like.
3. Accounting system is simplified as recording relates to the output of the group but not individuals.
4. Supervision is reduced because efficient workers compensate less efficient workers.
5. Indirect workers can also be included in the team by taking them into the team.

**Disadvantages**

1. This system is unfair to efficient and persons doing hard work as efficient workers are penalised for inefficiencies of other members of the team,
2. Workers do not easily accept this plan, and
3. It is difficult to fix group incentive and distribute it to employees.

The following are some of the important types of group bonus systems:

#### *1. Priestman production bonus*

Under this system, all employees are paid on a wage guaranteed basis. In this system, a production standard is fixed every month. When the actual production exceeds the standard, workers receive during the following month additional pay equal to the percentage in output over standard.

#### *2. Scanlon plan*

The plan was introduced by Scanlon in USA prior to Second World War. Under this system also, day wages are guaranteed. The bonus payable is calculated from the effective reduction in labour cost which is expressed as a ratio of labour cost of total sales value. If the labour cost is reduced or sale value increased, it results in increased pay for all employees. This method enables more workers' participation and increased interest to raise productivity in factories.

## VI. Other schemes of incentive system

This type of remuneration is paid to employees in addition to the usual remuneration based upon prosperity of the factories. Two systems fall under this category of employee remuneration, viz. (a) indirect monetary incentives, and (b) non-monetary incentives.

#### *A. Indirect monetary incentives*

Indirect monetary incentives are allowed on the understanding that employees contribute to the profit earning capacity of the factory. This can take two forms, viz. (1) profit sharing, and (2) co-partnership or co-ownership.

1. **Profit sharing:** Under this system, the employer agrees to pay a certain predetermined amount of profit in addition to usual salary payable to the employees. Profit sharing scheme differ from factory to factory in terms of coverage and method of distributing profit. In some factories, it is restricted only to executives. While in other factories, it is extended to all employees. Again, in some factories, it is paid for the year during which profit is earned while in others the payment of profit is deferred. This is to enable the employees to get a sizeable fund at the time of retirement, disability, or separation. The method of distributing profit also differs from factory to factory. In some factories, length of service is taken as the basis for determining the percentage of profit. In others, a fixed percentage of the total wages or merit ratings of employees constitute the basis.

**Advantages**

1. It reduces the excess labour turnover.
2. It increases production on account of increased efforts of workers with a view to earn profit.
3. It eliminates conflicts between employer and employee.
4. It leads to better cooperation team spirit and increased efficiency of workers.

**Disadvantages**

1. Usually, the worker has no control over profit and it is not directly related to his effort.
2. Unless merit rating is considered as the basis, both efficient and inefficient workers get profit at the same rate.
3. Payment of profit is at long intervals, usually once in a year and the share received by employees are negligible.
4. Employees share only profit but not losses.
5. When workers are in the habit of getting payment of profit on regular basis, non-payment of profit in any particular year leads to discontent.

2. **Co-partnership or Co-ownership:** Co-partnership confers upon employees the opportunity to share in the capital of the factory and to receive a part of the profits that accrue to their share of ownership.

Co-partnership differs from profit sharing in two respects: (1) In the co-partnership, employees invest capital into the factory, whereas in profit sharing scheme, the employees do not contribute capital. (2) In co-partnership, the employees share profit and losses if there is any, whereas in profit sharing scheme, the workers receive only profit but they are not called upon to bear losses.

### *B. Non-monetary incentives*

Non-monetary incentives are offered with a view to attract better employees, encourage loyalty, reduce labour turnover, promote better health and reduced absenteeism with a view to build up a happy and contended staff. Non-monetary, incentives are sometimes provided somefacilities free of cost while in some other cases, it may be subsidised. This usually takes the following forms:

(a) Canteens.

(b) Educational facilities for training the employees or to educate children of employees. Sometimes scholarships may also be awarded.
(c) Financial assistance in respect of housing.
(d) Medical facilities.
(e) Transport facilities.
(f) Recreational facilities.
(g) Cooperative societies.

## QUESTIONS

### A. Objective type

### I. Choose the correct answer from the following alternatives:

1. Under Emerson efficiency plan, the worker gets normal wage at

(a) $66\frac{2}{3}\%$ efficiency (b) $33\frac{1}{2}\%$ efficiency

(c) 75% efficiency (d) 100% efficiency

2. The basis on which bonus is calculated under Rowan system is

(a) $\frac{\text{Standard time}}{\text{Time saved}} \times \text{Std. time} \times \text{Time rate}$

(b) $\frac{\text{Standard time}}{\text{Time taken}} \times \text{Time saved} \times \text{Time rate}$

(c) $\frac{\text{Standard time}}{\text{Time rate}} \times \text{Time taken} \times \text{Time saved}$

(d) $\frac{\text{Time saved}}{\text{Standard time}} \times \text{Time taken} \times \text{Time rate}$.

3. Which one of the following is a system which combines both time and piece rate system?

(a) Priestmen's production bonus system
(b) Taylor's differential system
(c) Merrick's differential system
(d) Emerson's efficiency system

4. In which of the following incentive plan of wage payment, wage on time basis are not guaranteed?

(a) Halsey plan (b) Rowan plan
(c) Taylor's differential system (d) Emerson's efficiency system

5. Differential piece rate system
   (a) are discriminatory.
   (b) are complicated.
   (c) pay workers in proportion to their efficiency
   (d) is opposed by trade union.
6. Incentive system of wage payment
   (a) pay bonus for the time saved besides guaranteed wages for the time taken.
   (b) are a fraud on the employee compensation plan.
   (c) are intended to speed up work for the benefit of the employer.
   (d) pay increased bonus at an increasing rate as the efficiency increases.

**II. Write *True* or *False* for the following sentences:**

1. Taylor's differential piece rate system is an improvement over Merrick's differential piece rate system.
2. Time rate system is more suitable where strict supervision is possible.
3. In Merrick's differential piece rate system time wages are guaranteed to each worker.
4. Rowan system distributes the benefit of time saved equally between employees and employers.
5. In Halsey premium plan time wages are guaranteed.
6. Merrick's differential piece rate system is less punitive than Taylor's system.
7. Under the Rowan plan, bonus paid is fixed.

**III. Match the following:**

| | Column A | | Column B |
|---|---|---|---|
| 1. | Piece wage system | (a) | Based on time saved |
| 2. | Gantt task and bonus plan | (b) | Three piece rates |
| 3. | Premium bonus plan | (c) | Bonus is divided equally between employer and employee |
| 4. | Halsey plan | (d) | Speed is the basis of payment |
| 5. | Merrick's differential system | (e) | Combination of time and piece rate system |
| 6. | Halsey system | (f) | Indirect monetary incentive |
| 7. | Taylor's system | (g) | Group bonus system |
| 8. | Emerson's system | (h) | Combination of time and piece rate |
| 9. | Co-partnership | (i) | Premium bonus plan |
| 10. | Production plan | (j) | Piece rate system |
| | | (k) | Time rate system |
| | | (l) | Non-monetary incentive |
| | | (m) | 50% of time saved as bonus |

## B. Very short answer type

1. Distinguish between wages and salaries.
2. Define wage rate.
3. What do you mean by a standard wage rate?

4. Define salary.
5. What do you mean by time rate system of wage payment?
6. How are employees remunerated under piece rate system?
7. Give the feature of Taylor's differential piece rate system.
8. Give the features of Merrick's differential piece rate system.
9. State the features of Emerson's efficiency system.
10. State the features of Gantt task and bonus plan.
11. State the features of Halsey system of incentive payment.
12. State the features of Rowan system of incentive payment.
13. State the features of Priestman's production bonus.
14. State the features of Scanlon.
15. Distinguish between co-partnership and profit sharing.
16. List out four non-monetary incentives offered in factories.

### C. Short answer type

1. State the matters to be included in preparing a statement of wage policy.
2. Explain the characteristics of sound wage plan.
3. Explain the factors which influence wage payment.
4. Explain the three incentive systems of wage payment.

### D. Long answer type

Explain the various methods of wage payment.

## ANSWERS TO OBJECTIVE TYPE QUESTIONS

I. *Choose the correct answer:*

| 1. (a) | 2. (d) | 3. (d) | 4. (c) | 5. (c) | 6. (a) | |
|---|---|---|---|---|---|---|

II. *True or False:*

| (1) F | (2) T | (3) F | (4) F | (5) T | (6) T | (7) F |
|---|---|---|---|---|---|---|

III. *Match the following:*

| 1. (d) | 2. (e) | 3. (d) | 4. (c) | 5. (e) |
|---|---|---|---|---|
| 6. (m) | 7. (h) | 8. (h) | 9. (f) | 10. (g) |

# Chapter 35

# LABOUR ABSENTEEISM AND LABOUR TURNOVER

## ■ MEANING OF LABOUR ABSENTEEISM

Labour absenteeism means absence of workers from their regular duty without intimation to their employers. In other words, it means absence without seeking prior sanction from the seniors. Absenteeism amounts to unauthorised absence from duty. Labour absenteeism can be expressed as a ratio of man-days lost to the total number of days for which employment is available. It can also be expressed in the form of percentage taking into account the workers who are absent out of the total workers employed. Labour absenteeism, though common in factories, should not be allowed to exceed a maximum limit. The normal limit of absenteeism that can be allowed is in between 3 to 5%. However, efforts should be made to keep it at the lowest limit. Otherwise, it leads to delay in production and involves incurring of additional expenses in the form of overtime wages.

## ■ CAUSES OF LABOUR ABSENTEEISM

Several factors are responsible for excess in absenteeism from work. The most important among those are:

### 1. Monotonous work

Monotomy in the factory work leading to heavy physical and mental stress very often cause employees to stay away from work.

### 2. Bad working conditions

Lack of proper physical facilities, such as lighting, heating, ventilation, air-conditioning, and sanitation cause dissatisfaction among the employees. This is responsible for the excess of absenteeism of workers in factories.

### 3. Individual fatigue

Constant work subjects the employees to feel tiresomeness. Heavy work load also makes the employees to take long rest. Therefore, they stay away from work leading to absenteeism.

### 4. Absence of regular leave

When the normal leave of 15 to 20 days per year is not allowed, employees do not feel like attending the work continuously. This leads to more absenteeism.

### 5. Absence of welfare facilities

When welfare facilities, such as medical facilities, transport facilities, educational facilities, recreational facilities and monetary benefits are not extended to workers, they do not feel like attending to the work continuously. This is responsible for excess of absenteeism of employees in factories.

### 6. Miscellaneous causes

Miscellaneous causes, such as enforcing too much of discipline, strained relationship between seniors and subordinates, domestic problems, sickness of employees and their family members, accidents, etc., are also responsible for an increase in labour absenteeism.

## ■ EFFECTS OF LABOUR ABSENTEEISM

1. Excess absenteeism leads to delay in the production process. Often overtime work is to be engaged to complete the production which involves payment of double the normal wages to the employees.
2. Excess absenteeism leads to extra pressure of work on other employees.
3. Absenteeism of workers constituting a group weakens the team of working group. Where work is of inter-dependent nature, absenteeism of workers even leads to stoppage of production.
4. Due to absenteeism of workers, if orders are not promptly executed it leads to loss of reputation and good-will of the factory.
5. Excessive absenteeism also leads to discharge of employees from the factory.
6. It leads to incurrence of fixed expenses without corresponding increase in the production.
7. Workers suffer loss of pay during the period of absence from factory work.
8. Workers also lose promotion if they abstain themselves from the work for long period, and at frequent interval.

## ■ REMEDIAL MEASURE TO PREVENT ABSENTEEISM

1. Workers should be provided with annual leave as per the requirements of statute.
2. Provision of better working conditions to employees.
3. Establishment of good relation between seniors and subordinates.
4. Provision of recreational facilities and welfare measures to employees.
5. Taking strict disciplinary action against the workers who remain absent frequently.
6. Maintenance of surplus staff to take up the work of absentee workers.
7. Payment of incentives to those workers who are regular for the whole year.

## ■ DEFINITION OF LABOUR TURNOVER

Whenever the employees of a factory get better terms and conditions of employment, they leave the existing factory to join another one which offers better prospects. This change in the labour force is known as labour turnover. Thus, labour turnover refers to mobility of employees, from factory to factory, for getting better opportunities in terms of earnings and position of authority. In concrete words, labour turnover may be defined as the number of employees who leave the factory during a period in relation to the average number of workers employed during the year. In other words, labour turnover denotes the rate of displacement of labour employed in a factory. The National Employment

Managers conference held in USA, in the year 1918, indicated that "labour turnover for any period consists of the number of separations from service during that period. Separations include all quits, discharges, or lay-offs for any reason whatever".

Although a minimum labour turnover is quite normal and can be allowed in factories, an excess rate of labour turnover is not desirable. This is because efficient and experienced workers leave the factory and in their place new employees come and occupy. Naturally, the ability of such new workers less when compared to experienced workers. The percentage of labour turnover that can be provided is in between 3 to 5%; beyond this it is undesirable in factories.

## ■ CAUSES OF LABOUR TURNOVER

The causes for labour turnover may be listed under the following headings:

I. Causes arising from the point of view of employees:

The main causes of high labour turnover from the point of view of employees can be summed up under the following points:

(a) Incompetence to do a job satisfactorily.
(b) Insubordination of work.
(c) Accidents.
(d) Prolonged illness.
(e) Death
(f) Mariage in case of women employees.
(g) Housing problems.
(h) Discharge on disciplinary ground.
(i) Retirement.
(j) Personnel betterment.
(k) Domestic responsibilities.

II. Causes arising from the point of view of employers:

(a) Payment of low wages.
(b) Unsatifactory working conditions.
(c) Failure to protect the worker against the accident.
(d) Bad attitude on the part of senior towards subordinates.
(e) Unfair promotional policies.
(f) Inefficient management.
(g) Lack of proper amenities like medical, recreational facilities, etc.
(h) Lack of job security, improper training facilities and lack of social security measures.

## ■ EFFECTS OF LABOUR TURNOVER

The effects of labour turnover can be studied under the following headings:

### I. Effects of labour turnover on production

Excess labour turnover reduces the output owing to the following reasons:

1. Time span involved in filling up the vacancy caused by the separation.

2. Time involved in adjuting to the work by the new employee.
3. Performance of work by slow speed owing to lack of experience and familiarity with the job.
4. Time involved in training and induction of new employees.

### II. Effects of the extent of defectives and spoilages

Labour turnover increases spoilages and defectives owing to the following factors:

1. Handling the tools and equipments in an improper way.
2. Inability to operate the machine with the required speed and accuracy.
3. Lack of understanding and ability towards design and specifications.
4. Lack of required skill and experience.

### III. Effects on plant and machinery

Labour turnover has damaging effect over plant and machinery owing to the following reasons:

1. Defective material handling procedure followed by the employees.
2. Wrong setting of tools.
3. Wrong feeding of jobs into machines.
4. Non-lubrication of machines.
5. Inability to locate defects in machines at the early stages.

### IV. Effects of labour turnover on industrial accidents

The labour turnover increases the number of industrial accidents due to the following reasons:

1. Lack of adaptation by the new employees to the safety programme.
2. Failure to observe safety rules.
3. Inability to control the speed of machines.
4. Careless handling of tools and equipments.
5. Exceeding the safe working load and speed of operation.

### V. Effects of labour turnover on cost of production

Generally speaking, excessive labour turnover increases the cost of production due to the following reasons:

1. Increased wages due to diminution of less speed in production.
2. Additional expenses incurred in training the newly-recruited employees.
3. Increased cost of labour arising out of rectifying the spoilt and defective units.
4. Increase in idle time wages as new workers are always less efficient.
5. Overhead expenses increases per unit owing to lower volume of production.
6. Increase in the cost of repairs and maintenance.
7. Payment of higher compensation for employees involving industrial accidents.

## ■ MEASUREMENT OF LABOUR TURNOVER

Labour turnover can be measured by any one of the following three methods: In this connection, it is worthwhile to remember that once a particular method is adopted it should not be changed frequently as comparison of labour turnover becomes difficult.

### 1. Separation method

This is the most commonly used method of measuring the labour turnover. In this case, the total number of separations during a period (month or year) is divided by the average number of workers on roll during the period and multiplying the quotient by 100 to determine the percentage of turnover. The average number of workers during a period is obtained by adding the number of workers in the beginning and at the end of the year, and dividing the sum by 2. When expressed in the form of formula, it is

$$\text{Separation Method} = \frac{\text{Number of separation during the period}}{\text{Average number of employees during the period}} \times 100.$$

### 2. Replacement method

This method takes into consideration only the actual replacement of labour, i.e., the number required to be replaced during the period, irrespective of total leavings. This is obtained by dividing the number of replacements during the period by average number of employees during that period and then multiplying by 100 to determine the percentage. Expressed in the form of formula, it is

$$\text{Replacement Method} = \frac{\text{Number of replacement during a period}}{\text{Average number of employees during a period}} \times 100.$$

### 3. Flux rate method

This method takes into consideration both the leavings and the new entrants. This is obtained by adding the leavings and replacements, dividing the total by average number of employees during the period and multiplying the quotient by 100. Expressed in the form of formula:

$$\text{Flux Rate Method} = \frac{\text{Number of separations} + \text{Number of replacements}}{\text{Average number of employees during a period}} \times 100.$$

## ■ REMEDIAL MEASURES TO PREVENT LABOUR TURNOVER

The following measures are to be taken to control and reduce the percentage of labour turnover to the minimum:

1. Scientific recruitment, selection and training of labourers.
2. Provision of attractive wages, allowance and other monetary benefits.
3. Provision of better working conditions to workers.
4. Introduction of impartial promotion policy.
5. Provision of social security measures such as pension, provident fund, gratuity, etc.
6. Better motivation and provision of welfare facilities to employees.
7. Cordial labour-management relations.
8. Reducing fluctuations in the volume of work
9. Ensuring job satisfaction and job security.
10. Measures should be taken to reduce labour disputes to the minimum.

# QUESTIONS

## A. Very short answer type

1. Define labour absenteeism.
2. Define labour turnover.
3. State the methods of measuring labour turnover.
4. How is labour turnover measured under separation method?
5. How is labour turnover measured under replacement method?
6. How is labour turnover measured under flux rate method?

## B. Short answer type

1. Explain the causes and consequences of labour absenteeism.
2. Explain the various methods of measuring labour turnover.

## C. Long answer type

Explain the causes and consequence of high labour turnover. What remedial measures would you suggest to minimise high labour turnover in factories?

Chapter 36

# EMPLOYEE MORALE AND INDUSTRIAL PSYCHOLOGY

## ■ INTRODUCTION

Employee morale refers to an attitude of satisfaction with a desire to continue and strive for attaining the objectives of a factory. Good morale is evident from positive feelings of employees, such as enthusiasm, and by willingness to cooperate with co-workers. Poor morale is evident the negative feelings of employees, such as dissatisfaction, discouragement and dislike of job.

## ■ DEFINITION OF MORALE

Theo Haimann in his book, *Professional Management*, defines morale as "a state of mind and emotions affecting the attitude and willingness to work which, in turn, affect individual and organisational objectives".

Morale indicates the state of mind and emotional force of employees. Low morale adversely affects the quantity, quality and cost of output. It deteriorates the initiative, enthusiasm, discipline and cooperative attitude of employees.

## ■ HIGH AND LOW MORALE

High morale is indicated by less frustration whereas low morale is characterised by high frustration. High morale is created by introducing favourable climatic conditions in the factory. Good human relations leads to high morale among the employees. Other factors, which are responsible for high morale, are motivation, honouring dignity of human labour, good leadership, employees participation, effective communication and such other practices.

The chief symptoms of high morale, as listed by Ralph Davis in his book "Fundamentals of Top Management" are as follows:

1. Willing cooperation for the attainment of organisational objectives.
2. Loyalty to the organisation and its leadership.
3. Good discipline or voluntary conformance with rules, regulations and orders.
4. A high degree of employee interest in the job and in the organisation.
5. A reasonable display of employee initiative.
6. Pride in the organisation.

As against high morale denoted by the above symptoms, a low morale is characterised by the following symptoms:

1. Reduced productivity,

2. Excessive absenteeism,
3. Lack of interest in the rules and policies of the factory,
4. Excessive complaints,
5. High labour turnover,
6. Disputes among workers.

## ■ FACTORS INFLUENCING MORALE

Theo Haimann classifies the factors responsible for employee morale into three groups. They are:

1. Employees themselves,
2. Extra-organisational forces, and
3. Management practices.

The perception of employees about the organisation, its philosophy, feelings towards co-workers, and supervisors are some of the factors which affect employee morale. The ill-feelings purely depends upon the psychology of employees. The management has less influence over the low morale arising out of the above factors.

The extra-organisational forces responsible for a low morale are domestic problems, association with creditors, property matters, physical health of the workers, personal habits and extent of fatigue caused to them. Here also management cannot do much to improve the morale of the employees.

Those factors which are within the realm of management are organisation structure, effective leadership, adequate incentives, good relation between employer and employee. In this connection, it is worth mentioning that in addition to all the above factors certain variables of employees, such as age, sex, education, position of authority and income also decides the morale of employees. For example, women employees surpass their men counterparts in morale. Similarly, aged and experienced workers adjust better when compared to new employees. Likewise, job satisfaction is high in case of educated employees. Other factors which affect morale of the employee are size of the organisation and trade unionism. Regarding the size of the factory, as it grows big, job satisfaction tends to decline because the involvement of workers in decision-making process is far removed, and employees feel that they have lost their importance in the organisation. The morale of pro-union worker is less when compared to pro-management workers, as the former are more dissatisfied with wages, working conditions, and nature of work.

## ■ MEASURING MORALE

Morale is an intangible and subjective concept. As such, it cannot be directly measured or evaluated. However, the following methods are most commonly used to study employee morale:

1. Observation,
2. Attitude surveys,
3. Records and Reports, and
4. Counselling.

The above methods are briefly explained below:

### 1. Observation

When the Manager constantly and systematically observes attitudes of employees, it is possible to appraise the level of morale of lookers. As the Manager comes closer to the worker, he can to infer the behaviour and attitude of employees. But it involves a close watch and time-consuming process because the employee can change his mind on coming to know that he is being watched closely by the Manager.

### 2. Attitude surveys

In order to overcome the limitation of the above method, attitude survey method is being largely employed in modern days. This method includes conducting surveys through questionnaires and interviews. This reveals as to what is lacking in the workers and what steps should need be taken to improve their behaviour towards work. While preparing a questionnaire, other alternate solutions are provided or it can be left to the discretion of employees to suggest suitable measures. The former type is known as objective survey and the latter one is known as discipline survey.

### 3. Records and reports

The records and reports relating to absenteeism, labour turnover, idle time, late arrivals, excess wastage serve as an index of employee dissatisfaction. However, this method may not serve as a good method as it may show managerial deficiencies in fulfilling the needs of employees.

### 4. Counselling

Under this method, employees are advised to develop better mental health so that they can cultivate self-confidence, understanding and self-control. This method is used to find out the cause of dissatisfaction so as to advise the employees by way of remedial measures.

## ■ BUILDING MORALE

Having come to know about the low morale of employee, it is the duty of management to promote and maintain a high morale. Two approaches followed by management to develop high morale are: (1) group approach, and (2) individual approach.

Group approach is geared to the discovery of those areas of morale that have the broadest application to all employees. It is designed for an average man and is based upon common wants and levels expected by workers. Some of the benefits derived by employees in general are: (a) recreational facilities, (b) canteen facilities, (c) transport facilities, (d) housing facilities, and (e) pension benefits, etc.

The individual approach is oriented to unique feeling of each employee. However, it is difficult to meet the individual requirements of employees. Still, efforts can be made to enable the individual workers to adjust to the circumstances. Some of the morale building techniques applied to employees indivisually are: (a) Job evaluation and merit rating for fixing higher wages and promotion purposes, (b) payment of increased wages, (c) rewards for original ideas, and (d) employee recognition, and so on.

## ■ INDUSTRIAL PSYCHOLOGY

Industrial psychology is the study of human behaviour in the industrial setting and the application of psychological principles, knowledge and theory to workers, their behaviour and problems. Management can use the knowledge of psychology in the following ways:

1. Personnel Manager can make scientific selection of the staff required on the basis of the knowledge of his psychology. The main matters to be covered in this regard are job

requirements, matching with the job specification, psychological tests, training of interviewers, placement of staff to various departments on the basis of performance in the tests, study of skills, abilities, interest, aptitude of workers before recruitment.

2. Management can be effective if employees are involved in the participation of management. Besides this, cooperation of workers is also essential at all stages. In addition to this, interest must also be created among employees. Industrial psychology is useful to achieve all their requirements.
3. A manager is expected to give training, guidance and assistance to the staff working under his control. This job of training and guidance is a delicate one and requires the study of human mind, sentiments, reactions and so on. The study of industrial psychology enables a manager to give proper training and guidance to workers and make them efficient.
4. A manager can raise the morale of workers and develop cordial labour-management relations through a feeling or involvement, loyalty and satisfaction among the workers. For this the study of industrial psychology is useful. A manager is treated as efficient manager, if he is able to create favourable impact on the workers and avoid disputes, grievances and the like.
5. A manager can also prevent accidents in the factory by using the concept of industrial psychology. Accidents do occur when the worker's attitude become indifferent. Industrial psychology enables the manager to study this indifferent attitude and avoid occurrence of accidents.

## ■ EMPLOYEE FRUSTRATION AND INDUSTRIAL PSYCHOLOGY

Industrial employees get frustration because of various reasons like monotonous work, faulty machines, poor relations with fellow workers, wrong attitude of the workers himself. Due to frustration, a worker takes limited interest in his work and the mental health of a worker can even be the cause of an accident. The management has to give attention to such workers and try to ensure that the workers always remain mentally fit. It is desirable to take assistance of industrial psychologists to deal with such workers. Various counselling schemes are useful in order or develop a sense of confidence in workers's mind. Counselling refers to discussion with an employee as regards his emotional problem and to solve it.

## ■ INDUSTRIAL PSYCHOLOGY AND MORALE OF EMPLOYEE

High morale of employees is necessary to raise production in factories. It also creates good atmosphere in the factory as the attitudes of all persons move in the same direction for achieving certain well defined objectives. Industrial psychology suggests suitable methods for improving morale of workers. Such methods are:

### (a) Expert assistance

Here, an expert is asked to make a spot survey and assess the situation. The expert is also asked required to make recommendations to improve morale. Such suggestions are implemented by the management.

### (b) Industrial spy

Here, an expert is given a job in the organisation and his identity is kept secret. He studies the whole situation by meeting people and prepares a report with his recommendations for improvement in the situation.

### (c) Industrial counsellor

Here, an expert is appointed and he acts as a communication link between employees and management. He also helps management in raising the morale of employees.

### (d) Employee problem approach

Here, the problems are placed before the employees and their opinions, views, suggestions etc. are collected. This develops cooperation and proper understanding among the workers. The workers get the feeling that they are consulted and that their views carry weight.

## QUESTIONS

### A. Very short answer type

1. Define employee morale.
2. Distinguish between high and low morale.
3. Mention the different methods of measuring morale.
4. What do you mean by industrial psychology?

### B. Short answer type

1. Explain the characteristics of high and low morale.
2. Discuss the factors which affect employee morale.
3. Explain the various methods of measuring morale.
4. Explain the benefits of industrial psychology to management of a factory.
5. How should industrial psychology deal with
   (a) frustration and counselling of workers?
   (b) morale of workers?

Chapter 37

# WORKERS' PARTICIPATION IN MANAGEMENT

## ■ INTRODUCTION

The concept of worker's participation in management has acquired special significance in the recent times all over the world. It is the application of the concept of industrial democracy. Workers are no more treated merely as wage earners. They are treated as partners in the productive process. Naturally, they must be consulted and their suggestions taken into consideration while framing policies and managing day-to-day administration of a factory. Thus, labour participation in management means giving higher status to workers and associating them as partners in the management of a factory. The purpose is to create cordial labour-management relations and to avoid industrial unrest and disputes. It also creates mental and emotional involvement of workers in the working of a factory. In other words, workers' participation is a process where workers share authority and responsibility with the management in respect of managerial and administrative functions.

## ■ NEED OF WORKERS' PARTICIPATION IN MANAGEMENT

The importance of workers participation is clearly indicated in the following statement made in the Third Five Year Plan. "For the peaceful evaluation of economic system on a democratic basis it is essential that worker's participation in management should be accepted as a fundamental principle and an urgent need". The need for workers' participation in management arises on account of the following:

1. To give better status to workers and also for the creation of industrial democracy in the country.
2. To give psychological satisfaction to workers and also for giving them an opportunity to express their views freely as regards various administrative problems of an industrial unit.
3. To have uniform approach as regards various problems arising in factories. It is needed as it facilitates mutual understanding and cooperation among the two parties.
4. For raising industrial efficiency and productivity.
5. To create a sense of confidence among workers and to facilitate quick and direct negotiations between the two parties.
6. To make working class more responsible and responsive to the needs of the factories.
7. To create a feeling of involvement among workers and also give them an opportunity to study the problems of a factory.
8. To act as a bridge and to remove the gulf between the management and the workers.
9. To improve and create cordial labour-management relations and to avoid industrial disputes.

## ■ METHODS OR FORMS

The forms in which worker can participate in management varies depending upon pattern of management, levels of management, size of the factory, authority delegated to subordinates and the areas in which participation is sought. Again, participation may be ascending participation to influence managerial decisions at higher levels through their elected representatives. In "descending" participation, the workers may be given more power to plan and make decisions about their own work, i.e., delegation and job enrichment. The various forms of workers participation in management prevalent in India are as follows:

1. Works committees
2. Joint management councils
3. Workers prepresentation in Board of Management
4. Shop councils
5. Joint councils
6. Unit councils
7. Suggestion scheme
8. Co-partnership
9. Auto management.

The above forms have been discussed hereunder:

### 1. Works committees

Works committee is a committee on which equal representation is given to employer and employees. In any works committee, various problems connected with employees and management are discussed and periodical meetings are arranged for peaceful negotiations on various issues. As per the provisions of Industrial Dispute Act of 1947, setting up of works committees are obligatory in factories where 100 or more workers work. The basic purpose is to have direct communication between the two parties. In England, such committees are very useful and effective in creating cordial labour-management relations. Works committee can deal with various issues like conditions of work, amenities to workers, prevention of accidents, welfare facilities to workers, promotion scheme, administration of labour welfare funds, and so on. The success of works committee, moreover, depends upon (a) responsible attitude on the part of management, and (b) wholehearted implementation of the recommendations of the works committees.

### 2. Joint management councils

A joint management council consists of representatives of management, technicians, and workers. The suggestion for such council was made in 1956 by a group set up by the Ministry of Labour and Employment. The council is expected to be consulted on matters relating to the administration of standing orders, welfare measures, retrenchment, rationalisation, holidays, leave, etc.

The number of such councils was 150 in 1969 and was 80 in 1974. It has gone up to 1083 in 1976. The main functions of joint management councils, according to 15th Session of the Indian Labour Conference, held in 1957 are:

(a) To improve working and living conditions of the employees,
(b) To improve productivity,
(c) To encourage suggestions from the employees,

(d) To assist in the administration of laws and agreements,

(e) To serve employees, and

(f) To create in the employees a live sense of participation.

In India, large number of such councils are established but the real contribution of such councils is limited. This is because the situation on labour front is not favourable to effective working of such councils. The reasons for limited success of such councils are: (i) The attitude of employers is not progressive and favourable for their effective working, (ii) Trade unions are opposed to such councils as they feel that their importance may reduce in the course of time, and (iii) In India, labour participation is government sponsored. The concerned parties have not taken initiative in the establishment of such councils.

### 3. Workers representation on board of management

Appointments of employees representatives on the Board of Directors of a company is one of the methods of labour participation in management. Under this method, two or three representatives are elected/nominated by workers and such representatives attend the meetings of the board and participate in the discussion. The representatives of workers on the board are expected to bring to the notice of other directors, the views, suggestions, etc. of the workers. Thus, the views and suggestions of workers are given due consideration in the process of decision-making at the top level. However, this system is not very effective in bridging the gap between workers and employers. The reasons are:

(a) The representatives of workers are in minority and naturally are unable to put any pressure on other directors. Due to this, the suggestions of workers are not taken seriously and the gap between the two parties continues.

(b) The representatives of workers have limited education, skill, knowledge and capacity to participate in the meetings of the board. Naturally, they are not in a position to make positive suggestions in the discussion in such meetings.

(c) The meetings of the board are basically for managerial decisions and not simply for the discussion and decisions on labour problems. Naturally, the representatives of workers get limited opportunities to place the views and demands of workers before the management.

(d) Rivalry among unions is quite common in India. Naturally, representatives of workers on the board are unable to put forward the views and suggestions which are acceptable to all. The management also finds it difficult to accept completely the views expressed by the representations of workers.

### 4. Shop councils

This method of participation was launched in India in 1975. The main features of this scheme are as follows:

(a) In every factory, where the number of workers are more than 500, the employer shall constitute a shop council for each department or one council for more than one departments.

(b) There shall be equal number of representatives of employers and workers in each council.

(c) All decisions of a shop council is on the basis of consensus and not by process of voting.

(d) The decision taken in the shop council shall be implemented within a period of one month.

(e) A shop council shall work for a minimum period of two years.

The functions of shop council are as follows:

(a) To assist the management in achieving production targets.

(b) To improve production and productivity by eliminating waste and better utilisation of manpower and machine capacity.

(c) To recommend steps to reduce absenteeism.

(d) To provide safety measures.

(e) To provide for physical facilities, such as lighting, ventilation, noise control, dust control.

(f) To provide welfare measures.

## 5. Joint councils

Factories employing 500 or more employees shall constitute a joint council, according to 20-point economic programme. The feature of joint councils are:

(a) The joint council shall meet, at least, once in a quarter.

(b) The council shall function for a period of two years.

(c) Every decision of the joint council shall be on the basis of consensus and not by a process of voting.

The functions of Joint Council are as follows:

(a) To increase the output by fixation of standards.

(b) To consider matters which could not be solved by shop councils.

(c) To develop skills of workers by offering training facilities.

(d) To encourage research and to award the reward to workers involving creative work.

(e) To prepare schedule of working laws.

(f) To ensure full utilisation of raw materials and maintain quality of finished goods.

## 6. Unit councils

This scheme was launched in the year 1977 in commercial and service organisations in the public sector. Unit councils are set up in those units which employ at least 100 workers. The organisations where unit councils are set up include hotels, hospitals, transport undertaking, educational institutions, provident fund and pension organisations, banks, municipalities, and warehousing corporations. Such councils are set up to eliminate factors which hinders the progress and to improve the methods of operations. The main function of unit councils are to create conditions for attaining higher efficiency and to provide better customer service.

## 7. Suggestion scheme

Under this scheme, workers are associated with the management through their suggestions on various matters relating to administration of a factory. Workers are encouraged to give their suggestions to the management and such suggestions are considered carefully and accepted, if found suitable. Rewards are also given to those who give constructive suggestions for the benefit of all. In India, suggestions scheme exists in Tata's DCM, and in many other group of industries. Workers are free to make suggestions for their convenience and also for the improvement in the administrative set up of an organisation. Suggestion boxes are kept at convenient places for collection of suggestions of workers. The suggestions may be given to a joint committee of workers and employer, or departmental heads.

### 8. Co-partnership

In co-partnership, workers are made equal partners, i.e., owners of the business unit in which they work as employees. For this, the company offers equity shares to its employees. As a result, the workers are made the owners of their company. They are invited to meetings of the company and are also given all rights of shareholders. Workers are given higher status and are connected with the company in dual capacity. Workers can elect their representative as the director and can protect their interest.

### 9. Auto management

In this system, workers are given wide powers of management of their factory. The industrial unit is established by the state but the day-to-day management is given in the hands of workers working there. The production targets, etc. are decided at the government level but rest of the activities are managed by workers themselves collectively. This method is suitable in socialists or communist countries. It actually exists at present in Yugoslavia. It is not suitable to Indian economic system.

## ■ POSITION OF WORKERS' PARTICIPATION IN INDIA

The concept of workers' participation in management is accepted in India. However, Indian experience in this regard is not encouraging. Various measures are adopted in the planning period for purposeful participation of workers in management. Such efforts are being made in the private as well as public sector organisations. The Industrial Dispute Act of 1947 provides for the setting up of work committees. After 1957, a large number of joint management councils have been set up both in private and public sector units. Employee directorships are also introduced in many factories. However much need to be done to improve cordial labour-management relations, certain pre-requisites are to be considered for the successful workers participation in management. Such pre-requisites include constructive leadership of trade unions, progressive outlook of employers, atmosphere of mutual trust and confidence among employers and workers and finally genuine desire to deal with the labour-management problems in a democratic manner.

## ■ CONDITIONS NECESSARY FOR THE SUCCESS OF PARTICIPATION SCHEMES

The conditions necessary for the success of labour participation schemes are as follows:

1. The attitude of the employer must be constructive and progressive. He must sincerely accept the concept of labour participation and must be prepared to give fair trial to such schemes.
2. Both the parties should have a genuine faith in the system and in each other and be willing to work together.
3. Frequent meetings of representatives of workers and employer should be arranged for discussion or negotiation on administrative issues.
4. The trade union in the factory must be strong with genuine leadership. Trade union leaders must have genuine desire to participate in the management. The attitude of union leaders must be cooperative and not aggressive.
5. Workers must be given proper education and training as regards the schemes of labour participation. Along with workers, supervisory staff should also be associated with the management.

# SELECTED BIBLIOGRAPHY


1. Agarwal, A.N., Verma, H.W., and Gupta, H.C., India 1988-89, National Publishing House, New Delhi.
2. Alford, L.P. & Russell, H. Beatty, *Principles of Industrial Management*, the Ronald Press Company, New York, 1951.
3. Arun Monappa & Mirza, S. Saiyadain, *Personnel Management*, Tata McGraw-Hill Publishing Ltd., New Delhi.
4. Claude, S. George Jr, *Management for Business and Industry*, Prentice Hall of India Pvt. Ltd., New Delhi, 1985.
5. Department of Economics and Statistics, *Statistical Outline of India 1986-87*, Tata Service Ltd., Bombay, 1986.
6. Dexter, S. Kimball, *Principles of Industrial Organisation*, Vakils, Febber, and Simons Pvt. Ltd., Bombay, 1971.
7. Donald Delmur, *Operations and Industrial Management*, Mcgraw-Hill, USA, 1985.
8. Frank Finch, *A Concise Encyclopedia of Management Techniques*, Allied Publishers Pvt. Ltd., New Delhi.
9. Franklin, E. Folts, *Introduction to Industrial Management*, Tata Mcgraw-Hill Publishing Company Ltd., New Delhi, 5th Edition.
10. Gordon, B. Carson, *Production Handbook*, Ronald Anees USA., 1972.
11. Harold, T. Anrivet, et al., *Manufacturing, Organisation and Management*, Prentice Hall of India Pvt. Ltd., New Delhi, 1983.
12. Henry Marshal, *The New Business Encyclopedia*, Doublday & Co., New York, 1963.
13. Jame, L. Ribbs & Associates, *Industrial Organisation and Management*, Mcgraw-Hill Kogakusha Ltd., Tokyo, 6th Edition.
14. James, L. Lundy, *Effective Industrial Management*, Eurasia Publishing House (Pvt.) Ltd., New Delhi, 1979.
15. John, A. Shubin, *Business Management*, Barnes & Noble Books, New York, 1957.
16. Keith Lockyer, *Production Management*, ELBS, UK, 4th Edition.
17. Lockyer, K.G., *Factory Management*, A.H. Wheeler & Co. (P) Ltd., Allahabad, 1971.
18. Mahajan, S.P., *Pollution Control in Process Industries*, Tata Mcgraw-Hill Publishing Co., Ltd., New Delhi (Personal Management).

19. Robert, D. Hay & Associates, *Business and Society,* South-Western Publishing Co., 1976.
20. William, V. Wilmot, Jr. & John, R. Bangs, *Plant Management*, Alexander Hamilton Institute New York, 1968.

## Journals

1. *Commerce.*
2. *Business India.*

## Newspapers

1. *Economic Times.*
2. *The Hindu.*

6. The follow-up action on the decisions of the participating forums should be ensured. The government may also set up a machinery to act as a watch-dog for implementing the scheme.
7. Effective two-way communication is a must for the success of the programme.

**Advantages**

1. It improves the quality of decision-making as employees can offer suggestions and recommendations about a problem.
2. Employees readily accept the change without any resistance.
3. It leads to employees' commitment to the factory.
4. It eliminates differences of opinion between labour and management.
5. It facilitates team work.
6. It increases a sense of confidence and trust in the minds of employees towards management.
7. It helps in solving various problems of employers and thus avoids the possibility of strikes and lockouts.

**Disadvantages**

1. It leads to frustration among employees if their proposals are not accepted by management.
2. Employees lack initiative, expertise and self-confidence in participating with managerial decision-making.
3. Participation of unskilled leader of employees may result in unfavourable decisions which may adversely affect the interest of employees.

## QUESTIONS

### Very short answer type

1. What is meant by workers participation in management?
2. Mention the various forms of workers participation in management.
3. What is a work committee?
4. What do you mean by joint management council?
5. Distinguish between shop council and joint council.

### Short answer type

1. Explain the need for workers participation in management.
2. State the conditions necessary for the successful participation of workers in management
3. State advantages and disadvantages of workers participation in management.

### Long answer type

Explain the various forms of workers participation in management.